NATIONAL
GEOGRAPHIC

GUIDE TO
BIRDING
HOT SPOTS
of THE UNITED STATES

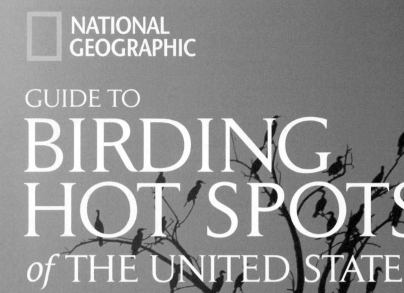

NATIONAL GEOGRAPHIC

GUIDE TO
BIRDING
HOT SPOTS
of THE UNITED STATES

MEL WHITE WITH PAUL LEHMAN
FOREWORD BY JONATHAN ALDERFER

CONTENTS

FOREWORD

*Lucifer
Hummingbird*

Wanderlust. You've started down the birding path and proceeded past your backyard and the local parks. You're starting to think of yourself as a "birder." Those little range maps in your field guide make it abundantly clear that an Elegant Trogon is not going to visit your backyard in Massachusetts, nor will a Sooty Shearwater be coming anywhere close to your apartment in Denver. You realize that if you want to experience these species (and lengthen your life list) you're going to have to bird new places. You start to feel the irresistible urge for distant horizons—akin to *Zugunruhe,* the German term for migratory restlessness in birds.

Just about anywhere you go you'll see birds—and the farther you go from home, the greater the changes in bird life you'll notice. Distance is just one variable. Habitat and time of year can be equally important. At special places, where geography, habitat, and season work together in the right mix, the result can be extraordinary birding. These places—birding hot spots—offer a visiting birder the best chances to see regional specialties, avian rarities, or concentrations of migrants.

No state or region of the lower 48 has a lock on great birding hot spots. A Californian might long to see a "fallout" of eastern warblers on spring migration. A New Yorker might crave the high mountain birds of the Rockies. Both might dream of arriving before dawn to witness Greater Prairie-Chickens strutting on a tallgrass prairie lek in Nebraska or Green Jays foraging in the streamside brush of the lower Rio Grande Valley in Texas. Some hot spots, like Cape May, New Jersey, and Hawk Mountain, Pennsylvania, have long histories. Others, like the Sax-Zim Bog in Minnesota and the Pawnee National Grassland in Colorado, are less storied, but still well known. At locations such as Corn Creek, Nevada, the story is just beginning. And other hot spots are yet to be discovered.

From Maine to California—state by state, from east to west—authors Mel White and Paul Lehman will help you find your way to all the best birding hot spots. There are entries for every state in the lower 48. Veteran birders and novices will appreciate the solid, up-to-date information: You'll find details on what species to look for, where to look for them once you arrive, and what time of year is optimal. Whether you're planning a cross-country birding expedition or just exploring the state next door, keep this guide right next to the road maps.

—Jonathan Alderfer

USING THE GUIDE

In this book you'll find more than 500 of the right places to go bird-watching in the 48 contiguous United States, from the Florida Keys to Maine's rugged coast; from the Texas Hill Country to Washington State's San Juan Islands. (Hawaii and Alaska are not covered because of the disparate bird life of the former and the complications of travel in the latter.) In consulting local birders, we've chosen top sites in each state: city and state parks, national wildlife refuges, national forests, nature preserves, lakes and marshes—even beaches and roads.

The text presents a short description of each area and a list of a few of the most typical or notable species found there. If you're new to this business of traveling to see birds, remember that birds travel, too. Some sites are rewarding year-round; others are at their best only in nesting season or winter, or in spring and fall migration.

States are grouped into chapters by region, with sites throughout each state arranged in a logical flow. Site numbers are keyed to the map at the beginning of each chapter (see sample map key on page 9), to aid you in finding your way from one site to the next. Throughout the book sidebars feature species of interest

At the end of each state section, we've included a "More Information" page, listing the sites that can help you plan your trip. First, you'll find telephone numbers of rare bird alerts. These are recorded messages, updated frequently, that list unusual species seen in a state or locality, often with directions to sites, or numbers to call for more information. Each list also includes web addresses and telephone numbers for the state sites or their administrative offices, so you can call or write ahead for additional information. Symbols indicate facilities at each site (see page 9), which can be seasonal or limited.

At the end of this guide, you'll find a listing of additional guidebooks by region and state, including Hawaii and Alaska.

A Few Other Ideas

New birders should first join their local National Audubon Society chapter or birding club. The leading national organization for bird-watchers is the American Birding Association, or ABA (*www.americanbirding.org*). Its bimonthly magazine, *Birding,* and monthly newsletter, *Winging It,* provide insight for birders. One of the benefits of ABA is its membership guide, published annually, which lists birders all over the country who will give advice to travelers or guide visitors to good birding sites in their home regions. If you join ABA, don't be shy about asking for help. Birders enjoy talking about their favorite places, and one inquiry to the right person could save you hours of driving or hiking in search of an elusive species.

Check the web sites of bird clubs and ornithological societies across the nation, which offer guides to birding spots, lists of local contacts, and schedules of field trips. Start your search with the National Audubon Society *(www.audubon.org);* check here for local chapters in the area you'll be visiting.

Also attend one of the birding festivals held annually across the nation, with programs and field trips led by experts, often concentrating on regional species. Find a list of festivals (and information on how to start your own) at the ABA web site.

Beyond Your List

Birding is fun and rewarding even if you approach it only as a sport or hobby. After they've been at it awhile, though, most birders become conservationists. Learning where to look for birds and understanding a bit about ecosystems and habitat requirements leads to some inescapable conclusions. For instance, Sprague's Pipits need naturally managed prairie; if all our grasslands are plowed or overgrazed, there won't be any more Sprague's Pipits. Increasingly, birders are realizing that their interest in, even love for, birds doesn't exempt them from responsibility. Playing a tape of a bird's song or call is often an effective way to bring it in close, but for some vulnerable species, or in heavily birded places, it is bad practice. Really wanting to see a Yellow Rail doesn't mean you can enter a marsh to flush one up, especially when it's nesting. Parks and refuges may close areas where a sensitive species—Peregrine Falcon, for example—is nesting; ethical birders obey such regulations, realizing that a bird's welfare comes before the desire to check it off a list.

Get Started

Birding ranks among the fastest growing outdoor pursuits in the country. All it takes to start is a pair of binoculars, a field guide, and a notebook; you can watch birds alone, or with friends. You're observing some of the earth's most colorful and interesting creatures; you'll travel, in many cases, to beautifully scenic wild places that you might otherwise never have discovered; and the challenges will last a lifetime, for no one will ever see all the different kind of birds there are.

—Mel White

INFORMATION

? Visitor Center/Information   **$** Fee Charged   **⅋** Food   **⅋** Rest Rooms

⅋ Nature Trails   **⅋** Driving Tours   **⅋** Wheelchair Accessible

Be advised that facilities may be seasonal and limited. We suggest calling or writing ahead for specific information. Note that addresses may be for administrative offices; see text or call for directions to sites.

MAP KEY AND ABBREVIATIONS

National Monument .... NAT. MON., N.M.
National Park ....N.P.
National Preserve .... NAT. PRES.
National Recreation Area ..........................N.R.A.
National Seashore .....................................N.S.
National Conservation Area ......................N.C.A.
National River

National Forest.......................... NAT. FOR., N.F.
State Forest ....S.F.
National Grassland

National Wildlife Refuge .... N.W.R.
National Wildlife Range

State Park .... S.P.

ADDITIONAL ABBREVIATIONS

Conservation Area .... C.A.
County .... CO.
Environmental Demonstration Area .... ENV. DEM. AREA
Fish and Wildlife Area .... F.W.A.
International .... INTL.
Memorial .... MEM.
National .... NAT.
National Battlefield Park .... N.B.P.
National Historical Park ...........................N.H.P.
National Lakeshore .... N.L.
Natural Area .... N.A.
Preserve .... PRES.
Recreation Area .... R.A.
Refuge .... REF.
Scenic Area .... S.A.
State Beach .... S.B.
State Conservation Park .... S.C.P.
State Game Area .... S.G.A.
State Historic Park .... S.H.P.
State Natural Area .... S.N.A.
State Nature Preserve ...............................S.N.P.
State Recreation Area .... S.R.A.
State Scenic Viewpoint .... S.S.V.
State Wildlife Area .... S.W.A.
State Wildlife Management Area .... S.W.M.A.
Wilderness .... WILD.
Wildlife Area .... W.A.
Wildlife Habitat Management Unit .... W.H.M.U.
Wildlife Management Area .... W.M.A.

Interstate Highway
U.S. Federal Highway
State Road
County, Local, or Other Road
Trans-Canada Highway
Other Canadian Highway
Ferry
State Boundary
National Boundary
National Forest Boundary

1 Featured Area
1 Additional Site
▪ Point of Interest
⊛ National Capital
⊛ State or Provincial Capital
| Dam
+ Peak

NEW ENGLAND

ALL THE NEW ENGLAND STATES SAVE VERMONT HAVE A seacoast, and it's along this meeting of land and water— rocky, sandy, or marshy; bluff-lined or flat—that many of the region's top birding sites are located.

One reason, of course, is seabirds. Given the relative uniformity of their ocean habitat, and including in their number some of the world's most accomplished fliers, these birds are notorious wanderers. Birders who brave the chilly winter wind of Rhode Island's Sachuest Point or Halibut Point in Massachusetts, or who take to the sea on a whale-watching boat, always hope for a true rarity to put an exclamation point on the day. Even species a bit more frequently seen make the coast an exciting place. Few birders become so jaded that their hearts don't speed up at the powerful flight of a jaeger or the beauty of a Harlequin Duck.

The coast is a great place to look for land birds, as well. In fall, north winds blow southbound migrants down against the coast, concentrating flocks into higher than normal numbers. The ocean acts as a barrier to their movement, so vagrants from the West often end their roaming on the coastline or on an island such as Block, off Rhode Island, or South Monomoy, in Massachusetts. You'll find famous and popular birding sites in New England, from Acadia National Park to Cape Cod. ∎

- Maine
- New Hampshire
- Vermont
- Massachusetts
- Rhode Island
- Connecticut

Atlantic Puffin

SPECIAL BIRDS OF NEW ENGLAND

Cory's Shearwater	Black Scoter	Black-legged Kittiwake	Gray Jay
Greater Shearwater	Long-tailed Duck	Roseate Tern	Boreal Chickadee
Sooty Shearwater	Spruce Grouse	Arctic Tern	Bicknell's Thrush
Wilson's Storm-Petrel	Piping Plover	Razorbill	Magnolia Warbler
Leach's Storm-Petrel	Purple Sandpiper	Black Guillemot	Blackburnian Warbler
Northern Gannet	Hudsonian Godwit	Atlantic Puffin	
Great Cormorant	Red-necked Phalarope	Snowy Owl	Saltmarsh Sharp-tailed Sparrow
Glossy Ibis	Red Phalarope	Northern Saw-whet Owl	Nelson's Sharp-tailed Sparrow
Mute Swan	Pomarine Jaeger	Black-backed Woodpecker	Snow Bunting
Brant	Parasitic Jaeger	Pileated Woodpecker	Rusty Blackbird
King Eider	Black-headed Gull	Yellow-bellied Flycatcher	Red Crossbill
Common Eider	Iceland Gull		White-winged Crossbill
Harlequin Duck	Glaucous Gull		
Surf Scoter			
White-winged Scoter			

MAINE

- Seabirds on whale-watch cruises
- Northern specialties in Baxter State Park

Somes Pond, Acadia National Park, Mount Desert Island

1 Though Maine's rugged, beautiful seacoast is the focus of much birding interest, it's the open-country species that make a visit to the **Kennebunk Plains** worthwhile. Walk the old roads in nesting season and look for Wild Turkey; Upland Sandpiper; Least Flycatcher; Horned Lark; Eastern Bluebird; Brown Thrasher; Prairie Warbler; Field, Vesper, Savannah, and Grasshopper Sparrows; Indigo Bunting; and Bobolink. Clay-colored Sparrow has been found here on occasion.

2 One of Maine's most famous birding spots is **Biddeford Pool.** Birding is best here a few hours before or after high tide, when waders (spring through fall) and migrant shorebirds

are feeding on mudflats near shore. Hudsonian Godwit is fairly regular in small numbers in late summer. Gulls are always present, and in summer or migration you may find Roseate, Common, Arctic (rare), or Black Terns.

Nearer the coast is **East Point Sanctuary.** Its shrubby vegetation provides good land birding in migration, and from the shoreline a scan of the ocean from fall through spring may turn up all sorts of seabirds. Common Eiders and Black Guillemots are regular. With luck you might find a Razorbill in winter. Look for wintering Purple Sandpiper on the rocks.

3 The Maine Audubon Society's **Scarborough Marsh Nature Center** is adjacent to the state's largest salt marsh. The center offers nature programs and canoe tours. Access the marsh by the **Dunstan River.** (Be aware that this is a popular duck-hunting area in fall.) Herons, ibises, and egrets feed here from spring through fall, and you might find an American Bittern in migration. Saltmarsh and Nelson's Sharp-tailed Sparrows nest here. Geese, ducks, and shorebirds use the marsh for resting and feeding in migration. The local public boat-launch area south of the marsh is another spot to find waders, shorebirds, gulls, and terns. This is a good place to see Roseate Tern in summer and Whimbrel and Hudsonian Godwit in late summer.

4 One of the most beautiful areas on the northeastern coast, **Acadia National Park** attracts millions of visitors each year. Among them are birders searching for seabirds and a good assortment of nesting land birds. Acadia is mostly located on **Mount Desert Island.** Other park areas are found on **Isle au Haut, Baker Island,** and the **Schoodic Peninsula.** A bird list is available at the visitor center.

Cadillac Mountain is a productive hawk-watching site in fall. From here you can look down on the islands off Bar Harbor, where Osprey and Bald Eagle nest and Common Raven gives its croaking call as it passes by. Trails around **Jordan Pond** make a good introduction to some of the park's nesting birds, including Ruffed Grouse, Black-capped Chickadee, Red-breasted Nuthatch, Brown Creeper, Winter Wren, Golden-crowned Kinglet, Hermit Thrush, Black-throated Blue and Black-and-white Warblers, Ovenbird, and Dark-eyed Junco. In spring, you'll hear the laughing call of Common Loon from the pond. From trails near **Acadia Wild Gardens,** view Yellow-bellied Sapsucker; Eastern Wood-Pewee; Alder and Least Flycatchers; Chestnut-sided, Black-throated Green, and Canada Warblers;

and American Redstart. Nearby, Peregrine Falcon nests on the cliffs of **Champlain Mountain,** and Common Eider, Black Guillemot, and other seabirds can be found at **Otter Point.**

Some of the park's best birding is found on the southwest part of Mount Desert, between the Seawall Campground and the Bass Harbor Head lighthouse. On the **Wonderland Trail** and the **Ship Harbor Nature Trail,** look for breeding Yellow-bellied and Alder Flycatchers, Blue-headed Vireo, Ruby-crowned Kinglet, Swainson's Thrush, and warblers including Nashville, Black-throated Green, Palm, Wilson's, Northern Parula, and American Redstart.

Seabird-watching tours are offered in the warmer months. Depending on the season and the luck of the day, one might see Common Loon; Greater, Sooty, and Manx Shearwaters; Wilson's Storm-Petrel; Northern Gannet; Double-crested and Great Cormorants; Common Eider; Osprey; Bald Eagle; Red-necked and Red Phalaropes; Arctic and Roseate Terns; Razorbill; and Atlantic Puffin.

WHITE-WINGED AND RED CROSSBILLS

The White-winged Crossbill and its relative the Red Crossbill are famous—perhaps notorious is a better word—for the irregularity and unpredictability of their movements. Some years they're seen all over the North Woods, using their specially adapted crossed bills to feed on seeds of pine, fir, spruce, and hemlock. Other years there are none to be found, and a visiting birder looking for one of these finches leaves frustrated, having searched in vain. ∎

5   For years, the *Bluenose* ferry between Bar Harbor and Yarmouth, Nova Scotia, was a favorite birding trip; birders scanned the waves for the species listed above as well as uncommon to rare birds such as Northern Fulmar, Cory's Shearwater, Leach's Storm-Petrel, Great and South Polar Skuas, Pomarine and Parasitic Jaegers, Black-legged Kittiwake, and Common and Thick-billed Murres. In 1998, the *Bluenose* was replaced with *The Cat.* While this pelagic birding isn't as leisurely as it once was, it is still a convenient way to search for birds seldom, if ever, seen from shore.

6   The Atlantic Puffin nests on a few islands off Maine's coast and in larger colonies in Canada. A boat trip to **Machias Seal Island** is a reliable way to see nesting puffins. When weather allows, visitors can land on the island and see not only puffins but Common Eider, Common and Arctic Terns, Razorbill, and Black Guillemot. Common Murre is also often seen in summer, though it doesn't nest on the

island, and at least a few pelagics, such as shearwaters and jaegers, are usually found on the trip out and back.

7 Nesting Nelson's Sharp-tailed Sparrow can be found in the vegetation bordering the salt marsh near **Quoddy Head State Park;** migrant shorebirds may be feeding and resting here in spring and in late summer and fall. The park is a good spot for seabirds and interesting land birds as well. At the **West Quoddy Head Light,** scan the water and offshore rocks for a seasonally changing list of birds including Common Eider; Surf, White-winged, and Black Scoters; Long-tailed Ducks; Red-throated and Common Loons; Great Cormorants; Black-legged Kittiwake; Common and Arctic Terns; Razorbill; and Black Guillemot. When winds blow shoreward, you might see migrant Northern Gannet, or Greater or Sooty Shearwater.

Trails lead though spruce-fir forest and boggy wetlands where nesting birds include Spruce Grouse and Black-backed Woodpecker (both scarce); Olive-sided and Yellow-bellied Flycatchers; Gray Jay; Boreal Chickadee; Golden-crowned and Ruby-crowned Kinglets; Tennessee, Yellow, Magnolia, Black-throated Green, Blackburnian, Blackpoll, and Black-and-white Warblers; Northern Parula; and Lincoln's and White-throated Sparrows. Red and White-winged Crossbills may be around any time of year.

8 Maine's famed **Baxter State Park** has 204,000 acres of fine birding for those prepared for its remoteness, wildness, and bugginess (bring insect repellent).

The park's high point is 5,267-foot **Mount Katahdin,** where Bicknell's Thrush sings on the sparsely wooded slopes at 3,000 feet and above. Deciduous and spruce-fir forest below hosts breeding birds such as Ring-necked Duck, Hooded Merganser, Common Loon, American Bittern, Northern Goshawk, Ruffed and Spruce Grouse, Black-backed Woodpecker (this bird prefers burned or disease-killed areas), Philadelphia Vireo, Gray Jay, Boreal Chickadee, more than 20 species of warblers, Rusty Blackbird, Purple Finch, Pine Siskin, and Evening Grosbeak.

The area around **Roaring Brook Campground** offers a good selection of birds in varied habitats along the trails to **Sandy Stream Pond.** Take trails into the highlands for upper-elevation birds including Bicknell's Thrush, or simply drive the park's main **Tote Road** and stop to investigate different habitats, from woodland to second growth to bogs and marsh.

MAINE | MORE INFORMATION

RARE BIRD ALERT
Statewide 207-781-2332

1 Kennebunk Plains
(Page 12)
www.state.me.us/spo/lmf
/projects
207-287-8000

2 East Point Sanctuary
(Page 13)
www.maineaudubon.org
207-781-2330

**3 Scarborough Marsh
Nature Center** *(Page 13)*
www.maineaudubon.org
207-883-5100

4 Acadia National Park
(Page 13)
www.nps.gov/acad
207-288-3338

**5 Bar Harbor Yarmouth
Ferry Service** *(Page 14)*
www.catferry.com
207-288-3395 or
888-249-7245
This company operates The
Cat *ferry (p. 14), which
travels between Bar Harbor,
Maine, and Yarmouth,
Nova Scotia—an opportunity
for pelagic birding.*

6 Norton's Tours
(Page 14)
www.machiassealisland
.com
207-497-5933
*Atlantic Puffins are easily
seen on summertime tours
to Machias Seal Island.
This company operates
out of Jonesport.*

**6 Bold Coast Charter
Company** *(Page 14)*
www.boldcoast.com
207-259-4484
*This company, which operates
out of Cutler, also runs trips
to Machias Seal Island for
viewing Atlantic Puffins.*

**7 Quoddy Head
State Park** *(Page 15)*
www.state.me.us/doc
/prkslnds/prkslnds.htm
207-733-0911(park season)
or 207-941-4014 (off season)

8 Baxter State Park
(Page 15)
www.baxterstatepark
authority.com
207-723-5140

NEW HAMPSHIRE

■ Seabirds along the Atlantic coast
■ Bicknell's Thrush on Mount Washington

Rye Harbor Marina

9 At **Seabrook Harbor,** you should check for unusual species among the more common gulls. Look for loons and waterfowl in migration and winter and for Great Blue Heron, Snowy Egret, and Glossy Ibis from spring through fall. Recently, the threatened Piping Plover has begun to nest here.

At **Hampton Beach State Park,** scan for Northern Gannet in spring and fall and sea ducks, Red-throated and Common Loons, Horned and Red-necked Grebes, and Cormorant in migration and winter. Check rock jetties for wintering Purple Sandpiper. At **Rye Harbor Marina,** look for waders, waterfowl, and gulls. You may see sea ducks and have another chance at a Purple Sandpiper on **Pulpit Rocks,** just offshore.

10 When at **Odiorne Point State Park,** look for migrant land birds in fall. Also scan the sea for waterbirds including the typical winter sea ducks of the region: Surf, White-winged, and Black Scoters; Long-tailed Duck; Common Goldeneye; Common Eider; and Red-breasted Merganser. Rarer are sightings of King Eiders or Harlequin Ducks.

  Wintering Bald Eagles and nesting Ospreys can be found at **Great Bay National Wildlife Refuge.** Look for a variety of migrant and winter waterfowl, from the Mute Swan to the Bufflehead, and for wading birds (spring through fall). Wood Duck and Great Blue and Green Herons in nesting season and Wild Turkey visit **Upper Peverly Pond.**

12 Osprey nests near the salt marsh by the **Sandy Point Discovery Center,** and migration can bring good viewing of shorebirds and waterfowl. Great Bay has the state's largest winter concentration of American Black Duck.

Female Spruce Grouse, an elusive North Woods bird

13 The drive up **Mount Washington** reveals species such as Ruffed Grouse; Olive-sided Flycatcher; Brown Creeper; Winter Wren; Swainson's and Hermit Thrushes; Northern Parula; and Magnolia, Black-throated Blue, Blackburnian, Bay-breasted, and Blackpoll Warblers.

The **Caps Ridge Trail** at **Jefferson Notch** affords good access to high-elevation species. Both Bicknell's Thrush and Black-backed Woodpecker (scarce) have been seen near the trailhead. Look for Olive-sided and Yellow-bellied Flycatchers; Gray Jay; Boreal Chickadee; Golden-crowned Kinglet; Magnolia, Blackburnian, Bay-breasted, and Blackpoll Warblers; and Pine Siskin.

14 The elusive Spruce Grouse, Gray Jay, Boreal Chickadee, various warblers, and Rusty Blackbird are attractions of the **Connecticut Lakes region.** Common Loons call in summer. Explore the **Connecticut Lakes State Forest** or private roads owned by timber companies. Along **Smith Brook Road** and **East Inlet Road,** you may find Ruffed and Spruce Grouse; Northern Saw-whet Owl; Black-backed Woodpecker; Olive-sided, Yellow-bellied, and Alder Flycatchers; Blue-headed and Philadelphia Vireos; Gray Jay; Common Raven; Boreal Chickadee; Winter Wren; Golden-crowned and Ruby-crowned Kinglets; Swainson's and Hermit Thrushes; Nashville, Magnolia, Yellow-rumped, Black-throated Green, Blackburnian, Bay-breasted, Blackpoll, Mourning, Canada, and Wilson's Warblers; Northern Parula; Northern Waterthrush; Rusty Blackbird; and Purple Finch.

NEW HAMPSHIRE | MORE INFORMATION

RARE BIRD ALERT
Statewide 603-224-9900

**9 Hampton Beach
State Park** *(Page 17)*
*www.nhstateparks.com
/hampton.html*
603-926-3784

**10 Odiorne Point
State Park** *(Page 17)*
*www.nhstateparks.com
/odiorne.html*
603-436-8043

**11 Great Bay National
Wildlife Refuge**
(Page 18)
*www.fws.gov/northeast
/nh/gtb.htm*
603-431-7511

**12 Sandy Point Discovery
Center** *(Page 18)*
*www.greatbay.org
/sandy_point/index.html*
603-778-0015

Open June–Oct.

**13 White Mountain
National Forest** *(Page 18)*
www.fs.fed.us/r9/white
603-528-8721

*Fee for toll road to summit.
Mount Washington
Observatory maintains a
weather station and research
facility on summit, as
well as a museum open
mid-May–late Oct.*

**14 Connecticut Lakes
Region** *(Page 18)*
www.nhconnlakes.com
603-538-7118

VERMONT

- Northern birds in the Northeast Kingdom
- Geese and wetland species at Dead Creek Wildlife Management Area

Fall flock of migrant Snow Geese, Dead Creek Wildlife Management Area, near Lake Champlain

 Look for Spruce and Ruffed Grouse at **Wenlock Wildlife Management Area,** and at nearby **Moose Bog,** as well as for Northern Saw-whet Owl; Black-backed Woodpecker; Olive-sided, Yellow-bellied, and Alder Flycatchers; Blue-headed and Philadelphia Vireos; Gray Jay; Boreal Chickadee; Red-breasted Nuthatch; Winter Wren; Golden-crowned and Ruby-crowned Kinglets; Tennessee, Nashville, Chestnut-sided, Magnolia, Cape May, Black-throated Blue, Yellow-rumped, Black-throated Green, Blackburnian, Mourning, and Canada Warblers; Northern Parula; Northern Waterthrush; Lincoln's and White-throated Sparrows; Rusty Blackbird; and White-winged Crossbill (erratic). Include some nearby roads (such as **Lewis Pond Road** or **Black Branch Road**) in your visit.

16 Many of these same boreal species can also be found at **Victory Basin Wildlife Management Area**. Bird along the road, and watch for parking areas and trails in the wildlife area.

17 **Mount Mansfield** is one of the best places to find Bicknell's Thrush. Its stunted spruce-fir forest has a good population of the thrush, best found in June and early July, when it

sings most often. On the way up, you may find Swainson's, Hermit, and Wood Thrushes; Yellow-bellied Sapsucker; Yellow-bellied and Least Flycatchers; Winter Wren; Golden-crowned Kinglet; Yellow-rumped, Blackpoll, and Black-throated Green Warblers; and Purple Finch. Near the top, look for Common Raven, White-throated Sparrow, and Dark-eyed Junco. Peregrine Falcon nests at nearby **Smuggler's Notch State Park.**

18   **Dead Creek Wildlife Management Area** is a famous birding site, and surrounding countryside can host migrant waterfowl and shorebirds. Nesting species include Northern Harrier; Upland Sandpiper; Horned Lark; Vesper, Savannah, and Grasshopper Sparrows; and Bobolink. In winter, Rough-legged Hawk, Snowy Owl, Northern Shrike, Lapland Longspur, Snow Bunting, and Common Redpoll could show up in area fields.

Wetlands at the **Stone Bridge Dam Access** in some years can have excellent migrant shorebirds and wading birds (including American and Least Bitterns and Black-crowned Night-Heron), ducks, Virginia Rail, Sora, and Common Moorhen.

South in **Addison** in spring and fall, Snow and Canada Geese may be present in roadside fields; a scan from the viewing shelter will reveal migrating waders, ducks, and shorebirds. Waders, rails, and other wetland birds may be found along Dead Creek.

The boat launch in **Chimney Point State Historic Site** is an excellent spot for winter ducks, loons, grebes, Bald Eagles, and gulls. Rolling cropland and pasture toward Middlebury host winter raptors, such as Rough-legged Hawk and the exceptionally rare Northern Hawk Owl, and Northern Shrike.

19   On the circuit through **West Rutland marsh,** look for nesting American and Least Bitterns, Virginia Rail, Sora, Common Moorhen, Alder and Willow Flycatchers, Warbling and Blue-headed Vireos, several species of swallows including Purple Martin, Marsh Wren, Yellow and Chestnut-sided Warblers, Swamp Sparrow, and Bobolink.

20   Migration is the peak time at **Herrick's Cove,** which can be filled with flycatchers, vireos, thrushes, warblers, and sparrows. Check the river and cove for waterfowl, which may include Canada Goose; Wood, American Black, and Ring-necked Ducks; American Wigeon; Mallard; Lesser Scaup; Bufflehead; Common Goldeneye; Hooded and Common Mergansers; and occasionally something unusual like Long-tailed Duck. Osprey and Bald Eagle also make appearances in migration.

VERMONT | MORE INFORMATION

RARE BIRD ALERT
Statewide 802-457-2779

15 Wenlock Wildlife Management Area
(Page 20)
*www.vtfishandwildlife.com
/wmaguide.cfm*
802-751-0100

16 Victory Basin Wildlife Management Area
(Page 20)
*www.vtfishandwildlife.com
/wmaguide.cfm*
802-751-0100

17 Mount Mansfield Natural Area *(Page 20)*
www.nature.nps.gov/nnl
802-241-3670
❓ 💲 🚶

*Toll road open Memorial
Day–Columbus Day. Trails
closed mid-Apr.–late May.*

18 Dead Creek Wildlife Management Area
(Page 21)
*www.vtfishandwildlife.com
/wmaguide.cfm*
802-759-2398
❓ 💲 🚻 🚶 〰 ♿

18 Chimney Point State Historic Site *(Page 21)*
*www.vtfishistoricvermont.
org/chimneypoint*
802-759-2412
❓ 🚻

*Exhibit center open Memorial
Day–Columbus Day.*

19 West Rutland Marsh
(Page 21)
*www.wrutland.org/bc
/marsh/marsh.html*
802-438-2381

20 Herrick's Cove
(Page 21)
vt.audubon.org/iba.html
802-434-4686

MASSACHUSETTS

- Excellent seabird sites
- Spring migration at Mount Auburn Cemetery in Cambridge

Marshland overlook, Cape Cod

21 Visit the **Newburyport** harbor and the **Joppa Flats Education Center and Wildlife Refuge** when traveling to Plum Island and the Parker River National Wildlife Refuge. The flats attract shorebirds in spring, late summer, and fall, along with wading birds, waterfowl, and gulls at various times. Arrive a few hours before or after high tide, when birds are concentrated on the exposed mudflats. The most common species are Black-bellied and Semipalmated Plovers, Greater and Lesser Yellowlegs, Semipalmated and Least Sandpipers, Dunlin, and Short-billed Dowitcher. A specialty fall bird is the Hudsonian Godwit. Check gull flocks in winter for uncommon to rare species, including Little, Black-headed, Iceland, and Glaucous. Marshy places host migrant geese and dabbling ducks; the warmer months bring herons and egrets. Also look for diving ducks such as Long-tailed Duck, Common Goldeneye, and Red-breasted Merganser.

Fields near the Plum Island airport attract "grasspipers" such as American Golden-Plover and Upland Sandpipers. On the bridge to Plum Island, look for wintering Rough-legged Hawk, Snowy and Short-eared Owls, and Northern Shrike.

22 Plum Island's **Parker River National Wildlife Refuge** is one of the region's best and most popular birding sites. With its beach, extensive salt marsh, freshwater impoundments, and scattered woodland and scrub, the refuge attracts a wide range of birds. Sample as many of the trails as you can.

COMMON EIDER

Of the four species of eider, the Common Eider is the only one that nests in the lower 48 states. These large sea ducks nest on islands off Maine and New Hampshire, where the female uses her famously soft down to line her nest (the bird's Latin name, *mollissima*, means "very soft"). Large flocks of Common Eiders are a common sight off the New England coast in winter. ∎

Check the marsh for Seaside and Saltmarsh Sharp-tailed Sparrows, Marsh Wren, in winter, Rough-legged Hawk and Short-eared Owl. Take a boardwalk to the beach to look for migrant or wintering loons, grebes, Northern Gannets, and sea ducks, or wintering Snow Bunting. (Some areas close in nesting season to protect Piping Plover.) At the **Salt Pannes,** look for shorebirds at high tide in spring, late summer, and fall.

The **Hellcat Interpretive Trail** offers two loops, one through dunes and the other through a man-made freshwater marsh where bitterns and rails are possible. Walk the dike between the North and Bill Forward Pools to look for herons and migrant waterfowl and shorebirds. Also walk the **Pines Trail** in winter to look for inconspicuous Long-eared and Northern Saw-whet Owls roosting in the trees. The **Stage Island Pool** can be excellent for shorebirds, particularly at high tide in late summer. Check the Atlantic for seabirds, and look for Purple Sandpiper on offshore rocks in winter.

23 A drive around **Cape Ann** in late fall and winter can be productive for loons, grebes, ducks, gulls, and other waterbirds. You may want to stop in Gloucester at **Stage Fort Park** or **Pavilion Beach** to look over the harbor. Great numbers of gulls are attracted to the fishing fleet here, and you'll often find Iceland and Glaucous among the common species.

Two spots on the north part of the cape are especially fine lookout points: In **Rockport,** visit Cathedral Ledge on Phillips Avenue, a prime spot to look for small rafts of Harlequin Ducks from November to May. Expect to see Common Eider;

Surf, White-winged, and Black Scoters; Long-tailed Duck; Common Goldeneye; Red-breasted Merganser; Red-throated and Common Loons; Horned and Red-necked Grebes; Northern Gannet; Great and Double-crested Cormorants; Razorbill; Black Guillemot; gulls; and, down on the rocks, small flocks of Purple Sandpipers. Watch for King Eider. When northeast winds blow, uncommon species such as shear-waters, jaegers, and other alcids may appear. .

The observation point at **Halibut Point State Park** offers an even better panorama of the Atlantic's bird life. The headland here, certainly one of the state's premier birding spots, provides good chances of seeing the pelagic species that fly past this Cape Ann extremity in fall and winter. During onshore winds in summer and fall, this spot can be good for shearwaters and jaegers, too.

24 Celebrated as a spring "migrant trap," where songbirds pause to rest and feed on their northbound flight, is the famed **Mount Auburn Cemetery,** which has more than 10 miles of roads and paths to explore. In spring, a board at the entrance lists recent sightings, and local birding clubs lead guided walks most mornings.

25 The eastern part of Cape Cod—the **Outer Cape**—is a fine birding destination. More than 43,000 acres are pro-tected as national seashore, while a national wildlife refuge and a Massachusetts Audubon Society sanctuary provide additional birding opportunities.

Walk onto **Morris Island** and the headquarters of **Monomoy National Wildlife Refuge,** which owns land where you're free to walk the beaches and observe herons, waterfowl, shorebirds, gulls, and terns. Be sure to ask at refuge headquarters about commercial tours to **North Monomoy Island** and nearby **South Beach.** The latter can have amazing numbers of shorebirds, gulls, and terns at high tide, and in recent years has become one of the top birding spots on the cape.

Wellfleet Bay Wildlife Sanctuary offers guided boat trips around Cape Cod and to **South Monomoy Island,** where a visit in spring or fall migration may bring sightings of excellent num-bers of shorebirds and, on occasion, abundant land birds in the thickets and scrub. Rarities sometimes show up on this tiny patch of land. Despite South Monomoy Island's potential, it can be difficult for a first-timer; a guided trip is by far the best option here.

South Monomoy Island once hosted greater numbers of terns, but increases in populations of Herring and Great Black-backed Gulls caused a huge drop in tern numbers. Recent measures to control gulls, however, have allowed Roseate Tern and Black Skimmer to return, as well as dramatic increases in nesting Common and Least Terns. The number of Piping Plover nests has also increased.

Pick up a map and obtain information about nature programs at the Salt Pond Visitor Center of **Cape Cod National Seashore.** Continue to **Coast Guard Beach** to scan for sea ducks, loons, grebes, and shorebirds. On your return, scan the marsh near Fort Hill for herons and migrant waterfowl and search scrubby areas for migrant songbirds.

26 The **Wellfleet Bay Wildlife Sanctuary** protects 1,000 acres of salt marsh, pinewoods, beach, and fields, home to an excellent diversity of species. Shorebirding can be superb here in spring, late summer, and fall, and spring migration can also bring good numbers of songbirds to woods and thickets. Follow trails out to the shore, past marshes where you may find herons and egrets in summer and waterfowl in migration. Piping Plover and Least Tern breed here, and guides are on hand to show these threatened species to visitors. Sanctuary staff members are an excellent source of advice on birding in the area. Varied natural history programs, including birding cruises, are offered throughout the year.

27 The Province Lands Visitor Center of the **Cape Cod National Seashore** is found near the north tip of Cape Cod. In spring and fall, bird along the trails in the **Beech Forest,** a fine spot for migrant songbirds. From late summer though winter, continue to the parking lot at **Race Point Beach,** which provides a convenient place from which to scan the Atlantic for loons and ducks, as well as for passing pelagic species such as shearwaters, Northern Gannet, phalaropes, jaegers, Razorbill, and Black Guillemot.

For those who want a better chance at pelagic species—birds such as the "tubenoses" (Northern Fulmar, shearwaters, and storm-petrels), phalaropes, skuas, jaegers, and alcids that spend most of their lives at sea—whale-watching boats provide a way to get out on the ocean at a reasonable cost. Late spring through fall usually offers the best seabirding. While these cruises are aimed at finding whales, often some members of the crew are knowledgeable about birds.

MASSACHUSETTS | MORE INFORMATION

RARE BIRD ALERT
Statewide 888-224-6444

21 Joppa Flats Education Center and Wildlife Refuge
(Page 23)
www.massaudubon.org
978-462-9998

22 Parker River National Wildlife Refuge *(Page 24)*
parkerriver.fws.gov
978-465-5753

23 Halibut Point State Park *(Page 25)*
www.mass.gov/dcr /forparks.htm
978-546-2997

24 Mount Auburn Cemetery *(Page 25)*
www.mountauburn.org
617-547-7105

25 Monomoy National Wildlife Refuge*(Page 25)*
monomoy.fws.gov
508-945-0594

Call regarding boat tours.

26 Wellfleet Bay Wildlife Sanctuary
(Page 26)
www.wellfleet.org
508-349-2615

27 Cape Cod National Seashore *(Page 26)*
www.nps.gov/caco
508-255-3785

Salt Pond Visitor Center open weekends Jan.–mid-Feb. and daily rest of year. Province Lands Visitor Center open daily mid-Apr.–Nov.

RHODE ISLAND

■ Fall migration on Block Island
■ Harlequin Ducks at Sachuest Point National Wildlife Refuge

Southeast Lighthouse, Block Island

28 Most of Rhode Island's best birding spots are near, or in, the Atlantic. **Block Island** is renowned for the number and variety of fall birds it attracts. At the peak time (early September to late October), birders come to spot rarities and marvel at the hunting flights of Merlin and Peregrine Falcon. Nearly any migrant eastern bird might show up on the island in fall, as well as western rarities like Say's Phoebe and Western Kingbird (a regular visitor). Start your birding at **Block Island National Wildlife Refuge,** but be discreet, as most of the island is private property.

The ferry takes about an hour; by air the trip is a quick hop. Rental bikes and cars are available on the island, but first-timers should try to experience Block Island in fall on a group tour.

29 Back on the mainland, **Trustom Pond National Wildlife Refuge** is a popular year-round birding destination, with a mix of woods, fields, and wetlands. The 642-acre refuge includes the brackish Trustom Pond, the only undeveloped coastal salt pond in the state. Observation platforms permit scanning for Mute Swan (or rare Tundra Swan), geese, and a variety of ducks from fall through spring.

Waders including Great Blue and Green Herons, Great and Snowy Egrets, and Glossy Ibis feed on the pond from spring through fall. Look for Osprey in spring and summer. When the water level is right, the pond attracts migrant shorebirds in numbers. The threatened Piping Plover nests on the beach south of the pond. The refuge still has extensive grassland, now uncommon in Rhode Island. Bobolink and Eastern Meadowlark sing in fields in summer, and in winter Northern Harrier, Rough-legged Hawk, and Short-eared Owl search for prey.

30 From fall through spring, a visit to **Point Judith** can turn up an interesting list of seabirds. At the park just before the lighthouse, scan the Atlantic for species such as Common Eider; Surf, White-winged, and Black Scoter; Long-tailed Duck; Red-breasted Merganser; Common Goldeneye; Red-throated and Common Loons; Horned and Red-necked Grebes; and Northern Gannet. Birders hope for rarer finds from Barrow's Goldeneye to jaegers to Black-legged Kittiwake to Razorbill.

31 The strategic location of the **Sachuest Point National Wildlife Refuge** makes it an excellent spot for seabirds fall through spring. Perimeter trails offer views of loons, grebes, cormorants, and sea ducks. Check the rocks for Purple Sandpiper, and look over flocks of Common Eider for the rare King Eider.

The star attraction is Harlequin Duck, regularly seen here in winter, quite often around the offshore **Island Rocks.** Uncommon to rare over much of the Northeast coast, the beautiful Harlequin makes braving the cold winds of the point more than worthwhile. Rough-legged Hawk and Short-eared Owl are regular winter visitors to the refuge, and Snow Bunting frequents grassy places. As you scan the surrounding waters here, look for all the seabird species listed above for Point Judith.

32 Providence's most famous site for spring songbird migration is **Swan Point Cemetery,** next to the Seekonk River. The most popular area is the wooded section in the northwest part of the cemetery.

RHODE ISLAND | MORE INFORMATION

RARE BIRD ALERT
Statewide 401-949-3870

28 Block Island National Wildlife Refuge
(Page 28)
www.fws.gov/blockisland
401-364-9124

29 Trustom Pond National Wildlife Refuge
(Page 29)
www.fws.gov/northeast
401-364-9124

Barrier beach closed Apr.–mid-Sept.

30 Point Judith Lighthouse *(Page 29)*
www.cr.nps.gov /maritime/light/ptjudith.htm
401-789-0444

31 Sachuest Point National Wildlife Refuge
(Page 29)
www.fws.gov/northeast /sachuestpoint
401-847-5511

32 Swan Point Cemetery
(Page 29)
swanpointcemetery.com
401-272-1314

CONNECTICUT

- Fall hawk migration at Lighthouse Point Park
- Fine birding all year at White Memorial Foundation

Snowy Owl, an irregularly occurring winter visitor from the Arctic

33 The diverse habitat of the **Audubon Center in Greenwich** draws flycatchers, vireos, thrushes, and warblers in spring migration. Nesting birds include Ruffed Grouse; Wood Duck; Green Heron; Pileated Woodpecker; White-eyed and Warbling Vireos; Carolina Wren; Eastern Bluebird; Veery; Blue-winged, Yellow, Chestnut-sided, and Worm-eating Warblers; Louisiana Waterthrush; Swamp Sparrow; and Rose-breasted Grosbeak.

34 **Milford Point** is a favorite birding spot. At the **Connecticut Audubon Coastal Center,** look for herons and egrets (spring through fall) and for migrant and wintering waterfowl. Osprey, gulls, and terns may fly over, while Clapper Rail skulks below. Black-crowned and Yellow-crowned Night-Herons breed in this area. Migrating shorebirds can be abundant. In late summer, Roseate Tern may fly with Common Tern; in fall, Peregrine Falcon may appear. Winter brings Red-throated Loon, Greater Scaup, possibly a scoter or Old-squaw, and Purple Sandpiper in rocky spots. Snowy Owl is an irregular winter visitor. Watch for wading birds, waterfowl, shorebirds, gulls, and terns near the **Stewart B. McKinney National Wildlife Refuge,** where small numbers of Piping Plover, American Oystercatcher, and Least Tern breed.

35 Varied habitats make **Hammonasset Beach State Park** one of the state's top birding sites. In spring or fall, head to **Willard's Island Nature Trail,** where songbirds can be abundant and marshland draws waders and shorebirds. Clapper Rail, Willet, and Saltmarsh Sharp-tailed and Seaside Sparrows nest in the marsh. Great Blue Heron, Great and Snowy Egrets, and Glossy Ibis are seen often here. In winter, the marsh is a hunting ground for Northern Harrier and Short-eared Owl.

36 **Devil's Hopyard State Park** is known for a variety of breeding species. In spring and summer, look along its trails for Pileated Woodpecker; Acadian and Least Flycatchers; Blue-headed, Yellow-throated, and Warbling Vireos; Brown Creeper; Chestnut-sided, Black-throated Green, Cerulean, and Worm-eating Warblers; American Redstart; Ovenbird; Louisiana Waterthrush; Scarlet Tanager; and Rose-breasted Grosbeak.

37 The **White Memorial Foundation and Conservation Center** offers excellent year-round birding, with many of the following birds found in spring and summer only. **Catlin Woods** is a favorite spot, with nesting Ruffed Grouse; Pileated Woodpecker; Red-breasted Nuthatch; and Yellow-rumped, Black-throated Green, and Blackburnian Warblers. **Little Pond** is home to Green Heron, Mute Swan, Wood Duck, Virginia Rail, Eastern Phoebe, Common Yellowthroat, Swamp Sparrow, and Red-winged Blackbird. Fields and scrubby areas have Alder and Willow Flycatchers; Warbling Vireo; Eastern Bluebird; Blue-winged, Yellow, and Chestnut-sided Warblers; and Field and Song Sparrows. **Laurel Hill** hosts several warblers, and **Point Folly** makes a good lookout from which to search for migrant Common Loon, Horned Grebe, and a variety of ducks.

38 Near Kent, **River Road** offers excellent spring-migration birding and interesting breeding birds (e.g., Acadian Flycatcher and Cerulean Warbler). Migrating Osprey and Bald Eagle fish along the river. During the spring and summer, look and listen for Ruffed Grouse; Blue-winged, Yellow, Chestnut-sided, Black-throated Blue, and Worm-eating Warblers; Scarlet Tanager; and Rose-breasted Grosbeak.

CONNECTICUT | MORE INFORMATION

RARE BIRD ALERT
Statewide 203-254-3665

33 Audubon Center in Greenwich *(Page 31)*
greenwich.center
.audubon.org
203-869-5272

The Quaker Ridge hawk-watch site is staffed in fall. Sharp-shinned, Cooper's, Broad-winged, and Red-tailed Hawks and American Kestrel are the most common raptors.

34 Connecticut Audubon Coastal Center *(Page 31)*
www.ctaudubon.org
/visit/milford.htm
203-878-7440

34 Stewart B. McKinney National Wildlife Refuge
(Page 32)
www.fws.gov/refuges
860-399-2513

35 Hammonasset Beach State Park *(Page 32)*
dep.state.ct.us/stateparks
203-245-2785

At Meig's Point, scan the sound in winter for typical North Atlantic species. Purple Sandpiper is often found on rocks just offshore.

36 Devil's Hopyard State Park *(Page 32)*
dep.state.ct.us/stateparks
860-873-8566

37 White Memorial Foundation and Conservation Center
(Page 32)
www.whitememorialcc.org
860-567-0857

ADDITIONAL SITES

1 Lighthouse Point Park
www.cityofnewhaven.
com/parks
203-946-8005

This is a noted fall hawk-watch spot. From late summer to Nov., Sharp-shinned and Broad-winged Hawks and a dozen or more other species pass over the park. Fall song-bird migration is another highlight. Shorebirds can make a good showing from late summer through fall.

2 East Rock Park
cityofnewhaven.com/parks
203-787-6086

Many consider East Rock Park to be the state's best spring migrant-songbird site. In late Apr. and May, flycatchers, vireos, thrushes, warblers, and other birds appear in excellent numbers near Mill River.

3 Bluff Point State Park and Coastal Reserve
dep.state.ct.us/stateparks
860-445-1729

Bluff Point hosts migrant and winter waterbirds and shorebirds, but most birders hope for a good fall concentration of migrant songbirds.

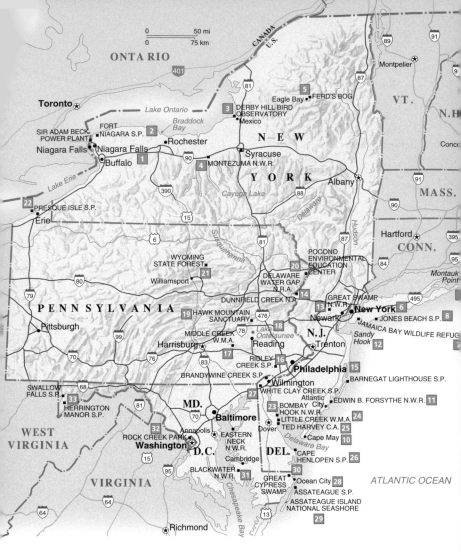

ONTARIO

Toronto

CANADA
U.S.

Montpelier

VT.

N.H.

Lake Ontario
Braddock Bay

3 DERBY HILL BIRD OBSERVATORY
Mexico

Eagle Bay · **5** FERD'S BOG

N E W

Conco

SIR ADAM BECK POWER PLANT
FORT NIAGARA S.P. **2**
Niagara Falls
Niagara Falls · Rochester
1 · Buffalo
Syracuse
4 MONTEZUMA N.W.R.

Albany

MASS.

Y O R K

Cayuga Lake

Hartford

CONN.

22 PRESQUE ISLE S.P.
Erie

Lake Erie

Susquehanna

Delaware

Hudson

Montauk Point

WYOMING STATE FOREST
21
Williamsport

POCONO ENVIRONMENTAL EDUCATION CENTER

20 DELAWARE WATER GAP N.R.A.

14 GREAT SWAMP N.W.R.
13 Newark
6 New York
8 JONES BEACH S.P.

P E N N S Y L V A N I A

Pittsburgh

DUNNFIELD CREEK N.A.

19 HAWK MOUNTAIN SANCTUARY

18
Lake Onteaunee
MIDDLE CREEK W.M.A.
Reading
Harrisburg

JAMAICA BAY WILDLIFE REFUG
Sandy Hook
12

N. J.
Trenton

17
RIDLEY CREEK S.P. **16**
BRANDYWINE CREEK S.P.

Philadelphia **15**

SWALLOW FALLS S.P.
33 HERRINGTON MANOR S.P.

27 WHITE CLAY CREEK S.P.
Wilmington

BARNEGAT LIGHTHOUSE S.P.

MD.
32 ROCK CREEK PARK
Annapolis
Baltimore
Washington **D.C.**

23 BOMBAY HOOK N.W.R.
Atlantic City
EDWIN B. FORSYTHE N.W.R. **11**
LITTLE CREEK W.M.A. **24**
TED HARVEY C.A. **25**

EASTERN NECK N.W.R.
Dover
Cambridge

Cape May **10**

DEL.
CAPE HENLOPEN S.P. **26

WEST VIRGINIA

BLACKWATER N.W.R. **31**
30 GREAT CYPRESS SWAMP
Ocean City **28**
ASSATEAGUE S.P.

ATLANTIC OCEAN

VIRGINIA

Richmond

Chesapeake Bay

Delaware Bay

ASSATEAGUE ISLAND NATIONAL SEASHORE
29

MID-ATLANTIC

- New York
- New Jersey
- Pennsylvania
- Delaware
- Maryland

HERE SPRAWLS THE SOUTHERN PART OF ONE OF THE world's great urban corridors, the Washington-to-Boston supermetropolis. Here highways entwine with rail lines and more highways, and city and suburb alternate seemingly without end along Atlantic shore and harbors, until from an airplane the landscape seems one glowing band of light. Here in large part we have reconfigured the natural landscape to serve our own purposes, for better or worse.

Here, too, is Cape May, New Jersey, unquestionably one of America's top birding spots, where hawks and land birds pass by each fall, sometimes by the hundreds of thousands. Northern New Jersey holds Great Swamp National Wildlife Refuge, where conservationists fought off a proposed airport in the days before ecology was a buzzword. In the expansive tidal marshes along Delaware Bay, rails carry on their furtive affairs as they did in the days before the first Europeans appeared. To the north, herons, egrets, and shorebirds enthrall watchers next door to John F. Kennedy and Philadelphia international airports, at Jamaica Bay Wildlife Refuge and John Heinz National Wildlife Refuge, respectively.

Nature yet endures in our largest metropolitan agglomeration, and so do opportunities for birding. For a beginner, the great thing about the mass of people in the Northeast is the fact that there are just that many more birders and a valuable body of collective expertise to exploit. Gulls in their multifarious plumages can seem impossible to sort out, for example, but visit Niagara Falls in early winter and you will find people peering through telescopes who will point out the darker underside of the primary feathers of the one Black-headed Gull amid all those Bonaparte's. Spend a weekend at one of the region's excellent hawk-watching sites and you'll learn a lot about the shapes and sizes and wing-flapping patterns of raptors. While you'll encounter the inevitable can't-be-bothered birder who is single-mindedly pursuing one particular species, you'll find many more friendly folks who are willing and happy to share their knowledge with others. ■

Ruddy Turnstone

SPECIAL BIRDS OF THE MID-ATLANTIC

Cory's Shearwater	Common Eider	Pomarine Jaeger	
Greater Shearwater	Surf Scoter	Parasitic Jaeger	
Sooty Shearwater	White-winged Scoter	Little Gull	
Wilson's Storm-Petrel	Black Scoter	Lesser Black-backed Gull	Yellow-bellied Flycatcher
Northern Gannet	Long-tailed Duck		Bicknell's Thrush
Great Cormorant	Ruffed Grouse	Black-legged Kittiwake	Golden-winged Warbler
Glossy Ibis	Black Rail	Least Tern	
Brant	Piping Plover	Gull-billed Tern	Cerulean Warbler
Mute Swan	American Oystercatcher	Roseate Tern	Prothonotary Warbler
Tundra Swan		Black Skimmer	Saltmarsh Sharp-tailed Sparrow
Eurasian Wigeon	Purple Sandpiper	Pileated Woodpecker	
Black Scoter	Ruff		Seaside Sparrow

NEW YORK

- Winter gulls at Niagara Falls
- Spring hawk-watching at Derby Hill Bird Observatory
- Fall shorebirds at Jamaica Bay Wildlife Refuge

Niagara Falls, on
the United States–
Canada border

1 **Niagara Falls,** famous the world over for its thundering walls of water, is celebrated by birders for a related phenomenon: The area from the rocky rapids above the falls down through the Niagara River Gorge to its outlet at Lake Ontario has been called "the gull capital of North America." In late fall and winter, gulls attracted to the churning water, which remains mostly unfrozen through the coldest weather, sometimes congregate by the tens of thousands. Mixed in with the abundant Bonaparte's, Ring-billed, and Herring are always assorted uncommon to rare species, from Little and Black-headed to Iceland, Glaucous, and Great Black-backed—sometimes totaling a dozen or more species.

At **Goat Island,** which separates the American Falls from the Horseshoe, or Canadian, Falls, check the rapids above the falls for gulls and for ducks, which may include Canvasback, Greater Scaup, Bufflehead, Common Goldeneye, and Common and Red-breasted Mergansers. Many birders agree that the Canadian side of the river provides better views, so cross the border and visit the many observation points in the park both above and below the falls.

Stop at the **Sir Adam Beck Power Plant** on the Canadian side, where flocks of gulls feed in the outflow. Then cross to the American side again and check the power-plant outlet between Niagara Falls and Lewiston. Finally, continue to **Fort Niagara State Park,** and scan the river and lake for gulls and waterbirds, which might include Common or King Eider, Harlequin Duck, scoters, Long-tailed Duck, or Barrow's Goldeneye, Red-throated Loon, and Red-necked Grebe.

2 One of western New York's best all-around birding spots, **Braddock Bay** on Lake Ontario is a mix of city park, state wildlife management area, and private property that offers marsh and wading birds, waterfowl, owls, migrant songbirds, and an exciting spring hawk-watch. In spring, hawks pass along the lakeshore by the thousands: Sharp-shinned, Broad-winged, and Red-tailed are most frequent, but several other species are common as well. Also, scan the bay here for Double-crested Cormorant in spring, migrant and wintering waterfowl, migrant Caspian and Common Terns in spring (plus Forster's in fall), and nesting Black Tern, a seriously declining species in the Northeast. Beginning near the hawk-watching platform, a nature trail leads to **Cranberry Pond,** where at times you can spot waders (including occasional American and Least Bitterns), ducks, rails, and migrant shorebirds. On nearby Island Cottage Road, stop to check the ponds on the south as you go. Park and explore **Island Cottage Woods** (taking care to stay on the trails), where spring songbird migration can bring excellent numbers of vireos, thrushes, and warblers.

3 Spring hawk-watching has made the **Derby Hill Bird Observatory** one of the state's most famous birding sites. From this high point on the southeastern corner of the Lake Ontario shoreline, watchers tally the sometimes spectacular numbers of hawks that stream past from late winter into May. (Here, as at Braddock Bay, weather can make the hawk flight either exciting or slow. The best days have moderate southerly winds and some cloud cover.) Broad-winged Hawk is by far the most numerous species, but anything from Bald and Golden Eagles to Northern Goshawk and Peregrine Falcon might happen by. Osprey; Northern Harrier; Sharp-shinned, Cooper's, Red-shouldered, Red-tailed, and Rough-legged Hawks; and American Kestrel are all regular migrants at various times throughout the spring.

PURPLE SANDPIPER

The Purple Sandpiper, which breeds in the Arctic, might better be called a "rockpiper," since in winter it's almost always found on wave-splashed rocks along the North Atlantic coast. It especially favors rock jetties, and with the building of these structures where once there was only sand and marsh, it now winters much farther south than before. Look for this sandpiper at Barnegat Lighthouse State Park in New Jersey and the Ocean City jetty in Maryland. ▪

4 Situated at the northern end of Cayuga Lake in New York's Finger Lakes region, the more than 7,000 acres of **Montezuma National Wildlife Refuge** protect marshland that can host well over 100,000 waterfowl in spring and fall migration, including Snow and Canada Geese, Tundra Swan, and up to 25 species of ducks, several of which remain to nest. Naturally, all this marsh attracts other birds, too: Breeding species include Pied-billed Grebe, American and Least (rare) Bitterns, Great Blue Heron, Black-crowned Night-Heron, Virginia Rail, Sora, Common Moorhen, Common and Black Terns, and Marsh (and rarely Sedge) Wren. Scan the refuge **Main Pool** from the visitor center or nearby observation platform before beginning the wildlife drive. Watch for Osprey and Northern Harrier, both of which nest here, and for various waterbirds including Double-crested Cormorant, herons, egrets, gulls, and terns. Check **Tschache Pool** for nesting Bald Eagle and **May's Point Pool** for fall migrant shorebirds, which sometimes take flight at the approach of a hunting Peregrine Falcon.

5 One well-known spot to find many of the northern birds of the Adirondack Mountains is **Ferd's Bog,** a suitably boreal-looking spot near the small town of Eagle Bay. A trail here leads into an open bog where pitcher plants, sundews, and orchids grow. Nesting birds in the vicinity are a roll call of mostly higher latitude species, Northern Saw-whet Owl; American Three-toed (scarce) and Black-backed Woodpeckers; Olive-sided and Yellow-bellied Flycatchers; Blue-headed Vireo; Gray Jay; Boreal Chickadee; Red-breasted Nuthatch; Brown Creeper; Winter Wren; Golden-crowned

Kinglet; Nashville, Magnolia, Black-throated Blue, Black-throated Green, Blackburnian, and Canada Warblers; Northern Parula; Lincoln's, Swamp, and White-throated Sparrows; Dark-eyed Junco; and Purple Finch. Osprey nests nearby, and Red Crossbill is an irregular visitor. Spruce Grouse occurs elsewhere in the Adirondacks; with luck you'll see one here. Walk carefully, as the bog environment is fragile.

6 Any list of New York's birding hot spots must mention one of the best, and seemingly unlikeliest, of them all. **Central Park,** right in the heart of Manhattan, is a magnet not only for migrants but for city-bound birders. The park's 840 acres must seem tremendously inviting to birds looking for shelter in a forest of buildings, and nearly any patch of trees or shrubs may host interesting species in spring and, to a lesser extent, in fall. Most favored is the **Ramble,** a wooded area near the Great Lawn. In late April and May, you will find plenty of birders exploring the pathways for flycatchers, vireos, thrushes, warblers, sparrows, and anything else that might drop in. Central Park isn't just a convenient urban substitute for a "real" birding trip. When a migrant wave hits, it can hold its own with nearly any place on the East Coast. While not as famous as Central Park, **Prospect Park,** across the East River in Brooklyn, deserves mention as another fine migrant site.

7 Year-round, New York City's most rewarding birding site is the **Jamaica Bay Wildlife Refuge** in southern Queens. (The parking lot at the refuge visitor center is easy to miss, so watch for it carefully on the west side of Cross Bay Boulevard.) Herons, ibises, waterfowl, and shorebirds are the attraction at this preserve hard by John F. Kennedy International Airport; an amazing total of 330 species have been seen here. Stop at the refuge visitor center for information and a necessary free permit to walk the trails, and check the sightings book for interesting recent finds. Then walk around the **West Pond,** where depending on the season you will find geese and ducks, or waders (such as Great and Snowy Egrets, Tricolored Heron, Yellow-crowned Night-Heron, and Glossy Ibis), or shorebirds, gulls, and terns. American Oystercatcher, Willet, Marsh Wren, Saltmarsh Sharp-tailed and Seaside Sparrows, and Boat-tailed Grackle are among the nesting birds. In winter, look for Brant in Jamaica Bay, for Northern Harrier and Short-eared Owl over the marshes, and for an occasional Snowy Owl perched regally on the ground. The "garden" area near the visitor center can be

excellent for migrant land birds in spring and fall (especially).

This much visited refuge, part of **Gateway National Recreation Area,** is best known for shorebirds, especially in late summer and early fall at the **East Pond,** across from the visitor center. High tide is most productive, and at times the mudflats may be crowded with hundreds of Black-bellied and Semipalmated Plovers, Greater and Lesser Yellowlegs, Semipalmated and Least Sandpipers, Red Knot, and Dunlin, to name just a few of the common species. Less numerous species include Hudsonian Godwit, Stilt Sandpiper, and Wilson's Phalarope, plus the occasional Old World rarity.

8 **Jones Beach State Park** is one of the top sites on Long Island. (It is actually on one of the barrier islands that parallel Long Island's southern coast.) From fall through spring, follow Bay Parkway to the west end of the island. In fall—especially with a northwest wind, which pushes southbound migrants to the ocean's edge—the vegetation in this area can be alive with songbirds, often including western strays. Also keep an eye out for migrant raptors, including Merlin and Peregrine Falcon. Walk west along the beach, watching in winter for Northern Harrier, Snowy Owl, Horned Lark, the Ipswich race of Savannah Sparrow, and Snow Bunting. Check the jetty at the west end of the island for wintering Purple Sandpiper, and scan the sea and inlet for seabirds and possibly Harlequin Duck.

Cross over to Fire Island and **Robert Moses State Park,** another excellent spot in migration. An annual hawk-watch here records good numbers of raptors, and here, as at Jones Beach, fall songbird migration can be exciting. Piping Plover and Least Tern, two species hurt by beach development and recreational use, nest along these barrier islands. In summer, watch for Roseate Tern among flocks of the more common terns.

9 At Long Island's eastern tip, **Montauk Point** has long been a favorite spot from which to see waterbirds from fall through spring. Near the historic lighthouse, scan the waters and you may find many Common Eider; Long-tailed Duck; Surf, White-winged, and Black Scoters; Common Goldeneye; Red-breasted Merganser; Red-throated and Common Loons; Northern Gannet; and gulls of various kinds, to list a sampling. Look for alcids (auks) such as Dovekie and Razorbill in the sea. Check fields, scrub, and dunes in nearby parklands for sparrows, Lapland Longspur, and Snow Bunting, and expect to see Northern Harrier and Rough-legged Hawk on the hunt.

NEW YORK | MORE INFORMATION

RARE BIRD ALERT
Albany 518-439-8080
Buffalo 716-896-1271
Chautauqua County
 716-595-8250
Ithaca 607-254-2429
Lower Hudson Valley
 914-666-6614
New York City
 212-979-3070
Rochester 716-425-4630
Syracuse 315-668-8000

1 Fort Niagara State Park *(Page 37)*
nysparks.state.ny.us/parks
716-745-7273

2 Braddock Bay Fish and Wildlife Management Area *(Page 37)*
www.dec.state.ny.us
/website/reg8/wma
/braddock.html
716-948-5182

3 Derby Hill Bird Observatory *(Page 37)*
www.dec.state.ny.us
/website/education
/drbyhill.html
315-963-8291

4 Montezuma National Wildlife Refuge *(Page 38)*
www.fws.gov/r5mnwr
315-568-5987

5 Ferd's Bog *(Page 38)*
www.nybirds.org/Articles
/ferds_bog.htm

6 Central Park *(Page 39)*
www.centralparknyc.org
212-310-6600

7 Jamaica Bay Wildlife Refuge *(Page 39)*
www.nature.nps.gov/jbi
718-318-4340

Free permit required and available at visitor center.

8 Jones Beach State Park *(Page 40)*
nysparks.state.ny.us/parks
516-785-1600

8 Robert Moses State Park *(Page 40)*
nysparks.state.ny.us/parks
631-669-0470

9 Montauk Point *(Page 40)*
nysparks.state.ny.us/parks
631-668-3781

NEW JERSEY

- Fall migration at Cape May
- Winter waterbirds at Barnegat Lighthouse State Park
- Year-round birding at Edwin B. Forsythe National Wildlife Refuge

Belted Kingfisher, perched here, but often seen diving for fish

10 Fall migration at **Cape May** ranks with the most dramatic and rewarding birding adventures in the country. Situated at the end of a peninsula dividing Delaware Bay from the Atlantic Ocean, Cape May is home to seabirds or shorebirds throughout the year. In fall, southbound migrant songbirds following the coast (or pushed against it by westerly winds) arrive at the cape and face the challenge of flying at least 12 miles over water. Many stop to feed and rest before flying on; others, forced out to sea by north and west winds, fight their way back to land to regain their strength before continuing. In addition, tens of thousands of migrant hawks pass over the cape, their numbers concentrated by the funnel shape of the land.

All these birds, inevitably including rarities, attract many birders. Like a happy convention of migration-watchers, they leave few trees or fields or patches of sky unexamined and pass word rapidly of some outlandish discovery, perhaps a Calliope Hummingbird from the Pacific Northwest or a Swallow-tailed Kite from the Southeast or a Brown-chested Martin from South America. A major wave, or "fallout," of birds at Cape May is often dependent on the weather. In fall, the best wind is northwest, but anything between southwest and north-northeast can be good. In spring, the best flights occur with southwesterly winds and overcast conditions.

Newcomers should begin exploration at the Northwood Center of **Cape May Bird Observatory.** Across from the observatory information center is **Lily Lake,** a popular birding spot. The observatory's hawk-watch at **Cape May Point State Park** is staffed from September through November. Usually 16 to 18 species of raptors are seen each fall, with peak numbers from late September to mid-October and the greatest diversity from late October to early November. On a good day with northwest winds, there can be huge numbers of Sharp-shinned Hawk, and often amazing flights of American Kestrel, Merlin, and Peregrine Falcon.

The beach at Cape May Point is also a good place from which to scan for seabirds, and there may be flocks of all sorts of vireos, thrushes, warblers, and other songbirds in fall.

The Nature Conservancy's **Migratory Bird Refuge,** also called South Cape May Meadows, is another favorite birding spot, where Least Bittern, Virginia Rail, Piping Plover, and Least Tern nest. Wetlands attract waders and waterfowl, and beach access allows searching for shorebirds and seabirds. **Higbee Beach Wildlife Management Area** is Cape May's finest spot for migrant songbirds and for nesting Yellow-breasted Chat and Blue Grosbeak. For the best birding be sure to arrive here early, as on some days the show may pretty well be over by 9 a.m.

11 New Jersey's second most famous birding site is the **Brigantine Division** of the **Edwin B. Forsythe National Wildlife Refuge.** Migrant shorebirds are the main attraction at Brigantine; they can be abundant in numbers and exciting in diversity both in spring and in late summer and fall, when 30 or more species might be found in the refuge's **West** and **East Pools** and in **Turtle Cove.** Uncommon to rare species such as Black-necked Stilt, Hudsonian and Marbled Godwits, Baird's and Curlew Sandpipers, and Ruff make occasional stops here.

These wetlands attract wading birds and waterfowl: Migrant and wintering Tundra Swan, Snow Goose, Brant (which rest on the bay but fly to the West Pool to drink fresh water); summer concentrations of herons, egrets, and ibises; and more than 20 species of ducks from fall through spring. Nesting birds include Osprey, Peregrine Falcon (reintroduced here), Gull-billed Tern, Black Skimmer, Fish Crow, Saltmarsh Sharp-tailed and Seaside Sparrows, and Boat-tailed Grackle. In winter, Short-eared Owls, eagles, and Rough-legged Hawks hunt over fields and marshes.

NORTHERN GANNET

With its pointed bill and tail and tapered body, the Northern Gannet seems as aerodynamic as a winged rocket ship as it flies over the ocean. Spotting a fish, it dives into the water with a spectacular impact from as high as 50 to 60 feet. From large nesting colonies in eastern Canada, gannets roam the East Coast from fall through spring, sometimes coming quite close to shore. ▪

Barnegat Lighthouse State Park is one of New Jersey's hot spots in the cold of winter. From the park or the long jetty that extends along **Barnegat Inlet,** scan for wintering birds including Common and King Eiders; Harlequin Duck; Long-tailed Duck; Surf, White-winged, and Black Scoters; Red-throated and Common Loons; Double-crested and Great Cormorants; Black-legged Kittiwake and Razorbill (both rare); and Snow Bunting. Purple Sandpiper is usually present on jetty rocks in winter. In late fall and spring, look east across the Atlantic, where you may find Northern Gannet fishing offshore.

12 Like Jamaica Bay Wildlife Refuge in New York, **Sandy Hook** is part of **Gateway National Recreation Area**. It's another good spot for wintering ducks and other waterbirds, and especially for spring and fall migrant songbirds, which rest and feed in any patch of trees or scrub. In addition, the narrowness of the spit here concentrates migrant raptors and can create a good hawk flight in spring and fall. Osprey, Piping Plover, and Least Tern are among the breeding birds.

Parking lots on the east side offer views of the ocean, where some of the same sea ducks listed for Barnegat Lighthouse may be present in winter, and an east wind in spring or fall may bring Northern Gannet close in. Anywhere you find beach dunes, look for Snow Bunting and the Ipswich race of Savannah Sparrow in winter. Stop at the visitor center and walk west to **Spermaceti Cove** to check for waterbirds and (at low tide) for shorebirds. A mile-long nature trail begins here. Check the woods to the north for migrant songbirds, visit the observation tower to scan **North Beach** for raptors and waterbirds, and walk the dune trail along **North Pond** for bitterns, waterfowl, rails, and passerines. **Horseshoe Cove** to the west is good for waterbirds, while the Boy Scout camp opposite the boardwalk is an excellent "migrant trap."

13 The **Great Swamp National Wildlife Refuge** was almost an airport. Today, the *who-cooks-for-you?* of Barred Owl and the *chur-lee* of Eastern Bluebird are heard instead of the whine of jet turbines. The Great Swamp—with 7,425 acres of woods and wetlands—is a relict of a glacial lake formed after the last ice age. Its Wildlife Observation Center has short trails and a boardwalk that lead through forest and wet areas. Here Wood Duck, Least Bittern, Great Blue and Green Herons, Virginia Rail, Marsh Wren, Wood Thrush, Black-and-white Warbler, American Redstart, and Common Yellowthroat can be found in breeding season.

The refuge wilderness area can be explored via trails. Easier birding is available along Pleasant Plains Road, which is closed to through traffic and traverses open areas where Eastern Bluebird and Bobolink nest and through woods and second growth with breeding Wild Turkey, American Woodcock, Willow Flycatcher, White-eyed and Yellow-throated Vireos, Blue-winged and Yellow Warblers, and Baltimore Oriole.

14 In northwestern New Jersey, **Delaware Water Gap National Recreation Area** makes a fine destination in winter, when numbers of Bald Eagle roost along the Delaware River, and also in breeding seasons. Sample the trails at the nearby **Dunnfield Creek Natural Area** before heading north on Old Mine Road, which parallels the river.

This road offers excellent possibilities over the next 12 miles. Some of the birds here are Pileated Woodpecker; Acadian and Least Flycatchers; Yellow-throated, Blue-headed, and Warbling Vireos; Cliff Swallow; Brown Creeper; Veery; Wood Thrush; Blue-winged, Chestnut-sided, Black-throated Green, Blackburnian, Pine, Cerulean, Worm-eating, and Hooded Warblers; Northern Parula; American Redstart; and Louisiana Waterthrush. For a selection, check several different habitats: Shady ravines, tall riverside trees, conifers, hardwoods, and scrubby second growth. Stop along the road and at as many parking lots and picnic spots as you can. The recreation area encompasses the Pennsylvania side of the Delaware River, too. **45**

NEW JERSEY | MORE INFORMATION

RARE BIRD ALERT
Statewide 908-766-2661
Cape May 609-861-0466

10 Cape May Bird Observatory *(Page 43)*
www.njaudubon.org
/Centers/CMBO
609-884-2736
[?]

10 Cape May Point State Park *(Page 43)*
www.state.nj.us/dep
/parksandforests/parks
609-884-2159
[?] [‖] [人] [⅃]

10 Higbee Beach Wildlife Management Area
(Page 43)
www.state.nj.us/dep/fgw
609-628-2103
[人]

11 Brigantine Division, Edwin B. Forsythe National Wildlife Refuge
(Page 43)
www.fws.gov/northeast
/forsythe
609-652-1665
[$] [‖] [人] [∿] [⅃]

11 Barnegat Lighthouse State Park *(Page 44)*
www.state.nj.us/dep
/parksandforests/parks
609-494-2016
[‖] [人] [⅃]
Open Nov.–Apr.

12 Sandy Hook, Gateway National Recreation Area
(Page 44)
www.njaudubon.org
/Centers/SHBO
732-872-2500
[?] [$] [ǁ] [‖] [人] [⅃]

13 Great Swamp National Wildlife Refuge
(Page 45)
www.fws.gov/northeast
/greatswamp
973-425-1222
[‖] [人] [∿] [⅃]

14 Delaware Water Gap National Recreation Area
(Page 45)
www.nps.gov/dewa
570-588-2452
[?] [‖] [人] [∿] [⅃]

PENNSYLVANIA

- Waterfowl at Middle Creek Wildlife Management Area
- Fall raptors at Hawk Mountain Sanctuary
- Migrants and rarities at Presque Isle State Park

Fall at Hawk Mountain Sanctuary, north of Reading

15 Good birding spots don't have to be remote: Just ask birders walking the trails at **John Heinz National Wildlife Refuge at Tinicum**, just a mile north of Philadelphia's international airport. Tinicum attracts herons, waterfowl, shorebirds, and a good variety of other species to its wetlands and fields. In late summer, Great Blue and Green Herons, Great and Snowy Egrets, and Black-crowned Night-Heron feed in the wetlands, sometimes joined by Little Blue Heron, and Yellow-crowned Night-Heron and Glossy Ibis (both rare). Least Bittern, Common Moorhen, Marsh Wren, and Swamp Sparrow nest in these marshes, as do a selection of dabbling ducks; in winter, Northern Harrier hunts the open spaces along with a rare Short-eared Owl.

When water levels are right, you may find common migrant shorebird species like Black-bellied Plover; Greater and Lesser Yellowlegs; and Semipalmated, Least, and Pectoral Sandpipers. As fall arrives, so do flocks of geese and ducks—mostly dabblers such as Northern Shoveler, Northern Pintail, and Green-winged Teal, with an assortment of divers intermixed.

47

16 In Philadelphia's western suburbs, **Ridley Creek State Park** is a favorite spot to see migrant and nesting songbirds. Head to the **Multi-Use Trail** along the creek. Nesting birds in the area include Yellow-billed Cuckoo; Acadian Flycatcher; White-eyed and Yellow-throated Vireos; Carolina Chickadee; Veery; Wood Thrush; Blue-winged, Chestnut-sided, Yellow-throated, Prairie, Cerulean, and Kentucky Warblers; Northern Parula; American Redstart; and Louisiana Waterthrush. Trails in the park connect with the adjacent **Tyler Arboretum,** worth checking in migration. Pine Warbler nests in the pinetum here, where crossbills sometimes show up in November.

17 **Middle Creek Wildlife Management Area** ranks as one of the state's best places to see concentrations of migrant Snow Goose and Tundra Swan, with the possibility of finding Ross's Goose (seen annually in early spring). Barnacle Goose, a stray from Greenland, has recently appeared here, though the "wildness" of the birds seen has been subject to debate. Late winter is the best time for the swans, with good numbers of ducks present from fall through spring. Though waterfowl are Middle Creek's claim to fame, its nesting birds include Ruffed Grouse, Black-crowned Night-Heron, Willow Flycatcher, Grasshopper Sparrow, and Bobolink. Shorebirds arrive in fair numbers in migration, when its water levels are low.

18 At **Lake Ontelaunee,** waterbirds make an impressive showing. At the dam area, from fall through spring, look for thousands of Snow Geese, as well as loons, grebes, ducks, and gulls. Tundra Swan; Long-tailed Duck; White-winged, Surf, and Black Scoters; Red-throated Loon; Osprey; Bald Eagle; and Iceland and Lesser Black-backed Gulls are just a few of the notable birds seen at times from spring through fall. When the water is low, mudflats on the upper part of the lake attract interesting herons and shorebirds.

19 One of the greatest landmarks of the American conservation movement can be found on Kittatinny Ridge. **Hawk Mountain Sanctuary** attracts tens of thousands of visitors each fall to experience the phenomenon of eagles, hawks, and falcons streaming along this Appalachian crest.

Watchers begin gathering on the sanctuary's **North Lookout** as early as mid-August, looking for southbound Osprey, Bald Eagle, and American Kestrel. In mid-September, thousands of Broad-winged Hawks pass by; with October come thousands of Sharp-shinned and Red-tailed Hawks. Falcons are not as common here as along the Atlantic coast, but Northern Goshawk (most likely in Nov.) and Golden Eagle (peak in early Nov.) are specialties. Hundreds of Turkey Vulture, Northern Harrier, Cooper's and Red-shouldered Hawks, and American Kestrel are seen annually, with lesser numbers of Black Vulture, Merlin, and Peregrine Falcon. Weather is the vital factor in hawk flights: Try to be at Hawk Mountain in the days immediately after a cold front passes, with northwest winds following.

20 **Delaware Water Gap National Recreation Area** is famed for winter gatherings of Bald Eagle along the river, where a determined seeker may find dozens of these birds perched along the shoreline in January. Watch, too, for waterfowl along the river. Common Merganser nests in the area and may be seen throughout the year.

For land birds, walk trails at the **Pocono Environmental Education Center**. Both the **Scenic Gorge** and **Tumbling Waters Trails** pass through ravines where Acadian Flycatcher, Blue-headed Vireo, Red-breasted Nuthatch, and Blackburnian Warbler nest. In second-growth areas, look for both Blue-winged and Golden-winged Warblers; the latter is being pushed out of its nesting areas while the former expands its range.

21 The wooded hills and steep valleys of north-central Pennsylvania are home to a set of northern-affinity species seldom or never found as breeders in the rest of the state. A number of them are among the breeding birds of **Wyoming State Forest**. Fine northern hardwood-hemlock forest is home to Northern Goshawk; Northern Saw-whet Owl; Yellow-bellied Sapsucker; Alder (in shrubby wetlands) and Least Flycatchers; Blue-headed Vireo; Common Raven; Winter Wren; Hermit Thrush; Magnolia, Black-throated Blue, Black-throated Green, Blackburnian, Mourning (in thickets in clear-cut areas), and Canada Warblers; Northern Waterthrush; White-throated Sparrow; Dark-eyed Junco; and Purple Finch. Unpaved roads throughout the forest provide access to good habitat. Stop at forest headquarters for a map, essential for getting the most from your visit. To the east, Dry Run and Ogdonia Roads are easy places to begin exploring. Drive to the overlook at the end of Slab Run Road, where road birding is good and a number of trails loop through woods and wetlands. The **Loyalsock Trail** meanders through the forest, intersecting roads often and allowing hikes of varying lengths.

22 When it comes to variety and rarity, Pennsylvania's birdiest place is a 7-mile-long spit of land that extends into Lake Erie from the city of Erie. Though it's made of sand, **Presque Isle State Park** seems to have magnetic qualities for migrant birds, both regularly occurring eastern species and long-distance wanderers. More than 320 species have been found in this relatively minuscule sliver of beach, ponds, marsh, and woods. Though many records are of once-in-a-lifetime vagrants, the odds are better here than anywhere else in the state that something unusual will turn up.

In spring, northbound migrant songbirds following the Lake Erie shoreline move out onto the peninsula here and find themselves at the end of a cul-de-sac, nearly encircled by water. At the peak of migration, in mid-May, it's sometimes possible to see two dozen or more species of warblers while strolling only a few hundred yards.

In early spring, more than 25 species of waterfowl may occur in the lake, bay, or interior ponds of Presque Isle. Shorebirds appear along the beaches in spring and fall, and winter brings flocks of more common waterfowl species. A lucky visitor may sight such species as King Eider, Harlequin Duck, Purple Sandpiper, jaegers, Iceland or Glaucous Gulls, Snowy Owl, Northern Shrike, or Snow Bunting. While Presque Isle is home to some interesting nesting birds, it's also a very popular summer playground, and most birders seeking peace visit here from fall through spring.

Birding can begin immediately upon arrival, with an excellent opportunity to view Presque Isle Bay from the three parking lots on the right. A mile from the entrance, an observation deck overlooks one of the peninsula's marshes, a good place for waterfowl and songbirds. Continue to West Fisher Drive and turn east—a keen eye along this stretch can spot wonderful nesting and migrant birds. At the end of this dead-end road, look for ducks in the marina to the left and Presque Isle Bay to the right. **Sunset Point** is the best place from which to scan the lake for passing migrant waterfowl. **Gull Point,** to the east, is partially closed to entry April through November, but a platform allows observation of shorebirds, gulls, terns, and anything else in the area. In winter, it's a good place to look for Snowy Owl, Horned Lark, and Snow Bunting.

Red-headed Woodpecker can be found along the **Sidewalk Trail,** and Prothonotary Warbler has nested in both natural and man-made cavities. To the south, the trees at **Frys Landing** can be excellent for warblers and other songbirds in spring.

PENNSYLVANIA | MORE INFORMATION

RARE BIRD ALERT
Central 717-255-1212
  ext. 5761
Eastern 610-252-3455
Philadelphia 215-567-2473
Reading 610-376-6000
  ext. 2473
Schuylkill County
  570-622-6013
Western 412-963-0560
Wilkes-Barre
  717-825-2473

**15 John Heinz National
Wildlife Refuge** *(Page 47)*
*www.fws.gov/northeast
/heinz*
215-365-3118

**16 Ridley Creek State
Park** *(Page 48)*
*www.dcnr.state.pa.us
/stateparks*
610-892-3900

16 Tyler Arboretum
(Page 48)
www.tylerarboretum.org
610-566-9134

**17 Middle Creek Wildlife
Management Area**
(Page 48)
*www.dep.state.pa.us/dep
/deputate/enved
/mcreek.htm*
717-733-1512

Closed late Nov.–Jan.

18 Lake Ontelaunee
(Page 48)
www.hamburgpa.org
610-562-3106

**19 Hawk Mountain
Sanctuary** *(Page 48)*
www.hawkmountain.org
610-756-6000

**20 Delaware Water Gap
National Recreation Area**
(Page 49)
www.nps.gov/dewa
570-588-2452

**20 Pocono Environmental
Education Center**
(Page 49)
www.peec.org
570-828-2319

Visitor center open May–Oct.

21 Wyoming State Forest
(Page 49)
*www.dcnr.state.pa.us
/forestry*
570-387-4255

**22 Presque Isle State
Park** *(Page 50)*
www.presqueisle.org
814-833-7424

DELAWARE

- Spring migration at White Clay Creek State Park
- Concentrations of shorebirds along Delaware Bay

Geese in flight,
Bombay Hook
National Wildlife
Refuge, near Leipsic

The marshy Delaware Bay shoreline encompasses some of the Atlantic coast's finest birding sites. Waterbirds of one sort or another, from loons to terns, are present throughout the year. This is one of the country's best places to find Curlew Sandpiper, a rare wanderer from breeding grounds in Siberia, and Ruff, another sandpiper that nests in northern Europe and Asia. Even if no rarities are present, though, waders, massed shorebirds, or waterfowl will reward a visit.

23 **Bombay Hook National Wildlife Refuge** protects some 13,000 acres of tidal salt marsh, much of which is inaccessible to the casual visitor. An auto tour route leads to impoundments managed for waterfowl and shorebirds and to walking trails and observation towers. A leisurely trip along the roads could take several hours, especially in migration, when throngs of shorebirds await study through a spotting scope. Peak shorebirding

is in May and again from mid-July to late September. Common birds (such as Black-bellied and Semipalmated Plovers, Greater and Lesser Yellowlegs, Ruddy Turnstone, Red Knot, Semipalmated Sandpiper, Dunlin, and Short-billed Dowitcher) will be accompanied by many other species in the impoundments and marsh. In fall, when adults and juveniles in their varying plumages are present, you'll need a specialized guide concentrating on shorebird identification.

Nesting birds include Least Bittern; Bald Eagle; Clapper, King (check the **Boardwalk Trail**), and Virginia Rails; Black-necked Stilt; Willet; Forster's Tern; Acadian and Willow Flycatcher; Marsh Wren; and Seaside and Saltmarsh Sharp-tailed Sparrows. In summer, Great and Snowy Egrets, Great Blue and Little Blue Herons, Blacked-crowned Night-Heron, and Glossy Ibis roost in wetlands (especially **Bear Swamp**); in fall, Snow and Canada Geese, and many ducks, take up winter residence.

24 South along the coast are two other wildlife areas also known for extraordinary shorebird viewing: **Little Creek Wildlife Management Area** and **Port Mahon**. The tiny Black Rail, one of America's most sought-after and elusive birds, calls in the marshes along County Road 89 (Port Mahon Road) during a couple weeks in May. About a mile south, scan the impoundment, part of Little Creek, for shorebirds in spring and fall and waterfowl from fall through spring. Black-necked Stilt usually nests here. Continue east to the bay at Port Mahon, another excellent shorebird site in migration. Look for Royal Tern here in summer among the Caspian, Common, Forster's, and Least Terns. Black Tern and Black Skimmer can be found, too. The marsh before the bay is good for nesting Seaside and Saltmarsh Sharp-tailed Sparrows, and Nelson's Sharp-tailed Sparrow in fall. An observation platform a few miles past the main entrance offers views of the wetlands, host to summer waders and, from fall through spring, flocks of waterfowl; walk the dike for better views.

25 Take Del. 9 south from Port Mahon to Kitts Hummock Road on the east, just before intersecting with US 113. Two miles east is the entrance to the **Ted Harvey Conservation Area** and more waterbird viewing. Some of the roads in this tract may be gated, but you can drive or walk to the various parking lots and viewing areas, especially the road leading to Delaware Bay, where herons, egrets, ibises, waterfowl, and migrant shorebirds can be diverse and abundant.

26 Just east of Lewes, **Cape Henlopen State Park** occupies a thin spit of land pointing north where Delaware Bay meets the Atlantic Ocean. Nearly surrounded by water, this strategic location is a superb place from which to search ocean and bay for waterbirds. On certain days with northwest winds, Sharp-shinned Hawk, Merlin, Peregrine Falcon, and other species appear in good numbers. Spring, too, can bring good hawk-watching, especially for falcons. Piping Plovers nest on the long sandspit.

From fall through spring it's often productive to scan the Atlantic from **Herring Point Overlook.** You may spot Red-throated and Common Loons, Northern Gannet, and gulls. Sea ducks here can include Greater Scaup, Common Eider (rare), Long-tailed Duck, and all three scoters. At the fishing pier, search the bay and shore for winter Brant, ducks, loons, Great and Double-crested Cormorants, and gulls. Look for nesting Osprey and Least Tern in summer, and check the park's pinewoods for Brown-headed Nuthatch and Pine Warbler. On a spring or summer evening listen for Whip-poor-will, Chuck-will's-widow, and Common Nighthawk.

27 Two spots in northern Delaware provide terrific birding for songbirds in spring and fall migration, as well as interesting nesting species. In Newark, take Del. 896 north 3 miles to **White Clay Creek State Park,** where trails lead through woods alive with flycatchers, vireos, thrushes, and warblers from mid-April into June. Past the nature center, cars are not allowed on the road, and walking it north can be productive.

Here and elsewhere in the park you might find nesting Wood Duck; Barred Owl; Acadian Flycatchers; White-eyed, Yellow-throated, and Warbling Vireos; Veery; Blue-winged, Yellow, Cerulean (this park is Delaware's only breeding site), Kentucky, and Hooded Warblers; Northern Parula; and sometimes Black-and-white Warbler. Investigate not only the woods but also second-growth areas and fields where Prairie Warbler and Grasshopper Sparrow nest. Check the trees around the bridge and walk part of the blue-blazed trail.

North of Wilmington, **Brandywine Creek State Park** offers more great birding in spring and fall migration. In addition, a marsh here is home to wetland species including Great Blue and Green Herons and Virginia Rail, which nests. Walk trails, especially those through the old-growth woods and along the creek. A side road east of the main entrance leads to a hawk-watching spot where birders scan for migrant raptors in fall.

DELAWARE | MORE INFORMATION

RARE BIRD ALERT
Statewide 302-658-2747

**23 Bombay Hook
National Wildlife Refuge**
(Page 52)
*www.fws.gov/northeast
/bombayhook*
302-653-6872

**24 Little Creek Wildlife
Management Area**
(Page 53)
*www.dnrec.state.de.us
/fw/wildlifemaps.htm*
302-739-5297

**25 Ted Harvey
Conservation Area**
(Page 53)
*www.dnrec.state.de.us
/fw/wildlifemaps.htm*
302-284-4795

**26 Cape Henlopen State
Park** *(Page 54)*
*www.destateparks.com
/chsp/chsp.htm*
302-645-8983

**27 White Clay Creek
State Park** *(Page 54)*
*www.destateparks.com
/wccsp/index.asp*
302-368-6900

**27 Brandywine Creek
State Park** *(Page 54)*
*www.destateparks.com
/bcsp/bcsp.asp*
302-577-3534

MARYLAND

■ Seabirds at Ocean City
■ Wintering Bald Eagles at Blackwater National Wildlife Refuge

American Wigeon, once called "baldpate" for its white crown

28 From fall through spring, the area around the seaside town of **Ocean City** is an excellent birding destination, primarily for seabirds and shorebirds, but including fall land birds, raptors, and waterfowl. Check the ponds south of Griffin Road for migrant and wintering waterfowl, and scan the pond west of Golf Course Road for waterfowl including wintering Tundra Swan and Canvasback, and for Black-crowned Night-Heron and other waders.

After crossing the bridge to Ocean City, turn south on Philadelphia Avenue and drive to the jetty protecting the inlet here. A check of the surrounding waters from fall through spring will turn up ducks (Common and King Eiders and Harlequin Duck, though rare, are seen most winters, and all three scoters are likely), loons, grebes, and gulls. Purple Sandpiper winters on the rocks. East winds may bring Northern Gannet close to shore, or, in May, a lucky sighting of Sooty

Shearwater, Wilson's Storm-Petrel, or Parasitic Jaeger. On the bay west from Fourth Street, scan the mudflats and islands for Brown Pelican, shorebirds, waders, gulls, and terns. Royal, Common, and Least Terns; American Oystercatcher; and Black Skimmer are among the many possibilities.

29 When approaching **Assateague Island National Seashore** and **Assateague State Park,** stop at the Barrier Island Visitor Center for a map. Park at the pedestrian bridge to scan the bay. On the island, beachside parking lots provide access across the dunes to lookout points for searching for seabirds. In the national seashore, walk the **Life of the Marsh Nature Trail.** In fall, especially after a cold front has passed, migrant songbirds can be abundant in trees and shrubs here and around the campground. The **Life of the Forest Nature Trail** is also worth checking in migration. Fall can also bring southbound hawks along the shore, with Peregrine Falcon occurring regularly from mid-September through October. (See page 62 in the South Atlantic chapter for Chincoteague National Wildlife Refuge on the southern part of Assateague Island, in Virginia.)

30 A very different sort of environment attracts birders in spring to **Great Cypress Swamp** and its surroundings. Stop and observe where Sheppards Crossing Road meets the Pocomoke River before continuing your drive through the swamp. The route through the Pocomoke Swamp (which includes Nelson Road, Swamp Road, Blueberry Road, and Ebenezer Road) is complicated, but the roadside birding is rewarding: Spring migrants can be abundant and exciting, and nesting birds include Barred Owl; Pileated Woodpecker; Acadian and Great Crested Flycatchers; White-eyed and Yellow-throated Vireos; Wood Thrush; Yellow-throated, Prothonotary, Worm-eating, and Hooded Warblers; Northern Parula; and American Redstart.

31 While Pocomoke Swamp is usually visited only in spring and early summer, **Blackwater National Wildlife Refuge** south of Cambridge offers fine birding all year. Look for wintering waterfowl (including Tundra Swan), herons and egrets from spring through fall, and migrant shorebirds. Nesting species include Osprey, Bald Eagle (common year-round, with as many as 200 birds present in winter), Chuck-will's-widow, Prothonotary Warbler, Summer Tanager, Grasshopper and Saltmarsh Sharp-tailed Sparrows, and Blue Grosbeak. Refuge woodlands include both deciduous trees and loblolly pines. Look in the latter for Brown-headed Nuthatch and Pine Warbler and for the endangered Delmarva fox squirrel.

The wildlife refuge drive passes several freshwater impoundments and crosses woodlands and an extensive area of brackish marsh beside the tidal Blackwater River. Along the way, the **Marsh Edge Trail** offers the chance to see waders and waterfowl, nesting Osprey and Bald Eagle, and pinewoods birds. A nearby observation point provides another view of open water. Farther along, in the marshes, look for herons and egrets, rails, wintering waterfowl, and migrant shorebirds. Snow and Canada Geese and Tundra Swan are common, as are many species of ducks. Marsh Wren nests in the bulrush. Check tall, isolated loblolly pines for roosting Bald Eagle, and in winter watch for Northern Harrier, Rough-legged Hawk, and Short-eared Owl (at dusk) over fields and marshland.

32 Birders who enjoy spring migration in **Rock Creek Park** in adjacent Washington, D.C., are following a distinguished tradition: The great conservationist and sportsman Teddy Roosevelt liked to watch birds here as well. The park hosts 25 or more species of warblers—not to mention cuckoos, flycatchers, vireos, wrens, thrushes, tanagers, and sparrows—that might be seen in May in this 1,754-acre forested park, where tulip trees, white oaks, sycamores, black gums, and beech trees create a long green oasis. After you stop at the nature center on Glover Road, walk the trails that lead south and east to Rock Creek. Though migration is the best time to visit, the lush woodland is home to typical nesting birds of eastern deciduous forest, including Broad-winged Hawk, Yellow-billed Cuckoo, and Barred Owl.

33 Out where Maryland's western extension rises with the Appalachian Mountains, **Herrington Manor State Park** and nearby **Swallow Falls State Park** are home to an assortment of highland breeding birds, as well as to beautiful scenery of woodland and rugged gorges. The parks' mixed coniferous-deciduous woods have nesting Ruffed Grouse; Black-billed Cuckoo; Blue-headed Vireo; Golden-crowned Kinglet; Magnolia, Black-throated Green, Blackburnian, and Canada Warblers; Northern Waterthrush; and Rose-breasted Grosbeak. Herrington Manor has more open habitats where Alder Flycatcher and Golden-winged Warbler nest, while Swallow Falls might be more reliable for Veery and Hermit Thrush.

MARYLAND | MORE INFORMATION

RARE BIRD ALERT
Maryland and
 District of Columbia
 301-652-1088

28 Ocean City
(Page 56)
www.ococean.com
410-250-0125

**29 Assateague Island
National Seashore**
(Page 57)
www.nps.gov/asis
410-641-1441

**29 Assateague State
Park** *(Page 57)*
www.dnr.state.md.us
410-641-2120

30 Great Cypress Swamp
(Page 57)
302-378-2736
*Write or call ahead to arrange
on-site visits; otherwise bird
from road.*

**31 Blackwater National
Wildlife Refuge** *(Page 57)*
www.fws.gov/blackwater
410-228-2677

Fee for wildlife drive.

32 Rock Creek Park
(Page 58)
www.nps.gov/rocr
202-426-6070

**33 Herrington Manor
State Park** *(Page 58)*
www.dnr.state.md.us
301-334-9180

**33 Swallow Falls State
Park** *(Page 58)*
www.dnr.state.md.us
301-387-6938

SOUTH ATLANTIC

- Virginia
- North Carolina
- South Carolina
- Georgia

THE NATURAL WORLD SEEMS ESPECIALLY NEAR ON THE Atlantic coastal islands, out on the sunrise frontier of America. Perhaps it's the elemental nature of the landscape—sea, sky, sun, wind, sand—or our awareness, conscious or not, that these are, by earth's measuring, fragile and transient places. But here our senses seem keener, the environment more immediate. The fecund smell of a salt marsh, the raucous cries of gulls, the stirring sight of a flock of Dunlins whirling in unison as they come to rest on a beach—

we experience these and realize instinctively that we are witness to earth's grand and endless cycle of renewal.

If we look more closely we may see a pale little Piping Plover running along the sand, a secretive Virginia Rail materializing in the marsh grass, or a fierce Merlin skimming over the dunes. Places like Assateague Island and Cape Hatteras, despite their great popularity as recreational areas, still offer the opportunity for solitary observation and contemplation.

This region brings birders some spectacular sights, including the fall hawk migration at Kiptopeke State Park and the gathering of thousands of Tundra Swans at Mattamuskeet National Wildlife Refuge. Imagine more subtle encounters: a Black-throated Blue Warbler singing in a dark Appalachian hemlock forest or a Least Bittern picking its way through the cattails. Nesting birds here include southern Purple Gallinule and Painted Bunting and northern Red-breasted Nuthatch and Dark-eyed Junco. Habitats range from ocean beach to the highest mountain east of the Mississippi River. In between lie brackish estuaries, bottomland hardwood swamps, pine forests, the unique Sandhills ecosystem, lakes, and ponds.

Every season in the South Atlantic area has its own birding highlights. Spring sees waves of beautiful warblers heading up the mountains. From coastal lookouts, seabird migration can provide exciting viewing. In early summer, heronries are full of noisy life, mountain breeders are singing, and regional specialties are nesting. Shorebirds throng beaches in late summer and fall, hawks move south, and songbird migration can be excellent along the coast. In winter, waterfowl are in every watery environment—from sea to marsh to lake—and birders check hot spots for rarities. ∎

Band-rumped
Storm-Petrel

SPECIAL BIRDS OF THE SOUTH ATLANTIC

Black-capped Petrel	Swallow-tailed Kite	Black Skimmer	Nelson's Sharp-tailed Sparrow
Cory's Shearwater	Mississippi Kite	Common Ground-Dove	Saltmarsh Sharp-tailed Sparrow
Audubon's Shearwater	Black Rail	Red-cockaded Woodpecker	Seaside Sparrow
Band-rumped Storm-Petrel	Purple Gallinule	Brown-headed Nuthatch	Painted Bunting
White-tailed Tropicbird	Wilson's Plover	Swainson's Warbler	
White Ibis	Purple Sandpiper	Bachman's Sparrow	
Wood Stork	Royal Tern		
	Sandwich Tern		
	Bridled Tern		

VIRGINIA

- Year-round birding at Chincoteague National Wildlife Refuge
- Fall hawk migration at Kiptopeke State Park
- Appalachian specialties at Shenandoah National Park

View from
Hawksbill Mountain,
Shenandoah
National Park,
south of Luray

1 **Chincoteague National Wildlife Refuge** occupies the southern end of **Assateague Island National Seashore.** Its mix of habitats and its strategic position make it an appealing destination.

Several species of waterfowl nest here (Mute Swan, Canada Goose, Wood and American Black Ducks, and others), but in autumn swans, geese, and ducks begin arriving by the thousands. Refuge roads and the wildlife loop around **Snow Goose Pool** may bring sightings of Tundra Swan, Snow Goose, Brant, dabbling ducks, and divers including Greater and Lesser Scaup, Bufflehead, and Ruddy Duck. Fall is also when wooded areas, such as that found along the **Woodland Trail** loop, may harbor good numbers of southbound warblers and other songbirds.

Sharp-shinned and Cooper's Hawks, Merlin, and Peregrine Falcon pass in migration, and Red-throated and Common Loons and Horned Grebe arrive to spend the winter.

Shorebirds can be abundant in impoundments and along the beach, especially from late summer through fall when two dozen or more species may gather, including Black-bellied and Semipalmated Plovers, Greater and Lesser Yellowlegs, Semipalmated and Least Sandpipers, and Dunlin, along with occasional Hudsonian and Marbled Godwits and Buff-breasted Sandpiper. Herons also congregate in impressive numbers.

The threatened Piping Plover nests at the southern end of the island (closed during breeding season). Other nesting birds include Osprey; American Oystercatcher; Black Skimmer; Common, Forster's, and Least Terns; Chuck-will's-widow; Fish Crow; Brown-headed Nuthatch (check pinewoods); and sometimes Saltmarsh Sharp-tailed Sparrow. Peregrine Falcon has nested on a hacking tower reached by taking the trail that leads north to Wash Flats.

2 In fall, southbound migrants often gather in great numbers near the tip of Cape Charles, where the peninsula and the birds' reluctance to cross the Chesapeake Bay can result in spectacular birding. **Kiptopeke State Park** is a center of fall songbird migration-watching, beginning with the first Eastern Kingbirds and Blue-gray Gnatcatchers in July and continuing through straggling Gray Catbirds and Common Yellowthroats in late November. In between, Black-throated Blue and Yellow-rumped Warblers, American Redstart, and other species appear by the hundreds in woods, shrub lands, and fields. Kiptopeke is a good place to scan for Brant and ducks from fall through spring and for shorebirds, gulls, and terns year-round.

Fall hawk migration, though, may be Kiptopeke's biggest birding thrill: In recent years as many as 70,000 raptors have been counted from the park observation platform.

Nearby, the **Eastern Shore of Virginia National Wildlife Refuge** is also a fine spot for fall migrant songbirds and hawks. At road-accessible ponds and wetlands you'll find waders, ducks, and shorebirds. Take the wildlife trail through woods to a marsh overlook, and check for wintering American Bittern, Sora, American Woodcock (at dusk), and Nelson's and Saltmarsh Sharp-tailed Sparrows. Herons, Clapper and Virginia Rails, Marsh Wren, and Seaside Sparrow are found here year-round. Fisherman Island has nesting Brown Pelican, White Ibis, and terns, but access is restricted.

The **Chesapeake Bay Bridge-Tunnel** is one of the more unusual birding spots on the Atlantic coast. Four man-made islands make excellent lookouts for coastal seabirds from fall through spring. The public is usually allowed only on the southernmost island; the other three can be difficult and costly to access. King (rare) and Common Eiders, Harlequin Duck, all three scoters (Surf is most common), Long-tailed Duck, Red-breasted Merganser, Red-throated and Common Loons, Northern Gannet, Great Cormorant, Purple Sandpiper (on rocks), and many gulls are among the possibilities. Check for migrant land birds in autumn. Many rarities have appeared on the islands over the years, bringing birders back again and again.

AMERICAN OYSTERCATCHER

With its pied plumage and blood-red bill, the American Oystercatcher is one of our most attractive shorebirds. It inserts its long, compressed bill into oysters, mussels, clams, and other mollusks to cut the muscle that holds the halves of their shells together and proceeds to feast on fresh seafood. Usually seen singly or in small groups, American Oystercatchers are fairly common all along the Atlantic coast. ∎

South of Virginia Beach, **Back Bay National Wildlife Refuge** protects a segment of coastline and bay encompassing sand beach, dunes, marsh, woods, bay islands, and impoundments enclosed by dikes. Access to the impoundments is limited in winter to create a waterfowl sanctuary, but in other seasons they host waders and shorebirds. Wooded and shrubby areas are full of migrant songbirds in spring and fall. Shorebirds, gulls, and terns are almost always on the beach, where there's a chance of seeing an endangered Piping Plover in spring and early fall.

In **Great Dismal Swamp National Wildlife Refuge,** bald cypress, Atlantic white cedar, tupelo, sweet gum, and red maple grow in a bottomland forest. Listen for the hoots of Barred Owl and the *zweet zweet zweet* whistle of Prothonotary Warbler, and at night for the calls of Chuck-will's-widow and Whip-poor-will. This is possibly the northernmost breeding area for the Wayne's subspecies of Black-throated Green Warbler, and a good spot to find Swainson's Warbler as well. A boardwalk off White Marsh Road brings you near many of the typical nesting birds of this habitat, from Red-shouldered Hawk and Yellow-billed Cuckoo to Yellow-throated Vireo and Louisiana Waterthrush. Walking Washington Ditch Road is a good way to find Black-throated Green and Swainson's Warblers; also walk the trails along Jericho Ditch and Lynn Ditch. Other breeding birds here include Red-headed and Pileated Woodpeckers; Acadian Flycatcher; Fish Crow; Wood Thrush; Yellow-throated, Worm-eating, Kentucky, and Hooded Warblers; American Redstart; and Summer Tanager.

6 **Huntley Meadows Park** is one of the most popular birding areas in the greater Washington, D.C., region. As you stroll here at dusk in early spring, you might hear an American Woodcock in display flight. In spring or summer you may flush up a Green Heron or see a family of Hooded Mergansers or King Rails. The boardwalk through a wetland area often provides excellent looks at marsh birds, and viewing areas make it easy to sit and watch in summer for Great Egret and Yellow-crowned Night-Heron or for a migrant Virginia Rail or Sora. Other common nesting birds include Wood Duck, Barred Owl, Belted Kingfisher, Wood Thrush, Ovenbird, Scarlet Tanager, Eastern Towhee, and Song Sparrow.

7 The beauty of the Appalachian Mountains in **Shenandoah National Park** makes it one of the most visited of America's parks. It's popular with birders primarily as a place to see upper-elevation northern birds. The 105-mile **Skyline Drive** is dotted with overlooks and intersects more than 500 miles of hiking trails (the Appalachian Trail runs through the park), providing convenient access to fine birding. In addition, persons with limited mobility can find a good number of species simply by stopping, looking, and listening at Skyline Drive parking areas.

The handicapped-accessible **Limberlost Trail** runs through a hemlock-dominated woodland good for nesting birds including Ruffed Grouse; Blue-headed Vireo; Common Raven; Veery; Cedar Waxwing; Chestnut-sided, Blackburnian, Kentucky, and Canada Warblers; Ovenbird; Scarlet Tanager; Dark-eyed Junco; and Rose-breasted Grosbeak. The most popular birding location in the park may be the **South River Falls Trail,** where on a late-spring or summer visit you may find Yellow-throated and Blue-headed Vireos; Veery; Wood Thrush; Chestnut-sided, Black-throated Blue, Black-throated Green, Cerulean, Canada, and Hooded Warblers; Northern Parula; American Redstart; Scarlet Tanager; Eastern Towhee; and Dark-eyed Junco.

At **Rockfish Gap,** local birders hold a fall hawk-watch. Here starts the **Blue Ridge Parkway** (see p. 70), which has 275 overlooks and miles of nature trails where birders can enjoy highland birds. One favorite birding location is **Peaks of Otter.**

VIRGINIA | MORE INFORMATION

RARE BIRD ALERT
Statewide 757-238-2713

1 Chincoteague
National Wildlife Refuge
(Page 62)
*www.fws.gov/northeast
/chinco*
757-336-6122

2 Kiptopeke State Park
(Page 63)
*www.dcr.state.va.us
/parks/kiptopek.htm*
757-331-2267

2 Eastern Shore
of Virginia National
Wildlife Refuge
(Page 63)
*www.fws.gov/northeast
/easternshore*
757-331-2760

3 Chesapeake Bay
Bridge-Tunnel
(Page 64)
www.cbbt.com
757-331-2960

*Birders are advised to write
or call well in advance for
information about permits
and rules.*

4 Back Bay National
Wildlife Refuge
(Page 64)
www.fws.gov/backbay
757-721-2412

*No autos allowed. Trails
closed Nov.–Mar.*

5 Great Dismal Swamp
National Wildlife Refuge
(Page 64)
*www.fws.gov/northeast
/greatdismalswamp*
757-986-3705

6 Huntley Meadows
Park *(Page 65)*
*www.fairfaxcounty.gov
/parks/huntley*
703-768-2525

Closed Tues.

7 Shenandoah National
Park *(Page 65)*
www.nps.gov/shen
540-999-3500

7 Blue Ridge Parkway
(Pages 65 and 70)
www.nps.gov/blri
828-271-4779

NORTH CAROLINA

- Ocean birds at Cape Hatteras
- Wintering Tundra Swans at Mattamuskeet NWR
- Appalachian specialties along the Blue Ridge Parkway

Autumn foliage along the Blue Ridge Parkway, western North Carolina

8 Birders know North Carolina's easternmost barrier islands, the **Outer Banks,** as a place where sea, sand, and marsh combine to create exciting birding opportunities year-round. Hatteras Island's **Pea Island National Wildlife Refuge,** within **Cape Hatteras National Seashore,** ranks with the top birding spots on the south Atlantic coast. Approaching the refuge, stop first at the **Bodie Island Visitor Center,** where a nature trail provides access to wetlands excellent for waterfowl, herons, egrets, White and Glossy Ibises, rails, and shorebirds. Patient birders may spot a Clapper Rail skulking through the vegetation or, in winter, an American Bittern, Virginia Rail, or Sedge Wren.

At the northern edge of **North Pond,** an observation platform provides a view of this impoundment and of salt flats where Snow and Canada Geese winter and Black-necked Stilt and Willet nest. Along the half-mile nature trail at the southern edge of North Pond, the live oaks can be excellent for songbirds in fall

67

migration. The pond itself has waders and wintering waterfowl, including Tundra Swan and several species of ducks. Look for Eurasian Wigeon, seen almost annually in flocks of American Wigeon, as well as shorebirds. The observation tower at the end of the trail offers a view over Pamlico Sound, where Brown Pelican and Royal and Sandwich Terns nest. Anywhere along the Hatteras Island beach, you can see an array of shorebirds, gulls, and terns. In fall, check the skies frequently for migrant raptors: Sharp-shinned Hawk is common; Merlin and Peregrine Falcon are seen often. Early October is best for Peregrine.

In fall through spring at the "elbow" of Cape Hatteras, dedicated birders journey to the end of the point to watch for seabirds, from loons and grebes to shearwaters, storm-petrels, jaegers, and gulls. If you don't want to go that far, explore the salt flats for shorebirds, gulls, and terns. Nesting birds may include Piping Plover; American Oystercatcher; Gull-billed, Common, and Least Terns; and Black Skimmer.

Some of the most exciting birding takes place on chartered boat trips. Species seen on these pelagic trips (which usually last ten hours or more) vary seasonally. Between late May and September, they can include Black-capped Petrel; Cory's, Greater, Sooty, and Audubon's Shearwaters; Wilson's, Leach's, and Band-rumped Storm-Petrels; Pomarine Jaeger; and Bridled and Sooty Terns. Rarer possibilities include Herald and Fea's Petrels, Manx Shearwater, White-tailed Tropicbird, Masked Booby, South Polar Skua, and Parasitic and Long-tailed Jaegers.

9 **Mattamuskeet National Wildlife Refuge,** across Pamlico Sound, has a tremendous population of wintering waterfowl (Tundra Swan is the highlight) that peaks in November at more than 100,000 birds. Snow and a few Ross's Geese join more than 20 species of ducks on the waters of Lake Mattamuskeet and in surrounding fields. Several Bald Eagles are always present in winter, as well. Good views are found along the causeway across the lake and along the road leading to the refuge headquarters. Check the impoundment south of the entrance road for herons and shorebirds in spring and fall migration. Breeding Osprey are common here, with 60 to 80 nests scattered around the lake.

10 South of New Bern, **Croatan National Forest** is home to several notable birds, such as Red-cockaded Woodpecker, Brown-headed Nuthatch, the Wayne's subspecies of Black-throated Green Warbler, Swainson's Warbler, and Bachman's Sparrow. Before exploring, pick up a map at the Forest Service office or the Croatan ranger station. Areas both north and south along Forest Road 121 (Little Road) are good for Red-cockaded Woodpecker (roost trees are marked with blue bands) and the Brown-headed Nuthatch. In breeding season, listen for the song of Black-throated Green Warbler. The Atlantic coastal Wayne's subspecies has a slightly smaller bill than the typical form of this bird. Listen, too, in swampy places for the loud whistle of Swainson's Warbler. Take Forest Road 3000 to reach **Catfish Lake Waterfowl Impoundment** (check with the Forest Service office during fall hunting season). The "moist soils" impoundments here often host good numbers of herons, egrets, and shorebirds.

Scan the open pinewoods along the route from Morehead City to Forest Road 128 (Millis Road) for Bachman's Sparrow as well as Red-cockaded Woodpecker; Swainson's Warbler is also a possibility in appropriate habitat.

11 Birders visit **Fort Fisher State Recreation Area** for its beach, mudflats, ocean, and bay habitats, which attract a good variety of birds year-round. In nesting season, Painted Bunting is a good bet at the feeders of the North Carolina Aquarium. The **Hermit Trail** here provides access to marsh (look for rails), open water, and beach. In fall, warblers and other songbirds may throng shrubs and scrubby trees; in winter, ducks, loons, and Northern Gannet repay visitors who scan the Atlantic. Determined birders can continue south more than 3 miles along a narrow spit of land where Brown Pelican, Wilson's Plover, American Oystercatcher, and Black Skimmer are among the many shorebirds and waterbirds present seasonally.

12 **Weymouth Woods–Sandhills Nature Preserve** preserves a remnant of the once-widespread Sandhills ecosystem. Noted for its old-growth longleaf pines and pinewoods birds such as Red-cockaded Woodpecker, Brown-headed Nuthatch, and Pine Warbler, the preserve also encompasses bottomland deciduous woods, with excellent birding accessible along its trails. Red-cockaded Woodpecker can be found on the **Pine Barrens** and **Bower's Bog Trails** near the visitor center; Brown-headed Nuthatch is common throughout pine areas. Bachman's Sparrow has recently begun nesting at the preserve, as the habitat is restored. The **Gum Swamp Trail** is good for Red-tailed Hawk, Wood Thrush, Prothonotary and Kentucky Warblers, Louisiana Waterthrush, and Ovenbird. Other nesting species here include Great Horned and Barred Owls, Acadian Flycatcher, Prairie Warbler, Chuck-will's-widow, Blue-headed Vireo, and Eastern Towhee.

13 The rugged, beautiful Blue Ridge mountains harbor many northern birds found nesting nowhere else in the state. Excellent access to birding sites can be found along the stunning **Blue Ridge Parkway**. A good starting point is the area around the mountain town of Blowing Rock. Both **Moses H. Cone** and **Julian Price Parks** offer fine high-country forest and miles of trails to explore. Here breeding birds include a mix of both middle- and high-elevation species: Ruffed Grouse; Yellow-bellied Sapsucker; Blue-headed Vireo; Golden-crowned Kinglet; Red-breasted and White-breasted Nuthatches; Black-throated Blue, Chestnut-sided, Black-throated Green, Blackburnian, Black-and-white, Canada, and Hooded Warblers; Louisiana Waterthrush; Ovenbird; Eastern Towhee; Scarlet Tanager; Dark-eyed Junco; and Rose-breasted Grosbeak.

TUNDRA SWAN

Even a single wild swan can yield a red-letter day in the field. No wonder, then, that one of the birding highlights of the mid-Atlantic coast is its concentration of wintering Tundra Swans. North Carolina's Mattamuskeet National Wildlife Refuge is the most famous winter home for Tundra Swans, offering tens of thousands of these magnificent birds from November through February. Swans may be seen just about anywhere waterfowl gather near the coast, from Chesapeake Bay south into South Carolina. ∎

14 Above the parkway, **Grandfather Mountain** rises to 5,964 feet. Common Ravens soar above the cliffs, and lucky birders may hear the call of Northern Saw-whet Owl between March and early May. (They'd be luckier still to see one.) Grandfather Mountain is privately owned, and a fee is charged for entry and to hike its trails. The Blue Ridge Parkway winds around the mountain on the **Linn Cove Viaduct**. The information center at Mile 304 (closed in winter) offers guidebooks and other information, and nearby trails, such as the **Tanawha Trail**, provide more birding opportunities.

The parkway climbs into the Black Mountains to **Mount Mitchell State Park** and the summit of the highest mountain east of the Mississippi River. The red spruce and Fraser fir forest surrounding 6,684-foot mountain has suffered from insect infestations and disease but is still rewarding to visit. Red Crossbill and Pine Siskin, both unpredictable nesting species in the southern Appalachians, have been seen in the park in summer.

The parkway reaches its highest point (6,053 ft.) near Richland Balsam. Here and elsewhere, overlooks and short trails make convenient birding spots. The parkway ends at the edge of **Great Smoky Mountains National Park** (see p. 96).

NORTH CAROLINA | MORE INFORMATION

RARE BIRD ALERT
Statewide 704-332-2473

8 Pea Island National Wildlife Refuge
(Page 67)
www.fws.gov/peaisland
252-473-1131

8 Cape Hatteras National Seashore
(Page 67)
www.nps.gov/caha
Bodie 252-441-5711
Hatteras 252-995-4474
Ocracoke 252-928-4531

9 Mattamuskeet National Wildlife Refuge
(Page 68)
www.fws.gov/mattamuskeet
252-926-4021

10 Croatan National Forest *(Page 68)*
www.cs.unca.edu/nfsnc
252-638-5628

11 Fort Fisher State Recreation Area
(Page 69)
www.ils.unc.edu/parkproject/ncparks.html
910-458-5798

12 Weymouth Woods–Sandhills Nature Preserve
(Page 69)
www.ils.unc.edu/parkproject/ncparks.html
910-692-2167

13 Blue Ridge Parkway
(Pages 65 and 70)
www.nps.gov/blri
828-271-4779

14 Grandfather Mountain
(Page 70)
www.grandfather.com
828-733-2013

14 Mount Mitchell State Park *(Page 70)*
www.ils.unc.edu/parkproject/ncparks.html
828-675-4611

SOUTH CAROLINA

- Excellent year-round birding at Huntington Beach State Park
- Pinewoods birds in Francis Marion National Forest
- Wetland species at Savannah National Wildlife Refuge

Cape Romain
National Wildlife
Refuge, south
of Georgetown

15 **Huntington Beach State Park** is one of South Carolina's top birding spots. Freshwater and saltwater marshes flank the main entrance road, and assorted herons and, in winter, ducks are easily seen. A closer look can turn up Pied-billed Grebe, Least Bittern (absent in winter), Black-crowned Night-Heron, Common Moorhen, Marsh Wren, Clapper Rail, or Seaside Sparrow. On the beach, shorebirds, gulls, and terns congregate. Look for Brown Pelican, Wilson's and Piping (mostly in winter) Plovers, American Oystercatcher, Willet, and Black Skimmer.

Fall through spring, the walk to **Murrell's Inlet jetty** is a must. Look for Greater Scaup, Common Eider (rare), Harlequin Duck (rare), Red-throated Loon, Great Cormorant, Razorbill, scoters, Purple Sandpiper, and other coastal specialties.

Among the many species in this park are Tundra Swan (winter), Osprey, Common Ground-Dove, and (in breeding season)

Prairie and Yellow-throated Warblers and Painted Bunting. Fall can bring excellent numbers of migrant songbirds; Merlin and Peregrine Falcon along the beach; and the endangered Wood Stork, whose numbers here are increasing.

16 Farther south, **Francis Marion National Forest** and **Cape Romain National Wildlife Refuge** share the **Sewee Visitor and Environmental Education Center,** where you can stop for maps and birding advice. Look for Wild Turkey, Mississippi Kite, Yellow-billed Cuckoo, Barred Owl, and warblers (including Yellow-throated, Prothonotary, Kentucky, Hooded, and Northern Parula) on I'on Swamp Road. You may find the Wayne's Black-throated Green Warbler here. The I'on Swamp's most famous bird is the extinct Bachman's Warbler, not seen since the early 1960s.

The endangered Red-cockaded Woodpecker, Brown-headed Nuthatch, and Bachman's Sparrow may be found along Forest Road 202. Check scrubby areas and clear-cuts for Painted Bunting and Prairie Warbler. The bridge over Wambaw Creek is a good lookout for Swallow-tailed Kite during nesting season; lucky birders might spot this species anywhere in this area, especially where US 17 crosses the South and North Santee Rivers.

The **Moore's Landing** area of Cape Romain National Wildlife Refuge is an excellent place to see marsh birds. A pier extends into a salt marsh where American Oystercatcher, Gull-billed Tern, and Black Skimmer can be found, along with shorebirds when the tide is low. This is a good spot for Marbled Godwit in winter, and Painted Bunting nests around the parking lot.

The **Pitt Street Causeway** near Charleston provides easy access to salt marsh and tidal mudflats where Clapper Rail, Marsh Wren, and Seaside Sparrow breed, Saltmarsh and Nelson's Sharp-tailed Sparrows have been found in winter, and waders and American Oystercatcher are present all year. Another worthwhile site is **Folly Beach:** A walk along a closed road is excellent for songbirds during fall migration. Painted Bunting breeds here, and nearby are lookout points where you can scan the Atlantic in winter for sea ducks and Northern Gannet.

17 The **Francis Beidler Forest Sanctuary and Center** protects bald cypress-tupelo swamp. Among the birds seen along its boardwalk are Anhinga; Yellow-crowned Night-Heron; White Ibis; Barred Owl; Red-headed and Pileated Woodpeckers; Yellow-throated Vireo; Red-shouldered Hawk; Fish Crow; and Yellow-throated, Prothonotary, Swainson's, and Hooded Warblers. Ask about bird walks, canoe trips, and night walks.

18 **Bear Island Wildlife Management Area** is a terrific location for herons and marsh birds, with 12,000 acres of wetlands, woods, and fields where nesting birds include Least Bittern, Mottled Duck, White and Glossy Ibises, Bald Eagle, Clapper and King Rails, Common Moorhen, Black-necked Stilt, Marsh Wren, and Painted Bunting. Wood Stork is commonly seen among the throngs of herons, egrets, and ibises. Seasonally abundant waterfowl and shorebirds are easily seen from roads. Although the area is closed in the winter, some impoundments can be seen from a viewing platform adjacent to Bennett's Point Road.

PAINTED BUNTING

The flamboyant Painted Bunting is one of the South's most sought-after birds. It comes to the South Carolina and Georgia coasts to nest, preferring scrubby areas with dense thickets. Good spots include Carolina Sandhills and Santee National Wildlife Refuges, Huntington Beach State Park, and the Francis Marion National Forest in South Carolina; Jekyll Island in Georgia; and the Fort Fisher area in North Carolina. Surprisingly, the Painted Bunting often perches inconspicuously. To find one, listen for its short, rather patternless warbling song. ■

19 Large areas of marsh (freshwater and tidal) can also be found at **Savannah National Wildlife Refuge.** Part of the refuge can be seen from pull-offs along S.C. 170 southwest of Hardeeville and the 4-mile **Laurel Hill Wildlife Drive** south of the highway. From dikes throughout the impoundment area, one can view thousands of wintering ducks; waders (including egrets, herons, and ibises) can be found year-round. The endangered Wood Stork is frequently seen (summer) along with the King Rail and wintering Virginia Rail and Sora, and the striking Purple Gallinule is a breeding specialty. Shorebirds can be numerous in impoundment areas with low water.

20 On the shores of Lake Marion, **Santee National Wildlife Refuge** is usually considered the best place in South Carolina to find wintering geese. On the refuge's **Bluff Unit,** pick up a map and consult with refuge staff at the visitor center. The nearby **Wright's Bluff Nature Trail** leads to an observation tower from which Canada Geese, along with Snow, and occasional Greater White-fronted can be seen from late fall to spring. Around a hundred Tundra Swans also winter on or near the refuge. The trail leads to viewpoints over Cantey Bay, where waterfowl gather, and passes swampy and marshy spots good for waders and other wetland birds. Osprey and Bald Eagles nest on the lake, and depending on (unpredictable) water levels, the shore may have good numbers of herons or migrant shorebirds.

21 Protecting more than 22,200 acres of Congaree River bottomland, **Congaree Swamp National Monument** comprises America's largest old-growth floodplain forest. Breeding birds here include Wood Duck; Yellow-crowned Night-Heron; Red-shouldered Hawk; Mississippi Kite; Red-headed and Pileated Woodpeckers; Wood Thrush; Yellow-throated, Prothonotary, and Hooded Warblers; Northern Parula; and Summer Tanager. You'll find Brown-headed Nuthatch, Pine Warbler, and an occasional Bachman's Sparrow in the loblolly pines.

Near the beginning of the boardwalk by the visitor center, watch for Barred Owl. Weston Lake is good for herons, egrets, and an occasional Anhinga. **Kingsnake Trail,** which traverses fine bottomland forest, is another favorite birding walk. Congaree can be flooded, so consider birding from a canoe.

22 The Sandhills is a rolling landscape covered in deep sandy soil, as seen in **Carolina Sandhills National Wildlife Refuge.** Red-cockaded Woodpeckers are fairly common here. Brown-headed Nuthatch is common on the refuge, and Bachman's Sparrow (uncommon) can be found when males are singing in spring.

Red-cockaded Woodpeckers are often seen in (white-banded) roost trees near headquarters and in the Martins Lake area off the wildlife drive, also favored by many for all-around birding. The **Lake Bee Recreation Area** is also a choice site for Red-cockaded Woodpecker and Brown-headed Nuthatch. Wild Turkey; Northern Bobwhite; Chuck-will's-widow; Red-headed Woodpecker; Whip-poor-will; Pine, Prairie, Prothonotary, and Hooded Warblers; and Blue Grosbeak are among the nesting species. Ponds, streams, and fields provide habitat for a good variety of migrants and wintering birds.

23 South Carolina also encompasses some Appalachian highlands where Common Ravens and Black-throated Blue Warblers and other up-country birds can be found. In **Caesars Head State Park,** in the **Mountain Bridge Wilderness,** nesting species include Ruffed Grouse; Blue-headed Vireo; Chestnut-sided, Black-throated Green, Black-and-white, Worm-eating, and Hooded Warblers; Scarlet Tanager; and Dark-eyed Junco. Red Crossbill has nested here, and Cerulean Warbler has been seen in summer. Local birders recommend **Raven Cliff Falls Trail** and **Pinnacle Pass Trail.** The **Caesars Head** rock formation can be a productive hawk-watching site in autumn migration, with more than 2,000 raptors occasionally seen in a day. Most are Broad-winged Hawks, but other species are spotted as well.

SOUTH CAROLINA | MORE INFORMATION

RARE BIRD ALERT
Statewide 704-332-2473

15 **Huntington Beach State Park** *(Page 72)*
www.discoversouthcarolina
.com/stateparks/
843-237-4440
🔲🔲🔲🔲🔲🔲

16 **Francis Marion National Forest and Cape Romain National Wildlife Refuge** *(Page 73)*
www.fws.gov/seweecenter
843-928-3368
🔲🔲🔲🔲
Visitor center open Thurs.–Sun.

17 **Francis Beidler Forest Sanctuary and Center**
(Page 73)
www.beidlerforest.com
843-462-2150
🔲🔲🔲🔲🔲🔲🔲

18 **Bear Island Wildlife Management Area**
(Page 74)
www.dnr.sc.gov/managed
843-844-8957
🔲
Closed Sun. and Nov.–late Jan. Some impoundments can still be seen from a viewing platform adjacent to Bennett's Point Road.

19 **Savannah National Wildlife Refuge**
(Page 74)
www.fws.gov/savannah
912-652-4415
🔲🔲🔲🔲
Portions of refuge may be closed in Oct. for wheelchair-dependent hunters and Dec.–Feb. to reduce disturbance to wintering birds.

20 **Santee National Wildlife Refuge** *(Page 74)*
www.fws.gov/santee
803-478-2217
🔲🔲🔲🔲🔲

21 **Congaree Swamp National Monument**
(Page 75)
www.nps.gov/cosw
803-776-4396
🔲🔲🔲🔲

22 **Carolina Sandhills National Wildlife Refuge**
(Page 75)
www.fws.gov
/carolinasandhills
843-335-8401
🔲🔲🔲

23 **Caesars Head State Park** *(Page 75)*
www.discoversouthcarolina
.com/stateparks/
864-836-6115
🔲🔲🔲
Caesars Head is part of, and provides access to trails into, the 10,883-acre Mountain Bridge Wilderness.

GEORGIA

- Spring migration at Kennesaw Mountain
- Wetland species in Okefenokee Swamp
- Shorebirds and seabirds at Jekyll and Tybee Islands

Okefenokee Swamp, southeastern Georgia

24 The Georgia landscape includes coastline, piedmont, and highlands. The state's highest point is **Brasstown Bald,** in the **Chattahoochee National Forest.** Brasstown Bald is more accessible than some similar areas: A shuttle bus runs to the summit, but most birders prefer to walk the trail to the top.

Nesting birds include Ruffed Grouse, Blue-headed Vireo; Common Raven; Winter Wren; Veery; Chestnut-sided, Blackburnian, Black-throated Blue, Black-throated Green, and Canada Warblers; Ovenbird; Scarlet Tanager; Dark-eyed Junco; and Rose-breasted Grosbeak. With a map, explore nearby public lands for a wider range of species. Nearby **Lake Winfield Scott** and **Cooper Creek Recreation Areas** and **Vogel State Park** offer the chance for some highland species and for Broad-winged Hawk, Eastern Wood-Pewee, Acadian Flycatcher, Wood Thrush, Black-and-white and Kentucky Warblers, and many other birds more typical of this latitude.

25 Outside Atlanta, **Kennesaw Mountain National Battlefield Park** acts as a magnet for migrant songbirds in spring and, to a lesser extent, in fall. Walk to the top of the mountain and watch for migrants of dozens of species, from treetop birds such as Blackburnian and Cerulean Warblers to ground dwellers such as Swainson's Thrush and Ovenbird. On peak days in late April or early May, 20 or more species of warblers may be seen or heard. On weekends, birders can take a shuttle bus to the summit.

26 Some of Atlanta's best birding is found at the Clayton County Water Authority's **Wetlands Center** and **E. L. Huie Land Application Facility.** Check the sightings list at the center, and then take the nature trail and boardwalk through woods and wetlands that are excellent for warblers and other songbirds in spring and fall migration. Red-shouldered Hawk; Eastern Screech-Owl; Great Horned and Barred Owls; Prothonotary, Kentucky, and Hooded Warblers; and Louisiana Waterthrush nest here. The Huie site is Atlanta's best spot for shorebirds and wintering ducks. Birders can drive on levees to scan water and mudflats; ducks are always present in winter, but shorebird numbers depend on water levels. In spring and summer, check nearby Blalock Lake, where Osprey nests.

27 **Sparks Reservoir** in **Sweetwater Creek State Conservation Park,** west of Atlanta, presents a fine opportunity to look for ducks, loons, grebes, and gulls during winter. Scan the water from the park's north and south entrances and from the park office. Wintering or migrant species may include Wood Duck (nests here), Ring-necked Duck, several dabbling ducks, Lesser Scaup, Bufflehead, Red-breasted Merganser, Ruddy Duck, Common Loon, Pied-billed and Horned Grebes, American Coot, and Ring-billed and Herring Gulls. Great Blue Heron can be present year-round; Green Heron is here spring through fall, and an occasional Osprey stops in migration. Unusual species include Greater Scaup, Harlequin Duck, and Long-tailed Duck. Trails through the southern part of the park offer opportunities for pleasant woodland birding. For a variety of habitats, take the path from the picnic grounds up the Jack Hill area as well as the trails alongside Sweetwater Creek.

28 **Piedmont National Wildlife Refuge,** north of Macon, is known for good all-around birding as well as for the southern pinewoods specialties of Red-cockaded Woodpecker, Brown-headed Nuthatch, and Bachman's Sparrow. The woodpeckers

can be found at several spots, including along the **Red-cockaded Woodpecker Trail.** Look for Bachman's Sparrow here and elsewhere in open pine forest with grassy understory.

Little Rock Wildlife Drive passes a variety of habitats, including a pond, bottomland hardwoods, and scrubby openings where nesting species include Northern Bobwhite, Prairie Warbler, Yellow-breasted Chat, Field Sparrow, Blue Grosbeak, and Indigo Bunting. In woodland, watch for Wild Turkey; Red-shouldered Hawk; Blue-headed Vireo (here at the southern limit of its range); Pine (in pines), Kentucky, and Hooded Warblers; and Orchard Oriole.

29 The fabled **Okefenokee Swamp,** one of America's most important wetland areas, lies on the Florida state line. Nearly 400,000 acres of the swamp are protected as **Okefenokee National Wildlife Refuge.**

The major gateway to the swamp is the **Suwannee Canal Recreation Area,** at the refuge's east entrance. You'll find a Red-cockaded Woodpecker cluster (family nesting group) near the entrance station, and more Red-cockaded Woodpeckers, along with Brown-headed Nuthatch and Bachman's Sparrow, at the **Upland Discovery Trail** on the Swamp Island Drive south to **Chesser Island.** Watch for Wild Turkey along the road. At Chesser Island, a boardwalk leads to an observation tower; a few Great Blue Herons and Sandhill Cranes usually nest near the boardwalk. Here the resident Sandhills are joined in winter by hundreds of migrating cranes. You'll see herons and ibises here. Anhinga, Wood Stork (formerly nested, but not in recent years), Osprey, Swallow-tailed Kite (rare, but believed to nest in the area), Red-shouldered Hawk, Barred Owl, and Red-headed and Pileated Woodpeckers are a few of the many other possibilities.

To get closer to the swamp, rent a canoe or johnboat or take a commercial tour out into the **Suwannee Canal** and its side channels. In addition, tours and rental boats are available at **Stephen C. Foster State Park,** where your chances of seeing Osprey and Purple Gallinule improve.

30 One accessible birding spot among Georgia's coastal islands is **Jekyll Island.** Before crossing the causeway to the island, stop at the welcome center and check the mudflats behind it for herons and shorebirds. A few hundred yards ahead, a wetland beyond the trees on the right may have White Ibis, Roseate Spoonbill (rare), Wood Stork, and other waders.

Once on the island, visit **St. Andrew Picnic Area,** one of many spots where you'll find beach access and views of waterfowl, loons, grebes, and American White Pelican in winter; and Brown Pelican, Double-crested Cormorant, herons, Wood Stork (scarce), shorebirds, gulls, and terns year-round. Wilson's Plover, American Oystercatcher, Willet, Laughing Gull, Royal Tern, and Black Skimmer are among the nesting birds to be seen on the coast, and large numbers of migrant shorebirds stop in during spring and fall. Jekyll's extreme southern end is most favored by birds and birders. Don't neglect Jekyll's woods and marshes, with nesting birds like Wild Turkey; Clapper Rail; Brown-headed Nuthatch; Yellow-throated, Prairie, and Hooded Warblers; and Painted Bunting.

Purple Gallinule, a colorful inhabitant of southern swamps and marshes

31 Up the coast, **Harris Neck National Wildlife Refuge** is worth a visit during any season. Thousands of waders and waterbirds make their nests here, including Wood Duck; Anhinga; Great, Snowy, and Cattle Egrets; Little Blue, Tricolored, and Green Herons; Black-crowned Night-Heron; White Ibis; Clapper Rail; Purple Gallinule; and Common Moorhen. Of particular interest is the endangered Wood Stork; an artificial nesting platform at the refuge has encouraged the birds to breed. Breeding Painted Buntings are common throughout spring and summer, while in winter dabbling ducks such as Gadwall, American Wigeon, Mallard, Blue-winged Teal, Green-winged Teal, Northern Shoveler, and Northern Pintail are common on ponds, along with divers such as Ring-necked Duck, Bufflehead, and Ruddy Duck. Grassy fields host a variety of sparrows.

32 **Tybee Island,** east of Savannah, is another easily accessible spot to look for seabirds and shorebirds. Approaching the island, stop at **Fort Pulaski National Monument** for trails and dikes that provide access to brackish marsh, good for waders, waterfowl, rails (Clapper year-round, Virginia and Sora in winter), Sedge (winter) and Marsh (year-round) Wrens, and Saltmarsh Sharp-tailed and Nelson's Sharp-tailed (both in winter), and Seaside Sparrows (resident).

On Tybee, look along the island's northern end, where rock jetties host the rare Purple Sandpiper. Black Skimmer is common all year, and American Oystercatcher is seen fairly often among the seasonally changing mixed flocks of shorebirds. Tybee's southern end also has beach and mudflats worth checking. Large rafts of wintering ducks can be found offshore.

GEORGIA | MORE INFORMATION

RARE BIRD ALERT
Statewide 770-493-8862

24 Brasstown Bald
(Page 77)
www.fs.fed.us/conf/rec
/btb_overview.htm
706-745-6928

? ⑤ ♦ ♿

Area in the Chattahoochee
National Forest.

25 Kennesaw Mountain
National Battlefield Park
(Page 78)
www.nps.gov/kemo
770-427-4686

? ♦ ⚡ ∿ ♿

26 CCWA Wetlands
Center and E. L.
Huie Land Application
Facility
(Page 78)
www.ccwa1.com/facilities
770-603-5606

? ♦ ⚡ ∿ ♿

27 Sweetwater Creek
State Conservation Park
(Page 78)
gastateparks.org/info
/sweetwater
770-732-5871

? ⑤ ♦ ♦ ⚡ ♿

28 Piedmont National
Wildlife Refuge
(Page 78)
www.fws.gov/piedmont
478-986-5441

? ♦ ⚡ ∿ ♿

29 Okefenokee National
Wildlife Refuge
(Page 79)
www.fws.gov/okefenokee
912-496-7836

? ♦ ⚡ ♿

Also provides information
on Suwannee Canal
Recreation Area.

29 Stephen C. Foster
State Park *(Page 79)*
gastateparks.org/info
/scfoster
912-637-5274

? ♦ ⚡ ♿

30 Jekyll Island
(Page 79)
www.jekyllisland.com
912-635-3636

♦ ⚡ ∿ ♿

31 Harris Neck National
Wildlife Refuge
(Page 80)
www.fws.gov/harrisneck
912-652-4415

♦ ⚡ ∿ ♿

Portions of refuge periodically
closed for hunting and to
reduce disturbance to wildlife.

32 Fort Pulaski National
Monument *(Page 80)*
www.nps.gov/fopu
912-786-5787

? ⑤ ♦ ⚡ ♿

FLORIDA

The flocks of birds that covered the shelly beaches,
and those that hovered overhead,
so astonished us that at first we could scarcely believe our eyes.

THIS WAS JOHN JAMES AUDUBON'S REACTION ON VISITING the Florida Keys in the early 1830s, and it's still the vision that appears to many travelers when they think of Florida: masses of herons, egrets, ibises, spoonbills, and storks feeding in shallow wetlands or flying to roost at dusk, in a setting of lush, subtropical vegetation. In places this scene is just what you'll find, an avian spectacle that still has the power to astonish.

Unfortunately, persecution in the late 19th and early 20th centuries and, lately, the burgeoning human population of South Florida and the attendant loss and degradation of habitat mean that never again will we see numbers of wading birds comparable to those that once throve here. It's sobering to imagine, as you look out over a teeming, colorful flock of waders in Big Cypress National Preserve or the famed J. N. "Ding" Darling National Wildlife Refuge, that once there were many more of these birds—in some cases ten times as many—and many more places where they could nest and feed.

Florida has more to entice birders than flashy herons and egrets, beautiful as they are. As a continental extremity, the peninsula is home to species seldom or never found elsewhere in the United States. Apart from regularly occurring specialties, Florida also sees rare strays that wander from the Bahamas and the Caribbean islands. Among the sought-after regular species are Swallow-tailed and Snail Kites, Short-tailed Hawk, Limpkin, Roseate Tern, White-crowned Pigeon, Mangrove Cuckoo, Smooth-billed Ani, Antillean Nighthawk, Gray Kingbird, Black-whiskered Vireo, the endemic (and threatened) Florida Scrub-Jay, and Shiny Cowbird. The pinelands, scrub, and prairies of central and northern Florida harbor Crested Caracara, Sandhill Crane, Red-cockaded Woodpecker (endangered), and Bachman's Sparrow, among other species. With a huge pet trade, abundant fruit trees, and a subtropical climate that allows escaped birds to survive, southern Florida is home to a broad and colorful variety of free-flying exotic birds. And beaches (less than two hours away no matter where you are in the state) host an array of shorebirds that changes with the seasons. ■

Mangrove Cuckoo

SPECIAL BIRDS OF FLORIDA

Fulvous Whistling-Duck	Snail Kite	White-crowned Pigeon
Masked Booby	Short-tailed Hawk	Mangrove Cuckoo
Brown Booby	Crested Caracara	Smooth-billed Ani
Magnificent Frigatebird	Limpkin	Burrowing Owl
Roseate Spoonbill	Sandhill Crane	Antillean Nighthawk
Wood Stork	Roseate Tern	Red-cockaded Woodpecker
Greater Flamingo	Bridled Tern	Gray Kingbird
Swallow-tailed Kite	Sooty Tern	Black-whiskered Vireo
	Brown Noddy	
	Black Noddy	
		Florida Scrub-Jay
		Cave Swallow
		Yellow Warbler (golden race)
		Bachman's Sparrow
		Shiny Cowbird

SOUTHERN EVERGLADES REGION AND THE KEYS

- Varied waterbirds in Everglades wetlands
- Seabirds and exciting spring migration in the Dry Tortugas

Whitewater Bay,
Everglades
National Park

1   By now, those with an interest in conservation know the story of **Everglades National Park.** Despite its 1.5-million-acre size, this portion of the "river of grass" and its inhabitants have suffered enormously from pollution and changes in water flow brought about by agriculture, urban growth, and other human activities. New public awareness, though, has led to massive and far-ranging efforts to restore the Everglades ecosystem. Time will tell of their effectiveness.

Most people get acquainted with the park at the Ernest F. Coe Visitor Center or the Royal Palm Visitor Center, farther inside the park. The 0.5-mile **Anhinga Trail** at the latter center is excellent for close views of alligators and various waterbirds, including Anhinga, a pelican relative that looks something like a sharp-billed cormorant. Many other waders and waterbirds are found here as well, from Green Heron and Purple Gallinule to White Ibis and Yellow-crowned Night-Heron.

As you drive through the park, watch for the South Florida race of Red-shouldered Hawk, smaller and much paler than birds elsewhere in the country. A Swallow-tailed Kite, one of the world's most beautiful and graceful raptors, may sail overhead during spring and summer. But the bird of prey most sought after here is Short-tailed Hawk, a small buteo (the same genus as Red-shouldered and Red-tailed) that often eludes visiting birders. Short-tailed is easier—though not necessarily easy—to find in winter when birds from farther north migrate to the tip of the Florida Peninsula. Take time to check all soaring hawks and vultures; Short-tailed often soars quite high, above other birds.

One of the most famous birding locales in Everglades National Park is **Snake Bight Trail,** a couple of miles past the canoe ramp and rest rooms at West Pond. One reason it's famous, unfortunately, is its almost indescribably dreadful mosquitoes. (In truth, this could apply to nearly all the Everglades from spring through fall.) The 2-mile trail leads alongside an old borrow ditch to Snake Bight (a shallow bay), which, short of taking a boat out into Florida Bay, is the likeliest place in the United States to see Greater Flamingo between early fall and early spring. High tide pushes the birds closer to shore to feed, making them easier to sight, and the birds are seen most often from late summer through midwinter. Don't be fooled by Roseate Spoonbill, which is smaller with a much longer bill. The origin of these flamingos has long been debated, with continuing disagreement over whether they're truly wild or descendants of birds escaped from captivity. Snake Bight is also a good place to see throngs of herons, shorebirds, gulls, terns, and Black Skimmer, again with high tide being by far the best time to visit—otherwise the birds will be far out on the mudflats in the heat haze.

White-crowned Pigeon, an attractive South Florida specialty, is seen often here. Mangrove Cuckoo, one of Florida's most prized birds, also occurs, but is quite elusive—hard to see even when located by its call. If you miss this species on your first trip to Florida, you'll be joining a very large club; just think of it as an excuse to come back again.

At the park's **Flamingo Visitor Center,** at the end of the main park road on the shore of Florida Bay, look for the white-plumaged form of Great Blue Heron known as the "Great White Heron," once considered a separate species. Its larger size, body shape, and leg color (yellow, not black) help distinguish it from Great Egret. Reddish Egret, Roseate Spoonbill,

Osprey, Bald Eagle, and a variety of shorebirds are likely, and in winter this is another spot to watch for Short-tailed Hawk.

Shiny Cowbird, a rarity found sporadically throughout Florida and occasionally seen here, is a recent invader from the Caribbean that is not illustrated in most field guides. The male is shiny purplish in color; the female is very difficult to differentiate from the common Brown-headed Cowbird female. Check around the campground and other grassy areas for this species.

Near **Homestead** and **Cutler Ridge,** watch from February through summer for Cave Swallow, which nests very locally in highway culverts and under bridges in the area. These birds belong to the distinct West Indian race of Cave Swallow, darker on the undersides and on the rump than the southwestern subspecies, which may someday be designated as a separate species. One favorite spot is near the S.W. 216th Street overpass of Florida's Turnpike (Fla. 821).

"Great White Heron" form of Great Blue Heron

2 Begin your exploration of the **Florida Keys** by taking Card Sound Road east from US 1 at Florida City, crossing the bridge to north Key Largo and Fla. 905. Because of criminal activity, law-enforcement officers are very strict about trespassing in this area. Bird only along roads unless public access is clearly permitted, such as at a short nature trail at the botanic site less than a half-mile east of the intersection with US 1 on Key Largo. Black-whiskered Vireo and Mangrove Cuckoo nest here, and White-crowned Pigeon can be common except in winter. Gray Kingbird is frequent along the highway in spring and summer.

Continuing south, you'll find Osprey nesting along the road, and "Great White Heron" may be seen along the shore anywhere. Keep an eye out for soaring Magnificent Frigatebird, as well as Short-tailed Hawk in winter. In summer, the airport at **Marathon** can be a good spot for one of the keys' specialty birds, the Antillean Nighthawk, active beginning just before sunset. Though slightly smaller than Common Nighthawk, Antillean is best distinguished by its insect-like call, usually described as *pity-pit-pit.* Check the Marathon golf course for Burrowing Owl, a declining species in Florida.

At **Sugarloaf Key,** turn south at the light at Milepost 17; at a T intersection, turn right and follow County Road 939A to its end. This drive passes through extensive mangrove habitat good for spotting White-crowned Pigeon, Mangrove Cuckoo, Gray Kingbird, and Black-whiskered Vireo. Check periodically all along the way.

As you approach Key West (and quite literally the end of the road), the parking lot at Florida Keys Junior College on **Stock Key** provides the best chance to find Antillean Nighthawk at dusk between late April and August. The nearby Key West Botanical Gardens are good for land birds during migration. On **Key West** itself, Antillean Nighthawk feeds at night over the Key West airport, in the southeastern part of the island. Roseate Tern, a bird with a very limited and disjunct breeding range in the United States, nests in the lower keys and should be looked for from April through summer anywhere you find terns gathering; **Fort Zachary Taylor State Historic Site** is a favorite spot.

3 **Dry Tortugas National Park** comprises seven tiny islands and about 100 square miles of ocean. The park centers on **Garden Key** and Fort Jefferson. Most birders visit in spring, when an astonishing variety of migrants use these islands as a rest stop and several localized breeding specialties can be found.

Visiting the Dry Tortugas requires a boat trip or seaplane ride, both of which run daily out of Key West. One way to go is with a bird-tour company, a few of which offer three-day boat trips that allow close reconnaissance of the islands and the chance to see seabirds en route (including Audubon's Shearwater, Northern Gannet, Pomarine Jaeger, and Bridled Tern). You can also set up a one-day trip via boat or seaplane operating under a National Park Service permit.

The Dry Tortugas definitely rank on the short list of top U.S. birding sites. Sooty Tern and Brown Noddy nest by the thousands on **Bush Key.** A few Black Noddy may also be found here but are difficult to see.

Magnificent Frigatebird and Masked Booby breed in the Dry Tortugas. The former is easily seen at Garden Key; the latter is usually identified only from a boat, as it nests on **Hospital Key.** Brown Booby, while not a local nester, is sometimes seen on navigation towers; the Red-footed Booby is much rarer.

In spring, thousands of trans-Gulf land-bird migrants use the Dry Tortugas as a rest stop. On good days, Garden Key can resemble an overstocked aviary. Naturally, all this activity attracts raptors, so it's not unusual to find a Sharp-shinned Hawk, Merlin, or Peregrine Falcon. South Florida specialties such as Gray Kingbird, Black-whiskered Vireo, and Shiny Cowbird are regularly found here as well.

SOUTHEAST AND SOUTHWEST

- Regional specialties in some of America's most famous natural areas
- Good sites for Florida Scrub-Jay

Big Cypress
National Preserve,
southeast of Naples

4 Among Florida's tourist-thronged beaches, birders come to coastal parks not only for spring migrants, but also for rare vagrants from the Bahamas and the Caribbean, such as La Sagra's Flycatcher and Western Spindalis. The size and diverse habitats of **Jonathan Dickinson State Park** make it a fine destination anytime. The park hosts breeding Osprey and Bald Eagle, as well as Bachman's Sparrow in pinewood; one specialty is the symbolic Florida Scrub-Jay.

5 Northwest of Boca Raton, **Arthur R. Marshall Loxahatchee National Wildlife Refuge** is a possible spot to find the declining, elusive Smooth-billed Ani. The impoundments here have a good variety of waders and waterfowl, often including Fulvous Whistling-Duck, and a Snail Kite (endangered) spotted in slow, floppy-winged flight. Although boat tours are not allowed, one option is **Swampland Tours,** on the north shore of Lake Okeechobee, where the odds of seeing the kite are pretty good. Purple Gallinule and Limpkin are seen commonly.

6 A bit farther west, you'll enter **Big Cypress National Preserve.** The 26-mile County Road 94—first paved, then unpaved and rough—offers close views of herons and egrets. Ten miles farther west, unpaved County Road 839 parallels a swampy canal and offers abundant waders and waterbirds, including Wood Stork. Once breeding across much of the Southeast, with a population as high as 50,000 in Florida alone, Wood Storks have declined to only a few thousand pairs nesting in Florida, Georgia, and South Carolina.

Stop at the Big Cypress Bend area of **Fakahatchee Strand State Preserve,** where a boardwalk leads into a swamp forest with very old, very large bald cypresses. Bald Eagle nests here, and this is a good area to see Pileated Woodpecker.

7 **Corkscrew Swamp Sanctuary** ranks among the state's finest natural areas. The sanctuary's 10,560 acres (with other adjacent protected lands) is home to the country's largest colony of Wood Storks. Recently, the number of nests here has ranged from around 200 to nearly 1,000.

A boardwalk loops through a splendid cypress swamp where you may see an Anhinga drying its wings beside the trail, a Limpkin searching for snails, a Little Blue Heron patiently waiting at a pond full of water lettuce for an unwary crayfish, or a small flock of glowing White Ibis flying away. Red-shouldered Hawk screams its evocative call as it soars overhead. Barred Owl is common.

8 On Sanibel Island lies one of America's most famous nature preserves, **J. N. "Ding" Darling National Wildlife Refuge,** where many birders have seen their first Black-whiskered Vireo. As you cross the causeway to Sanibel, look for Magnificent Frigatebird, Reddish Egret, Wilson's Plover, American Oystercatcher, Black Skimmer, and a variety of terns.

The main attraction is the wildlife drive, where impressive birds such as these are seen seasonally in varying numbers: American White and Brown Pelicans; Anhinga; Great Blue, Little Blue, Tricolored, and Green Herons; Great, Snowy, and

Reddish Egrets; Yellow-crowned Night-Heron; White Ibis; Roseate Spoonbill; and Wood Stork. Black-whiskered Vireo nests here and is easy to find along the wildlife drive and refuge walking trails in late spring and summer, when males are singing. Mangrove Cuckoo nests, too, but is elusive.

Gray Kingbird can be found anywhere on the island, perching in plain sight, more cooperatively than the vireo or the cuckoo. Osprey is also conspicuous, its bulky nests set atop various supports, from channel markers to platforms erected specially for this popular raptor.

SNAIL KITE

The Snail Kite's distinctive bill is adapted for feeding on apple snails, large gastropods common in South Florida marshes. The curved, pointed bill easily reaches inside the snail's shell. The kite's ability to find snails is greatly affected by water levels, so the birds wander widely. Once reduced to just a few pairs in Florida, the Snail Kite has made something of a comeback, though it remains vulnerable to drought and human-caused disruptions in water flow through the "river of grass." ∎

9 In Sarasota, **Myakka River State Park** comprises grassland, marshes, and the Myakka River, which attract a fine selection of species. Nesting birds include Wood Duck, Wild Turkey, Anhinga, Least Bittern, Black-crowned and Yellow-crowned Night-Herons, Osprey, Bald Eagle, Red-shouldered Hawk, Black-necked Stilt, and Common Ground-Dove. In addition, Glossy Ibis, Roseate Spoonbill, Wood Stork, Swallow-tailed Kite, Limpkin, and Sandhill Crane are seen regularly. Stop at the bridge where the main park road crosses the Myakka River, and don't miss the boardwalk at Upper Myakka Lake.

The woodlands and prairies from north toward Sebring and Avon Park are worth exploring for several special species. Crested Caracara, a strikingly marked large raptor, may be seen scavenging along Fla. 70 east of Arcadia, County Road 74 east of Babcock, or the part of US 27 connecting them. Short-tailed Hawk (which occurs in both light and dark morphs), difficult to find in the nesting season, is occasionally seen near Palmdale.

The **Avon Park Air Force Range** is a good place to look for Swallow-tailed Kite, Crested Caracara, Sandhill Crane, and Florida Scrub-Jay. The endangered Red-cockaded Woodpecker is found here with Brown-headed Nuthatch and Bachman's Sparrow, which frequent the same open pine habitat. The best place in Florida to find Grasshopper Sparrow is along Kissimmee Road. It's also a great location for Wild Turkey. Call or check in at the range and visit the natural resources office on County Road 64 for a map and permission to bird.

NORTHERN PENINSULAR FLORIDA

■ Concentrations of waterbirds at Merritt Island
National Wildlife Refuge

Cattle Egret in
Merritt Island
National Wildlife
Refuge

10 Adjacent to the Kennedy Space Center, **Merritt Island National Wildlife Refuge** is famous for its varied birding opportunities. Encompassing beach, marsh, oak scrub, pinelands, and grassland, the refuge has seen more than 310 species recorded since its establishment in 1963.

Mottled Duck, herons, ibises, Osprey, Bald Eagle, and Florida Scrub-Jay are among the many nesting species here. In fall, shorebirds are found on ponds and Atlantic beaches, while Peregrine Falcons are frequently seen hunting during their southbound migration. In winter, thousands of ducks congregate on the refuge; Tree Swallow sometimes feeds in enormous flocks; Clapper, King, and Virginia Rails and Sora skulk along the edges of wetlands. Laughing, Ring-billed, and Herring Gulls are the common species, but a few Great Black-backed Gulls can also be found along with Caspian, Royal, and Forster's Terns and Black Skimmer. Northern Gannet is frequently seen offshore in winter, with dozens of birds sometimes sighted daily.

Just beyond the refuge visitor center, the **Oak Hammock Trail** is good for songbirds in spring migration. At nearby Playalinda Beach, scan for seabirds, shorebirds, gulls, and terns. The 6-mile **Black Point Wildlife Drive** traverses marshes where waders are abundant. A hiking trail here leads to an observation tower with views over the surrounding wetlands.

11 Located about 10 miles south of Gainesville, **Paynes Prairie State Preserve** comprises an expanse of wet prairie with pine flatwoods, hardwood hammocks, and wetlands intermixed. Sandhill Crane winters here in the thousands and can be seen from observation towers in various parts of the preserve, including at the visitor center north of Micanopy. Stop here for a bird checklist and a map locating several short hiking trails. Wild Turkey, herons, Osprey, Bald Eagle, King Rail, and Purple Gallinule breed here, along with Sandhill Cranes of the resident Florida population.

FLORIDA PANHANDLE

- Red-cockaded Woodpecker at Apalachicola National Forest
- Spring "fallouts" at Fort Pickens

RED-COCKADED WOODPECKER

One of the few birds found only in the U.S., the Red-cockaded Woodpecker is endemic to southeastern pine forests. Loss of its habitat—mature pines with the fungus red heart disease—has resulted in its endangered status. **Apalachicola National Forest** is central to its population. Look for roost trees marked by whitish resin; the birds' drilling creates these sap flows, which may repel predators. ■

12 St. Marks National Wildlife Refuge covers over 68,000 acres along the Gulf of Mexico, including wetlands and forest (pine flatwoods and hardwoods).

As you enter, check near the visitor center for Yellow-throated Warbler. Great numbers of ducks winter in the ponds along the road to the lighthouse (peaking in December). Bald Eagle pairs nest here as early as November or December; Ospreys wait until spring is nearer. You may find Brown-headed Nuthatch along **Mounds Trail** near the fire tower. Herons are abundant year-round.

Several trails wind through the refuge, including some that follow dikes. These can be good places to see such marsh birds as rails, Purple Gallinule, Sedge (winter) and Marsh Wrens, and Nelson's Sharp-tailed Sparrow (winter). Marshes near the coast are home to Seaside Sparrow year-round, and the elusive Black Rail is sometimes heard. Wilson's Plover nests along the shore.

13 Fort Pickens—part of the **Gulf Islands National Seashore** and one of the most famous birding spots on the upper Gulf Coast—is known primarily for spring "fallouts" of migrant songbirds. After checking trees or shrubs near the campground store for vireos, thrushes, warblers, orioles, and other migrants (mid-March to mid-May), follow the biking trail parallel to the main road and several nature trails to birding locations.

Two other parks to visit during fallouts are **St. Joseph Peninsula State Park** and **St. George Island State Park.** Snowy Plover, Least Tern, Black Skimmer, and Gray Kingbird breed along the coast. Fall can bring migrant songbirds and southbound raptors. Sprague's Pipit is rare but regular on the causeway to St. George from mid-November through December. These parks host large breeding colonies of Least Tern and Black Skimmer.

FLORIDA | MORE INFORMATION

RARE BIRD ALERT
Statewide 561-640-0079

1 Everglades NP
(Page 84)
www.nps.gov/ever
305-242-7700

2 Florida Keys
(Page 86)
www.fla-keys.com

3 Dry Tortugas NP
(Page 87)
www.nps.gov/drto
305-242-7700

4 Jonathan Dickinson SP
(Page 88)
www.floridastateparks.org
772-546-2771

5 Arthur R. Marshall Loxahatchee NWR
(Page 88)
loxahatchee.fws.gov
407-732-3684

6 Big Cypress National Preserve *(Page 89)*
www.nps.gov/bicy
239-695-2000

6 Fakahatchee Strand State Preserve *(Page 89)*
www.floridastateparks.org
239-695-4593

7 Corkscrew Swamp Sanctuary
(Page 89)
www.audubon.org
239-348-1522

8 J. N. "Ding" Darling NWR *(Page 89)*
www.fws.gov/dingdarling
239-472-1100

9 Myakka River SP
(Page 90)
www.myakkariver.org
941-361-6511

9 Avon Park Air Force Range *(Page 90)*
www.avonparkafr.com
863-452-4254

10 Merritt Island NWR
(Page 91)
www.fws.gov/merittisland
321-861-0667

11 Paynes Prairie State Preserve *(Page 91)*
www.floridastateparks.org
352-466-3397

12 St. Marks NWR
(Page 92)
www.fws.gov/saintmarks
850-925-6121

13 Gulf Islands National Seashore *(Page 92)*
See p. 107 for contact info.

See p. 107 for contact info.

ADDITIONAL SITES

① John U. Lloyd Beach SRA

② Hugh Taylor Birch SRA
www.floridatateparks.org

③ Shark Valley
www.nps.gov/ever/visit

④ Conservancy Nature Center
www.conservancy.org

⑤ Oscar Scherer SP

⑥ Edward Ball Wakulla Springs SP
www.floridastateparks.org

⑦ Apalachicola NF
www.fs.fed.us/r8

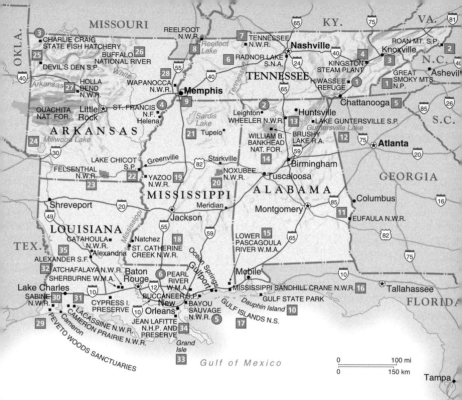

SOUTH-CENTRAL

- Tennessee
- Alabama
- Mississippi
- Arkansas
- Louisiana

ROSEATE SPOONBILL AND CANADA WARBLER are seldom mentioned in the same paragraph, much less the same sentence. Here, though, they will be—to illustrate the avian extremes of this mid-southern chapter, which encompasses the salt marshes of Louisiana and the 6,000-foot peaks of eastern Tennessee, with a correspondingly broad range of birding possibilities. In one corner of the region, Fulvous Whistling-Duck and Purple Gallinule nest; in the other, Northern Saw-whet Owl, Common Raven, Black-capped Chickadee, and other northern birds extend their ranges south along the Appalachian Mountains.

Between these extremes lies the land that many people picture when they think of the South: meandering rivers lined with bald cypresses and tupelos, bottomland hardwood forests, and flat cropland. Southern birds favoring these temperate lands include Anhinga, Little Blue Heron, Swallow-tailed Kite,

Prothonotary and Swainson's Warblers, and Painted Bunting.

Other habitats reward birders, too. Pinewoods are home to Red-cockaded Woodpecker, Brown-headed Nuthatch, and Bachman's Sparrow, all southern specialties. Sandy beaches provide nesting sites for Snowy and Wilson's Plovers, Least Tern, and Black Skimmer. Some of America's most famous spring migration "fallout" sites lie along the Gulf Coast, and great inland reservoirs such as Alabama's Guntersville Lake attract wintering loons, grebes, waterfowl, Bald Eagles, and gulls.

Here, as in so many places, human activities have worked immense changes on the land. The same rich alluvial soil that once grew huge oaks, hickories, and sweet gums was "invaded" to grow cotton, soybeans, and rice. Rivers and creeks that once annually overtopped their banks, spreading renewing silt and nurturing productive wetlands, were ditched and leveed. Pine forests where trees once grew to staggering sizes were planted and harvested like wheat or corn. Such human intervention affected wildlife as well. Due in part to habitat loss the Carolina Parakeet is gone, as is the Bachman's Warbler, both once widespread in the South. Nature, too, has had a hand in the loss. In 2005 Hurricanes Katrina and Rita ravaged land and life along the Gulf Coast. In places, the comeback may be a long one.

On the other side of the scale, Ospreys and Bald Eagles are beginning to breed in places where they were long absent, their huge nests appearing beside lakes and rivers. Brown Pelicans have made a strong comeback after declines in population caused by pesticides. Colonies of wading birds, once vulnerable to hunting and harassment, enjoy strong protection. And a growing corps of conservationists works to safeguard the natural areas that remain in the South, from old-growth forests to lowland swamps. Many of them are among America's finest places to see birds.∎

Scissor-tailed Flycatcher

SPECIAL BIRDS OF SOUTH-CENTRAL STATES

Brown Pelican	Glossy Ibis	Purple Gallinule	Red-cockaded Woodpecker
Neotropic Cormorant	Fulvous Whistling-Duck	Snowy Plover	Scissor-tailed Flycatcher
Anhinga	Ross's Goose	Wilson's Plover	
Reddish Egret	Mottled Duck	American Oystercatcher	Brown-headed Nuthatch
Roseate Spoonbill	King Rail	Royal Tern	
Yellow Night-Heron	Swallow-tailed Kite	Sandwich Tern	Swainson's Warbler
White Ibis	Mississippi Kite	Common Ground-Dove	Bachman's Sparrow
			Painted Bunting

TENNESSEE

- Northern species in the eastern mountains
- Migration hot spots in Knoxville and Nashville
- Excellent shorebirds in Memphis

Rhododendrons on Roan Mountain, in eastern Tennessee

1 Clingmans Dome, in **Great Smoky Mountains National Park,** is the second highest point east of the Mississippi River. For birders, this means the chance to see breeding species such as Northern Saw-whet Owl; Common Raven; Black-capped Chickadee; Red-breasted Nuthatch; Brown Creeper; Winter Wren; Golden-crowned Kinglet; Veery; Chestnut-sided, Black-throated Blue, Black-throated Green, Blackburnian, and Canada Warblers; Dark-eyed Junco; and Red Crossbill (irregular).

The best place to see many of these northern birds is the road up from Newfound Gap. The parking lot at Newfound Gap can have some interesting birds, as can several pull-offs and trail junctions. Saw-whets call here in spring, and you may even hear the Red Crossbill.

The beautiful **Cades Cove** area is a good choice to see lower-elevation birds, including Ruffed Grouse, Wild Turkey, Acadian and Willow Flycatchers, Yellow-throated and Hooded Warblers, Blue Grosbeak, and Orchard Oriole.

2 Many of the same highland birds can be found at Roan Mountain. Visit **Roan Mountain State Park** for nesting birds such as Ruffed Grouse; Golden-winged, Chestnut-sided, and Worm-eating Warblers; Scarlet Tanager; and Rose-breasted Grosbeak. In late spring and early summer, listen for Alder Flycatcher (in alders) and Winter Wren at **Carver's Gap**. Hermit Thrush is heard in nesting season. Vesper Sparrow nests on grassy balds.

3 Knoxville's favorite birding spot, **Sharp's Ridge Memorial Park** is an excellent place to observe songbird migration in warblers, vireos, thrushes, tanagers, and other migrants. The wooded slopes offer good views of birds usually seen only high in treetops. Fall migration can also be productive.

4 **Kingston Steam Plant Wildlife Observation Area,** one of the best all-around birding spots in eastern Tennessee, encompass-es ponds, marsh, grassy fields, and woodland. Check pines near the entrance road for Brown-headed Nuthatches and nesting Yellow-throated and Pine Warblers. Migration may bring Sora or Marsh Wren to marshy spots. Ducks winter by the hundreds on ponds here; Snow Goose is rare but regular, and Greater White-fronted Goose is found occasionally. Osprey and Grasshopper Sparrow nest in the area, and spring, late summer, and fall can bring good numbers of shorebirds.

5 The easy access to wetlands at Chattanooga's **Brainerd Levee** is good for sighting wintering waterfowl (especially dab-bling ducks), migrant rails and shorebirds, and postbreeding waders. Walk the levee beside South Chickamauga Creek and look for Great Blue and Green Herons (both common). Least Bittern nests here, and American Bittern is seen in migration. When water levels are right, this can be the region's best s horebird spot, and grassy places can harbor sparrows and Sedge and Marsh Wrens in migration. Purple Gallinule is seen occa-sionally, and Common Moorhen is a nearly annual sighting.

6 Nashville birders treasure **Radnor Lake State Natural Area,** which is most popular in spring migration, when more than 20 species of warblers pass through, and in winter, when a good variety of ducks can be seen. American Woodcocks perform courtship flights in late winter, when Ring-necked Duck, Lesser Scaup, Bufflehead, and Hooded Merganser cruise the lake. In summer, the songs of Wood Thrush, Prothonotary Warbler, and Summer and Scarlet Tanagers can be heard throughout the forest.

7 The **Pace Point Area** of **Tennessee National Wildlife Refuge** can be one of the region's best birding spots from fall through spring. Low water levels on the Kentucky Lake create shallows that attract large numbers of herons, shorebirds, gulls, and terns. In late summer, Great Blue and Little Blue Herons and Great and Snowy Egrets congregate; fall brings flocks of Caspian and Black Terns. Canada Geese and dabbling and diving ducks can be abundant. Check the small coves along the entrance road for mergansers; Barred Owl is seen often near the road down to the lake. In spring, woods west of the entrance road and near the refuge office are excellent for viewing flycatchers, vireos, and warblers. Both Osprey and Bald Eagle nest on the lake.

8 Western Tennessee's most famous birding location, **Reelfoot Lake** typifies one image of the South: Great Egrets wading through the shallows, with the squeal of Wood Ducks, the scream of Red-shouldered Hawks, and the whistle of Prothonotary Warblers in the air. Of the several birding locations around the lake, the most accessible is the auto tour route at **Reelfoot National Wildlife Refuge.** Nesting birds include Hooded Merganser, Least Bittern, Black-crowned Night-Heron, Osprey, and Mississippi Kite. Migration brings shorebirds to muddy pools, late summer can see flocks of herons and egrets, and in winter thousands of ducks and geese mass on the lake and in fields (some years more than half a million). The Black Bayou area has marsh where King Rail nests, and grassy places where Short-eared Owl (rare) winters. Reelfoot is also known for its wintering Bald Eagles.

9 The most famous birding site in Memphis is the **EARTH Complex** in the southwestern part of town, where the shorebirds can be terrific. In spring and fall migrations, you can see Black-bellied and Semipalmated Plovers; Greater and Lesser Yellowlegs; Solitary, Spotted, Semipalmated, Western, Pectoral, Least, and Stilt Sandpipers; and Short-billed Dowitcher. Black-necked Stilt nests, and from fall through spring, ducks, gulls, and terns offer a break from a confusing peep or dowitcher.

TENNESSEE | MORE INFORMATION

RARE BIRD ALERT
Statewide 615-356-7636
Chattanooga
 423-821-4381
Knoxville 423-577-4717
 ext. 80

1 **Great Smoky
Mountains National Park**
(Page 96)
www.nps.gov/grsm
865-436-1200

2 **Roan Mountain
State Park** *(Page 97)*
*www.state.tn.us
/environment/parks*
423-772-0190 or
800-250-8620

3 **Sharp's Ridge
Memorial Park** *(Page 98)*
*www.ci.knoxville.tn.us
/parks/sharpsridge.asp*
865-215-2000

4 **TVA Kingston
Steam Plant Wildlife
Observation Area**
(Page 97)
ww.tva.gov
865-632-2101
*Located off US 70;
closed to public access
mid-Oct.–Jan.*

5 **Brainerd Levee**
(Page 97)
*www.chattanooga.gov
/PRAC/30_1000.htm*
423-757-5167

6 **Radnor Lake State
Natural Area** *(Page 97)*
*www.tennessee.gov
/environment/parks*
615-373-3467

7 **Tennessee National
Wildlife Refuge**
(Page 98)
*www.fws.gov
/tennesseerefuge*
731-642-2091

8 **Reelfoot National
Wildlife Refuge**
(Page 98)
www.fws.gov/reelfoot
731-538-2481

8 **Reelfoot Lake State
Park** *(Page 98)*
*www.state.tn.us
/environment/parks*
731-253-7756 or
800-250-8617

*Reelfoot Lake State Park offers
guided bus tours to see eagles.
Call for information about
these popular trips.*

9 **EARTH Complex
T.E. Maxson Wastewater
Treatment Plant**
(Page 98)
901-789-0510

*Check in at the office for
advice on birding areas and
road conditions. A spotting
scope is essential to get the
most from a visit.*

ADDITIONAL SITE

1 **Blythe Ferry Unit of
Hiwassee Refuge**
www.state.tn.us/twra
931-484-9571

*This site (about 8 mi. N of
Georgetown via County Road
131) offers many of the stan-
dard attractions of a waterfowl area. In recent years,
though, Sandhill Cranes have
become the refuge stars, some
wintering and others stopping
in migration. The concentration has grown to more than
6,000 at times, making this
one of the state's premier
wildlife spectacles Nov.–Mar.
Though closed mid-Oct.–Feb.,
the area can be viewed from
adjacent roads and an observation deck anytime.*

ALABAMA

- Spring migrants on Dauphin Island
- Winter waterbirds at Guntersville Lake
- Nesting warblers in Bankhead National Forest

Gulf State Park, along the Gulf of Mexico east of Gulf Shores

10 Alabama's most famous birding spot, **Dauphin Island** is a top-ranked Gulf Coast spring migration "fallout" site. Dauphin can be mobbed with migrants the day after a front brings north winds or rain. Beaches, bay, and Gulf waters make for productive birding at other times of year as well.

Many birders make their first stop the **Audubon Bird Sanctuary,** where Brown-headed Nuthatch can be found year-round. Another equally favored location is the **Shell Mounds** area. At either spot, when conditions are right, migrant song-birds—flycatchers, vireos, thrushes, warblers, tanagers, and other species—may be present in amazing concentrations.

Watch in spring for Black-whiskered Vireo, which is a rare

but regular visitor, and for Gray Kingbird in open areas from May through August. Also check the marshes south of the airport for Mottled Duck, wading birds, rails, American Oystercatcher, and sparrows. On the western end of the island (heavily damaged by Hurricane Katrina in 2005 and recovering at this printing), scan beaches for Reddish Egret, shorebirds (including Snowy, Wilson's, and Piping Plovers and American Oystercatcher), gulls, terns, and Black Skimmer. Northern Gannet is often seen in the Gulf from fall through spring, and Magnificent Frigatebird may soar overhead in summer.

A ferry runs from the island to **Fort Morgan,** which attracts regular trans-Gulf migrants and frequent rarities. Western Kingbird and Scissor-tailed Flycatcher are regular here in October. The trees just east of the ferry landing can be productive in migration, as can the old stables area near the park entrance; check grassy areas around the fort for migrant Upland and Buff-breasted Sandpipers. The old airstrip is good for sparrows and migrant Bobolink.

The mostly undeveloped **Bon Secour National Wildlife Refuge** has nature trails. Scan for seabirds at the **Gulf State Park** pavilion, and check the shoreline around **Perdido Pass** for waders and shorebirds. Snowy and Piping Plovers are often found here.

11 The fields, woods, and water of **Eufaula National Wildlife Refuge** host a broad range of species, including abundant wintering ducks and geese; Wood Stork is possible in late summer and Sandhill Crane in winter. Osprey and Bald Eagle nest around the lake, and the refuge has several rookeries where Anhinga, Great Blue and Little Blue Herons, and Great and Cattle Egrets nest. White Ibis appears regularly in summer. Tour the **Upland** and **Houston Units** to bird in a variety of habitats, including marshes that may have migrant rails and shorebirds, as well as nesting Purple Gallinule and Common Moorhen. Some refuge roads are closed in winter, but two observation towers are always open. The platform at the Upland Unit is best to see wintering waterfowl.

12 The long expanse of **Guntersville Lake** is the state's best location to find wintering loons and grebes; it's also an excellent spot to see other waterbirds and Bald Eagles. The lakeshore at **Lake Guntersville State Park** is a good place from which to scan the water. A favorite lookout is the area behind Harbor House restaurant: Several rare gulls have appeared here over the years. The best lookout is the causeway where Ala. 69

crosses the lake just west of Guntersville. Stop carefully along the road and watch for loons (Common is most frequent, but Red-throated is seen almost annually; even Pacific has showed up), grebes, and waterfowl. The **Guntersville Dam** makes another good viewpoint. Bald Eagles and gulls winter by the river.

BLACK SKIMMER

Those who speak French in southern Louisiana, a state over from Alabama, call the Black Skimmer *bec à ciseaux*, or scissor-beak—an appropriate name considering the skimmer's distinctive bill shape. This bird and other closely related species of skimmer are the only birds in the world with the lower mandible longer than the upper. Skimmers feed by flying just above the water, slicing the surface with their long lower bill. When skimmers touch a fish or other prey, they quickly snap their beak closed to make the catch. ■

13 **Wheeler National Wildlife Refuge,** downstream on the Tennessee River, sees some of Alabama's largest concentrations of wintering waterfowl. Several species of dabbling ducks are common, along with divers such as Bufflehead, Ruddy Duck, Canvasback, and Common Goldeneye. The refuge also hosts the state's largest population of wintering Canada Geese. Hooded Merganser and Wood Duck are common breeders.

The observation building at the Wheeler visitor center overlooks water where thousands of wintering ducks congregate in late afternoon. **Limestone Bay** is a good spot for observing geese and the best spot for Snow Goose—and a few Ross's are found annually. Although the refuge is usually considered a winter birding site, good opportunities exist year-round. Swainson's Warbler has been found regularly near the headquarters, and trails provide access to spring migrants and common nesters.

14 Alabama's **Bankhead National Forest** invites exploration with a fine assortment of nesting birds, not to mention wild and rugged scenery. Here in the lower Cumberland plateau, wooded ravines with mature hemlock and hardwood forest are home to a number of breeding warblers including Black-throated Green, Yellow-throated, Cerulean, Swainson's, and Worm-eating, and Northern Parula. Look for Blue-winged and Prairie Warblers in regenerating clear-cuts. Some of the best birding is found in and around the 35-acre **Brushy Lake Recreation Area,** with a trail system that loops through a wide variety of habitats. A few miles north, Forest Road 208 has fine roadside birding, as does Forest Road 210 on the western edge of the wilderness.

ALABAMA | MORE INFORMATION

RARE BIRD ALERT
Statewide 256-751-4788

10 Dauphin Island Bird Sanctuaries *(Page 100)*
www.dauphinisland.org/bird.htm
251-861-3607

🍴 🚻 🚶 〰 ♿

As you drive across the causeway to Dauphin Island, watch for waders, waterfowl, and Seaside Sparrow.

10 Fort Morgan
(Page 101)
www.alabama coastalbirdingtrail.com
334-540-7125

❓ 💲 🚻

10 Bon Secour National Wildlife Refuge *(Page 101)*
www.fws.gov/bonsecour
251-540-7720

❓ 🚻 🚶 〰 ♿

10 Gulf State Park
(Page 101)
www.alapark.com
251-948-7275

❓ 🍴 🚻 🚶

11 Eufaula National Wildlife Refuge
(Page 101)
www.fws.gov/eufaula
334-687-4065

🚻 🚶 〰 ♿

12 Lake Guntersville State Park *(Page 101)*
www.alapark.com
256-571-5444

❓ 🍴 🚻 🚶 〰 ♿

13 Wheeler National Wildlife Refuge
(Page 102)
www.fws.gov/wheeler
256-353-7243

❓ 🚻 🚶 〰 ♿

14 Bankhead National Forest and Brushy Lake Recreation Area
(Page 102)
www.fs.fed.us/r8/alabama
205-489-5111

❓ 💲 🚻 🚶 〰 ♿

ADDITIONAL SITE

2 Leighton
www.colbertcountytourism.org
256-383-0783
In migration, northern Alabama birders keep a watch on several small ponds near the town of Leighton, southeast of Florence. When water conditions are right, these ponds can be excellent places to see shorebirds. Rarities found here have included Roseate Spoonbill, Wood Stork, and Black-bellied Whistling-Duck. Black-necked Stilt has nested in this area. Town Creek Marsh, a wetland area on Wilson Lake, is good for rails and waders.

MISSISSIPPI

- Nesting Least Tern at Gulfport
- Red-cockaded Woodpecker at Noxubee National Wildlife Refuge

Reddish Egret, found along the length of the Gulf Coast

15 **Lower Pascagoula River Wildlife Management Area** may well be Mississippi's most important natural area. Breeding birds are those typical of such southern woods, and the Swallow-tailed Kite attracts birders from late spring through summer.

From the wildlife management area office, continue west to Deep Slough Road, which is a good (usually) unpaved road that leads north into woods productive for birding. Though there is a substantial population of Swallow-tailed Kites here, seeing one is not guaranteed. Your best chance for a sighting is to watch for soaring birds just over the treetops in late morning. There are several other old roads off Miss. 614, which, while usually not drivable, can be walked.

16 The **Mississippi Sandhill Crane National Wildlife Refuge** preserves habitat for an endangered nonmigratory subspecies of the tall gray cranes. While most of the refuge is closed to visitation to protect the birds, tours are offered in January and February. On the refuge nature trail, Bachman's Sparrows sing their sweet song and Brown-headed Nuthatches squeak. Along the way, look for wading birds and migrant Osprey at **Bayou Castelle**. Both Henslow's and Le Conte's Sparrows may be found here, with effort, in winter in weedy or tallgrass open areas.

17 Ocean Springs is among the areas heavily damaged by Hurricane Katrina in 2005, and recovering at this printing. A favorite site to visit here has been the **Davis Bayou Unit** of **Gulf Islands National Seashore** for land birding and waterbirding. It is full of birds in spring migration, especially during a "fallout." Marshes have wading birds and rails. A boat-launching area and a fishing pier have provided lookout points over the bayou, where, depending on the season, loons, grebes, pelicans, ducks, waders, gulls, or terns may be present. Accessible by boat, the islands also have Ospreys, eagles, and spring and fall migrants.

At **Gulfport**, sections of beach, also ravaged by the hurricane, have been dedicated as Least Tern nesting areas, and here hundreds of these delicate little terns have traditionally bred, along with Black Skimmers. Other beach and harbor areas have offered loons, shorebirds, gulls, and terns from fall through spring and Magnificent Frigatebird, regular in summer. One favorite spot has been the beach just east of Moses Pier. A quieter beachfront is at **Buccaneer State Park**, which itself can be worth a visit in spring for migrant songbirds. Along the way you may find Reddish Egret or American Oystercatcher.

18 South of historic Natchez, **St. Catherine Creek National Wildlife Refuge** hosts an amazing number of wading birds in the postbreeding season from midsummer through fall. The thousands of birds present include Great Blue, Little Blue, and Green Herons; Great, Snowy, and Cattle Egrets; and White Ibis. Wood Stork is an annual visitor, and Roseate Spoonbill appears occasionally. The refuge can be productive for shorebirds, and waterfowl are abundant in winter.

19 To the north, **Yazoo National Wildlife Refuge** offers similar attractions: wintering flocks of ducks and geese (mostly Snow, with large numbers of Greater White-fronted and some Canada) and summer waders. Nesting birds include Wood

Duck, Hooded Merganser, Pied-billed Grebe, Anhinga, Purple Gallinule, Common Moorhen, and Painted Bunting. The last can be difficult to find. It helps to learn its rather nondescript song, a series of warbling phrases.

ANHINGA

A swamp dweller, the Anhinga eats fish as do its pelican relatives. Instead of scooping them up, though, it spears its prey with its long, pointed bill. Three of its folk names derive from its appearance and behavior: "Black darter" from its ability to dart its head forward quickly and forcefully to stab fish; "snakebird" from its habit of swimming partly submerged with only its head and sinuous neck showing; and "water turkey" from its fanlike tail's resemblance to a Wild Turkey's. ■

20 The 48,000 acres of **Noxubee National Wildlife Refuge** combine extensive bottomland hardwood forest, lakes, and pinewoods to create one of Mississippi's finest birding areas. The refuge manages part of its pine forest for the endangered Red-cockaded Woodpecker. Noxubee's short **Woodpecker Trail,** near the headquarters, passes through a cluster where the birds are usually found easily (early morning and late afternoon are best). Brown-headed Nuthatch, another pine specialist, can be seen here, too. In addition, a boardwalk at Bluff Lake leads to a deck offering a view of wintering waterfowl and a colony of 5,000 nesting Cattle Egrets and nonbreeding Wood Storks and White Ibises in late summer. The 2-mile **Beaver Dam Trail** passes through the refuge's bottomland forest, where nesting birds include Yellow-throated Vireo; Yellow-throated, Black-and-white, Prothonotary, Kentucky, and Hooded Warblers; American Redstart; and Louisiana Waterthrush. Swainson's Warbler is a rare breeder.

21 The 58,000 acres of **Sardis Lake** host loons, grebes, waterfowl, and Bald Eagle, which can be seen from lookout points on the dam from late fall through early spring, and Osprey has begun to nest in the area. Birding is often better on the lower lake, where American White Pelican and gulls feed. In addition to the usual Bonaparte's, Ring-billed, and Herring Gulls, rarities such as Black-headed Gull and Black-legged Kittiwake have appeared in late fall and winter. Sandbars in the lower lake can attract shorebirds (occasionally American Avocet), gulls, and terns. West of the Little Tallahatchie River, a side road leads to the **Clear Springs Nature Trail.** Pass through a bald cypress-tupelo swamp where Red-headed Woodpeckers call year-round and Wood Thrushes sing in breeding season.

MISSISSIPPI | MORE INFORMATION

RARE BIRD ALERT
Coastal 228-435-7227

15 Lower Pascagoula River Wildlife Management Area
(Page 104)
www.mdwfp.com
228-588-3878

As is often the case with this sort of habitat, access is a bit problematical, with the few interior roads sometimes under water. For advice on road conditions, visit the wildlife management area office. This is also a popular hunting area—exercise caution in fall and winter.

16 Mississippi Sandhill Crane National Wildlife Refuge *(Page 105)*
www.fws.gov
/mississippisandhillcrane
228-497-6322

While most of the refuge is closed to visitation to protect the birds, tours are offered in Jan. and Feb.; call for information.

17 Gulf Islands National Seashore *(Page 105)*
www.nps.gov/guis
228-875-9057

Check the visitor center for exhibits on Gulf ecology and maps of the area.

Buccaneer State Park
(Page 105)
www.mdwfp.com
228-467-3822

18 St. Catherine Creek National Wildlife Refuge
(Page 105)
www.fws.gov
/saintcatherinecreek
601-442-6696

Areas of the refuge flood in late winter through spring.

19 Yazoo National Wildlife Refuge *(Page 105)*
www.fws.gov/yazoo
southeast.fws.gov
662-839-2638

Cox's Ponds, a former catfish farm in the northwestern part of the refuge, is one of the region's top birding locations. Now managed as a "moist soils" area, it should be scanned any time of year for waders and shorebirds, especially in the peak fall migration period of Aug. and Sept.

Noxubee National Wildlife Refuge
(Page 106)
www.fws.gov/noxubee
662-323-5548

21 Sardis Lake
(Page 106)
www.sardislake.com

ARKANSAS

- Excellent variety of waterbirds at Millwood Lake
- Winter waterfowl and raptors at Holla Bend National Wildlife Refuge

The Ozarks, at Devil's Den State Park, south of Fayetteville

22 You'll find some of Arkansas's finest birding near **Lake Chicot State Park,** with woods and wetlands that provide habitat for a variety of breeding species and locally rare wanderers from points south. In late summer and early fall, Lake Chicot attracts thousands of wading birds, which feed in nearby wetlands and roost in bald cypress trees in the lake's northern reaches. Part of this impressive gathering can be seen from shore, but for the best view sign up for a sunset boat tour with a park naturalist. Great Blue and Little Blue Herons and Great and Cattle Egrets are abundant on this strikingly pretty lake, accompanied by smaller numbers of American White Pelican, Snowy Egret, Tricolored Heron, Black-crowned and Yellow-crowned Night-Herons, White Ibis, and Wood Stork.

Any time of year, drive the gravel road atop the Mississippi River levee for a look at waterbirds and other species. In late summer the swampy borrow pits alongside the levee can teem with waders, including Wood Stork and, rarely, a visiting Roseate Spoonbill. Wood Duck, Hooded Merganser, and

Pied-billed Grebe breed here, and a variety of other ducks winter. In addition, Mississippi Kite and Painted Bunting occur spring through fall, and you may see Wild Turkey, Red-shouldered Hawk, or Red-headed Woodpecker anytime.

23 **Felsenthal National Wildlife Refuge** is known for hosting the state's largest population of the endangered Red-cockaded Woodpecker. Much of this refuge is swampy bottomland forest, but Pine Island and Shallow Lake Roads provide access to the pine forest the woodpeckers frequent. Watch for pines with painted white bands, indicating trees with roost cavities, and look for the fresh flow of sap that marks an active tree. The same areas also host Brown-headed Nuthatch, Pine Warbler, and Bachman's Sparrow. Explore roadsides for typical birds of southern woodlands, including Barred Owl; Red-headed and Pileated Woodpeckers; Acadian Flycatcher; Yellow-throated Vireo; Wood Thrush; Northern Parula; and Prothonotary, Kentucky, and Hooded Warblers.

24 The state's best location for waterbirds is **Millwood Lake.** From fall through spring, hundreds of loons, grebes, cormorants, ducks, coots, and gulls can be seen from spots along the shore, especially the **Beard's Bluff** area at the eastern end of the huge dam. Bald Eagles have nested here; look for a mammoth nest in the top of a dead tree in the middle of the lake. Osprey is common in spring and fall.

Millwood is most famous for its regional rarities, including the Red-throated Loon; Magnificent Frigatebird; all three species of scoters; all three species of jaegers; Little, Laughing, Black-headed, Glaucous, and Sabine's Gulls; and Black-legged Kittiwake. Checking duck flocks of common species might turn up a Cinnamon Teal or a Long-tailed Duck. Greater Scaup, while uncommon, is regular, especially along the dam. Mid-October through early January is the optimal time for searching through the masses of Ring-billed, Bonaparte's, and Herring Gulls for the rarer gulls. Jaegers can be seen in fall only. Sabine's Gull tends to appear between mid-September and mid-October and doesn't necessarily associate with other species, except occasionally with Franklin's Gull.

Millwood's land bird potential is excellent as well, especially at the **Okay Levee,** where sparrows can be found. Land bird rarities noted in the past have included Say's Phoebe, Vermilion Flycatcher, and Couch's and Western Kingbirds. The levee provides good scope views of waterfowl.

25 **Devil's Den State Park** in the Ozarks is a good place to see migrant and nesting birds. Watch for Greater Roadrunner along the highway as you approach the park. Down in the **Lee Creek Valley,** look for nesting species including Wild Turkey; Red-shouldered Hawk; Yellow-throated Vireo; Yellow-throated, Worm-eating, and Kentucky Warblers; Northern Parula; American Redstart; Ovenbird; Louisiana Waterthrush; Chipping and Field Sparrows; and American Goldfinch.

26 **Buffalo National River,** one of the most beautiful natural areas east of the Rockies, offers good spring and summer birding, with possibilities of seeing locally uncommon breeding species such as Cerulean, Worm-eating, and Swainson's Warblers and American Redstart. Look for Worm-eating on shady slopes, Cerulean in streamside trees and ravines with large trees. Swainson's is not a certainty, but has been seen.

27 Waterfowl and Bald Eagles make **Holla Bend National Wildlife Refuge** a well-known winter site, although you'll find fine birding opportunities year-round. The refuge hosts thousands of Snow and Canada Geese in winter. White-fronted Goose is occasionally found, and Ross's Goose is regularly spotted. Look for wintering Bald Eagles along the river or the oxbow lakes. In spring and fall, American White Pelican, Osprey, and Caspian Tern migrate along the river. Northern Harrier is common in winter. Red-shouldered Hawk is often seen, and Broad-winged Hawk nests. Golden Eagle and Peregrine and Prairie Falcons are very rare visitors, and migrant Sandhill Cranes have occasionally stopped to feed. Holla Bend is also a good place to find Yellow-headed Blackbird in spring, and Long-eared Owl has wintered in thick stands of cedar. Scissor-tailed Flycatcher, Bell's and Warbling Vireos, Lark Sparrow, Painted Bunting, and Dickcissel can be found in open areas in spring and summer. Wood Duck, Wild Turkey, Barred Owl, Fish Crow, Northern Parula, and Kentucky Warbler breed in the bottomland woods.

28 In the swampy woods in **Wapanocca National Wildlife Refuge,** Wood Duck, Hooded Merganser, Mississippi Kite, Red-shouldered Hawk, Red-headed and Pileated Woodpeckers, Yellow-throated and Prothonotary Warblers, and Orchard and Baltimore Orioles nest. Find vagrant land birds in spring. Marshy spots attract herons in late summer, and geese winter in fields. Horned Lark, Yellow-breasted Chat, and Dickcissel breed in open places, and Bald Eagle winters around Wapanocca Lake.

ARKANSAS | MORE INFORMATION

RARE BIRD ALERT
Statewide 501-753-5853

22 Lake Chicot
State Park *(Page 108)*
www.arkansasstateparks
.com
870-265-5480

For the best view of gathering migrant wading birds, call to sign up for a sunset boat tour with a park naturalist.

23 Felsenthal National Wildlife Refuge
(Page 109)
www.fws.gov/felsenthal
870-364-3167

The birds often change roost sites from year to year, so be sure to ask at the refuge office for advice on current locations.

24 Millwood State Park
(Page 109)
www.arkansasstateparks
.com
870-898-2800

25 Devil's Den State
Park *(Page 110)*
www.arkansasstateparks
.com
479-761-3325

26 Buffalo National River
(Page 110)
www.nps.gov/buff
870-741-5443

Other good birding spots

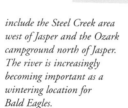

include the Steel Creek area west of Jasper and the Ozark campground north of Jasper. The river is increasingly becoming important as a wintering location for Bald Eagles.

27 Holla Bend National Wildlife Refuge
(Page 110)
www.fws.gov/southeast
479-229-4300

28 Wapanocca National Wildlife Refuge
(Page 110)
www.fws.gov/southeast
870-343-2595

ADDITIONAL SITES

3 Charlie Craig State Fish Hatchery
www.agfc.com
877-795-2470

The ponds here, by far northwestern Arkansas' best shorebirding spot, also host numbers of ducks in winter. Grassy spots along pond edges and in ditches provide habitat for such uncommon migrants as American and Least Bitterns, rails, and Sedge and Marsh Wrens. Among the locally rare land birds that have been found here are Prairie Falcon, Alder Flycatcher, Nelson's Sharp-tailed Sparrow, and Yellow-headed Blackbird.

4 St. Francis National Forest
www.fs.fed.us/oonf/ozark
479-968-2354

St. Francis National Forest, near Helena, is a fine place to find Wild Turkey, Red-headed Woodpecker, and Swainson's Warbler. Forest Roads 1900 and 1901 wind through hardwood forest that supports a variety of breeders.

LOUISIANA

- Coastal hot spots for spring migration
- Vast marshlands in national wildlife refuges

Little Blue Heron with frog prey, Atchafalaya Swamp near New Iberia

29 The small patch of low, windswept woods west of Holly Beach, now recovering from damage by Hurricane Rita in 2005, is noted among the most exciting birding spots on the Gulf Coast. During spring migration songbirds can throng these trees at the **Peveto Woods Sanctuaries.** Cuckoos, flycatchers, vireos, thrushes, warblers, tanagers, buntings, and orioles are among the species present from late March into May. Low vegetation provides excellent looks at birds usually seen only in treetops.

30 Great expanses of wetlands are encompassed within several wildlife refuges in southwestern Louisiana, all currently recovering from 2005 hurricane damage. One place to get close to marsh inhabitants is **Sabine National Wildlife Refuge.** At Sabine's 1.5-mile **Marsh Trail,** you may find Mottled Duck, Neotropic

Cormorant, Least Bittern, White and White-faced Ibises, Roseate Spoonbill, Clapper and King Rails, Purple Gallinule, and Marsh Wren among many other species.

Cameron Prairie National Wildlife Refuge offers another way to observe the marsh. Its **Pintail Wildlife Drive** loops through fields and wetlands where waders and shorebirds are common. From fall into spring, Snow Geese are abundant, and more than a dozen species of ducks may be present.

31 Also worth a visit is **Lacassine National Wildlife Refuge.** Drive the gravel roads and walk the levees that skirt Lacassine Pool, another spot to see waders, waterfowl (huge concentrations of ducks and geese), and marsh birds. Purple Gallinules swim in roadside ditches, and Roseate Spoonbills feed in open water. Anhingas perch and spread their wings to dry; King Rails skulk in reeds; Gull-billed Terns hawk for insects above the marsh; and Least Bitterns clamber about vegetation. Fulvous Whistling-, Wood, and Mottled Ducks nest here. Be sure to look for evidence of the growing population of Black-bellied Whistling-Ducks.

32 The **Atchafalaya Swamp** is one of America's great wild places, a wide stretch of river bottom with towering trees and lazy backwaters. To see a sample of this habitat, drive La. 975 between I-10 and US 190, skirting **Atchafalaya National Wildlife Refuge** and **Sherburne Wildlife Management Area,** which has a short nature trail. You can see the soaring, stunning Swallow-tailed Kite in breeding season or Wood Storks in post-nesting dispersal. The Swainson's Warbler is fairly common here, which is home to typical southern wetland birds from Anhinga to Mississippi Kite to Wood Duck to Prothonotary Warbler.

A lively, noisy heron rookery is accessible at the **Cypress Island Preserve** on the southern end of Lake Martin. From March through June, up to 11 species nest here, including Anhinga, Black-crowned and Yellow-crowned Night-Herons, White Ibis, and Roseate Spoonbill. Watch for alligators waiting under nests.

33 Spring birding has been called "fabulous" at **Grand Isle,** a barrier island at the mouth of Barataria Bay. Now recovering from hurricane damage, the island looks to the future to once again host trans-Gulf migrants in its woods, fields, and beach, and to have birders wandering the streets, checking for typical eastern migrant songbirds, and also for strays such as Groove-billed Ani, Vermilion and Scissor-tailed Flycatchers,

Western and Gray Kingbirds, Black-whiskered Vireo, and Yellow-headed Blackbird, all of which have appeared here. Along the beach, especially at **Grand Isle State Park,** Brown Pelican, Reddish Egret, Black Skimmer, and flocks of shorebirds, gulls, and terns have traditionally appeared. Magnificent Frigatebird, soaring above the Gulf in summer, has been a highlight.

34 Rich swamp woodland can be explored along trails in the **Barataria Preserve Unit** of **Jean Lafitte National Historical Park and Preserve** just south of New Orleans. Stop at the visitor center to gather maps and information, then head north to the **Bayou Coquille Trail,** a short paved-and-boardwalk path that passes through several ecological zones on its way from live-oak forest through bald cypress-tupelo swamp to marsh. Nesting birds in the swamp or in higher, drier forest include Wood Duck; Yellow-crowned Night-Heron; Great Horned and Barred Owls; Red-shouldered Hawk; Pileated Woodpecker; Acadian Flycatcher; White-eyed and Yellow-throated Vireos; Northern Parula; and Yellow-throated, Prothonotary, Swainson's (uncommon), and Hooded Warblers. Least Bittern, King Rail, and Purple Gallinule nest in the marsh, where herons, egrets, and ibises are common, and Painted Buntings breed in scrubby places around the preserve.

35 To find the southern pinewoods trio of Red-cockaded Woodpecker, Brown-headed Nuthatch, and Bachman's Sparrow, explore **Alexander State Forest.** The forest also has nesting Prairie Warbler, Painted Bunting, and Blue Grosbeak in cutover and scrubby spots. In recent winters, Henslow's Sparrow has been found consistently in weedy and scrubby places. White rings on pines indicate roosting cavities of the endangered Red-cockaded Woodpecker. Listen for the sweet song of the Bachman's Sparrow in spring and summer, and for the squeaky call of the Brown-headed Nuthatch anytime. The road leading to the **Indian Creek Recreation Area** is a good place to begin.

Nearby, **Catahoula National Wildlife Refuge** offers good birding all year; it may be best known for its flocks of thousands of wintering ducks (Mallard, Blue-winged Teal, Northern Pintail, and Wood and Ring-necked Ducks are the most common species). In late summer, flocks of postbreeding egrets and herons may include Tricolored Heron, White Ibis, Roseate Spoonbill, or Wood Stork. A 9-mile loop drive around Duck Lake provides access to an observation tower and trails. **Catahoula Lake,** a Wetland of International Importance, is adjacent to the refuge.

LOUISIANA | MORE INFORMATION

RARE BIRD ALERTS
Statewide 877-834-2473
Baton Rouge 504-768-9874
Southeast 504-834-2473
Southwest 318-988-9898

**29 Peveto Woods
Sanctuaries** *(Page 112)*
www.braudubon.org
225-768-9874

*Formerly known as Holliman
Sheely. The east jetty at
Cameron is a great place to
see concentrations of pelicans,
wading birds, shorebirds,
gulls, and terns.*

30 Sabine NWR
(Page 112)
www.fws.gov/sabine
337-762-3816

30 Cameron Prairie NWR
(Page 113)
www.fws.gov
337-598-2216

31 Lacassine NWR
(Page 113)
lacassine.fws.gov
337-774-5923

32 Sherburne WMA
(Page 113)
www.wlf.state.la.us
318-566-2251

*Visitors must have a hunting
or fishing license or a
Louisiana Wild Stamp...*

**32 Cypress Island
Preserve** *(Page 113)*
nature.org/wherewework
225-338-1040

**33 Grand Isle State
Park** *(Page 114)*
www.lastateparks.com
985-787-2559 or
888-787-2559

**34 Jean Lafitte National
Historical Park and
Preserve** *(Page 114)*
www.nps.gov/jela/
504-589-3882

**35 Alexander State
Forest** *(Page 114)*
*www.ldaf.state.la.us
/divisions/forestry*
318-487-5172

35 Catahoula NWR
(Page 114)
www.fws.gov/catahoula
318-992-5261

ADDITIONAL SITES

5 Bayou Sauvage NWR
bayousauvage.fws.gov
985-882-2000

*Check with the refuge office
about guided trips on spring
weekends to view a rookery
where thousands of herons
and egrets nest.*

Pearl River WMA
225-765-2360

*Swallow-tailed Kites nest in
the vicinity, and Swainson's
Warbler can also be seen here.
Visitors must have a hunting
or fishing license, or a
Louisiana Wild Stamp.*

115

EASTERN TEXAS

- Upper Texas Coast
- Central Texas Coast
- Lower Texas Coast and Rio Grande

I N AN ELECTION TO CHOOSE THE BIRDING CAPITAL OF THE United States, the Texas coast would be a serious contender. The geographic range of this 370-mile sweep of Gulf of Mexico shoreline, combined with the subtropical environment of the lower Rio Grande Valley, attracts birders on regular pilgrimages.

Sandy beaches, salt marshes, and prairie make up much of the Texas Gulf Coast. Some of the region's scattered woodlands are famed for spring songbird migration. Bolivar Flats is the best known of several excellent shorebird-watching sites, while rice fields and other agricultural areas west of Houston can attract impressive flocks of waterfowl from fall through spring, as well as migrant shorebirds. Farther south, an array of Mexican species are in the brushlands along the lower Rio Grande.

Every season has something to offer in this diverse, extensive region. Even midsummer, perhaps the least appealing time of year, affords birders interesting breeding species and such post-nesting wanderers as Magnificent Frigatebird and Wood Stork. Fall shorebird migration begins as early as July. In fall, Hazel Bazemore County Park has one of the great hawk-watching spectacles. Winter brings flocks of waterfowl and the annual return of Whooping Cranes to Aransas National Wildlife Refuge. Spring means the excitement of migration, from warblers on the upper coast to hawks moving north in flocks.

Making planning easier for the traveling birder, the Great Texas Coastal Birding Trail (see sidebar p. 122) directs visitors to excellent birding sites with maps and special road signs.

More and more, communities along the Gulf Coast and in the lower Rio Grande Valley are waking up to their birding possibilities and working to spread the word about them. One of the ways they're doing this is by holding birding festivals, most of which feature field trips aimed at finding local specialties, guest speakers, and workshops on improving identification skills. Attending these is a great way for birders to get an introduction to the wonders of this marvelous area. ■

Neotropic Cormorant

SPECIAL BIRDS OF EASTERN TEXAS

Least Grebe	Harris's Hawk	Ferruginous Pygmy-Owl	Chihuahuan Raven
Northern Gannet	Yellow Rail	Elf Owl	Cave Swallow
Brown Pelican	King Rail	Lesser Nighthawk	Clay-colored Robin
Neotropic Cormorant	Purple Gallinule	Common Pauraque	Long-billed Thrasher
Magnificent Frigatebird	Sandhill Crane	Buff-bellied Hummingbird	Tropical Parula
Reddish Egret	Whooping Crane	Ringed Kingfisher	White-collared Seedeater
Roseate Spoonbill	Snowy Plover	Green Kingfisher	Olive Sparrow
Black-bellied Whistling-Duck	Plain Chachalaca	Golden-fronted Woodpecker	Botteri's Sparrow
Fulvous Whistling-Duck	Wilson's Plover	Northern Beardless-Tyrannulet	Nelson's Sharp-tailed Sparrow
Muscovy Duck	Piping Plover	Brown-crested Flycatcher	Seaside Sparrow
Ross's Goose	American Oystercatcher	Great Kiskadee	Pyrrhuloxia
Mottled Duck	Hudsonian Godwit	Couch's Kingbird	Bronzed Cowbird
Masked Duck	Gull-billed Tern	Scissor-tailed Flycatcher	Altamira Oriole
White-tailed Hawk	Sandwich Tern	Green Jay	Audubon's Oriole
Crested Caracara	Red-billed Pigeon	Brown Jay	
Hook-billed Kite	White-tipped Dove	Tamaulipas Crow	
White-tailed Kite	Green Parakeet		
Gray Hawk	Red-crowned Parrot		
	Groove-billed Ani		

UPPER TEXAS COAST

- Spring "fallouts" at Sabine Woods and High Island
- Shorebirds at Bolivar Flats

Great Egret,
Anahuac National
Wildlife Refuge,
east of Houston

Visually unexciting—mostly agricultural areas, marshes, scrubby fields, and small towns—the upper Texas coast more than makes up in avian diversity what it lacks in aesthetics. Interesting birds can show up almost anywhere in this region. Roseate Spoonbills feed in farm ponds; White and White-faced Ibises, Snowy Egrets, and Tricolored Herons stream by overhead; Gull-billed Terns flap with deliberate wingbeats over marshes, hunting insects; and American Bitterns or Yellow-crowned Night-Herons flush up from roadside ditches. Don't feel that you need to reach a particular destination to begin seeing things—keep your eyes open all the time in this delight-fully birdy part of the world.

1 Two spots near **Port Arthur** can be covered in a relatively short time, though hurried travelers might want to begin with Anahuac National Wildlife Refuge (below). **Sabine Woods,** just south of Port Arthur, is small open woodland. Owned by the Texas Ornithological Society, this spot can be terrific in spring migration, attracting much the same birdlife as High Island (see p. 120). With good weather conditions and luck, Sabine Woods can be even better than High Island.

Continue along to **Sea Rim State Park,** best known among birders for its short marsh boardwalk, which often allows close views of rails, Least Bittern, and wintering Sedge Wren. Occasional close views of alligators provide another stimulating experience. Seaside Sparrows, permanent residents, are easy to see when males are singing in spring. The park's beach hosts birds ranging from Sanderlings to Reddish Egrets. Cliff Swallows nest in the park boathouse on the north side of Tex. 87, where a few Cave Swallows have recently been regular breeders.

2 **Anahuac National Wildlife Refuge** provides easy vehicle access (on gravel roads) to coastal prairie and marshlands. Just a short drive from legendary High Island, Anahuac is a fine alternative when birding at High Island is slow.

As you approach the refuge along Farm Road 1985, inspect wet fields and croplands along the road. During spring and fall these fields can host multitudes of shorebirds and waders. Watch to the south 3.1 miles from Tex. 124 for the **East Bay Bayou Tract,** where you can witness shorebirds and waders in bordering moist-soil units and rice fields, as well as songbirds in the narrow woodland along the bayou. One spring specialty is Hudsonian Godwit, which prefers inland terrain. American Golden-Plover and Baird's, Upland, White-rumped, and Buff-breasted Sandpipers are among the many other shorebird species more likely to be found here.

Once you enter the refuge itself, turn right at the first road past the gate, and check the willow trees. Trees are scarce, so even this wee woods can attract migrant songbirds. Continue to **Shoveler Pond,** watching roadside ditches for Mottled Duck (a Gulf Coast specialty), Purple Gallinule (easily seen spring through fall), King Rail (a permanent resident), Least Bittern, and other waterbirds. A good variety of ducks is usually present on the pond from fall through spring, while surrounding grassy areas are home to wintering Snow, Ross's, Greater White-fronted, and Canada Geese. Also in winter, Bald Eagles watch for sick or injured waterfowl, Northern Harriers hunt over the prairies, and Sedge Wrens can be found in the tall grass.

Alligators are abundant here, sunning themselves in ponds and ditches. The venomous water moccasin is also common, so watch before hopping out of your car for a closer look at a Roseate Spoonbill or Yellow-crowned Night-Heron.

Rails are as secretive at Anahuac as anywhere, but look for them along the edges of openings in the grass. Clapper Rail is most common in saltwater areas; King Rail generally prefers freshwater marshes. From fall through spring Virginia Rail and Sora are also seen. Yellow (wintering) and Black Rails are much rarer.

ROSEATE SPOONBILL

The Roseate Spoonbill's odd-looking (in fact, spoon-shaped) bill is an adaptation to its feeding tactics. The bird swings its open bill back and forth in shallow water, using touch rather than sight to find prey; when it feels a small fish or crustacean, it quickly snaps its bill shut. Immature birds are white and very pale pink, with feathered heads. The bright-pink and orange adults lose their head feathers, developing a masklike naked greenish face. Once nearly killed off along the Gulf Coast, spoonbills have made a strong comeback in recent decades. ■

3 Long one of the mythic places of American birding, **High Island** is a subterranean salt dome that approaches the surface here, creating an area of slightly higher ground that early settlers called an "island." Oaks and other hardwoods offer rest and shelter to songbirds that have just completed their spring migration across the Gulf of Mexico. When conditions are right in April or early May, birds drop from the sky in numbers that are almost staggering—a phenomenon birders call a "fall-out." Note the qualifier "when conditions are right": For every fabulous day at High Island there are ten or more when birding ranges from very good to mediocre to slow. The best birding usually occurs after a front has pushed through bringing north winds or rain. (The usual birding rule about getting up at dawn doesn't necessarily apply here: A wave of migrants may not arrive at High Island until mid-morning or, during a fallout, even later.) Fall migration, while not as impressive as spring migration, is still very good birding in its own right.

On any spring day, **Boy Scout Woods** and the **Smith Oaks Bird Sanctuary** are likely to be full of birders from around the globe, but the birds are so exhausted that they pay no attention to their watchers. Many observers means that any rarity is almost certain to be seen and news of it quickly circulated.

The list of possible species here includes virtually every eastern warbler, vireo, thrush, grosbeak, tanager, flycatcher, bunting, and oriole, and, not infrequently, western rarities as well.

Species composition varies as the season progresses. In March, early migrants such as Eastern Kingbird; Yellow-throated Vireo; Northern Parula; Louisiana Waterthrush; and Yellow-throated, Black-and-white, Worm-eating, and Hooded Warblers begin showing up. The great mass of species arrives in April; later migrants such as Mourning Warbler are more likely in May.

A big day may bring a tree full of Scarlet Tanagers, a shrub laden with Gray Catbirds, or more than 20 species of warblers in a few hours. If you're a new birder, don't be shy about visiting such a famously popular hot spot. High Island is a great place to see the field marks of lots of species in a short time, and there's always a friendly veteran around to share identification tips.

West of High Island, a small channel called **Rollover Pass** leads from the Gulf to East Galveston Bay. On the bay side, scan the mudflats and sandbars. Depending on the season and the state of the tide, you may see Double-crested and Neotropic Cormorants, American White Pelican, Roseate Spoonbill, shorebirds (including American Oystercatcher, Black-necked Stilt, American Avocet, Marbled Godwit, and the ubiquitous Willet), several kinds of herons and egrets (including Tricolored Heron, Reddish Egret, and Black-crowned Night-Heron), gulls, terns (including Caspian, Royal, Sandwich, Common, Forster's, Least, and Black), and Black Skimmer.

4 As diverse and abundant as birds may be at Rollover Pass, it's just a preview of the scene at **Bolivar Flats.** Just before you reach Port Bolivar (on Rettilon Road), drive to the beach, turn right, and park at the barrier. This shorebird sanctuary and the adjacent tidal flats and Gulf comprise one of Texas' most famous birding locations. All the birds mentioned for Rollover Pass can be seen here, and more. You may find all four small plovers within a few yards of each other and be able to compare several of the small sandpipers known as peeps. Lift your eyes and you may see Brown Pelicans fly by, a migrant Peregrine Falcon, or in late summer a Magnificent Frigatebird soaring overhead. In winter, scan the Gulf for Northern Gannet and scoters.

As at High Island, continual scrutiny here means that few rare birds go unnoticed. Most gulls are the abundant Laughing and the common Ring-billed, Herring, and Bonaparte's (fall through spring), but such rare gulls as California, Thayer's, Lesser Black-backed, Glaucous, Great Black-backed, Black-legged Kittiwake, and Kelp can also be seen here or just across the bay on Galveston Island. Watch for Horned Larks in short-grass areas; the salt marsh can be good for Seaside and Nelson's Sharp-tailed Sparrow, the latter in winter and spring. In late winter and spring, throngs of American Avocets can be found.

 Farther down the coast, **San Bernard National Wildlife Refuge** offers another excellent chance to look for waders, water-fowl, and shorebirds; and spring "fallouts" bring neotropical migrants. Almost any bird possible at Anahuac could show up here, as could Crested Caracara, Barred Owl, and Painted Bunting (spring and summer). Sometimes Wood Storks (late summer) and Sandhill Cranes (winter) can be seen here.

GREAT TEXAS COASTAL BIRDING TRAIL

Recognizing the Gulf Coast's fame among birders, government agencies and private enterprise cooperated to establish the Great Texas Coastal Birding Trail (GTCBT), an auto tour route of more than 400 miles that links more than 300 sites from the Sabine River to the Rio Grande. Travelers can obtain special maps showing birding locations, and road signs depicting a Black Skimmer point the way to sites ranging from such well-known areas as Anahuac National Wildlife Refuge to small-town parks. ■

Inland from the coast and north towards Houston, **Brazos Bend State Park**, encompasses hardwood forest, extensive fresh-water marsh and swamp, coastal tallgrass prairie, and several small lakes. Wood Duck, Anhinga, Black-bellied Whistling-Duck, King Rail, Pileated Woodpecker, Prothonotary Warbler, and Painted Bunting are among the park's breeding species. Waders such as American and Least Bitterns, Yellow-crowned Night-Heron, and Roseate Spoonbill are seen with varying regularity, as is the western Cinnamon Teal in winter. Heed signs warning about the park's many alligators.

Attwater Prairie Chicken National Wildlife Refuge protects a dwindling population of the endangered Attwater's race of the Greater Prairie-Chicken. Both White-tailed Hawk and Crested Caracara are seen here, along with many wintering waterfowl and migrant shorebirds. Scan the sky often for a variety of raptors, from migrant Broad-winged and Swainson's Hawks to wintering Ferruginous Hawk and American Kestrel. Mountain Plover and Sprague's Pipit are two often elusive migrant or wintering species found along the refuge driving route, along with Northern Bobwhite; Sedge Wren; and Grasshopper, Le Conte's, and Harris's Sparrows. Check road-side ditches for King Rail and fields in spring for American Golden-Plover and Upland and Buff-breasted Sandpipers.

CENTRAL TEXAS COAST

- Winter Whooping Cranes at Aransas National Wildlife Refuge
- Hawk migration at Hazel Bazemore County Park

Great Blue Heron, Aransas National Wildlife Refuge, Gulf Coast

8 One of the most famous nature preserves in America, **Aransas National Wildlife Refuge** comprises more than 55,000 acres of woods, prairie, and coastal marsh along the Gulf Coast. Its prominence rests largely on its most famous winter visitor, the endangered Whooping Crane.

However, visiting Aransas is not the best way to see a Whooping Crane. Instead, reserve a spot on a commercial boat that traverses the Intracoastal Waterway from about November through early April, and you will almost certainly find success. You will also see a variety of other species, including pelicans, waders, waterfowl, shorebirds, gulls, and terns.

Aransas is still a fine place to visit: The bird checklist here totals 394 species, second most of any site in the National Wildlife Refuge system. Refuge roads pass near ponds where Anhinga (spring and fall); Double-crested and Neotropic Cormorants; King, Clapper, and Sora Rails; Purple Gallinule (spring through fall); Common Moorhen; and waterfowl may be found (as can alligators). Shoreline roads expose the usual Texas assortment of waders and shorebirds. Additionally, several (mosquito-filled) nature trails give access to oak woodlands that can provide excellent sightings during spring and fall migration.

Views from the observation tower encompass an expanse of marsh where Whooping Cranes occasionally feed. Do not mistake other birds (such as Great or Snowy Egrets or white-morph Reddish Egrets) for cranes. Flying Snow Goose, American White Pelican, and White Ibis can also be mistaken for cranes.

9 On the way to Port Aransas, scan passing beaches and bay fronts for pelicans, herons, gulls, terns, or flocks of shorebirds. Take the free ferry to Port Aransas, where a boardwalk at the **Port Aransas Birding Center** leads into a wetland where you may find Black-bellied Whistling-Duck, Mottled Duck, the diminutive Least Grebe (a south Texas specialty that nests here), Neotropic Cormorant, most of the locally occurring herons and egrets (including nesting Least Bittern), and Roseate Spoonbill. On the Gulf side of the island, the **Port Aransas jetty** provides a good lookout point for such oceanic birds as Northern Gannet (winter and early spring) and Magnificent Frigatebird (fairly common in summer and early fall).

10 **Padre Island National Seashore** protects a nearly 70-mile stretch of undeveloped ocean shoreline: beach and sand dunes with the Gulf of Mexico on one side and Laguna Madre on the other. Much of the park south of the Malaquite Beach visitor center is accessible only by four-wheel-drive vehicles, but there's still plenty of shoreline to search for shorebirds, gulls, and terns. This is a great place to see migrating Peregrine Falcons in spring and especially in fall, when several of these magnificent birds are likely to be seen cruising south along the beach daily. Keep your eyes open anywhere in this area for White-tailed Kite and White-tailed Hawk.

11 West of Corpus Christi, **Hazel Bazemore County Park** is the site of one of the country's premier hawk-watches. In recent years, of the more than a million birds seen between mid-August and mid-November, almost all were Broad-winged Hawks; occasional daily totals in mid- to late September were more than 100,000 individuals. Lesser numbers of Osprey, Mississippi Kite, Sharp-shinned and Cooper's Hawks, American Kestrel, Peregrine Falcon, and other species are also seen.

LOWER TEXAS COAST AND RIO GRANDE

- Mexican specialties along the Rio Grande
- Winter waterfowl at Laguna Atascosa National Wildlife Refuge

Bronzed Cowbirds and Great-tailed Grackles

As you travel through the flat, mesquite brushland south of Corpus Christi, you are entering a world that, uniquely in America, blends birds of east, west, and south—south as in Mexico, that is.

Eastern birds are represented especially well during spring migration, when any patch of trees may host an assortment of warblers, vireos, and thrushes (though migrants are not as abundant here as farther up the coast), and certain days bring the astounding spectacle of thousands of Broad-winged Hawks circling in "kettles." Western birds include White-tailed Kite, Harris's Hawk, Inca Dove, Black-chinned Verdin, Cactus Wren, Curve-billed Thrasher, Cassin's Sparrow, Pyrrhuloxia, Bronzed Cowbird, Hooded and Bullock's Orioles, and Lesser Goldfinch.

Most birders are drawn to the Mexican species usually found only in south Texas. Some of these, such as Plain Chachalaca, Great Kiskadee, and Green Jay, are easy to find, while others are rare or secretive. Some range northward up the coast; some are mostly confined to the immediate vicini-

125

ty of the Rio Grande. With planning and luck, a birder can hope to see a good percentage of them at south Texas' parks and refuges.

12 **King Ranch,** an area slightly larger than the state of Rhode Island that is well known for cattle ranching, recently added birding to its attractions. While a fine assortment of south Texas birds have found a de facto refuge on the ranch, three species in particular—Ferruginous Pygmy-Owl, Northern Beardless-Tyrannulet, and Tropical Parula—are specialties. The little owl was once thought to be extremely rare in the United States, until a thriving population was discovered on brushlands of ranches well north of the Rio Grande. The tyrannulet and Tropical Parula can be found elsewhere in the area but are probably easier to see here. Birders, who pay fees for a variety of guided tours of the ranch, will also see Wild Turkey in abundance, and probably White-tailed Kite, Harris's and White-tailed Hawks, Crested Caracara, and Green Jay, among many others.

Look out for raptors on the long stretch of US 77 between Kingsville and Raymondville. One recent winter, rare vagrant Masked Ducks settled in some of the small ponds along the highway here. Many a birder has seen his or her first Golden-fronted Woodpecker, Couch's Kingbird, Green Jay, Black-crested Titmouse, Long-billed Thrasher, or Hooded Oriole at the rest stops along US 77 south of Sarita, where Tropical Parula has nested with some regularity. Watch for both Cliff and Cave Swallows nesting in highway culverts, with small numbers of Cave Swallows seen even in winter.

13 Another of Texas' highly and deservedly celebrated birding meccas is **Laguna Atascosa National Wildlife Refuge,** which includes Laguna Madre shoreline, thorn forest, grassland, agricultural fields, and bays, lakes, and ponds of various sizes. Like most such refuges, it was established to provide a sanctuary for waterfowl, but it includes nongame species as well. In recent years the refuge has been a release site for captive-raised Aplomado Falcons, raptors extirpated in Texas in the 1950s. The refuge is also home to a small number of ocelots, rare and ultrasecretive cats barely holding on in the United States.

The roll call of Laguna Atascosa birds is very long, and only a few highlights may be noted here. Its shoreline can host nearly every type of waterbird listed previously in this chapter. Wilson's Plover nests here, and the refuge is an important winter home for the threatened Piping Plover. Marshy areas can harbor rails and other wetland species. Winter flocks of Snow Geese and Sandhill Cranes feed in fields, and ducks throng lakes and bays. (Laguna Madre is noted as the most important wintering ground for Redheads in the U.S.) Black-bellied Whistling-Duck; Plain Chachalaca; Least Grebe; White-tipped Dove; Groove-billed Ani; Brown-crested Flycatcher; Common Pauraque; Great Kiskadee; Green Jay; Long-billed Thrasher; and Cassin's, Olive, and Botteri's Sparrows are among the south Texas specialties nesting here, with Greater Roadrunner, Ladder-backed Woodpecker, Verdin, Cactus Wren, Painted Bunting, and Pyrrhuloxia.

Laguna Atascosa's **Bayside Drive** and **Lakeside Drive** pass through varied habitats and lead to good walking trails. They provide great birding for visitors unable to leave their vehicles. Don't speed around the loop drive on a hot summer afternoon and expect to see a teeming host of birds, though. Arrive early from fall through spring, take time to explore, give yourself a midday break, and return in late afternoon—and you'll undoubtedly realize Laguna Atascosa deserves its distinguished reputation as one of the country's finest birding sites.

14 Humans have greatly altered the environment of the lower Rio Grande Valley, but the natural areas that remain include some of the most famous and rewarding birding spots in the country. Here, among spreading suburbia and vegetable fields, pockets of woodland harbor birds that are more typical of the tropics than of temperate North America.

Brownsville, on the Rio Grande just a short stroll across the bridge from Mexico, is known for its free-flying flocks of parrots, the origin of which has long been in dispute. Some are undoubtedly escaped cage birds, while others may be wild birds that have wandered north from Mexico. The flocks move around for food, of course, but one reliable spot to look for them has been on **Los Ebaños,** a street a block west of Central Boulevard; listen for the birds' harsh shrieks and chattering calls. Red-crowned Parrots and Green Parakeets are the most common species, but others may also show up.

15 The **Sabal Palm Audubon Center and Sanctuary,** southeast of Brownsville off Farm Road 1419, ranks with Texas' most important natural areas. This 527-acre preserve protects the country's only significant remaining forest of sabal palms, a native species (as opposed to the exotic palms of sundry varieties ubiquitous in the valley) nearly extirpated in the United States by land clearing and damming. Birders know it as a beautiful spot to find Plain Chachalaca, Least Grebe, Buff-bellied Hummingbird, Green Jay, Long-billed Thrasher, Olive Sparrow, and many other species, occasionally including Tropical Parula. Here, as nearly anywhere along the Rio Grande Valley, very rare vagrants from Mexico may appear at any time. Rose-throated Becard, Yellow-green Vireo, Golden-crowned Warbler, Gray-crowned Yellowthroat, and Crimson-collared Grosbeak all have taken up temporary residence here in recent years. For those whose interest goes beyond birding, there are other rare animals and plants at the sanctuary as well, including the speckled racer, David's milkberry, and Barbados cherry (manzanita).

PLAIN CHACHALACA

Like phoebes and chickadees, the pheasant-like Plain Chachalaca was named for its call: in this case a loud, harsh *cha-cha-lac* that is initiated by a single individual and subsequently builds to a chorus of several birds that can be almost deafening in its intensity. With protection, Plain Chachalacas have expanded beyond the parks and refuges of the lower Rio Grande Valley into the suburbs of McAllen and Brownsville, where their dawn calling serves as nature's own alarm clock—welcome to some, an irritant to late sleepers. ▪

16 Occasionally a famous-golfer is asked which place he or she would play if restricted to just one course for life, and the answer is some legendary spot like Pebble Beach or Augusta National. Ask birders a comparable question about U.S. birding locations, and the choice would often be **Santa Ana National Wildlife Refuge.** The 2,088 acres bordering the Rio Grande host a great percentage of the region's specialties, attracted to an island of native forest and wetlands in an ocean of agriculture, cities, and suburbs.

Just a few of the birds found with some regularity here are Black-bellied and Fulvous Whistling-Ducks; Plain Chachalaca; Least Grebe; Anhinga; Hook-billed Kite; Gray and Harris's Hawks; King Rail; White-tipped Dove; Groove-billed Ani; Elf Owl; Common Pauraque; Buff-bellied Hummingbird; Ringed and Green Kingfishers; Northern Beardless-Tyrannulet; Brown-crested Flycatcher; Great Kiskadee; Couch's Kingbird; Green Jay; Long-billed Thrasher; Tropical Parula; Olive Sparrow; Bronzed Cowbird; and Hooded and Altamira Orioles. With near-daily scrutiny from expert birders, Santa Ana has seen the discovery of such rarities as Muscovy and Masked Ducks; Crane, Roadside, and Short-tailed Hawks; Ruddy Ground-

Dove; Green Violet-ear; Elegant Trogon; Rose-throated Becard; Clay-colored and Rufous-backed Robins; Gray-crowned Yellowthroat; Golden-crowned Warbler; Crimson-collared Grosbeak; and Blue Bunting. In general, winter offers the best chance to see Mexican rarities.

Santa Ana's official refuge bird list includes 9 vireos, 43 warblers, 24 flycatchers, and 29 waterfowl among its nearly 400 species. Remember, this is on a relatively tiny area, just 4 percent the size of Laguna Atascosa. Of course, no one can hope to see all these birds on a single visit, but the numbers indicate the refuge's potential. In short, go—and marvel.

Winter and spring are the most popular times to visit Santa Ana. To relieve traffic on refuge roads, private vehicles have been banned during the crowded winter season, when a tram makes a regular 7-mile circuit to drop off and pick up passengers. Some of the best birding areas are around **Willow** and **Pintail Lakes,** within easy walking distance of the refuge visitor center. Additionally, blinds in this area offer handicapped birders a chance to sit and wait for birds to come to them.

A note here about rarities in the valley: Because this area is so intensively birded, the odds are high that rare birds will be found and reported. It's especially important for visitors to check telephone rare bird alerts (see p. 131) as well as bulletin boards at parks and refuges, and to talk to other birders about what's been seen lately. Don't be shy about quizzing birders you meet at the various hot spots (and you will meet lots of them). You don't want to be walking the trail at Sabal Palm while a Crane Hawk is dining on a frog at Santa Ana.

17 Twenty miles upstream from Santa Ana, **Bentsen–Rio Grande Valley State Park** provides a chance to find a few birds you may have missed at Santa Ana, though its list is not quite as lengthy. The elusive Hook-billed Kite is seen relatively often here; the orange eye-shine of the Common Pauraque is frequent on park roads at night; and a pair of tiny Elf Owls commonly nests in a cavity in a tree or telephone pole near the picnic area. Once a favorite spot for visitors with RVs, the camping area was recently closed here, and there are no longer feeder setups. Still, a picnic stop or a leisurely hike around the park gives visitors much opportunity to find White-tipped Dove, Green Jay, Bronzed Cowbird, and many other species.

18 About 10 miles north of Roma, turn south off US 83 to **Salineno,** where the road dead-ends at the Rio Grande.

You can scan here for Muscovy Duck and for Hook-billed Kite, which often soars above the treetops as the air warms up in mid-morning, as well as for Red-billed Pigeon early and late in the day. Audubon's Orioles appear regularly at locals' feeders, which may also attract the rare and local Brown Jay. Watch, too, for Groove-billed Ani in late spring and summer, and for Ringed Kingfisher along the river. Also look for species such as Golden-fronted Woodpecker; Couch's Kingbird; Ash-throated and Brown-crested Flycatchers; Green Jay; and Altamira Oriole.

19 **Falcon Dam,** which contains sprawling Falcon Reservoir, serves as another access point to the Rio Grande. The expanse of short grass alongside the secondary road that runs below the large embankment is a fairly reliable spot for wintering Sprague's Pipit, a most elusive species. You'll have to walk the grassy area here (best with others to cover more ground) and hope to flush up a bird, which will then circle high in the air before performing its astounding "death dive" back toward earth. Once on the ground, the pipit may hesitate momentarily in a spot, allowing you a good look, or it may scurry off to hide.

Brushland this far upriver is home to such western species as Scaled Quail, Greater Roadrunner, Ladder-backed Woodpecker, Verdin, Cactus Wren, Curve-billed Thrasher, and Black-throated Sparrow. Habitat for these species is more than plentiful, but most is private, and ranchers generally disapprove of trespassing. One accessible spot is **Falcon State Park,** with first-rate nature trails.

20 One last bird must be included in this section: the White-collared Seedeater, a tiny finchlike species that barely reaches the United States (though it is very common in brushy places throughout most of Mexico and Central America). Its irregular occurrence has frustrated many birders.

Seedeaters once were seen with some regularity in the cattails of a wetland adjoining the public library in the small town of **Zapata;** this is no longer the case. The time-honored spot to find them is the even smaller town of **San Ygnacio.** Search the extensive area of reeds along the riverbank (where you might also find a Muscovy Duck, Red-billed Pigeon, or Ringed Kingfisher), as well as any feeders. Early and late in the day are the best times. Many of the characteristic scrub species listed under Salineno are found here as well.

EASTERN TEXAS | MORE INFORMATION

RARE BIRD ALERT
Statewide 713-964-5867

1 Sabine Woods
(Page 119)
www.texasbirds.org

1 Sea Rim SP *(Page 119)*
www.tpwd.state.tx.us
409-971-2559

2 Anahuac NWR
(Page 119)
www.fws.gov/refuges
409-267-3337

3 4 High Island Sanctuaries and **Bolivar Flats** *(Pages 120–121)*
www.houstonaudubon.org
713-932-1639

5 San Bernard NWR
(Page 122)
www.fws.gov/refuges
979-849-7771

6 Brazos Bend SP
(Page 122)
www.tpwd.state.tx.us
409-553-5101

7 Attwater Prairie Chicken NWR *(Page 122)*
www.fws.gov/refuges
949-234-3278

8 Aransas NWR
(Page 123)
www.fws.gov/refuges
361-286-3559

9 Port Aransas Birding Center
(Page 124)
www.cityof
portraransas.org
361-749-4158

10 Padre Island National Seashore *(Page 124)6*
www.nps.gov/pais
361-949-8068

11 Hazel Bazemore County Park *(Page 124)*
512-387-4231

12 King Ranch *(Page 124)*
www.king-ranch.com
361-592-8055

13 Laguna Atascosa NWR *(Page 126)*
www.fws.gov/refuges
956-748-3607

14 Brownsville *(Page 127)*
www.brownsville.org
800-626-2639

15 Sabal Palm Audubon Center and Sanctuary
(Page 127)

www.audubon.org/local
956-541-8034

16 Santa Ana NWR
(Page 128)
www.fws.gov/refuges
956-787-3079

17 Bentsen–Rio Grande Valley SP *(Page 129)*
www.tpwd.state.tx.us
956-519-6448

19 Falcon SP *(Page 130)*
www.tpwd.state.tx.us
956-848-5327

20 Zapata *(Page 130)*
www.zapatausa.com
956-765-4871

ADDITIONAL SITE

1 Galveston Island
www.tpwd.state.tx.us
409-737-1222

131

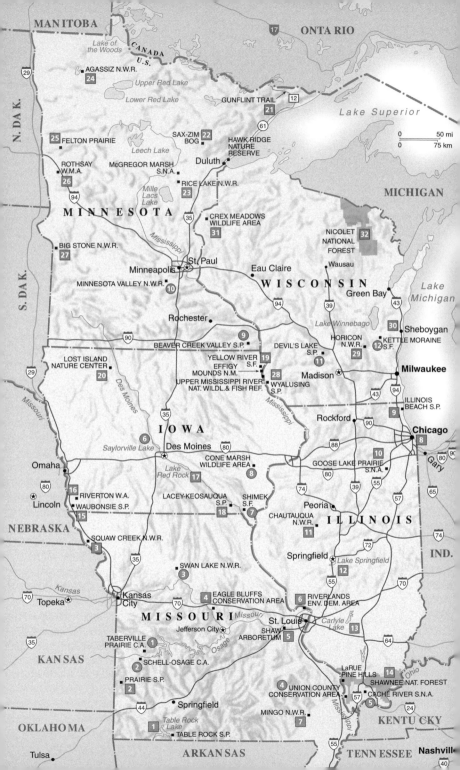

HEARTLAND

When birders think of the upper Midwest, one image often predominates in their collective imagination: A car winds slowly along a back road through a snowy forest, its occupants fighting off the cold with coffee and hopeful, half-hearted jokes. All eyes are on the roadside trees, constantly scanning. Someone calls, "Stop! Stop! There it is!" and all look up to see another set of eyes staring back at them in the piercing yellow gaze of a Great Gray Owl, that huge, elusive predator of the North Woods.

But perhaps this scenario is too specific. The subject might be an elusive Boreal Owl, a band of Common Redpolls, or a flock of sleek Bohemian Waxwings. The glamour birds of this region are mostly the species of the far north, which barely reach the lower 48 states in their breeding ranges or appear only as irregular winter visitors. A trip to northern Minnesota or Wisconsin in winter is as much a part of a birder's agenda as fall at Pennsylvania's Hawk Mountain or spring at the Texas coast.

Other seasons and other places have their own attractions. Spruce Grouse, Black-backed Woodpecker, and Gray Jay reward birders year-round, and the sought-after Connecticut Warbler nests here. Wisconsin's Crex Meadows is a premier birding area. Missouri's prairies are home to Greater Prairie-Chicken and Henslow's Sparrow. Refuges in Iowa and Illinois host migrant waterfowl and shorebirds. The Great Lakes attract many waterbirds, and their shorelines concentrate migrant raptors and songbirds. All these are just highlights in a region of surprising diversity, of prairies and lakes, of spruce-fir forests and Mississippi River bottomlands. ■

- Missouri
- Illinois
- Iowa
- Minnesota
- Wisconsin

Yellow-bellied
Flycatcher

SPECIAL BIRDS OF THE HEARTLAND

Northern Goshawk	Great Gray Owl	Bohemian Waxwing	Common Redpoll
Spruce Grouse	Boreal Owl	Connecticut Warbler	Hoary Redpoll
Sharp-tailed Grouse	Northern Saw-whet Owl	Henslow's Sparrow	Evening Grosbeak
Greater Prairie-Chicken	Black-backed Woodpecker	Chestnut-collared Longspur	Eurasian Tree Sparrow
Yellow Rail	Yellow-bellied Flycatcher	Pine Grosbeak	
Sandhill Crane	Gray Jay	Red Crossbill	
Snowy Owl	Boreal Chickadee	White-winged Crossbill	
Northern Hawk Owl			

MISSOURI

- Grassland birds in southwestern prairies
- Waterfowl at Squaw Creek National Wildlife Refuge
- Winter gulls at St. Louis's Riverlands area

Shaw Arboretum, an extension of the Missouri Botanical Garden, near St. Louis

1 Once upon a time waterbirds would have been nearly as scarce as hen's teeth in the rugged Missouri Ozarks— before the creation of reservoirs like **Table Rock Lake.** Now in winter, dabbling and diving ducks, Common Loon, and Pied-billed and Horned Grebes can be seen, along with Bald Eagle, perched in waterside trees and soaring overhead. The scarce Black Vulture also flocks here in winter with the common Turkey Vulture.

2 Just a few miles from the Kansas state line, **Prairie State Park** offers a glimpse back to a time when tallgrass prairie still stretched across vast areas of the Midwest. Big bluestem and Indian grass grow head high here, and wildflowers such as Indian paintbrush, pale purple coneflower, and coreopsis bloom in lovely profusion. Northern Harrier soars over the grassland, and other nesting birds include Upland Sandpiper,

Scissor-tailed Flycatcher, Loggerhead Shrike, Bell's Vireo, Grasshopper and Song Sparrows, Rose-breasted Grosbeak (near its southern range limit), and Dickcissel. The two breeding birds most sought, though, are Greater Prairie-Chicken and Henslow's Sparrow, both quite local. In winter, Rough-legged Hawk and Short-eared Owl are possible.

3 Visitors to the expanse of wetlands at **Squaw Creek National Wildlife Refuge** occasionally witness the presence of hundreds of thousands of Snow Goose (with a few Ross's) and other waterfowl in migration. An auto route provides excellent viewing of refuge pools and croplands. The list of possible species is long and varied here: American White Pelican can be common in migration; both bitterns have nested (Least is numerous here and can sometimes be seen from the observation platform at the beginning of the drive), as have both night-herons; Osprey roosts in open pool trees in migration. From late fall to early spring, Bald Eagle is sometimes present by the dozens. In addition, Common Moorhen is sometimes seen swimming through water plants and migrant shorebirds congregate in large numbers when water conditions are right (look for Hudsonian Godwit in May). Le Conte's Sparrow is present in migration; Yellow-headed Blackbird nests in the taller reeds.

4 One of the best birding spots in central Missouri, **Eagle Bluffs Conservation Area** sits alongside the Missouri River. A series of wetlands and adjacent woodlands has attracted an impressive list of birds, including rarities such as Cinnamon Teal, Glossy Ibis, Tricolored Heron, Black-necked Stilt, Prairie Falcon, Piping Plover, Red-necked Phalarope, Sprague's Pipit, and Cape May and Black-throated Blue Warblers. Great-tailed Grackle has nested here.

Almost all the shorebird species on the Missouri list have been found here at one time or another, along with such marsh birds as American and Least Bitterns, Virginia Rail, Sora, Common Moorhen, and Sedge and Marsh Wrens. A road through the pond area provides good access for birders with physical disabilities. The adjacent **Katy Trail** passes woods where nesting warblers include Blue-winged, Yellow-throated, Black-and-white, Prothonotary, Worm-eating, and Louisiana Waterthrush.

5 Diverse habitats make the **Shaw Arboretum,** an extension of the **Missouri Botanical Garden,** a popular birding destination. The arboretum's 2,400 acres include bottomland forest along the Meramec River, fields, deciduous woods and conifer plantings, glades, wetlands, and scrubby second growth, all crisscrossed by 13 miles of hiking trails.

Conifer plantings near the visitor center can be good for winter finches. In spring and summer, mixed woodland and open fields may have White-eyed Vireo, Eastern Bluebird, Blue-winged and Prairie Warblers, Common Yellowthroat, and Indigo Bunting. Henslow's Sparrow and Sedge Wren are occasional nesters in the prairie. In wetter woods near the river, look and listen for Red-shouldered Hawk; Barred Owl; Acadian Flycatcher; Wood Thrush; and Yellow-throated, Prothonotary, Cerulean, and Kentucky Warblers. Listen for the Worm-eating Warbler's insectlike trill, sounding from wooded slopes.

6 **Riverlands Environmental Demonstration Area** encompasses grassland, marsh, and backwaters of the Mississippi River just upstream from a lock and dam. This fine area has yielded a long bird list, including 18 species of gulls. In colder weather, especially when flocks are resting on ice, chances are good to pick out a Thayer's, Lesser Black-backed, or Glaucous.

In migration or winter, look for loons and grebes, pelicans, cormorants, herons (including occasional Snowy Egret), waterfowl of all kinds (including scoters and Long-tailed Duck), raptors (Bald Eagle is common), shorebirds, and terns. Alongside the many native sparrows in grass and brush, the region's most famous bird, Eurasian Tree Sparrow, can usually be found.

7 Though suffering great damage in a 1993 storm, **Mingo National Wildlife Refuge** still offers birders access to some of the best bottomland woods, including a former channel of the Mississippi River. From spring through fall the graceful Mississippi Kite soars over the forest. Bald Eagle has nested in recent years, and Red-shouldered Hawk is quite likely year-round.

Hooded Merganser uses refuge Wood Duck boxes (as do many Wood Duck), and Least Bittern, Little Blue Heron, Yellow-crowned Night-Heron, Virginia Rail, and Sora might be seen in marshes. Other birds here range from Wild Turkey, Black Vulture (occasional), and Fish Crow to Willow Flycatcher, Northern Parula, and Worm-eating Warbler. Prothonotary and Hooded Warblers call in breeding season. Winter brings waterfowl, with thousands of gathering geese and ducks, and hungry Bald Eagle waiting patiently in tall trees, ready to swoop down and make a meal of any sick or wounded birds they notice among the gabbling and quacking flocks.

MISSOURI | MORE INFORMATION

RARE BIRD ALERT
Statewide 573-445-9115
Kansas City 913-342-2473
St. Louis 314-935-8432

1 Table Rock State Park
(Page 134)
www.mostateparks.com
417-334-4704

2 Prairie State Park
(Page 134)
www.mostateparks.com
417-843-6711

3 Squaw Creek National Wildlife Refuge
(Page 135)
www.fws.gov/midwest
660-442-3187

4 Eagle Bluffs Conservation Area
(Page 135)
www.mdc.mo.gov
573-445-3882

5 Shaw Arboretum of the Missouri Botanical Garden *(Page 135)*
www.mobot.org
314-577-9400

6 Riverlands Environmental Demonstration Area
(Page 136)

www.mvs.usace.army.mil /Rivers/eda.htm
636-899-2600

Call the Riverlands bird hotline at 888-899-2650.

7 Mingo National Wildlife Refuge *(Page 136)*
www.fws.gov/midwest
573-222-3589

ADDITIONAL SITES

1 Taberville Prairie Conservation Area
mdc.mo.gov/areas /natareas
417-876-5226

Taberville hosts many of the species found at Prairie State Park. Prairie-chickens have declined, but Henslow's Sparrow is fairly easily found in spring and summer. The elusive Smith's Longspur is a good possibility in Mar. and Nov. Look for it in areas of very short grass.

2 Schell-Osage Conservation Area
mdc.mo.gov/areas /natareas
417-876-5226

A few miles west of Taberville, Schell-Osage has long been a favorite of local birders. Its open water, bottomland forests, cropland, and marsh attract an excellent variety of birds. Since this is a hunting area, access may be limited during waterfowl season.

3 Swan Lake National Wildlife Refuge
www.fws.gov/midwest
660-856-3323

South of Chillicothe, this refuge offers many of the same attractions as Squaw Creek, from big flocks of migrant pelicans and waterfowl to fine shorebirding in spring and fall.

ILLINOIS

- Migration in Chicago's lakeshore parks
- Varied breeders in Shawnee National Forest

Snowy Owl with American Crows at Chicago's lakefront

8 Chicago, one of the most urbanized environments in America, boasts fabulous birding in spring and fall, when migrants throng parks on the shores of Lake Michigan. The most famous bit of vegetation in Chicago is the Magic Hedge at **Montrose Point.** This spot can have an overwhelming number of both species and individuals. Many of the birds of eastern North America have shown up here (along with a surprising number from the West). Cuckoos, flycatchers, vireos, thrushes, warblers, tanagers, and sparrows are, of course, present in varying numbers, and the list of vagrants seen in the area is long and diverse, from Reddish Egret to Groove-billed Ani to Kirtland's Warbler. Be sure to check the harbor, nearby beaches, and the lake itself for loons, grebes, waterfowl, shorebirds, and gulls.

A few blocks south, the **Lincoln Park Bird Sanctuary** offers similar birding. South of the Loop, the **Paul Douglas Nature Sanctuary,** also known as **Wooded Isle,** at **Jackson Park** is another birders' favorite. Watch, too, for Peregrine Falcon here and elsewhere in Chicago. Watch for the introduced Monk Parakeet, which builds its bulky nest on power poles.

9 North of the city, stretching along the shore almost to Wisconsin, **Illinois Beach State Park** has long attracted birders to its varied habitats of beach, marsh, grassland, and woods. All these can be found on the trails leading from the visitor center toward Dead River, where songbirds appear in good numbers in migration. Illinois Beach is also known as a fine spot to watch fall raptor flights.

10 **Goose Lake Prairie State Natural Area** is an excellent place to find marsh and grassland birds. It's probably the state's best spot to find nesting (or "breeding") Henslow's Sparrow. To see one, you may need to walk the trails some distance from the visitor center—try the far end of the **Marsh Loop.**

Among the other nesting birds here are Pied-billed Grebe; Northern Harrier (not every year, but common in winter); King and Virginia Rails; Sora; Field, Savannah, Grasshopper, Song, and Swamp Sparrows; and Bobolink. Rails are always elusive, so you may have better luck seeing them on exposed mudflats in late summer. Short-eared Owl is a winter visitor to the grasslands here, appearing at dusk to search for rodents.

11 **Chautauqua National Wildlife Refuge** is a favorite site for observing waterfowl from fall through spring. As many as 400,000 geese and ducks have been counted on the refuge at the peak of fall migration, along with the usual "camp follower" Bald Eagle. Swans, both native Tundra and Trumpeter from reintroduced populations, appear on occasion. Birding on the refuge is dependent on water levels. At the south pool of Lake Chautauqua, fall shorebirding can be excellent. The lake's north pool is deeper, attracting diving ducks.

12 To the southeast, **Lake Springfield** offers an excellent variety of wintering waterbirds. Discharge from a power plant creates an area of open water even in midwinter, and dabbling and diving ducks, loons (occasional Red-throated or Pacific), and grebes (the state's second record of Clark's Grebe came here) are often numerous. One winter, Harlequin Duck and all three scoters were present, and jaegers have appeared rarely in fall. Much of the lakeshore is private property, but boat ramps and parks provide birding access. One favorite lookout is

Lincoln Memorial Garden on the southeast part of the lake. Woods and prairies here afford a diversion when waterbirding is slow.

13 Located in the middle of farm country, **Carlyle Lake** is a regional hot spot for loons, grebes, herons, egrets, waterfowl, gulls, and terns. Late September may bring a Sabine's Gull, and winter may see rarities such as Thayer's, Lesser Black-backed (becoming fairly regular here), or Glaucous, though Bonaparte's, Ring-billed, and Herring are the common species. Bald Eagle winters here, and some remain to nest; Osprey appears in migration. **Eldon Hazlet** and **South Shore State Parks** provide viewpoints in the southern section of the lake. The **Carlyle Lake Wildlife Management Area** at the lake's upper end hosts large concentrations of waterfowl, especially Snow Goose in February and March (hunting can restrict birding here). This area also provides good shorebirding in late summer and fall.

Look for winter finches in conifers, and you might run across a Long-eared or Northern Saw-whet Owl perched in a pine or cedar. Winter drives through nearby agricultural lands may turn up Northern Harrier, Rough-legged Hawk, or Horned Lark.

14 **Shawnee National Forest** occupies a highland area where the Ozarks cross the Mississippi River into southern Illinois. Two spots here are especially favored by local birders. To reach the first, start in the small town of Pomona and head north, following signs to Pomona Natural Bridge. The forest has specifically designated some 2,000 acres in the vicinity as a nongame bird management area. Trails beginning here lead through forest where you may find Mississippi Kite; Fish Crow; Prothonotary, Yellow-throated, Pine, Prairie (occasional), Cerulean, Worm-eating, and Hooded (occasional) Warblers; Northern Parula; American Redstart; and Summer and Scarlet Tanagers, among many other nesting species. The varied landscape makes this area one of the region's best in spring and fall migration.

The second birding spot within the forest is the **LaRue Pine Hills/Oakwood Bottoms Research Natural Area** in extreme northwestern Union County, which encompasses outstanding biological diversity in a small area, with swamp and limestone bluffs side by side. Take County Road 2 east of Ill. 3, following the levee along the Big Muddy River. Where the road meets Forest Road 345, turn right to reach LaRue Swamp. Listen for the scream of Red-shouldered Hawk, a bird seldom seen in Illinois, and the call of Barred Owl here. Wood Duck, Green Heron, Red-headed Woodpecker, and Prothonotary Warbler brighten the woods.

ILLINOIS | MORE INFORMATION

RARE BIRD ALERT
Chicago 847-265-2118
Dupage 630-406-8111
Northwest 815-965-3095

8 Chicago Park District, Lakefront Region
(Page 138)
www.chicagoparkdistrict
.com
312-742-7529

Contact for Montrose Point, Lincoln Park Bird Sanctuary, and Jackson Park.

9 Illinois Beach State Park *(Page 139)*
dnr.state.il.us/lands
/landmgt/parks
708–662-4811

Watch for Peregrine Falcon, various hawks, Merlin, and others Sept.–Oct. Also visit Waukegan Harbor (fall through spring) for loons, waterfowl, and gulls.

10 Goose Lake Prairie State Natural Area
(Page 139)
dnr.state.il.us/lands
/landmgt/parks
815-942-2899

11 Chautauqua National Wildlife Refuge
(Page 139)
www.fws.gov/midwest
/Chautauqua
309-535-2290

12 Lincoln Memorial Garden *(Page 139)*
www.lmgnc.org
217-529-1111

Nature center closed Mon.

13 Eldon Hazlet and South Shore State Parks
(Page 140)
dnr.state.il.us/lands
/landmgt/parks
618-594-3015

13 Carlyle Lake Wildlife Management Area
(Page 140)
dnr.state.il.us/lands
/landmgt/parks
618-425-3533

14 Shawnee National Forest *(Page 140)*
www.fs.fed.us/r9/forests
/shawnee
618-253-7114

ADDITIONAL SITES

4 Union County Conservation Area
dnr.state.il.us/lands
/landmgt/parks
618-833-5175
Just southeast of Ware, this conservation area is worth a visit any time of year. Water-fowl are abundant from fall through spring (some 75,000 Canada Goose winter here), and both Bald and Golden

Eagles may be seen overhead. Pelicans, egrets, and shorebirds can be found seasonally, and Mississippi Kite nests.

5 Cache River State Natural Area
dnr.state.il.us/lands
/landmgt/parks
618-634-9678
Black Vulture occurs in this area year-round. The board-walk at Heron Pond leads through a beautiful bald cypress-tupelo swamp; the trail at Wildcat Bluff drops to lowland forest. In migration this is a terrific spot.

IOWA

- Waterbirds at Lake Red Rock
- Excellent wetlands in the Ruthven area

Lake Red Rock, southeast of Des Moines

 Bordering the Missouri River in southwestern Iowa stretches a line of hills formed of the fine, wind-deposited soil called loess. Atop this ridge, **Waubonsie State Park** offers visitors an oak-hickory forest, hiking trails, and excellent spring and summer birding. Wild Turkey is common, and Broad-winged Hawk soars over the woods. Barred Owl, Whip-poor-will, Ovenbird, Louisiana Waterthrush, Kentucky Warbler, and Summer and Scarlet Tanagers (Waubonsie is one of the best spots in Iowa for the former) nest here. Northern Parula is consistently seen in spring migration, and Black-and-white Warbler, a scarce breeder in the state, has nested here.

Northern Bobwhite, Chuck-will's-widow, Western King-bird, and Blue Grosbeak are other specialties of this region. To hear Chuck-will's-widow in spring and summer, go west from the state park on Iowa 2 to County Road L44. Drive north and take the first gravel road to the east, where you can hear the birds at dusk and dawn.

16 **Riverton Wildlife Area,** one of Iowa's finest birding spots, lies a few minutes east of Waubonsie. This 2,721-acre expanse of marsh, open water, and fields seasonally attracts waders, waterfowl, and shorebirds. Snow Goose numbers here can reach more than 200,000 in late fall, creating what one naturalist has called "the greatest wildlife spectacle in Iowa." Careful observers can often pick out a few Ross's Goose in these Snow flocks. Bald Eagle perches in tall cottonwoods and soars overhead; thousands of Gadwall, Mallard, Northern Pintail, Blue-winged and Green-winged Teals, and other dabbling ducks rest and feed.

Mid-May is the peak of shorebird migration at Riverton, when (if water conditions are right) perhaps 20 species may appear on mudflats. In late summer, herons including occasional Snowy Egret, Little Blue Heron, and Black-crowned and Yellow-crowned Night-Herons can be seen, and Buff-breasted Sandpiper can appear in numbers. Nesting birds at Riverton include Least Bittern, Barred Owl, Willow Flycatcher, Horned Lark, Tree Swallow, Sedge Wren, Prothonotary Warbler, Grasshopper Sparrow, and both Eastern and Western Meadowlarks.

17 Sprawling **Lake Red Rock** hosts loons, grebes, and waterfowl in migration, and Bald Eagle in winter. The long list of rare or uncommon gulls that have been seen on the lake or along tailwaters below the dam includes Laughing, Mew, California, Thayer's, Iceland, Lesser Black-backed, Glaucous, Great Black-backed, Sabine's, Ross's, Ivory, and Black-legged Kittiwake. Check the river below the dam for Bald Eagle, waterfowl, and terns as well. Nearby **Whitebreast Recreation Area** is a good spot to scan the lake for waterbirds. Northern Saw-whet Owl has been found roosting in cedars here in winter, and Long-eared Owl sometimes winters in pines. Ducks occasionally include Greater Scaup, Long-tailed Duck, and all three scoters. Hooded, Common, and Red-breasted Mergansers can number in the hundreds. An observation area on Iowa 316 overlooks a part of the lake that may have American White Pelican, waders, ducks, or shorebirds, depending on water levels.

18 Birders visit **Lacey-Keosauqua State Park** in southeastern Iowa for several species seldom found elsewhere in the state, as well as a good assortment of more common birds that frequent the woodland alongside the Des Moines River. Breeding species include Wild Turkey; Turkey Vulture; White-eyed Vireo; Acadian Flycatcher (rare elsewhere in Iowa); Carolina

Wren (at the northern edge of its range, and susceptible to severe winters); Northern Mockingbird (occasional, and also affected by bad winters); Northern Parula; Yellow-throated, Cerulean, and Kentucky Warblers; Yellow-breasted Chat; and Summer and Scarlet Tanagers. To reach an area where Henslow's Sparrow has nested in recent years, leave the park by the south entrance, turn west at a four-way stop, and continue 1.4 miles to a field on the left. In open areas near the park, you may also see Northern Bobwhite, Bell's Vireo, Grasshopper Sparrow, Dickcissel, and Orchard Oriole.

GULL-WATCHING

The dams on the upper Mississippi River make for great gull-watching from late fall through early spring, when flocks of Ring-billed (shown here) and Herring Gulls may be joined by rarities from Lesser Black-backed to Glaucous. The similarity of many species, along with the various plumages of immatures and hybrid possibilities, make gull identification daunting for beginners. Spending time at places with lots of gulls, such as Dam No. 15 at Davenport, Iowa, and becoming familiar with the common species are the first steps toward sorting out this challenging group. ◼

19 The spring "drumming" of Ruffed Grouse thrills birders walking trails through **Yellow River State Forest.** The grouse is a specialty of this part of the state, as is Pileated Woodpecker. Red-shouldered Hawk, largely confined to the eastern part of the state, nests here, as do Veery; Blue-winged, Cerulean, Kentucky, and Hooded Warblers; Ovenbird; and Louisiana Waterthrush. Yellow-bellied Sapsucker, Acadian Flycatcher, and Brown Creeper have nested in Allamakee County, and all might be seen in summer.

Spring migration of warblers and other neotropical birds peaks in early May along the Mississippi River migration corridor at **Effigy Mounds National Monument.** Fall raptor migration runs mid-September through October. Winter is the best time to see large numbers of Bald Eagle feeding near the Mississippi.

20 In Dickinson, Palo Alto, and Clay Counties, you'll find a birdy landscape of ponds and marshes often referred to as the **Ruthven** area, named for the town at its center. Several species of ducks and Forster's and Black Terns nest here, and large numbers of Franklin's Gull pass through in fall.

Begin your exploration at **Lost Island Nature Center.** Search wetlands where Pied-billed Grebe, American and Least Bitterns, Virginia Rail, Sora, Marsh Wren, and Yellow-headed Blackbird nest. A wide variety of species from American White Pelican to shorebirds to sparrows (including Le Conte's and the rare Nelson's Sharp-tailed) can appear in migration.

IOWA | MORE INFORMATION

RARE BIRD ALERT
Statewide 712-364-2863

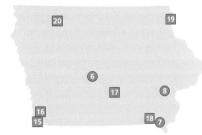

15 Waubonsie State Park
(Page 142)
*www.iowadnr.com/parks
/index.html*
712-382-2786

16 Riverton Wildlife Area
(Page 143)
*www.iowadnr.com/parks
/index.html*
712-374-2510
*Access can be limited in
waterfowl season.*

17 Lake Red Rock
(Page 143)
www.lakeredrock.org
641-828-7522

**18 Lacey-Keosauqua
State Park** *(Page 143)*
*www.iowadnr.com/parks
/index.html*
319-293-3502

**19 Yellow River State
Forest** *(Page 144)*
*www.iowadnr
.com/forestry
/yellowriver.html*
319-586-2254

*In fall or winter, stop by the
visitor center of the Upper
Mississippi River National
Wildlife and Fish Refuge for
advice on seeing waterfowl
and Bald Eagle (including*

*hundreds of Tundra Swan in
Nov.) on the Mississippi River,
above Dam No. 9 near
Ferryville, Wisc.*

**19 Effigy Mounds
National Monument**
(Page 144)
www.nps.gov/efmo
563-873-3491

**20 Lost Island Nature
Center** *(Page 144)*
*www.paccb.org
/WildlifeAreas.html*
712-837-4866

*For more excellent birding
opportunities, visit nearby
Deweys Pasture Wildlife Area.*

ADDITIONAL SITES

6 Saylorville Lake
www.saylorvillelake.org
515-276-4656

*Pacific Loon has been seen
here, as have both Red-necked
and Western Grebes. Parasitic
Jaeger has been seen several
times late Sept.–Nov.*

7 Shimek State Forest
*www.iowadnr.com/forestry
/shimek.html*
319-878-3811
*On these unmarked trails, you
may find Acadian Flycatcher;
White-eyed Vireo; Blue-
winged, Prairie (very rare),
Cerulean, Worm-eating (a
very rare breeder in Iowa),
Kentucky, and Hooded
Warblers; Carolina Wren;
Wood Thrush; and Northern
Parula.*

**8 Cone Marsh
Wildlife Area**
www.iowadnr.com/wildlife
319-335-1575
*All sorts of waders and water-
birds may be present here.
You'll also find Prothonotary
Warbler, American Woodcock,
and Smith's Longspur (late
Mar.–Apr.). Fall hunting may
interfere with birding.*

MINNESOTA

- Northern specialties on the Gunflint Trail
- Great fall hawk-watching in Duluth
- Greater Prairie-Chickens dancing in western grasslands

Poplar Lake, along the Gunflint Trail, northeastern Minnesota

21 Minnesota's most famous birding drive is Cook County Road 12, the **Gunflint Trail.** Winding north for 63 miles from Lake Superior toward Canada, the paved route gains elevation and passes through boreal forest of spruce, fir, pine, and white cedar, with hardwoods, boggy places, and cutover areas intermixed. It's worth driving any time of year, though winter travelers should be prepared for snow and intense cold.

At the top of the most wanted list here are Spruce Grouse, Boreal Owl (very rarely seen, but sometimes heard calling in early spring), and Black-backed Woodpecker (check burned areas). The list of other possibilities is long and enticing: Ruffed Grouse; Northern Goshawk; Great Gray and Northern Saw-whet Owls; Three-toed Woodpecker (very rare); Yellow-bellied and Alder Flycatchers; Gray Jay; Boreal Chickadee; up to 18 species of warblers including Cape May, Bay-breasted, Mourning, and Canada; and Rusty Blackbird nest here. Winter finches such as Pine Grosbeak, White-winged and Red Crossbills, and Common and Hoary Redpolls can be found from late fall into early spring. (Bohemian Waxwing is another sought-after winter visitor, though it's most often seen in towns, where fruiting trees and shrubs provide food.)

22 Another of Minnesota's most famous birding sites is **Sax-Zim Bog**, an area of conifer peatland, pasture, and open countryside. On the way there, stop often to look and listen for nesting species including Sharp-tailed Grouse; Upland Sandpiper; Great Gray Owl; Black-backed Woodpecker; Gray Jay; Boreal Chickadee; Golden-winged, Cape May, and Connecticut Warblers; and Le Conte's Sparrow. In winter, Sax-Zim is one of the state's best spots to search for Northern Hawk and Great Gray Owl. Other winter possibilities include Northern Goshawk, Snowy Owl, Northern Shrike, and Pine Grosbeak.

23 **Rice Lake National Wildlife Refuge** is excellent for geese and ducks in migration (as many as 100,000 Ring-necked Duck may gather in fall to feed). Its mixed conifer-hardwood forest, bogs, and grasslands attract a good variety of birds. Sharp-tailed Grouse, Common Loon, Bald Eagle, Northern Harrier, Black Tern, Short-eared Owl, Common Raven, and Le Conte's Sparrow are a few of the species you may see as you drive the refuge roads from spring through fall.

Among the most sought-after birds in North America, the secretive Yellow Rail spends its time in marshes and wet fields. This elusive species has made **McGregor Marsh State Natural Area** a popular Minnesota destination, although American Bittern, Sedge and Marsh Wrens, and Le Conte's and Nelson's Sharp-tailed Sparrows are among the other species that can repay a breeding-season visit here. An old railroad line converted to a hiking trail provides access, although many birders listen from roads bordering the marsh. Yellow Rails can be heard (mostly at night) fairly easily, but they're very difficult to actually see. Before tramping off into the marsh, bear in mind that "heard" birds count just as much on your life list as "seen" ones.

24 Northeast of Thief River Falls, **Agassiz National Wildlife Refuge** comprises 61,500 acres of open water, marsh, forest, and grassland. A fine assortment of birds is attracted by the diversity of habitat: for example, a colony of more than 20,000 Franklin's Gulls (possibly the largest in the U.S.), another colony of hundreds of Black-crowned Night-Herons, thousands of nesting ducks (Mallard and Blue-winged Teals are the most common, but at least 14 others breed), and five species of nesting grebes (Pied-billed, Red-necked, and Eared are seen often; Horned and Western are scarce). Other notable breeders include American and Least Bitterns, Bald Eagle, Yellow and Virginia Rails, Sora, Sandhill Crane, Forster's and Black Terns, Black-billed Magpie, Sedge and Marsh Wrens, and assorted sparrows. In fall, as many as 2,000 Sandhill Cranes gather here in migration.

DULUTH'S RAPTOR ROAD

Duluth sits at the extreme western end of Lake Superior, a location that becomes a virtual raptor superhighway in fall. Thousands of hawks migrating south, reluctant to cross the broad expanse of water before them, turn southwest and follow the shore. Duluth's renowned **Hawk Ridge Nature Reserve** provides a chance to see literally thousands of hawks on good days. Here beginners will often find experienced birders and naturalists who can provide tips on identifying the more than two dozen species that regularly pass by. ∎

25 **Felton Prairie** is a mix of private and public lands. (Two public prairie areas can be accessed by following County Road 108 east from Minn. 9, south of Felton.) The springtime call of the Greater Prairie-Chicken is a feature here, as are the songs of Clay-colored, Savannah, Grasshopper, Vesper, and Le Conte's Sparrows. There's a chance of seeing Swainson's Hawk and Loggerhead Shrike (scarce in Minnesota). Northern Harrier, Upland Sandpiper, Marbled Godwit, and Bobolink breed here, as sometimes does Chestnut-collared Longspur.

26 **Rothsay Wildlife Management Area** can seem magical in spring, with American Bittern giving its pumping call, Greater Prairie-Chicken booming, Sora whinnying, Marbled Godwit *kerwhit*-ing, Common Snipe in display flight, Bobolink in exuberant song, and Yellow-headed Blackbird shouting its odd creaks and screeches. Most birding is done from roads through adjacent private land.

27 Located on the South Dakota border, **Big Stone National Wildlife Refuge** offers a diversity of habitats from reservoir to marsh to prairie. Western Grebe, American White Pelican, American and Least Bitterns, Great and Snowy (rare) Egrets, and Swainson's Hawk breed in the refuge or nearby, along with a variety of rails, shorebirds, gulls, and terns. Along the 5-mile **Prairie Drive** loop you may see waders, ducks (13 species nest here), Ring-necked Pheasant, Upland Sandpiper, Marbled Godwit, or Sedge Wren.

MINNESOTA | MORE INFORMATION

RARE BIRD ALERT
Statewide 763-780-8890
Duluth 218-728-5030

21 Gunflint Trail
(Page 146)
www.gunflint-trail.com
800-338-6932

22 Sax-Zim Bog
(Page 147)
www.irontrail.org/
Attractions
218-749-8161

**23 Rice Lake National
Wildlife Refuge**
(Page 147)
midwest.fws.gov/ricelake
218-768-2402
🚻 🚶 〰 ♿

**23 McGregor Marsh
State Natural Area**
(Page 147)
www.dnr.state.mn.us
651-296-6157

**24 Agassiz National
Wildlife Refuge**
(Page 147)
www.fws.gov/midwest
/agassiz
218-449-4115
🚻 🚶 〰 ♿

*Be sure to bird along
Marshall County Road 7,
which crosses the refuge, and
from a 4-mile auto tour route.
Don't neglect the western and
northern boundary roads,
which often provide
excellent viewing.*

25 Felton Prairie
(Page 148)
www.dnr.state.mn.us
651-296-6157
*The prairie's public land
exists in disjunct tracts,
so first-time visitors might
do well to stop at nearby
Buffalo River State Park
for maps and advice.*

**26 Rothsay Wildlife
Management Area**
(Page 148)
www.dnr.state.mn.us
218-739-7576

**27 Big Stone National
Wildlife Refuge**
(Page 148)
www.fws.gov/midwest
/bigstone
320-273-2191
🚻 🚶 〰 ♿

*After driving the auto route,
check the viewpoints where
US 75 crosses the east end of
the refuge. Explore nearby
wetlands for waders and
marsh birds as well.*

ADDITIONAL SITES

**9 Beaver Creek Valley
State Park**
www.dnr.state.mn.us
507-724-2107
💲 🚻 🚶

*Beaver Creek Valley State
Park hosts several southern
species seldom seen elsewhere
in the state, among them
Wild Turkey, Acadian
Flycatcher, Tufted Titmouse,
Cerulean Warbler, and*

*Louisiana Waterthrush.
Among the other birds found
here are Ruffed Grouse, Least
Flycatcher, Blue-gray
Gnatcatcher, Wood Thrush,
Blue-winged Warbler, and
Scarlet Tanager.*

**10 Minnesota Valley
National Wildlife Refuge**
www.fws.gov/Midwest
/MinnesotaValley
952-854-5900
❓ 🚻 🚶 ♿

*Near the Twin Cities airport,
this refuge preserves lake,
marsh, bottomland forest,
oak savanna, and even bits
of prairie. Hiking trails
and observation points are
scattered through the refuge
tracts, themselves scattered
amid private land. Stop first
at the refuge visitor center for
maps and advice about areas
including Black Dog Preserve
and Louisville Swamp.*

WISCONSIN

■ Excellent waterbirding at Horicon Marsh
■ Northern breeders in Nicolet National Forest

Horicon Marsh, southwest of Fond du Lac

28 The Mississippi River and its tributaries provide pathways for some southern species to range into the northern states, so even in some of Wisconsin's bottomland woods one can hear Tufted Titmouse and Prothonotary Warbler. One such spot is **Wyalusing State Park.** This is probably the best place to find Kentucky Warbler in the state. Other noteworthy nesting species include Red-shouldered Hawk; Whip-poor-will; Acadian Flycatcher; Bell's Vireo; Winter Wren (unusual this far south in the state); Louisiana Waterthrush; and Yellow-throated, Cerulean, and Hooded Warblers. The best all-around birding spot is near the boat landing. Look for Cerulean Warbler near the **Wisconsin Ridge campground** and for Hooded along the **Bluff Trail** below.

29 **Horicon Marsh** encompasses 32,000 acres of marsh and lake and small areas of grassland, scrub, and woods. Hundreds of thousands of waterfowl gather in fall migration; the **Fourmile Island** area hosts the state's largest heronry, with nesting Great Blue Heron, Great Egret, and Black-crowned Night-Heron; more than 20 species of shorebirds have been seen in spring, late summer, or fall. Breeding birds also include more than a dozen species of ducks, Double-crested Cormorant, American and Least Bitterns, Northern Harrier, King (rare) and Virginia Rails, Sora, Common Moorhen, Sandhill Crane, Wilson's Phalarope, Black and Forster's Terns, Sedge and Marsh Wrens, Grasshopper Sparrow, Bobolink, and Yellow-headed Blackbird. American White Pelican has begun summering regularly in the marsh.

Pull-offs at the north end of the marsh are excellent places to scan for waders and shorebirds—and huge numbers of Canada Goose—in spring and fall. Watch also for Trumpeter Swan. The 3.2-mile **"TernPike"** auto tour route is in the northwestern part of the refuge, as are miles of hiking trails, including the handicapped-accessible **Egret Trail** through a marsh, where you may spot a bittern of either species or a rail. The **Bud Cook Hiking Trails** lead through grassland where you may find nesting Northern Harrier, American Kestrel, Sandhill Crane, or Bobolink.

30 From fall through spring, birders visit the Lake Michigan shore for migrant and wintering land birds and waterbirds. Among the best sites is **North Point Park** at Sheboygan. Here a bit of land sticks out into the lake, providing a vantage point to watch for ducks (including occasional Harlequin Duck, Long-tailed Duck, and scoters), loons, gulls, and terns. In migration, shorebirds (including occasional wintering Purple Sandpiper) can be common. The woodland attracts migrant songbirds and can be a good hawk-watching spot in fall.

31 **Crex Meadows Wildlife Area** is one of the Midwest's finest birding sites. Much of its 30,000 acres is brush-prairie. Marshes and other wetlands attract flocks of waterfowl and an excellent variety of shorebirds. Listen at dawn and dusk for Yellow Rail and Nelson's Sharp-tailed Sparrow, two of the area's most sought-after nesting species. Chances are better for Ruffed Grouse; Common Loon; Red-necked Grebe; American and Least Bitterns; Osprey; Bald Eagle; Northern Harrier; Virginia Rail; Sora; Sandhill Crane (thousands in fall); Upland Sandpiper; Wilson's Phalarope; Black Tern; Short-eared Owl; Horned Lark; Sedge and Marsh Wrens; Clay-colored, Vesper,

Savannah, Le Conte's, and Swamp Sparrows; and Yellow-headed Blackbird. Sharp-tailed Grouse is common in places. Crex's mixed deciduous-coniferous woodlands and scrub host nesting birds including Red-headed Woodpecker; Alder and Least Fly-catchers; Yellow-throated and Warbling Vireos; Scarlet Tanager; Chestnut-sided, Pine, Golden-winged, and Black-and-white Warblers; and Indigo Bunting.

GREATER PRAIRIE-CHICKEN

The spring courtship display of the Greater Prairie-Chicken ranks among the most thrilling natural spectacles in North America. As many as a dozen or more males gather at traditional "dancing" grounds, called leks, where they give their deep booming calls, inflate their orange neck sacs, raise their "horns," and charge each other—all the while posturing and promenading in an attempt to woo a watching female. At some leks, wildlife officials erect blinds to allow close observation. ∎

32 **Nicolet National Forest** harbors some of Wisconsin's most exciting birds. One favorite area is located between Argonne and Eagle River, where Wis. 55 meets Forest Road 2182 in the **Headwaters Wilderness.** Stop wherever you like, and look and listen for Ruffed Grouse; Black-backed Woodpecker; Olive-sided and Yellow-bellied Flycatchers; Blue-headed Vireo; Gray Jay; Boreal Chickadee; Hermit Thrush; Common Raven; Nashville, Magnolia, Black-and-white, Black-throated Green, Blackburnian, Palm, Mourning, and Canada Warblers; Northern Parula; Ovenbird; Lincoln's Sparrow; Red and White-winged Crossbills; and Evening Grosbeak. In winter, look for Bohemian Waxwing and Pine Grosbeak.

Dedicated or lucky birders might find a Spruce Grouse, Northern Goshawk, or Connecticut Warbler, but these species are hard to find. Those who are willing to hike into the interior of the Headwaters Wilderness might find the grouse and the warbler in pines at the edges of bogs. A bit farther south, the trail at **Shelp Lake** can be good for Black-backed Woodpecker, Olive-sided and Yellow-bellied Flycatchers, and Blackburnian Warbler, among many of the previously listed species. The Common Loon sounds across lakes in the forest, while overhead Osprey soars and occasionally gives its sharp whistle.

East of Eagle River, the **Anvil Lake Trail System** makes for good hiking and birding. Forest Road 2178 skirts the edge of the **Blackjack Springs Wilderness.** The squat jack pines north of this wilderness sometimes reward searchers with a Connecticut Warbler, and this is another area where Spruce Grouse might appear. Recently, the endangered Kirtland's Warbler has been found annually in jack pines near the Nicolet National Forest.

WISCONSIN | MORE INFORMATION

RARE BIRD ALERT
Statewide 414-352-3857
Madison 608-255-2476

28 Wyalusing State Park
(Page 150)
www.dnr.state.wi.us/org
/land/parks
608-996-2261

29 Horicon National Wildlife Refuge
(Page 151)
midwest.fws.gov/horicon
920-387-2658

Before you begin your explorations here, stop at the federal refuge visitor center north of Mayville for maps and information. Just north of the town of Horicon, the State Department of Natural Resources field office offers good views of a broad stretch of the marsh. A hiking trail leads through woodland, scrub, and wetlands. In winter, surrounding farmland may have flocks of Horned Lark, Lapland Longspur, and Snow Bunting.

30 North Point Park
(Page 151)
ci.sheboygan.wi.us
920-459-3444
Sheboygan Harbor may have thousands of resting ducks, especially when Lake Michigan is rough. Check the breakwaters here in winter for Snowy Owl. Peregrine Falcon nests nearby, on the local power plant.

31 Crex Meadows Wildlife Area
(Page 151)
www.dnr.state.wi.us
/org/land/wildlife
715-463-2739

A network of roads provides access to keep any birder busy for days, and the visitor center offers maps, a bird list, and advice. Blinds for observing the Sharp-tailed Grouse's "dancing" courtship displays are erected in Apr. (reservations are needed for viewing), but grouse may be seen throughout the year.

32 Nicolet National Forest *(Page 152)*
www.exploringthenorth
.com/nicolet/nicmain.html
715-362-1359

ADDITIONAL SITES

11 Devil's Lake State Park
www.dnr.state.wi.us/org
/land/parks
608-356-8301

This park is in the ancient uplands of the Baraboo Range, a landscape where diverse habitats and varying elevation create niches for an array of breeding species. The list of nesting birds here reflects a mingling of north and south. (Stop by the nature center on North Shore Road for a park map and bird list.) Two favorite locations for a good sampling of species are South Shore Road and Steinke Basin. Nearby Baxter's Hollow Preserve is known for its excellent variety of breeding birds and many of the species listed for Devil's Lake.

12 Kettle Moraine State Forest, Northern Unit
www.dnr.state.wi.us/org
/land/parks
262-626-2116

This forest has long been a favorite of birders. Nesting species at Spruce Lake Bog include Nashville and Canada Warblers and White-throated Sparrow. The restored prairie at Jersey Flats hosts grassland species, while Haskell Noyes Memorial Forest is good for woodland species. Obtain a map of the forest at the Ice Age Visitor Center, west of Dundee on Wis. 67.

NORTH-CENTRAL

T HE GREAT LAKES WRAP AROUND THE TOP OF THIS PART-
northern, part-eastern, part-midwestern section of the
country, acting as both a passageway and a barrier for
birds. They're a path mostly for waterbirds, of course—even
those usually thought of as seabirds, which find familiar territory on the broad expanses of these "inland seas." As a result, diligent birders can at times turn up such anomalies as King Eider
in Ohio or Parasitic Jaeger in Indiana.

- Michigan
- Indiana
- Ohio
- West Virginia
- Kentucky

The lakes are a barrier, too—a fact that birders put to good
use in spring migration. Northbound land birds arrive at the
lakes, look out over seemingly endless stretches of water offering
no food or place to rest, and often take a break before going on.
As a result, impressive numbers of birds can pile up along shorelines, especially at isolated patches of trees. On any day from
mid-April through May, or during September and October, one
is likely to find birders scanning such patches in anticipation of
a "fallout" day when 20 or more species of warblers may be
found in just a few hours. Beginning birders do well to visit such
popular sites, since there's always a veteran around willing to
share his or her knowledge, and more birds may be seen in one
place in a single morning than in days of solitary wandering.

This region's birds are as varied as its geography, from Ohio
River bottomland in Kentucky to Indiana beaches to the bore-
al forests of Michigan's Upper Peninsula. For city birding,
Columbus has its Green Lawn Cemetery and Arboretum,
Indianapolis its Eagle Creek Park, Louisville its Falls of the
Ohio. For solitude, travel to Kentucky's expansive Land
Between the Lakes, walk the trails at Michigan's Warren
Woods State Natural Area, or explore the highlands of West
Virginia, where great birding is set in one of the most beauti-
ful landscapes of the eastern United States. ■

Spruce Grouse

SPECIAL BIRDS OF THE NORTH-CENTRAL STATES

Spruce Grouse	Snowy Owl	Kirtland's Warbler
Sharp-tailed Grouse	Great Gray Owl	Henslow's Sparrow
Yellow Rail	Black-backed	Le Conte's Sparrow
Sandhill Crane	Woodpecker	Pine Grosbeak
Upland Sandpiper	Gray Jay	Red Crossbill
Common Tern	Bohemian Waxwing	

White-winged
Crossbill

Common Redpoll

Hoary Redpoll

MICHIGAN

- Wetland species at Pointe Mouillee
- Migration at Whitefish Point
- Tours to see Kirtland's Warbler

Seney National Wildlife Refuge in Michigan's Upper Peninsula

1 In the extreme southwestern corner of Michigan, **Warren Woods State Natural Area** attracts birders looking for southern species seldom seen elsewhere in the state. In addition, it's great for migrant songbirds in spring. Here you can explore trails through beech-maple forest (the largest undisturbed tract in the state) near the Galien River for Red-headed (population varies from year to year) and Pileated Woodpeckers and Carolina Wren (hard to find after bad winters). In breeding season, look for Acadian Flycatcher; Yellow-throated, Cerulean, Black-and-white, and Hooded Warblers; Louisiana Waterthrush; and Scarlet Tanager.

Warren Dunes State Park stretches along 2.5 miles of Lake

Michigan shoreline, with scenic sand dunes rising as high as 240 feet above the water. Some of the park's best birding is found in its northern section, on the trail system north of Floral Lane. The short **Golden Rod** and longer **Yellow Birch Loops** pass through varied habitats including marshy areas and old fields, excellent in spring migration (look for the elusive Connecticut Warbler in late May). Nesting birds include Black-throated Green, Hooded, and Canada Warblers, and occasionally Worm-eating Warbler. In addition, Prairie Warbler has nested along the **Blue Jay Trail**. Spring or fall days with east winds can be productive for migrant raptors here. Local birders sometimes set up a hawk-watching site at the Floral Lane parking lot (or on the nearby boardwalk trail), or you can climb one of the dunes for a high viewpoint. From fall through spring, scan Lake Michigan from the beach area in the southern part of the park for loons, ducks, gulls, terns, occasional jaegers (fall only), and other waterbirds.

2 Two areas on the Lake Erie shore south of Detroit rate among the state's most popular birding sites. **Lake Erie Metropark** is known for its excellent fall hawk migration on days with north or northwest winds. Over hundreds of thousands of Broad-winged Hawk may pass through in the second half of September, along with other raptors including Osprey, Bald Eagle, Sharp-shinned and Cooper's Hawks, American Kestrel, Merlin, and Peregrine Falcon. Long known as a prime waterfowl migration site, the lake and marsh attract thousands of geese and ducks and a wintering population of Tundra Swan.

Pointe Mouillee State Game Area is a 4,000-acre expanse of natural wetlands and diked marshes at the mouth of the Huron River. Walk the dikes in the marsh area (many birders use bicycles to cover more ground) and look for waterfowl, herons, rails, shorebirds, gulls, and terns. American and Least Bitterns, Great Egret, Black-crowned Night-Heron, and the state's best variety of shorebirds are found here seasonally. The south dike leads to a spit of land (locally called the Banana) extending into Lake Erie. Check the waters here for wintering scoters, Long-tailed Duck, Common Goldeneye, and many other waterfowl, and for occasional wintering Snowy Owl.

3 Michigan's most famous bird is undoubtedly the endangered Kirtland's Warbler. The heart of the bird's range is the north-central part of Michigan's **Lower Peninsula**; it's very rarely seen on migration to and from its winter home in the Bahamas. The warbler is strictly protected, and the best way to see it is on tours conducted by the U.S. Fish and Wildlife Service from **Grayling** and by the U.S. Forest Service from **Mio.** Though singing males are almost always heard, the chance of actually seeing one is about 80 percent.

KIRTLAND'S WARBLER

One of the rarest birds in the United States, Kirtland's Warbler nests only in areas of jack pine less than 15 feet tall. Its range is almost entirely restricted to north-central Michigan. Biologists there work to improve its habitat and to control harmful Brown-headed Cowbirds. After falling to only 167 territorial males in the late 1980s, the warbler's population has steadily increased. ∎

4 Michigan's Upper Peninsula has some excellent birding sites. One of the best is **Seney National Wildlife Refuge,** covering 95,212 acres of coniferous and hardwood forests, marshes, bogs, meadows, and lakes. The lengthy list of species that have nested here includes Hooded and Common Mergansers; Spruce and Sharp-tailed Grouse (rare); Common Loon; American Bittern; Osprey; Bald Eagle; Northern Harrier; Sora; Sandhill Crane; Common and Black Terns; Black-backed Woodpecker; Olive-sided Flycatcher; Nashville, Chestnut-sided, Magnolia, Cape May, Black-throated Blue, Blackburnian, Pine, Palm, Mourning, and Canada Warblers; Vesper and Le Conte's Sparrows; and Virginia and Yellow Rails. (The latter is the refuge's most famous nesting bird.) Trumpeter Swan has been successfully reintroduced here.

5 **Whitefish Point** and **Whitefish Point Bird Observatory** compose one of the legendary locations of American migration-watching. Tens of thousands of birds pass over, pass by, or stop here in spring and fall. In addition, boreal species such as Spruce Grouse, Gray Jay, Boreal Chickadee, and Pine and Evening Grosbeaks are often found. Ducks, loons (mostly Common but with good numbers of Red-throated), grebes (including thousands of Red-necked in fall), shorebirds, gulls, and terns fly past Whitefish Point. All three species of jaegers have been found, with the best chance to see these in September.

Among the thousands of raptors seen in spring, Sharp-shinned and Broad-winged Hawks are most common; other hawks, eagles, and falcons seen here include rare but regular Northern Goshawk, Golden Eagle, Merlin, and Peregrine Falcon. Whitefish Point is also known for owls: Snowy, Great Gray, Long-eared, Boreal (very rare), and Northern Saw-whet are all possible.

MICHIGAN | MORE INFORMATION

RARE BIRD ALERT

Statewide 616-471-4919
Detroit 248-477-1360
Sault Ste. Marie
705-256-2790

1 Warren Dunes State
Park *(Page 156)*
www.michigan.gov/dnr
269-426-4013

2 Lake Erie Metropark
(Page 157)
www.metroparks.com
734-379-5020

2 Pointe Mouillee State
Game Area *(Page 157)*
www.michigan.gov/dnr
734-379-9692

*Access restricted in
hunting season.*

3 U.S. Fish and Wildlife
Service, East Lansing
(Page 158)
www.fws.gov/midwest
517-351-2555

4 Seney National
Wildlife Refuge *(Page 158)*
midwest.fws.gov/seney
906-586-9851

*Visitor center and wildlife
drive open mid-May–
mid-Oct.*

5 Whitefish Point Bird
Observatory *(Page 158)*
www.wpbo.org

906-492-3596

*Visitor center open
mid-Apr.–mid-Oct.*

ADDITIONAL SITES

① Maple River State
Game Area
www.michigan.gov/dnr
517-373-9358

*This area, which is open to
public hunting, covers 9,000
acres of varied wetlands, fields,
and woods. At the dikes, look
for waders and for shorebirds
in spring and fall. Common
Moorhen breeds among the
marsh vegetation, and
Prothonotary Warbler nests
along the Maple River. Osprey
and Bald Eagle pass through
in migration. Near an observation tower on Taft Road,
large numbers of waterfowl are
present fall through spring.
King Rail has nested in this
area. Off Ranger Road, Northern Harrier and Short-eared
Owl winter, and Northern
Shrike is a winter possibility.*

② Nayanquing Point
State Wildlife Area
www.michigan.gov/dnr
989-697-5101
*Many areas along Saginaw
Bay, this one included, offer
excellent birding. Migrant
waterfowl are abundant here,
and several species of dabbling
ducks remain in summer to
nest. Stop at the area office on
Tower Beach Road for advice.*

③ Tawas Point
State Park
www.michigan.gov/dnr
989-362-5041

*This park is best known for
spring and fall songbird migration and for migrant waterbirds. In fall, watch for Merlin
or Peregrine Falcon along the
shore. Tawas Point is famed for
numerous rarities, including
such oddities as Wilson's Plover,
Say's Phoebe, and Black-
throated Gray Warbler.*

④ Sault Ste. Marie
www.saultstemarie.com
906-632-3366 or
800-647-2858
*A winter visit to Sault Ste.
Marie has long been a favorite
birding expedition for
Michiganders (be prepared for
occasional severe weather).
Gyrfalcon, that rare and
majestic raptor, has been seen
in winter regularly on the large
electric power plant near the
canal locks.*

159

INDIANA

■ Spring migration at Migrant Trap
■ Winter waterbirds at the Michigan City Harbor

Lake Michigan,
Indiana Dunes
National Lakeshore

6   The United States boasts many "migrant traps," but one spot on Indiana's Lake Michigan shoreline has become known as the **Migrant Trap** for its concentrations of flycatchers, vireos, thrushes, warblers, sparrows, and other birds. Officially called **Lakefront Park and Sanctuary,** this small patch of trees and scrub can be thronged with birds in spring (mid-April through May is best) and fall, from the expected eastern songbirds to occasional surprises like herons, rails, and owls. Good birding isn't guaranteed even at peak migration times, but the Migrant Trap is always worth a look in spring and fall.

7   The Lake Michigan shore between Chicago and Michigan is crowded with birding opportunities. Loons, grebes, waterfowl, shorebirds, and gulls frequent the lake and beaches. In spring, wetlands attract dabbling ducks and wading birds,

and hawks moving north cruise the shoreline. A substantial part of this area is preserved within the **Indiana Dunes National Lakeshore** and **Indiana Dunes State Park,** which encompass sand dunes, forests, and some swampy or marshy spots.

The **Paul H. Douglas Center for Environmental Education** has trails along dune ponds and through oak savanna, which can be full of birds in migration. The parking lot at nearby **Marquette Park** makes a good viewpoint for scanning the lake from fall through spring for waterfowl and gulls. Jaegers (rare) are seen here with some regularity in fall. Check **Long Lake** on the south side of the road to West Beach for waterfowl and herons. Trails beginning at the visitor center wind through dunes and along the lake.

Indiana Dunes State Park offers extensive trails through fine woodlands where breeding birds include Red-shouldered Hawk (rare), Acadian Flycatcher, Yellow-throated Vireo, Cerulean and Hooded Warblers, American Redstart, and Ovenbird. Check the beach here (as anywhere along the lake) for shorebirds, especially in late summer and fall, and for migrant Peregrine Falcon in September and October. At the eastern end of the national lakeshore, the high dune called **Mount Baldy** makes an excellent lookout for spring hawk migration. Watch also for flocks of Sandhill Crane passing overhead in early spring.

8 In Michigan City, visit **Washington Park** and the **Michigan City Harbor,** the top waterbird-watching spot on the Indiana lakeshore. In spring, the park can be a bit of a migrant trap itself, but the main focus here is on waterfowl, shorebirds, gulls, and terns from fall through spring. Many rarities have appeared in this area over the years, including King Eider, Harlequin Duck, many unusual gulls, and Snowy Owl. Look for the rare Purple Sandpiper on rock jetties in winter and gulls and ducks in open water near the electric power plant.

9 One of the state's top inland shorebirding sites is **Kingsbury Fish and Wildlife Area.** The mudflats exposed here can attract all the regularly occurring migrant shorebirds as well as scarcer species such as White-rumped (regular in late spring), Baird's, and Stilt Sandpipers and Long-billed Dowitcher. This marsh also hosts waterfowl from spring through fall and herons in the warmer months. American White Pelican, Bald Eagle, and Sandhill Crane are seen occasionally, and Reddish Egret and White-faced Ibis are among the rarities that have appeared. In recent winters Kingsbury has been a good spot for Merlin, and Rough-legged Hawk sometimes appears over open fields. **161**

10 **Willow Slough Fish and Wildlife Area** is known for fine marsh and grassland habitats and a good assortment of nesting birds. Least Bittern and Common Moorhen have nested in the marsh on the north side of J. C. Murphey Lake, and Virginia Rail and Sora can be heard calling in spring; King Rail may nest as well. American Bittern stops here in migration, and even the elusive Yellow Rail has been found by determined searchers. Elsewhere, Chestnut-sided Warbler, Lark and Henslow's Sparrows, and Blue Grosbeak breed. Tundra Swan is fairly regular in migration, along with good numbers of dabbling ducks, and by walking through grassy spots you may flush up a Le Conte's or Nelson's Sharp-tailed Sparrow in migration.

11 **Eagle Creek Park,** one of the largest municipal parks in America, is a superb destination near Indianapolis. It is excellent for spring songbird migration, with 30 species of warblers possible on a good day in the beautiful deciduous woods. Begin at an overlook above **Eagle Creek Reservoir;** also walk the trails circling the lake. Nesting birds are a mix of southern birds such as Yellow-throated and Worm-eating Warblers with species more typical of the north-central states.

The reservoir can be good for waterbirds. Parts are deep enough for Common Loon (both Red-throated and Pacific have also been found here), while the shallower north end attracts dabbling ducks. With low water levels, this area can also have migrant shorebirds and waders. Look in migration for Double-crested Cormorant, Osprey, and Bald Eagle.

12 At **Muscatatuck National Wildlife Refuge,** migrant and wintering waterfowl are the focus. As many as 15,000 geese and ducks may be present in spring and fall migration, including Canada Goose, Wood Duck, American Black Duck, Mallard, Blue-winged Teal, Gadwall, and Ring-necked Duck, but Tundra Swan and Greater White-fronted and Snow Geese appear occasionally. Waders (Least Bittern and Green Heron have nested) and rails can be seen seasonally in wetlands. Osprey and Sandhill Crane may pause at Muscatatuck in migration.

Diverse nesting birds include Northern Bobwhite; Red-shouldered Hawk; Great Horned and Barred Owls; Red-headed Woodpecker; Wood Thrush; Yellow-throated, Prothonotary, and Kentucky Warblers; Willow Flycatcher; White-eyed Vireo; Eastern Bluebird; Blue-winged Warbler; Indigo Bunting; Grasshopper and Henslow's Sparrows; and Dickcissel. In early spring, American Woodcock performs its courtship flight at dusk.

INDIANA | MORE INFORMATION

RARE BIRD ALERT
Statewide 317-259-0911

6 Lakefront Park and Sanctuary *(Page 160)*
hmdin.com/parks
219-853-6378

Known as the Migrant Trap

7 Indiana Dunes National Lakeshore
(Page 161)
www.nps.gov/indu
219-926-7561

7 Indiana Dunes State Park *(Page 161)*
www.IN.gov/dnr/parklake
219-926-1952

Drive east on Lakefront Drive for more lake and shoreline viewing. Beverly Drive, which parallels Lakefront Drive inland, passes through wetlands where Virginia Rail and Sora can be heard calling in spring. At nearby Porter Beach, local birders hold hawk-watches in spring.

8 Michigan City Parks and Recreation *(Page 161)*
www.emichigancity.com
219-873-1506

9 Kingsbury Fish and Wildlife Area *(Page 161)*
www.in.gov/dnr/fishwild
/publications/kings.htm
219-393-3612

10 Willow Slough Fish and Wildlife Area
(Page 162)
www.in.gov/dnr/fishwild
/publications/willow.htm
219-285-2704

11 Eagle Creek Park
(Page 162)
www.indygov.org/eGov
/City/DPR/Parks
317-327-7110

12 Muscatatuck National Wildlife Refuge
(Page 162)
www.fws.gov/midwest
/muscatatuck
812-522-4352

ADDITIONAL SITE

5 Minnehaha Fish and Wildlife Area
www.in.gov/dnr/fishwild
/publications/hillen.htm
812-268-5640

Just east of Sullivan, this area encompasses reclaimed strip mines now covered in extensive grasslands. In winter, Northern Harrier and Short-eared Owl fly low, and an occasional Rough-legged Hawk hovers in the wind. Le Conte's Sparrow is a rare winter resident, while nesting birds include Great Blue Heron (several heronries are in the area); Loggerhead Shrike; Bell's Vireo; Lark, Henslow's, and Grasshopper Sparrows; Blue Grosbeak; and Dickcissel. American Bittern and Common Snipe are possible breeders.

OHIO

- Spring migration at Crane Creek
- Winter birding at Killdeer Plains Wildlife Area

Canada Goose brood at Ottawa National Wildlife Refuge Complex, east of Toledo

13 Several adjoining sites on Lake Erie just east of Cleveland provide fine birding opportunities year-round. Park in the extreme eastern parking area of **Headlands Beach State Park,** and walk northeast to **Headlands Dunes State Nature Preserve,** a remnant beach dune ecosystem that can be excellent for spring songbird migration. Spring can also bring good hawk-watching; Merlin is fairly regular in spring and fall. Walking through the dunes may scare up a migrant Common Snipe, American Woodcock, or Grasshopper or Le Conte's Sparrow. In late fall and winter, look for Northern Saw-whet Owl (rare) roosting in shrubs, and Lapland Longspur and Snow Bunting along the beach.

Check the beach for migrant shorebirds and gulls and the offshore waters for diving ducks. From fall through spring, continue east to the breakwater for a view of **Fairport Harbor,** where loons, grebes, ducks, and gulls congregate. This has traditionally been a good spot for rarities, from King Eider to all three jaegers to Little, Mew, and Glaucous Gulls. In late fall, scan the breakwater for the rare Purple Sandpiper. **Shipman Pond** is also worth a look for waders and waterfowl.

Continue west to **Zimmerman Trail**, part of **Mentor Marsh State Nature Preserve,** which protects more than 600 acres of marsh with beech-maple and oak-hickory woodland around the edges. The trail provides access to wetlands where you may find nesting Wood Duck, Pied-billed Grebe, Virginia Rail, Sora, Common Moorhen, Red-headed Woodpecker, and Prothonotary Warbler, and in migration American and Least Bitterns (both rare but regular; Least may breed in the area) or Black-crowned Night-Heron. Mentor can also host a fine diversity of migrant songbirds in spring. More than 250 species of birds have been documented in the park in recent years.

14 Just north of Castalia, **Resthaven Wildlife Area** is worth a visit for its habitats of woods, lake, and the largest tract of prairie remaining in the state. Bald Eagle nests nearby, and winter can bring flocks of ducks to wetlands. Check grassy and scrubby areas for sparrows in migration and for nesting birds including Ring-necked Pheasant, American Woodcock, Yellow Warbler, and Indigo Bunting. Bell's Vireo has been seen in the area in summer.

15 The most famous birding site in Ohio is really two sites, side by side on Lake Erie, collectively called **Crane Creek** by local birders. The first, **Magee Marsh Wildlife Area,** is renowned as a spring "migrant trap" where phenomenal numbers of songbirds pause on northbound migration before flying over Lake Erie. A boardwalk through a patch of woods near the beach is immensely popular from mid-April through May, when cuckoos, flycatchers, vireos, thrushes, warblers (more than 30 species have been seen), tanagers, and other songbirds rest and feed in the trees. A second trail near the **Sportsmen's Migratory Bird Center** has an observation tower good for watching hawks in spring.

Bald Eagle nests at Magee Marsh, and Trumpeter Swan has been reintroduced here. Tundra Swan is one of many species of waterfowl common in migration. Nesting birds in the marshland may include American Black and Wood Ducks, Hooded Merganser, Pied-billed Grebe, Black-crowned Night-Heron, American and Least Bitterns, King (rare) and Virginia Rails, Sora, Common Tern, Sedge and Marsh Wrens, Yellow Warbler, and occasionally Yellow-headed Blackbird. Herons can be common from spring through fall, as are shorebirds in migration. Look for Northern Harrier and Short-eared Owl in winter.

Next door, **Ottawa National Wildlife Refuge Complex** offers more birding opportunities, with miles of trails through wetlands, scrubby areas, and woods. Tens of thousands of waterfowl gather on the refuge in late fall, including Snow and Canada Geese, Tundra Swan, and 18 or more species of ducks. Depending on water levels in "moist soil" areas, shorebirding can be excellent in spring and fall migration.

SHORT-EARED OWL

Though owls are often thought of as forest birds, Short-eared Owl prefers open grassland for nesting and wintering. At dusk it flies low over the ground like a huge moth, searching for mice and other rodents, or an occasional small bird. While mostly nocturnal, it is sometimes seen in daylight sitting on the ground. Look for it in prairies and fields such as those at Killdeer Plains Wildlife Area (below) in Ohio. Short-eared Owl is irregular in occurrence from year to year. ▪

16 Toledo's **Oak Openings Preserve Metropark** is one of the region's most popular birding locations. Check the sand dunes off Girdham Road for nesting Lark Sparrow, a very rare breeder in Ohio (about 20 pairs nest in the metropark). Be sure to keep disturbance of the birds to a minimum; do not leave the paths. Some of the noted breeding birds of the metropark include Barred Owl; White-eyed, Blue-headed, Yellow-throated, and Red-eyed Vireos; Eastern Bluebird; Chestnut-sided, Cerulean, Kentucky, and Hooded Warblers; American Redstart; and Summer and Scarlet Tanagers.

17 Northwest of Marion, **Killdeer Plains Wildlife Area** ranks with Ohio's favorite birding spots, known for wintering owls and hawks, migrant shorebirds and waterfowl, and nesting Bald Eagle. In winter, look for Northern Harrier, Rough-legged Hawk, American Kestrel, and Short-eared Owl in open places, along with flocks of Horned Lark, American Pipit, Lapland Longspur, and Snow Bunting. Check pine groves along County Road 71 for roosting Long-eared and Northern Saw-whet Owls.

Nesting birds at Killdeer Plains include Ring-necked Pheasant; Pied-billed Grebe; American Bittern; Great Blue Heron; Red-headed Woodpecker; Vesper, Lark, Savannah, and Grasshopper Sparrows; and Bobolink. In fall, huge numbers of Tree, Northern Rough-winged, Bank, and Barn Swallows feed over wetlands, and American Woodcock is common. Canada Goose and dabbling duck numbers can build to 40,000 or more. Depending on water level, shorebirding can be productive in migration; spring may bring White-rumped Sandpiper, and in fall Baird's and Buff-breasted Sandpipers may be seen along with more common species such as Black-bellied and Semi-palmated Plovers; Greater and Lesser Yellowlegs; and Solitary, Semipalmated, Least, and Pectoral Sandpipers.

18 **Mohican State Park** and **Mohican-Memorial State Forest** center on the beautiful gorge through which the Clear Fork of the Mohican River flows. The gorge shelters stands of white pine and hemlock where northern warblers—Magnolia, Black-burnian, and Canada Warblers, and Northern Waterthrush—have nested, along with Brown Creeper and Winter Wren. Blue-winged, Yellow, Chestnut-sided, Cerulean, and Worm-eating Warblers; Northern Parula; American Redstart; and Ovenbird are among more than 20 warblers that nest in the area, creating perhaps the greatest breeding diversity of this group in the state.

19 A diverse collection of nesting warblers is also the main attraction in the **Clear Creek Valley.** Part of the valley is protected as the **Clear Creek Nature Preserve,** and a few trails lead up from the road into the woods. Bird along the road and in the forest for nesting birds including Black Vulture; Red-shouldered and Broad-winged Hawks; Yellow-throated Vireo; Cedar Waxwing; Blue-winged, Yellow, Black-throated Green, Yellow-throated, Prairie, Cerulean, Black-and-white, Worm-eating, and Kentucky Warblers; American Redstart; Ovenbird; Louisiana Waterthrush; and Summer and Scarlet Tanagers, among others. Magnolia and Canada Warblers have nested in the valley.

20 Ohio birders travel to Adams County to look for a few southern species, specifically Chuck-will's-widow, Blue Grosbeak, and Summer Tanager. A walk around the lake at **Adams Lake State Park** can turn up nesting Warbling Vireo; Blue-winged, Pine, and Prairie Warblers; American Redstart; Summer Tanager; and both Orchard and Baltimore Orioles.

Follow Ohio 125 east about 8 miles from West Union to Waggoner Riffle Road and turn south along Ohio Brush Creek. After about 2.5 miles, Beasley Fork Road on the west leads to a bridge where Chuck-will's-widow calls after dark. Check scrub-by areas anywhere along the creek for Blue Grosbeak. In about 2 miles, take Abner Hollow Road to the northeast and park at the old cemetery. This area is good for warblers, including Yellow-throated, Cerulean, Worm-eating, and Hooded. Keep an eye out anywhere in this vicinity for Ruffed Grouse, Wild Turkey, Black Vulture, and Red-shouldered Hawk.

OHIO | MORE INFORMATION

RARE BIRD ALERT
Central 614-221-9736
Cleveland 216-556-0700
Northwest 419-877-9640
Southwest 937-640-2473
Youngstown 330-742-6661

**13 Headlands Beach
State Park** *(Page 164)*
www.dnr.state.oh.us/parks
216-881-8141

**13 Mentor Marsh State
Nature Preserve**
(Page 165)
www.dnr.state.oh.us/dnap
800-317-9155

*Nature center open Apr.–Oct.
Sat.–Sun., or by appt.; call for
program schedule. Note also
that warm water from nearby
power plants (one in Eastlake
and one at Avon Lake) attracts
large numbers of gulls and
flocks of waterfowl in winter.
The harbor at the western
Cleveland suburb of Lorain is
noted for hosting rare shorebirds in spring and fall.*

**14 Resthaven Wildlife
Area** *(Page 165)*
419-684-5049
*In nearby Castalia, Castalia
Pond is noted for amazing
concentrations of wintering
ducks, sometimes numbering
in the thousands.*

**15 Magee Marsh
Wildlife Area**
(Page 165)
www.dnr.state.oh
.us/parks
419-836-7758

*Known as Crane Creek.
Limited access in hunting
season (mid-Oct.–Nov.);
bird center remains open
year-round.*

**15 Ottawa National
Wildlife Refuge Complex**
(Page 166)
www.fws.gov/midwest
/Ottawa
419-898-0014

**16 Oak Openings
Preserve Metropark**
(Page 166)
www.metroparkstoledo.com
419-826-6463

**17 Killdeer Plains Wildlife
Area** *(Page 166)*
www.dnr.ohio.gov
/wanderings
740-496-2254
*Waterfowl area closed to the
public except by special permit*

18 Mohican State Park
(Page 167)
www.dnr.state.oh.us/parks
419-994-5125

**18 Mohican-Memorial
State Forest** *(Page 167)*
www.dnr.state.oh.us
/forestry
330-339-2205

**19 Clear Creek Nature
Preserve** *(Page 167)*
www.metroparks.net
614-891-0700

**20 Adams Lake State
Park** *(Page 167)*
www.dnr.state.oh.us/parks
740-858-6652

*A satellite of Shawnee State
Park, which has full facilities.*

ADDITIONAL SITE

6 Green Lawn Cemetery
*Birders in Columbus consider
this one of the state's finest
sites for spring migration. A
special Audubon Society kiosk
here shows bird lists and notes
on recent sightings.*

WEST VIRGINIA

- Wetland species at Green Bottom Wildlife Management Area
- Appalachian birds in eastern highlands
- Wintering waterfowl at Robert C. Byrd Locks and Dam

High-elevation vegetation at Dolly Sods, south of Thomas

21 **Green Bottom Wildlife Management Area** offers excellent birding year-round. Least Bittern, Virginia Rail, and Common Moorhen nest in the marshes here. Sora, found commonly in migration, has nested; King Rail (rare) has summered in the area. Also, American Bittern is seen in migration, and in late summer waders feed in wetlands: Great Blue and Green Herons and Great Egret are most common, with occasional sightings of Snowy and Cattle Egrets and both Black-crowned and Yellow-crowned Night-Herons. Little Blue Heron is regular in late summer or fall. In winter, Northern Harrier and an occasional Short-eared Owl hunt over the marshes, and Mute and Tundra Swans have appeared in the flocks of wintering waterfowl.

When low water levels expose mudflats, Green Bottom attracts migratory shorebirds; the state's first recorded Black-necked Stilt was found here. Nesting birds of the area include

169

Willow Flycatcher, Warbling Vireo, Tree Swallow, Prothonotary Warbler, Blue Grosbeak (one of the few places in the state for this species), and both Orchard and Baltimore Orioles.

 A few minutes upstream on the Ohio River, **Robert C. Byrd Locks and Dam** is a favorite birding location. Check grassy

and scrubby areas along the entrance road for nesting Willow Flycatcher, Savannah and Grasshopper Sparrows, Blue Grosbeak, and Dickcissel. In fall, American Golden-Plover and Upland and Buff-breasted Sandpipers may stop to rest. Snow Bunting has been found here in winter, when Short-eared Owl sometimes quarters the fields at dusk. Cross the locks to an island and walk north to scan another island just upstream for geese and shorebirds, which in spring may include Willet and Marbled Godwit (both rare). Along the river, look for migratory and wintering waterfowl, gulls, and terns.

Baltimore Oriole, a brightly colored relative of the blackbirds

Near the Maryland state line, the **Cranesville Swamp Nature Preserve** protects a peat bog and the country's southern-most tamarack forest. Intersecting trails lead to a boardwalk into a wetland. Nesting birds are the attraction here: Look for Sora (in migration, and a possible breeder); Northern Saw-whet Owl; Alder and Willow Flycatchers; White-eyed and Blue-headed Vireos; Veery; Wood Thrush; Golden-winged, Nashville, Chestnut-sided, Magnolia, and Black-throated Green Warblers; American Redstart; Northern Waterthrush; Scarlet Tanager; Eastern Towhee; and Savannah and Swamp Sparrows.

Fine birding lures travelers to the Allegheny Mountains. One quite accessible site to see distinctive high-country birds is **Cranberry Glades Botanical Area** in the 900,000-acre **Monongahela National Forest.** Stop at the Cranberry Mountain Nature Center for information and maps. Off the parking lot a mile north of the center, a boardwalk trail passes through low shrubland with scattered trees, and across two "glades," or peat bogs. In summer, look for Alder Flycatcher; Blue-headed Vireo; Common Raven; Black-capped Chickadee; Red-breasted Nuthatch; Winter Wren; Swainson's and Hermit Thrushes; Veery; Magnolia, Black-throated Blue, Mourning, Black-burnian, and Canada Warblers; and Northern Waterthrush. Purple Finch and Red Crossbill may also be present at times.

WEST VIRGINIA | MORE INFORMATION

RARE BIRD ALERT
Statewide 304-736-3086

21 Green Bottom Wildlife Management Area *(Page 169)*
wvweb.com/www
/hunting/area.html
304-675-0871

22 Robert C. Byrd Locks and Dam *(Page 170)*
www.lrh.usace.army.mil
/projects/locks/rcb
304-399-5211

23 Cranesville Swamp Nature Preserve *(Page 170)*
nature.org
304-637-0160

To reach the swamp from Terra Alta, take County Road 47 north about 7 miles and turn right on County Road 49. Drive a bit more than a mile and turn left; the preserve will be on your right.

24 Monongahela National Forest *(Page 170)*
www.fs.fed.us/r9/mnf
304-636-1800

Encompasses Cranberry Glades, Gaudineer, and Dolly Sods areas.

ADDITIONAL SITES

7 Highland Scenic Highway
www.fs.fed.us/r9/mnf/sp
/highland_hwy.html
304-846-2695
This highway offers more birding opportunities. Many of the same birds listed for Cranberry Glades can be seen in summer from overlooks and trails along this marvelous route, which climbs to over 4,500 feet. Look for Mourning Warbler in regrowing logged areas, and listen for Northern Saw-whet Owl after dark in spring.

8 Gaudineer Knob and **Gaudineer Scenic Area**
www.fs.fed.us/r9/mnf/sp/
gaudineer.html
304-456-3335
Drive to the summit of the 4,445-foot knob, and look for Red-breasted Nuthatch; Winter Wren; Golden-crowned Kinglet; several species of warbler including Chestnut-sided, Magnolia, and Yellow-rumped; and Dark-eyed Junco. At the
scenic area, four species of thrushes—Veery, Swainson's, Hermit, and Wood—nest in spruce woods in this general area, along with the species listed for Cranberry Glades.

9 Dolly Sods Wilderness
www.fs.fed.us/r9/mnf/sp
/dolly_sods_wilderness.htm
304-636-1800
This part of the Monongahela National Forest is known to birders for two reasons. Near the Red Creek Campground, members of a local bird club have conducted a birdbanding operation each fall since 1961. Visitors are welcome to observe the banding process—a great chance to see close-up many species usually observed flitting through foliage in the treetops. Only a short distance north on Forest Road 75, the overlook at Bear Rocks has become a regular fall hawk-watching site. While not recording the numbers or variety of some more famous spots, Bear Rocks provides good viewing on days with northeast winds.

KENTUCKY

- Waterbirds at the Falls of the Ohio
- Wintering Bald Eagles, gulls, and waterfowl at Land Between the Lakes

Red River Gorge Geologic Area, east-central Kentucky

25 The highlands of Kentucky's rugged Cumberland Mountains attract nesting birds rare or unknown elsewhere in the state. Big **Black Mountain** has been a favorite site to find many of these species in breeding season. Some of the area's uncommon to rare nesting songbirds can be seen during the ascent on Ky. 160, while others are found along the side road to the summit. Watch for Ruffed Grouse and Common Raven (both resident, but rarely seen); Black-billed Cuckoo (rare); Blue-headed Vireo; Veery; Golden-winged (uncommon), Chestnut-sided, Black-throated Blue, Blackburnian (rare), and Canada Warblers; Dark-eyed Junco; and Rose-breasted Grosbeak. In some years, Least Flycatcher sings from the scrubby woodland

edges. The entire summit area is privately owned, but strolling around the gravel roads has long been acceptable.

26 The **Minor E. Clark Fish Hatchery** has a reputation for attracting waterbirds and some outstanding rarities; the total list for the area is more than 250 species. The more than one hundred ponds at the hatchery can host waterfowl, herons, shorebirds, gulls, or terns depending on the season. Osprey may stop to fish in migration, and Bald Eagle is regularly seen in the trees along the adjacent **Licking River,** especially from November through March. Several species of herons and shorebirds are commonly observed from August to October. Some waterbirds are present during spring migration, but shorebirds may be scarce. Among the unusual sightings here have been Tundra Swan, Long-tailed Duck, Surf and Black Scoters, Wood Stork, Marbled Godwit, and American Avocet. A dam just upstream forms **Cave Run Lake;** check overlooks here and at several points farther along Ky. 801 from fall through spring for loons, grebes, waterfowl, and Bald Eagle.

27 Though the best access is across the Ohio River in Indiana, Louisville birders consider the **Falls of the Ohio** their home turf. Birding at the **Falls of the Ohio State Park** depends on water level: When the river is low, shallow pools in the exposed rocks can attract waders and shorebirds. Activity is best in late summer and fall, but spring can be good if the river is not high. Along with more common shorebirds, look for Baird's and Buff-breasted Sandpipers (August through September) and Dunlin (October). Gulls sometimes gather in numbers from November through March, and among the common Ring-billed and Herring have been such rarities as Laughing, Franklin's, Black-headed, Iceland, and Great Black-backed. Peregrine Falcon has begun nesting on a nearby bridge.

28 Although closed from mid-October to mid-March, the **Sauerheber Unit** of **Sloughs Wildlife Management Area** offers fine birding the rest of the year. Located in the bottomlands of the Ohio River, the area hosts thousands of wintering geese and ducks, some of which can be seen from observation platforms along Ky. 268 northwest of Geneva. These platforms and roadside birding allow limited waterfowl viewing even when the area is closed. Sloughs Wildlife Management Area can be a good place in migration to see American and Least Bitterns, rails (Virginia and King are sporadic; Sora is common here at

times), shorebirds, Sedge and Marsh Wrens, and locally uncommon sparrows such as Le Conte's and Nelson's Sharp-tailed (mostly early October). A pair of Bald Eagle nests, and the area is home to a colony of Great Blue Heron. Eastern song-birds are well represented in woods during migration.

29 Tennessee Valley Authority and U.S. Army Corps of Engineers dams on the Tennessee and Cumberland Rivers have created two huge adjacent and parallel reservoirs, **Kentucky Lake** and **Lake Barkley,** as well as one of the region's finest sites for wintering waterfowl and gulls. Kentucky and Barkley Dams and lakes have rewarded birders with a long list of rari-ties, as well as amazing numbers of common waterbirds. Thousands of Bonaparte's, Ring-billed, and Herring Gulls sometimes gather in fall and winter below the dams or on the lakes. Both lakes offer many access points and recreation areas from which to scan for waterbirds (best from September to May), including waterfowl, Common Loon, Pied-billed and Horned Grebes, Double-crested Cormorant, Great Blue Heron, and gulls. November through March are the best months to view gulls.

Both Osprey and Bald Eagle nest around the lakes, and the state resort parks of **Kentucky Dam Village, Kenlake,** and **Lake Barkley** offer special programs and tours in winter to see some of the many eagles that winter here.

30 The strip of land between the two lakes makes up a national recreation area called, logically enough, **Land Between the Lakes National Recreation Area:** 170,000 acres of most-ly forested terrain open to hiking, biking, camping, picnicking, hunting, fishing, and, of course, birding. Begin your visit at the **Land Between the Lakes Nature Station.** Check feeders here, and ask about guided walks and special wildlife events such as canoe trips, nocturnal "owl prowls," and winter Bald Eagle viewing excursions. Then walk trails to **Hematite Lake** or **Honker Bay** for a diversity of forest and wetland habitats, keeping an eye out for breeding Cerulean Warbler in large trees.

Land Between the Lakes is an excellent destination for migrant songbirds in spring and fall, and a good variety of war-blers nest here, including Blue-winged and Prairie (old fields), Northern Parula, Yellow-throated and Pine (pine plantings), American Redstart, Prothonotary, Worm-eating, Ovenbird, and Louisiana Waterthrush. You might want to make a special effort to find the Kentucky Warbler, the state's namesake.

KENTUCKY | MORE INFORMATION

RARE BIRD ALERT
Statewide 502-326-0878

25 Black Mountain
(Page 172)
www.kingdomcome.org
606-589-5812

**26 Minor E. Clark Fish
Hatchery** *(Page 173)*
www.kdfwr.state.ky.us
606-784-6872

**27 Falls of the Ohio
State Park** *(Page 173)*
www.fallsoftheohio.org
812-280-9970

Access via I-65, in Indiana.

**28 Sauerheber Unit of
Sloughs Wildlife
Management Area**
(Page 173)
www.kdfwr.state.ky.us
800-858-1549

*Closed mid-Oct.–mid-Mar.;
elevated observation
areas along Ky. 268
open year-round.*

**29 Kentucky Lake Visitor
Center** *(Page 174)*
*www.tva.gov/sites
/kentucky.htm*
502-362-4128 or
800-467-7145

*An observation point is located
below the dam on Barkley
Dam Rd.*

29 Lake Barkley
(Page 174)
*www.orn.usace.army.mil
/pao/lakeinfo/BAR.htm*
270-362-4236

*An observation point is
located below the dam on
US 62/641.*

**30 Land Between the
Lakes National
Recreation Area**
(Page 174)
www.lbl.org
270-924-2000 or
800-525-7077

*Stop at the North Welcome
Station, south of Grand
Rivers, to pick up a map
before continuing south along
the main north-south road,
called the Trace. The nature
station, on Silver Trail Rd. E
(off the Trace), is usually
closed in winter.*

ADDITIONAL SITE

**10 Red River Gorge
Geologic Area**
www.fs.fed.us/r8/boone
859-745-3100

*Interesting breeders are the
attraction at this site in the
Daniel Boone National
Forest. In spring and summer,
watch for Ruffed Grouse,
Blue-headed Vireo, and warblers including Northern
Parula, Black-throated Green
(in hemlocks), Yellow-throated
and Pine (on the ridges),
Black-and-white, Worm-
eating, Ovenbird, Louisiana
Waterthrush, and Hooded.
Two special breeding birds of
this area are Red-breasted
Nuthatch, which has nested
near Rock Bridge, and
Swainson's Warbler, regularly
found along Swift Camp
Creek, especially in the thick
patches of rhododendron.*

THE PLAINS

L OOKING AT THIS STRIP OF STATES IN AMERICA'S MIDSEC-
tion, a birder is bound to think: prairie. Yet while many
adaptable grassland species are still common, prairie in its
various forms is one of our most imperiled habitats.

- Oklahoma
- Kansas
- Nebraska
- South Dakota
- North Dakota

The grassland of Lostwood National Wildlife Refuge, in
North Dakota, is one of the best places in the country to find
the scarce Sprague's Pipit and Baird's Sparrow. Lesser Prairie-
Chicken, another dwindling species, still dances at leks in
Cimarron National Grassland in Kansas. Its relative, the Greater
Prairie-Chicken, is more widespread and can be seen at numer-
ous sites throughout the region, including Fort Pierre National
Grassland in South Dakota and Burchard Lake Wildlife
Management Area in Nebraska.

These states are also appealing because of the "East meets
West" aspect of their bird life. Areas in the west, like South
Dakota's Black Hills, host birds with Rocky Mountain affinities.
Eastern species find deciduous-forest habitat at places such as
Little River National Wildlife Refuge in Oklahoma.

There are superb wetlands here, too. Quivira National
Wildlife Refuge and Cheyenne Bottoms in Kansas and
Nebraska's Rainwater Basin are two of the best.

And any list of America's most thrilling birding phenomena
has to include the gathering of Sandhill Crane on Nebraska's
Platte River in spring migration. The sights and sounds of
countless thousands of these impressive birds has become one of
the "must see" spectacles of North American natural history.

Each of these states offers more diversity than residents of
other parts of the country might realize, and each will reward
exploration with a surprising variety of birds. ■

Sprague's
Pipit

SPECIAL BIRDS OF THE PLAINS

Trumpeter Swan	Snowy Plover	Sprague's Pipit	
Sharp-tailed Grouse	Piping Plover	Cassin's Sparrow	
Greater Prairie-Chicken	Burrowing Owl	Baird's Sparrow	Smith's Longspur
Lesser Prairie-Chicken	Scissor-tailed Flycatcher	Le Conte's Sparrow	Chestnut-collared Longspur
Black Rail	Bell's Vireo	Nelson's Sharp-tailed Sparrow	Painted Bunting
Sandhill Crane	Black-capped Vireo	Harris's Sparrow	
Whooping Crane	Chihuahuan Raven	McCown's Longspur	

OKLAHOMA

- **Waterfowl and Bald Eagles at Sequoyah National Wildlife Refuge**
- **Waders and shorebirds at Salt Plains National Wildlife Refuge**
- **Western species at Black Mesa**

Footbridge over the Mountain Fork River, Beavers Bend Resort Park, near Broken Bow

1 Birders travel to the southeastern corner of Oklahoma to explore the excellent bottomland-hardwood habitat at the **Little River National Wildlife Refuge,** a bit of southern swamp. The sloughs and river channels lined with bald cypresses, sweet gums, and oaks ring with the songs of migrant warblers and other species in spring. Northern Parula and Yellow-throated, Prothonotary, Kentucky, and Hooded Warblers nest here, but the most sought-after of the breeding warblers is Swainson's. Great Blue Heron and Great Egret breed in colonies in the refuge, as does Anhinga, a local specialty that's present from spring through summer. Other breeding species include Wood Duck, Mississippi Kite, Red-shouldered Hawk, Chuck-will's-widow, Yellow-throated Vireo, and Fish Crow.

2 Not far to the north, **Beavers Bend Resort Park** occupies a beautiful and rugged setting on the Mountain Fork River just below Broken Bow Lake. The park is at its best in spring migration, when the mix of pine and hardwood forest attracts a

good variety of songbirds. The **Dogwood Trail,** which loops along the river, is a particularly nice area. Pileated Woodpecker, Yellow-throated and Pine Warblers, and American Redstart nest in the park; in winter waterfowl and Bald Eagle can be found along the river. Brown-headed Nuthatch is seen occasionally, but it's more likely along the nature trail in the **McCurtain County Wilderness Area.**

3 **Sequoyah National Wildlife Refuge** attracts great flocks of wintering geese and ducks to wetlands and croplands on the shore of Robert S. Kerr Lake. Wintering Bald Eagle are common, and a few pairs nest around the lake and might be seen year-round. Double-crested Cormorant is abundant around the lake for much of the year. Though Sequoyah is known for waterfowl, including Oklahoma's largest concentration of Snow Goose, a birding trip here can be worthwhile anytime. Breeding birds include Red-headed Woodpecker, Scissor-tailed Flycatcher, Bell's and Warbling Vireos, Prothonotary Warbler, Lark Sparrow, Indigo and Painted Buntings, and Dickcissel. In summer, Great Blue and Little Blue Herons and Great and Snowy Egrets are common in marshes and along the lake. In migration, look for American and Least Bitterns, rails, and Sedge and Marsh Wrens in marshy places.

4 **Oxley Nature Center,** near Tulsa, is a relatively small area comprising prairie, marsh, and forest, and a correspondingly diverse selection of birds. Nearby **Lake Yahola** is a local favorite. It can have excellent numbers of waterfowl, grebes, and gulls in migration and winter, and many rarities have appeared over the years, from Surf Scoter to California and Lesser Black-backed Gulls.

Several fine trails wind through varied habitats around the nature center, and a boardwalk crosses a marsh where waders, rails, and other wetland birds may be seen. The grassland near the interpretive building can be excellent for migrants and wintering sparrows, especially Harris's and occasionally Le Conte's. In migration, be sure to visit the deciduous forest in the North Woods area for songbirds; the road to the parking lot here also provides another viewpoint of Lake Yahola.

5 The most popular birding sites in Oklahoma City are two lakes located just a few miles apart in the northwestern part of town. **Lake Overholser** is known for migrants and ducks, wintering loons (both Red-throated and Pacific have been found along with Common), grebes (Western is seen often), and gulls. Least Bittern and rails are at times found in the marshy area at the lake's north end, and Prothonotary Warbler breeds in nest boxes here. Exposed mudflats mean good shorebirding. Nearby **Rose Lake,** a wetland where shorebirds may be present in migration, also has several rarities. White Ibis, Roseate Spoonbill, and Wood Stork have appeared here over the years.

LEAST TERN

Though Lewis and Clark observed the interior Least Tern often, this small gull-like bird is now endangered. The terns perform an elaborate courtship after arriving at breeding sites from late April to early June. The tern's nest is a shallow cup scraped in bare ground on exposed salt flats, sandbars, and reservoir beaches—a habitat that is fragile and increasingly rare—and adults and young stay in the area, feeding on shallow-water fish, until fall migration. ■

At **Lake Hefner,** a lake viewpoint local birders call **Prairie Dog Point** can be an excellent site for migrant shorebirds and wintering gulls. The first state records of Little and Lesser Black-backed Gulls came from here, though such sightings are not to be expected. Ring-billed is the abundant species; Herring is seen often; and Bonaparte's and Franklin's are common in migration. Hefner is deeper than Overholser, so more likely to have loons and diving ducks. Be sure to check the ponds at the northeast corner of the lake for waterfowl.

6 In **Wichita Mountains National Wildlife Refuge,** a striking setting of prairie and rugged granite hills, eastern species such as Chuck-will's-widow, Eastern Phoebe, Carolina Wren, Eastern Bluebird, and Eastern Meadowlark nest near western birds such as Common Poorwill, Western Kingbird, and Bewick's Wren. Look for Rock and Canyon Wrens and Rufous-crowned Sparrow on the rocky slopes of Mount Scott. Other nesting birds include Wild Turkey, Mississippi Kite, Greater Roadrunner, Painted Bunting, and Lark and Grasshopper Sparrows. The endangered Black-capped Vireo has made a comeback in scrub-oak areas since programs were begun to control brood-parasitic Brown-headed Cowbird. In spring and summer, ask refuge personnel about productive spots for this species. In winter, venture south of Quanah Parker Lake, where you'll have a good chance of finding Chestnut-collared Longspur in the grassland.

7 Southwest Oklahoma's most important wetlands is **Hackberry Flat Wildlife Management Area,** a few miles from the municipal airport at Frederick. You can bird from county roads

or park and walk dikes around the impoundments. (Roads can be a problem in wet weather.) The largest wetlands restoration project in Oklahoma's history is creating an expanse of marsh and open water where waterfowl, heron, shorebirds, gulls, and terns are found seasonally. Look for Sandhill Crane (the number sometimes may be in the thousands) from fall through spring, and for Ferruginous Hawk and Prairie Falcon in winter, when geese and ducks are known to throng the area. Peregrine Falcon may appear in migration or winter. Upland grassy areas host winter sparrows and longspurs. Twenty-three species of shorebirds have been seen at Hackberry Flat in a single day during spring migration, when hundreds of Wilson's Phalarope might be found, along with fair numbers of Hudsonian Godwit. Buffbreasted Sandpiper has occurred in fall. Nesting species include Pied-billed Grebe, King Rail, Black-necked Stilt, American Avocet, and Wilson's Phalarope.

8 You'll find good birding, as well as Oklahoma's most otherworldly landscape, at **Salt Plains National Wildlife Refuge.** Bordering the Great Salt Plains Reservoir on the west is a vast expanse of gleaming white salt atop underlying mudflats, a strange and exotic sight in the midst of rolling agricultural land. Snowy Plover, American Avocet, and Least Tern nest on these salt flats, and can often be seen in spring and summer from the selenite crystal area in the refuge's southwest section (open April to mid-October).

Near the refuge headquarters you'll find the **Eagle Roost Nature Trail** and the refuge auto tour route, both offering fine birding opportunities. Prothonotary Warbler nests in the swampy marsh. The trail runs alongside Sand Creek Bay, where a variety of waterbirds can be found seasonally. Thousands of American White Pelican and Sandhill Crane appear in migration (an occasional Whooping Crane shows up, too), and flocks of geese and ducks are present from fall through spring, along with dozens of Bald Eagles.

Shorebirding is often excellent around the edge of the bay, with migrants such as Greater and Lesser Yellowlegs; Semipalmated, Western, Least, Baird's, and Stilt Sandpipers; Longbilled Dowitcher; and Wilson's Phalarope common in spring and fall. Nesting birds you might find along the auto tour route include Wild Turkey, several species of herons and egrets, White-faced Ibis, Mississippi Kite, Swainson's Hawk, King Rail, Red-headed Woodpecker, Western and Eastern Kingbirds, Scissor-tailed Flycatcher, Bell's and Warbling Vireos, and

Painted Bunting. Be sure to walk to Casey Marsh Tower for another chance to see waterfowl and Sandhill Crane.

9 Ranking near the top of Oklahoma's favorite birding spots, the **Black Mesa** country at the western extremity of the panhandle is home to several species seldom or never found anywhere else in the state. As you drive west from Boise City, watch for Chihuahuan Raven in agricultural lands; Common Raven is usually found around Black Mesa, farther west, but these species can overlap in range, and they can be difficult to distinguish. Look also for Scaled Quail, Greater Roadrunner, Say's Phoebe, Ash-throated Flycatcher, Horned Lark, Curve-billed Thrasher, Cassin's (sings in spring from the top of shrubby vegetation) and Black-throated Sparrows, and Lark and Lazuli Buntings, and in winter for Ferruginous and Rough-legged Hawks and Sage Thrasher.

Take the west turn toward **Black Mesa State Park,** but where the road turns north toward the park about 4 miles from Okla. 325, go south about a half mile to a large prairie dog town where you should find Burrowing Owl. Then return north to the state park, where Lake Carl Etling, one of the few bodies of water in the area, can attract interesting waterbirds. In spring and summer, look for Cassin's Kingbird here among the more common Western Kingbirds. Several pairs of Vermilion Flycatcher now nest in the park.

From the state park, drive north to Okla. 325, turn east, and in 3 miles turn north on a county road to reach the Cimarron River in less than a mile. Check the cottonwoods along the river for migrants in spring and fall, when you might find Black-throated Gray, Townsend's, or MacGillivray's Warblers or Western Tanager (rare in fall). Ladder-backed Woodpecker is a common resident, and Bullock's Oriole and Lesser Goldfinch nest here. Return to Okla. 325 and continue west. Before the tiny town of Kenton, turn north on a road marked "Colorado"; drive to the parking lot for **Black Mesa Preserve.** Here a one-way hike of 4 miles leads up the slope of an ancient lava flow to the highest point in Oklahoma, 4,973 feet above sea level. Nesting birds in the vicinity include Common Poorwill, Western Scrub-Jay, Pinyon Jay (can be hard to find), Golden Eagle, Prairie Falcon, Black-billed Magpie, Juniper Titmouse, Bushtit, Rock and Canyon Wrens, Rufous-crowned Sparrow, and Canyon Towhee. In winter, the Black Mesa region can host Steller's Jay (rare), Clark's Nutcracker (rare), Mountain Chickadee (uncommon), Mountain Bluebird, and Townsend's Solitaire.

OKLAHOMA | MORE INFORMATION

RARE BIRD ALERT
Statewide 918-669-6646

1 Little River National Wildlife Refuge
(Page 178)
www.fws.gov/refuges
580-584-6211

Roads in the largely undeveloped refuge are primitive in places; check with the office in Broken Bow for a map and travel advice.

2 Beavers Bend Resort Park *(Page 178)*
www.beaversbend.com
580-494-6300

3 Sequoyah National Wildlife Refuge *(Page 179)*
www.fws.gov/refuges
918-773-5252

The refuge offers a 6-mile auto tour route. Another site to explore is just to the southeast: The Arkansas River below the Robert S. Kerr Lock and Dam attracts good numbers of gulls (most will be Ring-billed) from late fall through early spring.

4 Oxley Nature Center
(Page 179)
www.oxleynaturecenter.org
918-669-6644

5 Lake Overholser
(Page 179)
www.okc.gov
405-297-3882

6 Wichita Mountains National Wildlife Refuge *(Page 180)*
wichitamountains.fws.gov
580-429-3221

In spring and summer, ask refuge personnel about productive spots for the endangered Black-capped Vireo.

7 Hackberry Flat Wildlife Management Area *(Page 180)*
580-335-5262

8 Salt Plains National Wildlife Refuge
(Page 181)
saltplains.fws.gov
580-626-4794

The refuge is open Apr.–mid-Oct. On the south side of Okla. 11, about 5 miles west of Okla. 38, walk along the short Sandpiper Trail to see migrant shorebirds along the Salt Fork of the Arkansas River. On the eastern side of the reservoir, explore the area around Great Salt Plains State Park and the dam for waterfowl and Bald Eagle from late fall through early spring.

9 Black Mesa State Park *(Page 182)*
touroklahoma.com
580-426-2222

9 Black Mesa Preserve
(Page 182)
nature.org
918-585-1117

KANSAS

- Eastern breeders and migrants at Weston Bend Bottoms
- Diverse waterbirds at Quivira National Wildlife Refuge
- Western species at Cimarron National Grassland

Geese over Quivira
National Wildlife
Refuge, southeast of
Great Bend

10 Fort Leavenworth, founded in 1827 to protect trade on the Santa Fe Trail, has coincidentally also protected one of the finest tracts of bottomland hardwoods in the Midwest. **Weston Bend Bottoms** attracts a superb variety of migrant songbirds in spring and fall and is also home to an interesting selection of nesting species. Nesting birds include Pileated Woodpecker; Acadian Flycatcher; Wood Thrush; Northern Parula; Yellow-throated, Yellow, and Prothonotary Warblers; American Redstart; Scarlet Tanager; and Rose-breasted Grosbeak. Sedge Wren occasionally nests in grassy marshes in late summer. Great Blue Heron and a few Great Egrets occupy a heronry here.

11 Northeast of Topeka, **Perry Lake** makes a fine year-round birding destination. From fall through spring, drive across the dam and visit **Thompsonville** and **Rock Creek Recreation Areas** to scan for waterfowl, loons, grebes, and Bald Eagle. Below the dam, check the spillway area for wintering gulls, and the nature

trail through the marsh off Spillway Road for waterfowl, herons, and migrant rails. Any of the recreation areas on the east side of the lake—such as **Slough Creek, Longview,** and **Old Military Trail**— can be good for migrant songbirds.

When water levels are down at nearby **Paradise Point,** herons and migrant shorebirds can be common. Where Ferguson Road bends northeast, continue north into **Upper Ferguson Marsh;** you can walk along the dike westward here to see waders, waterfowl, rails, and possibly nesting Sedge Wren. **Lassiter Marsh,** north off Kans. 16, offers good birding for wetlands species along the road through this wildlife area, or you can walk the trail through marsh where Prothonotary Warbler sings in spring and early summer and Least Bittern may nest.

12 Just a few miles from the Missouri state line in east-central Kansas, **Marais des Cygnes Wildlife Area** is known for spring songbird migration, interesting breeding species, winter waterfowl, and, when water levels are right, for migrant shorebirds. The **Unit A** impoundment, on the Marais des Cygnes River, will have geese and ducks from fall through spring and can be good for shorebirds when mudflats are present.

As you approach the settlement of Boicourt, turn north just east of the railroad track. After this road bends west under the rail line you'll pass through woods that are excellent in spring migration. Look for typical deciduous-hardwood nesting species such as Pileated Woodpecker; Yellow-throated Vireo; Acadian Flycatcher; Wood Thrush; Yellow-throated, Black-and-white, Prothonotary, and Kentucky Warblers; Louisiana Waterthrush; and Scarlet Tanager. Soon you'll reach **Unit G** of the wildlife area. A road runs around the perimeter of this impoundment, which can have waders and waterfowl, as well as shorebirds when water levels are low. Here and anywhere in the area, look for resident Wood Duck, Red-shouldered Hawk, Barred Owl, and Red-headed Woodpecker, migrant American White Pelican and Osprey, and wintering Bald Eagle. If you have time, explore other units of the area; note that changing water levels can create habitat for varied waterbirds, and that grassy places can be good for Upland Sandpiper, Scissor-tailed Flycatcher, longspurs, and sparrows in season.

At **La Cygne Lake and Wildlife Area,** check the lake for wintering waterfowl. Just over 2 miles east of US 69, turn south on a county road that leads through grasslands where you might find wintering Rough-legged Hawk, Prairie Falcon, Short-eared Owl, or Lapland Longspur, and migrant Smith's Longspur or Sprague's

Pipit. Upland Sandpiper and Grasshopper Sparrow nest here, and Swainson's Hawk is often seen in migration. This is private land, so bird from the roadside.

13 **Quivira National Wildlife Refuge** is the favorite birding destination of many Kansans. Waterbirds are the main attraction here—nesting, passing through, and wintering in remarkable numbers and variety. Refuge roads make it easy to observe tens of thousands of migrant waterfowl (including occasional Trumpeter and Tundra Swans), flocks of American White Pelican and Sandhill Crane, herons and egrets from spring through fall, and a superb array of migrant shorebirds. Small groups of Whooping Crane may appear, passing through quickly during April on their northward journey, but often lingering in October and November on their way south to the Gulf Coast of Texas.

You should drive as many of Quivira's roads and scan as many of its marshes and impoundments as you have time for. Be sure to check **Little Salt Marsh** just north of refuge headquarters for waterbirds, and stop to walk the wheelchair-accessible **Migrant's Mile** interpretive trail for marsh birds. Quivira's highlight is its 4-mile **Wildlife Drive,** which loops alongside Big Salt Marsh in the northern part of the refuge. Tens of thousands of Sandhill Cranes can appear here in fall, and this is where Whooping Crane is most likely to appear. American and Least Bitterns, White-faced Ibis, King and Virginia Rails, Sora, American Avocet, Wilson's Phalarope, Forster's and Black Terns, and Yellow-headed Blackbird are just a few of the nesting species you might spot, and Black Rail is seen or heard regularly in spring. Look on the flats north of Big Salt Marsh for nesting Snowy Plover and Least Tern.

There's more to Quivira than waterbirds. Breeding birds of grasslands and cottonwood groves include Ring-necked Pheasant, Mississippi Kite, Northern Harrier, Swainson's Hawk, Upland Sandpiper, Western and Eastern Kingbirds, Scissor-tailed Flycatcher, Bell's Vireo, Dickcissel, and Eastern and Western Meadowlarks. Winter visitors can include Bald and Golden Eagles, Short-eared Owl, Ferruginous and Rough-legged Hawks, an occasional Northern Shrike, and Lapland and Chestnut-collared Longspurs.

14 **Wilson Lake** has a history of turning up rare waterbirds, including such oddities as Brown Pelican and Black Skimmer. Diving birds are a specialty here from fall through spring: Pacific Loon is fairly regular, and Yellow-billed Loon has been seen. Horned, Western, and Clark's Grebes are regular migrants, and at times thousands of Common Goldeneye gather on the water, along with good numbers of ducks such as Redhead, Lesser Scaup, and Bufflehead. American White Pelican and Franklin's Gull appear in large numbers in migration, and Bald Eagle frequents the shoreline.

Wilson State Park is a good spot from which to scan the lake, as is **Minooka Park** a few miles west. Long-eared Owl roosts in cedar trees in the state park and elsewhere around the lake in winter, when Mountain Bluebird can also be found. Riparian habitats along the Saline River west of the lake can be good for songbirds. The grasslands around the lake are home to a population of Greater Prairie-Chicken, but it usually takes luck to spot them along the roadsides. Watch for an occasional Rough-legged Hawk or Northern Shrike in the grasslands in winter.

15 The largest tract of publicly owned land in Kansas is the **Cimarron National Grassland.** Nearly 350 species of birds have been seen in this area of sagebrush, prairie, and riparian vegetation bordering about 25 miles of the Cimarron River, including birds of southwestern affinity, winter visitors and migrants from the Rockies, and many wanderers from East and West. In spring, stop at the ranger office in Elkart to ask about visiting the leks, or courtship grounds, of the rare and declining Lesser Prairie-Chicken, a regional specialty.

At the **Cimarron River Picnic Area,** cottonwoods grow along the streambed. Look here for resident Great Horned Owl, Red-headed and Ladder-backed Woodpeckers, and Northern Flicker (mostly Red-shafted, but some showing characteristics of this and the Yellow-shafted form). In spring and summer you'll find Western and Eastern Kingbirds, House Wren, and Bullock's Oriole. Ponds north of the Cimarron River harbor waterbirds.

As you drive through the grassland, other birds to look for from spring through fall include Mountain Plover (rare; try along Kans. 51 west of Kans. 27), Mississippi Kite, Long-billed Curlew, Burrowing Owl (at prairie dog towns), and Cassin's and Lark Sparrows. Year-round, watch for Scaled Quail, Black-billed Magpie, Chihuahuan Raven (rare), Horned Lark, and Curve-billed Thrasher (mostly in summer and scarce; nests in clumps of cholla cactus). In winter, the grassland is home to Ferruginous and Rough-legged Hawks, Golden Eagle, Northern Shrike, and mixed flocks of longspurs, with Lapland abundant and McCown's and Chestnut-collared present in lesser numbers.

KANSAS | MORE INFORMATION

RARE BIRD ALERT
Kansas City 913-342-2473

10 Weston Bend Bottoms
(Page 184)
www.mostateparks.com
816-640-5443

11 Perry Lake *(Page 184)*
www.nwk.usace.army.mil
/perry/perry_home.htm
785-597-5144

Pick up a lake map at the U.S. Army Corps of Engineers office. To see the huge nest of a pair of Bald Eagles, drive to the Slough Creek area and turn east off Ferguson Rd., following the road as it curves south to an overlook on the Slough Creek arm of the lake. The nest can be seen to the east. To reach Paradise Point, turn west from Ferguson Rd. 1.8 mi. north of Kans. 92; to reach Upper Ferguson Marsh, follow Ferguson Rd. where it bends northeast, about 5.5 mi. north of Kans. 92, and continue north; to reach Lassiter Marsh, turn north off Kans. 16 for 1.3 mi. west of Kans. 4.

12 Marais des Cygnes Wildlife Area and **La Cygne Lake and Wildlife Area** *(Page 185)*
maraisdescygnes.fws.gov
913-352-8941
Stop at the headquarters on the west side of US 69, where maps are available at a kiosk.

Then return south on US 69; 0.9 mi. south of Kans. 52 turn west into the area, following the Marais des Cygnes River. To reach La Cygne Lake and Wildlife Area, drive north on US 69 about 6 mi. beyond Kans. 52 and turn east.

13 Quivira National Wildlife Refuge *(Page 186)*
www.fws.gov/quivira
316-486-2393

Open June–Oct.

14 Wilson State Park
(Page 187)
www.kdwp.state.ks.us
/news/state_parks
785-658-2465

Pick up a map at the Corps of Engineers office, and explore other lake access points.

15 Cimarron National Grassland *(Page 187)*
www.fs.fed.us/r2/psicc
620-697-4621

In migration and winter, local birders check trees at the Elkhart cemetery and the shelterbelt across the street and the Tunnerville Work Center for

Red-naped Sapsucker, Western Scrub-Jay, Mountain Chickadee, Red-breasted and Pygmy Nuthatches, Townsend's Solitaire, Canyon Towhee, and other uncommon to rare visitors. Just north of the river, turn west off Kans. 27 and in a mile check the ponds for waterbirds and migrants. Another mile west, visit the Middle Spring Picnic Area for interesting migrants. You may also wish to visit Point of Rocks.

ADDITIONAL SITE

1 Cheyenne Bottoms
www.cheyennebottoms.net
877-427-9299
This 41,000-acre basin is renowned for waders, waterfowl, and shorebirds. A drive through it in spring can turn up shorebirds, grebes, herons, American White Pelican, geese, ducks, gulls, and terns, present in varying numbers throughout the year. (It is a popular hunting area in fall.) Visit the state wildlife area headquarters and the kiosk at N.E. 80th Rd. for a brochure on an auto tour route through adjoining Nature Conservancy property, where Burrowing Owl numbers are on the rise.

NEBRASKA

> * Eastern forest birds at Fontenelle Forest Nature Center
> * Huge flocks of Sandhill Crane on the Platte River in spring
> * Rocky Mountain birds in the Pine Ridge

Some of the nearly half-million Sandhill Cranes that stop to roost on the Platte River in spring migration

16 Nesting birds of eastern deciduous forest reward a visit to **Indian Cave State Park.** This extensive wooded area along the Missouri River is home in spring and summer to American Woodcock; Chuck-will's-widow; Whip-poor-will; Yellow-throated Vireo; Acadian Flycatcher; Wood Thrush; Northern Parula; Yellow-throated, Cerulean, Black-and-white, and Kentucky (in wooded ravines) Warblers; Summer and Scarlet Tanagers; and Rose-breasted Grosbeak. Barred Owl, Red-headed Woodpecker, and Carolina Wren are present all year, and Prothonotary Warbler, near the edge of its range, is found here. **Trail Number 9** in the eastern part of the park is a good all-around bird walk. As might be imagined, Indian Cave makes an excellent destination for migrant songbirds in spring migration.

17 Much the same can be said of **Fontenelle Forest Nature Center,** a 1,400-acre preserve set on a bend in the Missouri River. The scream of Red-shouldered Hawk is heard here at times, along with the slurred whistle of Louisiana Waterthrush beside streams, and the song of Ovenbird. Yellow-throated Warbler nests here, Prothonotary Warbler has bred, and Veery has been

189

heard in summer, though nesting hasn't been confirmed. In addition to deciduous-forest birds, Fontenelle also hosts waders, waterfowl, and other waterbirds in its wetland areas. Look for Pied-billed Grebe, Green Heron, Black-crowned Night-Heron, Wood Duck, and Virginia Rail in ponds and marshes. Sedge Wren has nested here. Songbird migration is good in spring.

18 Mid-March through May, you can see the courtship "dance" of the Greater Prairie-Chicken at **Burchard Lake State Wildlife Management Area.** Circle around the north side of the lake to reach the blind overlooking the "booming ground" on the west side. Scout the area in advance to learn the route, because you must be in the blind before dawn to avoid disturbing the birds (peak activity first two weeks in April). Henslow's Sparrow has nested in the grassland here, where you'll also find Grasshopper Sparrow and Dickcisssel.

19 Each spring, Nebraska's **Platte River** is the site of one of America's most impressive wildlife spectacles. Close to a half-million Sandhill Crane stop in migration to roost in the shallow river, most of them along the stretch from Grand Island to Lexington. The cranes usually begin to arrive in February; the population peaks in March, and the birds are mostly gone by late April. Cranes leave the river each dawn to feed in nearby farm fields and pastures, and return to the river at dusk in wave after wave. Seeing these long-legged birds fly in, giving their loud trumpeting call, their numbers growing until many thousands may be in view at one time, has been described by countless witnesses as an awe-inspiring vision. Occasionally an endangered Whooping Crane, or a small group, will pause here on migration from Canada to Texas, usually in April. During the day, Sandhills feed and rest within 5 miles of the river; driving county roads south of the Platte River between Grand Island and Kearney will bring views of many groups of cranes.

The Platte River cranes have become a significant tourist attraction. The National Audubon Society's **Lillian Annette Rowe Sanctuary** offers crane-viewing from blinds and general advice. Check their feeders for Harris's Sparrow. Farther to the east near Grand Island, **Crane Meadows Nature Center** also provides viewing blinds and towers as well as wildlife displays and public programs, or call the U.S. Fish and Wildlife Service for information on their free tours. The hike-bike trail bridge northeast of **Fort Kearny State Historical Park** is a good vantage point, and there are parking areas and viewing platforms on Platte River bridges south of Alda and Gibbon. Both the Kearney and Grand Island Visitors Bureaus can help with viewing advice and maps.

20 **Rainwater Basin** is one of Nebraska's premier birding areas. This natural lowland hosts staggering numbers of waterfowl in migration, along with a diverse array of migrant shorebirds and nesting marsh birds. At times nearly five million waterfowl may be present in the basin and along the Platte River, including huge numbers of Greater White-fronted, Cackling, and Snow Geese, Mallard, and Northern Pintail, to mention the most numerous of the 25 species of waterfowl that might be seen. Small numbers of Ross's Geese are present in just about every large flock of Snows. More than two dozen species of shorebirds stop to feed in spring, late summer, and fall.

Though there are dozens of publicly owned wetland sites in the region, perhaps the most accessible and productive for birding is **Funk Waterfowl Production Area.** In addition to hosting migrant waterfowl, shorebirds, gulls, and terns, Funk is home to summering birds including Pied-billed and Eared Grebes, American White Pelican, several species of herons, Virginia Rail, Sora, Sedge Wren, Yellow-headed Blackbird, and Great-tailed Grackle. In winter and early spring, a drive through the Rainwater Basin could turn up Rough-legged Hawk, Prairie Falcon, Short-eared Owl, Northern Shrike, Horned Lark, American Tree and Harris's Sparrow, or Lapland Longspur. Bald Eagle is common in winter and early spring, preying on the flocks of waterfowl.

21 Gull-watching is great at **Lakes McConaughy** and **Ogallala** in winter and early spring, when Ogallala may be the only open water for miles around. Huge numbers of gulls may be here, including some uncommon or rare species (especially Thayer's and Glaucous) among the thousands of Ring-billed and Herring; smaller numbers of gulls are present almost year-round. Viewing is easy here from roads, **Lake Ogallala State Recreation Area,** and an observation station set up to allow viewing of the numerous Bald Eagles that are present in winter. Lake Ogallala is also famed for migrant and wintering waterfowl. Birds such as Trumpeter and Tundra Swans; Greater Scaup; Surf, White-winged, and Black Scoters; Long-tailed Duck; and Barrow's Goldeneye show up with varying degrees of regularity among more common species such as Common Merganser. On Lake Ogallala and especially Lake McConaughy, look for migrant loons, grebes, and American White Pelican as well.

The Lake McConaughy and Lake Ogallala area isn't just a winter waterbird destination. Depending on water level, mud-flats attractive to migrant shorebirds may be exposed, and the marshes below the dam are worth exploring for rails and other wetland birds. Driving county roads through grasslands north and east of the dam might turn up a Greater Prairie-Chicken. Ferruginous and Rough-legged Hawks, Mountain Bluebird, and Lapland Longspur might be present from fall into spring. Investigate lake access on the north side of Lake McConaughy, where Piping Plover and Least Tern nest on sandy beaches.

22 **Oliver State Recreation Area** is an excellent spot for migrant songbirds. While waterbirds might be present on Lake Oliver in migration, and shorebirds when mudflats are exposed, it's mostly birds in the riparian vegetation around its shore that attract birders in spring and, especially, in fall. There's good access to recreation sites on the lake's north and east sides. In the scrub and woodland, scarce migrants such as Cassin's Kingbird, Cassin's Vireo, Sage Thrasher, Townsend's and MacGillivray's Warblers, and Western Tanager are among those sought.

23 Northwestern Nebraska's **Pine Ridge** region is in some ways like a bit of the Rocky Mountains extending to the edge of the High Plains. Here forests of ponderosa pine cover rugged sandstone hills, with eroded badland canyons where cotton-wood, ash, and hackberry grow. Birds found here year-round include Golden Eagle, Prairie Falcon, Northern Saw-whet Owl, Pinyon Jay, Pygmy Nuthatch, the white-winged race of Dark-eyed Junco, Red Crossbill, and Pine Siskin, while among the nesting-season species are Common Poorwill, White-throated Swift, Western Wood-Pewee, Plumbeous Vireo, Cordilleran Flycatcher, Say's Phoebe, Violet-green Swallow, Rock Wren, Mountain Bluebird, Yellow-rumped and Black-and-white Warblers, Ovenbird, Western Tanager, Black-headed Grosbeak, and Lazuli Bunting. In winter, Clark's Nutcracker and Townsend's Solitaire sometimes appear. Exploring areas near US 20 will give you a good chance to see many of these species. For example, at **Gilbert Baker Wildlife Management Area**, trails from parking areas lead through deciduous riparian vegetation into pinewoods. **Chadron State Park** is another good birding site. By walking the **Blackhills Overlook Trail** to Overlook Point, you may see Lewis's Woodpecker (scarce here). In spring or summer, drive US 20 west through grasslands to the Wyoming state line, looking for Ferruginous Hawk, Say's Phoebe, and Rock Wren.

NEBRASKA | MORE INFORMATION

RARE BIRD ALERT
Statewide 402-292-5325

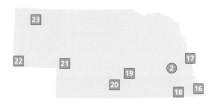

16 Indian Cave SP
(Page 189)
www.ngpc.state.ne.us
402-883-2575
⑤ 🚻 🏃 ⇌ ♿

**17 Fontenelle Forest
Nature Center** *(Page 189)*
www.fontenelleforest.org
402-731-3140
? ⑤ 🚻 🏃 ♿
Nature programs offered year-round; miles of trails include a handicapped-accessible boardwalk.

**18 Burchard Lake State
WMA** *(Page 190)*
www.ngpc.state.ne.us
402-335-2534

**19 Lillian Annette Rowe
Sanctuary** *(Page 190)*
www.rowesanctuary.org
308-468-5282
? 🚻 🏃 ⇌ ♿
Fee; reservations required

**19 Crane Meadows
Nature Center** *(Page 190)*
www.cranemeadows.org
308-382-1820
? ⑤ 🚻 🏃 ♿
Fee; reservations required. U.S. Fish and Wildlife Service (308-236-5015) offers free tours.

**19 Fort Kearny State
Historical Park** *(Page 190)*
www.ngpc.state.ne.us

308-865-5305
? ⑤ 🚻 🏃 ⇌ ♿
Both the Kearney (308-237-3101) and Grand Island (308-382-4400) Visitors Bureaus can help with viewing advice and maps.

20 Rainwater Basin
(Page 191)
www.rwbjv.org
308-865-5310
🏃 ⇌ ♿

**21 Lakes McConaughy
and Ogallala State
Recreation Areas**
(Page 191)
www.ngpc.state.ne.us
308-284-3542
? 🚻 🏃 ⇌ ♿
Stop at the Omaha Beach Recreation Area and the Clear Creek Refuge. Check stands of junipers for Townsend's Solitaire (fall–early spring).

**22 Oliver State Recreation
Area** *(Page 192)*
www.ngpc.state.ne.us
308-436-2383
⑤ 🚻

23 Gilbert Baker WMA
(Page 192)

www.ngpc.state.ne.us
308-665-2924
🚻

Another favorite Pine Ridge birding route is the road through Sowbelly Canyon. Ask local birders for advice about birding along the drive on US 20 to the Wyoming state line and on Henry Rd.

23 Chadron SP *(Page 192)*
www.ngpc.state.ne.us
308-432-6167
⑤ 🍴 🚻 🏃 ⇌ ♿

ADDITIONAL SITE

**2 Branched Oak Lake
State Recreation Area**
www.ngpc.state.ne.us
402-783-3400
⑤ 🍴 🚻 🏃 ♿
From fall through spring, a visit here can turn up varied waterfowl, shorebirds, and gulls. Common Loon is a regular migrant; Red-throated, Pacific, and Yellow-billed have been spotted over the years, along with an impressive list of winter gulls. Thousands of Franklin's Gulls can be found in migration at times. Branched Oak can have excellent migrant shorebirds.

SOUTH DAKOTA

- Eastern birds at Sica Hollow and Newton Hills State Parks
- Waterbirds at Sand Lake and Lacreek refuges
- Highland species in the Black Hills

Rock formations at Badlands National Park, south of Wall

24 The rugged uplands of what is now eastern South Dakota were called Coteau des Prairies by 19th-century French fur traders. Today these "prairie hills" are forested, an anomaly in the midst of rolling grasslands, and **Sica Hollow State Park** has become a favorite destination to find migrant and nesting birds of deciduous woodland. Here in a forest of basswood, ash, oak, elm, and maple, look for Broad-winged Hawk, Ruby-throated Hummingbird (a rare nesting bird in this region), Yellow-bellied Sapsucker, Willow and Least Flycatchers, Yellow-throated Vireo, Veery, Black-and-white Warbler (a scarce breeder in the state), Scarlet Tanager, and Rose-breasted Grosbeak. Wood Thrush has been found nesting in the area, and might be looked for, too.

25 At **Waubay National Wildlife Refuge,** lakes and sloughs host a good variety of waterbirds. Stop at the Spring Lake Overlook for a panoramic view of the area, and then continue to the headquarters. Here a half-mile trail through a wooded area that can be productive for migrant songbirds leads to Hillebrand's Lake and an observation tower. Among the nesting birds at Waubay are several species of ducks; Gray Partridge; Pied-billed, Horned, Red-necked (a few pairs), Eared, and Western Grebes; Double-crested Cormorant; American Bittern; Northern Harrier; Virginia Rail; Sora; Piping Plover (rare and irregular); Willet; Upland Sandpiper; Marbled Godwit; Wilson's Phalarope; Forster's and Black Terns; Western and Eastern Kingbirds; Horned Lark; Tree Swallow; Sedge and Marsh Wrens; Bobolink; and Yellow-headed Blackbird. American White Pelican is a common summering bird, and herons such as Great and Snowy Egrets can appear in summer and fall.

26 Like Waubay, **Sand Lake National Wildlife Refuge** can have hundreds of thousands of Snow Geese in early spring and thousands of Tundra Swans in late October, as well as abundant Canada and Cackling Geese, smaller numbers of Greater White-fronted and Ross's (Sand Lake is the state's best place for this species in fall) Geese, and more than 20 species of dabbling and diving ducks. All the birds listed for Waubay also nest at Sand Lake save Red-necked Grebe. Heronries are home to Great Blue Heron; Great, Snowy, and Cattle Egrets; Black-crowned Night-Heron; and White-faced Ibis. Little Blue Heron is a rare breeder some years. Sand Lake is the most likely place to find nesting Clark's Grebe in South Dakota, though it's rare. Here, as at many places in the region, tens of thousands of Franklin's Gulls sometimes congregate in fall before migrating south.

In addition to wetlands, Sand Lake provides habitat for grassland birds such as Swainson's Hawk; Upland Sandpiper; Short-eared Owl; Clay-colored, Vesper, Swamp, and Grasshopper Sparrows; Chestnut-collared Longspur; and Bobolink. Watch for Bald Eagle roosting in tall cottonwoods or soaring overhead in fall and spring.

27 The huge **Oahe Dam,** on the Missouri River just upstream from Pierre, is one of the state's best places to find gulls from fall through early spring, especially when the outflow may be the only open water around. In migration, Lake Oahe hosts loons, waterfowl, and grebes; Bald Eagle gathers around the lakeshore and along the river below the dam. U.S. Army Corps

of Engineers recreation areas below the dam and on the lakeshore above offer views of the east and west tailraces. Commonly occurring gulls include Franklin's, Bonaparte's, Ring-billed, California, and Herring, while Glaucous is regular, and rarities such as Mew and Thayer's Gulls and Black-legged Kittiwake have appeared.

RING-NECKED PHEASANT

So familiar is the Ring-necked Pheasant over much of the northern and western U.S. (it's South Dakota's state bird) that many people don't realize it's not a native species. Originally from Asia, this game bird was introduced here in the mid-19th century and has thrived in agricultural areas and grassy places. When encountered, it often runs away instead of flying. The male's *kok-cack* call is well known on the plains; rival males fight fiercely when one intrudes on another's territory. ∎

28 South Dakota's **Black Hills** offer birders a chance at a number of high-country birds in forests of aspen, ponderosa pine, and spruce. One of the most popular birding routes in the region is the **Spearfish Canyon Scenic Byway** in **Black Hills National Forest.** (Local traffic is lighter on an early morning visit.)

Some of the species to look for through the canyon area in late spring and summer include Ruffed Grouse, White-throated Swift (common around cliffs), Lewis's Woodpecker (scarce), Red-naped Sapsucker (in aspen and mixed woodland), Western Wood-Pewee, Dusky and Cordilleran Flycatchers, Pinyon Jay, Violet-green Swallow, Canyon Wren, Mountain Bluebird, Veery, MacGillivray's Warbler, Western Tanager, Black-headed Grosbeak, Lazuli Bunting, and Cassin's Finch. American Dipper can be seen along Spearfish Creek, but it's most likely found at Roughlock Falls.

As you ascend through the spruce and pinewoods of the Black Hills, some of the possibilities are Northern Saw-whet Owl, Black-backed Woodpecker (scarce), Plumbeous Vireo, Gray Jay, Red-breasted Nuthatch, Brown Creeper, Golden-crowned and Ruby-crowned Kinglets, Townsend's Solitaire, Swainson's Thrush, Yellow-rumped Warbler, Dark-eyed Junco (the white-winged race), Red Crossbill, and Pine Siskin.

Stop and explore recreation areas along the scenic byway, as well as along Forest Road 222 west of Savoy, such as Timon Campground. If you continue past Cheyenne Crossing, you can turn south to **Hanna Campground,** a good spot for many high-elevation species. American Three-toed Woodpecker is a possibility; it's easiest to find in spring when males are "drumming."

One more note about the Black Hills region: A population

of Virginia's Warbler nests in Boles, Roby, and Redbird Canyons in the southwestern part of the national forest, reached by taking Forest Road 117 north from US 16 at the Wyoming state line. The canyons are located along the first 10 miles from US 16, but continuing north will take you along a beautiful, less-congested drive good for many Black Hills birds.

29 **Badlands National Park** is a place of striking and stark beauty, where weirdly eroded sedimentary rocks rise up from arid grassland. If you can take your eyes off the landscape, simply driving park roads might turn up nesting species such as Sharp-tailed Grouse, Northern Harrier, Swainson's and Ferruginous Hawks, Golden Eagle, Prairie Falcon, Upland Sandpiper, Long-billed Curlew, White-throated Swift, Loggerhead Shrike, Black-billed Magpie, Mountain Bluebird, and Lark Bunting. Exploring roadsides and trails, you could find Say's Phoebe, Bell's Vireo, Rock Wren, and Lark and Grasshopper Sparrows. For varied birding, take a walk along the trails near the **Ben Reifel Visitor Center** at the eastern end of the park. The **Cliff Shelf Nature Trail,** steep but only a half-mile loop, traverses an oasis-like area of vegetation, while the longer **Castle Trail** passes through mixed-grass prairie and badlands formations.

30 A fine assortment of waterbirds is the primary attraction at **Lacreek National Wildlife Refuge.** Lacreek lies within the Sandhills region, a rolling grass-covered duneland area. Extensive marshland brings in thousands of waterfowl to rest and feed in spring and fall, along with flocks of Sandhill Cranes. When water levels expose mudflats, Lacreek can be excellent for viewing migrant shorebirds.

Trumpeter Swan nests at the refuge, and many Trumpeters winter here. Other nesting species include Eared and Western Grebes, American White Pelican, Double-crested Cormorant, American Bittern, Black-crowned Night-Heron, American Avocet, Forster's and Black Terns, and Marsh Wren. Swamp Sparrow breeds here, atypically for this part of the state, and Yellow-headed Blackbird nests alongside Red-winged Blackbird in marshes. Although Western Meadowlark nests in every county in South Dakota, this is the only part of the state where Eastern Meadowlark breeds. Bell's Vireo is common in shrubby thickets, and Ring-necked Pheasant, Sharp-tailed Grouse, Upland Sandpiper, Short-eared Owl, Loggerhead Shrike, and Bobolink are among the grassland nesters. Lacreek has two prairie dog towns where Burrowing Owl is seen frequently.

SOUTH DAKOTA | MORE INFORMATION

RARE BIRD ALERT
Statewide 605-773-6460
Western 605-584-4141

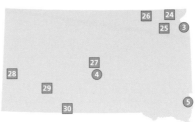

24 Sica Hollow SP
(Page 194)
www.sdgfp.info/Parks
605-448-5701
⑂ ⑂ ⑂ ⑂

25 Waubay NWR
(Page 195)
waubay.fws.gov
605-947-4521
⑂ ⑂ ⑂ ⑂

26 Sand Lake NWR
(Page 195)
sandlake.fws.gov
605-885-6320
⑂ ⑂ ⑂ ⑂ ⑂

The 15-mile auto tour route starts at the refuge head-quarters.

27 Oahe Dam *(Page 195)*
www.nwo.usace.army.mil
605-224-5862
⑂ ⑂ ⑂ ⑂ ⑂

Viewpoints are easily accessed by taking S. Dak. 1804 or S. Dak. 1806 north from US 14 at Pierre.

28 Black Hills National Forest *(Page 196)*
www.fs.fed.us/r2/blackhills
605-673-2251
⑂ ⑂ ⑂ ⑂ ⑂

Explore nearby Black Fox Campground, another favorite birding site.

29 Badlands National Park *(Page 197)*
www.nps.gov/badl
605-433-5361
⑂ ⑂ ⑂ ⑂ ⑂ ⑂ ⑂

Be sure to drive the Sage Creek Rim Road in the western part of the park to Roberts Prairie Dog Town, where you might find Burrowing Owls.

30 Lacreek NWR
(Page 197)
lacreek.fws.gov
605-685-6508
⑂ ⑂ ⑂ ⑂ ⑂

ADDITIONAL SITES

3 Hartford Beach SP
www.sdgfp.info/Parks
605-432-6374
⑂ ⑂ ⑂ ⑂ ⑂

This park is best known as the most likely place in South Dakota to find Pileated Woodpecker. Whip-poor-will occasionally nests here, right on the edge of its range. Set on the shore of Big Stone Lake, Hartford Beach also offers viewing of migrant loons, grebes, and waterfowl.

4 Fort Pierre National Grassland
www.fs.fed.us/r2/nebraska
605-224-5517
Greater Prairie-Chicken is fairly common here. Staffers set up blinds from which you can see males perform their courtship display (call for reservations). April and early May are the peak times for activity at the leks. You might see this large grouse anytime of year by driving gravel roads through the grassland accessed by US 83. With lots of luck, you might find a wintering Gyrfalcon as well, though Rough-legged Hawk is far more likely. Ferruginous Hawk nests on the grassland.

5 Newton Hills SP
www.sdgfp.info/Parks
605-987-2263
⑂ ⑂ ⑂ ⑂ ⑂

This is home to several notable birds of eastern deciduous forest. Walk the horse trail along Sargeant Creek, or take the Woodland Trail farther south. The woodland here is very good for migrant songbirds in spring and fall.

NORTH DAKOTA

- Western birds at Theodore Roosevelt National Park
- Prairie species and waterbirds at Lostwood National Wildlife Refuge
- Excellent diversity in the Devil's Lake region

Bends of the Souris River at J. Clark Salyer National Wildlife Refuge, north of Upham

31 **Sheyenne National Grassland** encompasses an expanse of tallgrass prairie where Grasshopper Sparrow buzzes and Bobolink performs its song flights in spring and summer. The bird most sought here is Greater Prairie-Chicken, a grassland grouse known for the male's courtship "dance," performed on leks to the accompaniment of low "booming" calls. To avoid disturbing the birds, you should be at the site before dawn and remain until the birds disperse, which may be several hours later. Quite often, males congregate at leks in late afternoon, though the exhibition is never as intense as at dawn. Sharp-tailed Grouse also is found.

32 Open water and extensive cattail marshes attract a varied list of waterbirds to the **Long Lake National Wildlife Refuge Complex.** Along the entrance road you'll pass through marshland where several species of ducks, American Bittern, Virginia Rail,

Sora, Sedge Wren, and Yellow-headed Blackbird nest. At a junction, turn north to cross a dike where you can scan the lake. Nesting birds on the refuge include Eared, Western, and Clark's Grebes; White-faced Ibis (numbers vary depending on water level); Willet; Marbled Godwit; American Avocet; Wilson's Phalarope; Franklin's Gull; and Common and Black Terns.

Piping Plover breeds here as well, although lake levels affect its occurrence, and American White Pelican is common from spring through fall.

Several Sharp-tailed Grouse dancing grounds are located in the area; ask at the office about visiting leks in spring. Away from the water, look for nesting Northern Harrier, Western and Eastern Kingbirds, Lark Bunting, Clay-colored and Nelson's Sharp-tailed (scarce) Sparrows, and Chestnut-collared Longspur. In migration, waterfowl and Sandhill Cranes stop at Long Lake. In fall, crane flocks can total 20,000, and Whooping Cranes are rare visitors. In late summer, shorebirds congregate along the shoreline.

BOBOLINK

Each fall, Bobolinks that nest in grasslands across the northern U.S. and Canada gather in flocks and fly thousands of miles to winter in similar habitat in the pampas and rice fields of southern South America. The male Bobolink is known for its "backwards" plumage—with the atypical pattern of lighter colors above and dark below—but by autumn it has molted to brown, buff, and yellow tones that match the female's. The Bobolink's penchant for feeding in rice fields led to its folk name of ricebird. ∎

33 **Garrison Dam,** which creates sprawling Lake Sakakawea, attracts great numbers of gulls to its tailrace waters. Ducks, Double-crested Cormorant, terns, and other waterbirds are present seasonally, but it's the chance for an uncommon or rare gull that brings birders here; the best time is October through December.

Take the road that leads below the dam to the **Garrison Dam National Fish Hatchery.** Just south of the hatchery ponds, a trail leads along the old channel of the Missouri River through a marshy nature area worth checking for migrants. Bald Eagle nests in this area and is seen often, and Northern Goshawk has been seen in fall and winter with some regularity. Wood Duck, Belted Kingfisher, Red-headed Woodpecker, Yellow Warbler, and Yellow-breasted Chat are just a few of the nesting birds here.

34 The Little Missouri River winds through both of the main units of **Theodore Roosevelt National Park,** set in the badlands of western North Dakota. Species such as Warbling and Red-eyed Vireos, White-breasted Nuthatch, American Redstart, Yellow-breasted Chat, Spotted Towhee, Black-headed Grosbeak, Lazuli Bunting, and Bullock's Oriole nest in the riparian zone along the river.

As you drive, watch for Sharp-tailed Grouse; Turkey Vulture; Swainson's and Ferruginous (rare) Hawks; Golden Eagle; Prairie Falcon; Say's Phoebe (nests on rock ledges); Black-billed Magpie; Rock Wren (on bluffs); Mountain Bluebird; and Clay-colored, Field, Vesper, and Lark Sparrows; and Bobolink. Brewer's Sparrow is found occasionally. Look for Burrowing Owl in the prairie dog towns from spring through fall, and listen for Common Poorwill on spring and summer evenings.

35 **Lostwood National Wildlife Refuge** is one of the best places anywhere to find Sprague's Pipit and Baird's Sparrow, which are fairly common here in late spring and summer. As you search the grassland for these target species, you'll likely come across Sharp-tailed Grouse; Northern Harrier; Upland Sandpiper; Marbled Godwit; Clay-colored, Savannah, Grasshopper, and Vesper Sparrows; Chestnut-collared Longspur; and Bobolink. With more effort you could find Le Conte's or Nelson's Sharp-tailed Sparrows, the latter in vegetation on the edges of sloughs.

In this "prairie pothole" region, every dip in the terrain is filled with a small pond hosting nesting ducks and other marsh birds. In Lostwood wetlands find a long list of ducks, Horned and Eared Grebes, American Bittern (scarce), Virginia Rail, Sora, Piping Plover (on alkaline lakeshores), American Avocet, Willet, Wilson's Phalarope, Black Tern, Sedge (uncommon) and Marsh Wrens, and Yellow-headed Blackbird. Other breeders include Long-eared and Short-eared Owls (both irregular in occurrence), Willow and Least Flycatchers (in aspen groves), Warbling Vireo (also in aspen), Black-billed Magpie, and Baltimore Oriole. Migrant waterfowl and shorebirds are abundant, as are great numbers of migrant Sandhill Cranes, peaking in early April and from late September to mid-October.

36 **J. Clark Salyer National Wildlife Refuge** hosts many of the same species noted for Lostwood, including an impressive list of breeding waterbirds on its marshy impoundments. On the 5-mile **Grassland Trail,** you can find Sharp-tailed Grouse (lek viewing is offered), several species of sparrows including Baird's and Le Conte's, and Chestnut-collared Longspur. Long-eared Owl has nested near the headquarters, and Ruffed Grouse nests at Salyer. In fall there can be more than 500,000 waterfowl here, with more than half that number Snow Geese. Like Lostwood, Salyer has flocks of migrant Sandhill Crane in spring and fall.

37 The aspen, birch, oak, and elm woodland at **Wakopa Wildlife Management Area** is known for diverse nesting birds. Look for Broad-winged Hawk, Ruffed Grouse, Ruby-throated Hummingbird, Least and Great Crested Flycatchers, Yellow-throated and Warbling Vireos, Mountain Bluebird (uncommon), Veery, Gray Catbird, Cedar Waxwing, Chestnut-sided and Mourning Warblers, American Redstart, Ovenbird, Northern Waterthrush, Rose-breasted Grosbeak, and Baltimore Oriole. White-throated Sparrow, a species with a very restricted range in the state, might be found here; it's a regular breeder at the nearby **International Peace Garden** at the Canadian border.

38 The region around **Devil's Lake** makes a fine birding destination, though changing water levels affect the area's potential. Still, Devil's Lake is one of the best areas in the state for waders and shorebirds. Great, Snowy, and Cattle Egrets and Black-crowned Night-Heron breed, and the rare Little Blue Heron may nest. Red-necked, Eared, Western, and possibly Clark's Grebes breed. It is a nesting place for Bald Eagle.

Nearby **Grahams Island State Park** can be good for songbirds in migration and offers lake viewing for waterfowl, herons, shorebirds, gulls, and terns. **Sullys Hill National Game Preserve** has more waterbird viewing at Sweetwater Lake, and the hardwood forest is home to a good variety of nesting birds, including Broad-winged Hawk (Red-shouldered has been seen here), Ruby-throated Hummingbird, Yellow-throated and Warbling Vireos, Black-and-white Warbler, American Redstart, Northern Waterthrush, Eastern Towhee, and Baltimore Oriole.

39 Eastern deciduous birds highlight a nesting-season visit to **Icelandic State Park.** Within the park, the **Gunlogson Nature Preserve** is a favorite. Look here for Ruffed Grouse, Wild Turkey, American Woodcock, Black-billed Cuckoo, Barred Owl (occasional), Ruby-throated Hummingbird, Pileated Woodpecker, Yellow-throated Vireo, Veery, Black-and-white and Mourning Warblers, American Redstart, Northern Waterthrush, Scarlet Tanager, and Rose-breasted Grosbeak. This is an excellent spot for migrant songbirds in spring and fall, and it's one of the places birders hope to find Gray Jay and Northern Hawk Owl in winter, though these species are rare finds in the state.

NORTH DAKOTA | MORE INFORMATION

RARE BIRD ALERT
Statewide 701-355-8554

31 Sheyenne National Grassland *(Page 199)*
www.fs.fed.us/r1
701-683-4342
🚶

32 Long Lake National Wildlife Refuge Complex
(Page 199)
longlake.fws.gov
701-387-4397
🚻🌊🚻

33 Garrison Dam National Fish Hatchery
(Page 200)
www.r6.fws.gov
701-654-7451
❓🚻🚶🚻

34 Theodore Roosevelt National Park *(Page 200)*
www.nps.gov/thro
701-623-4466
❓💲🚻🚶🌊🚻

The South Unit stretches along I-94 near Medora; the North Unit is located on US 85 about 50 miles north.

35 Lostwood National Wildlife Refuge *(Page 201)*
lostwood.fws.gov
701-848-2722
🚻🚶🌊🚻

Auto tour route open May–Sept. The refuge offers a blind for viewing Sharp-tailed Grouse's courtship leks.

36 J. Clark Salyer National Wildlife Refuge *(Page 201)*
www.fws.gov/jclarksalyer
701-768-2548
❓🚻🌊🚻

22-mile auto tour route, 13-mile canoe trail

37 Wakopa Wildlife Management Area
(Page 202)
www.state.nd.us/gnf
701-662-3617
🚻🚶🌊🚻

38 Grahams Island State Park *(Page 202)*
www.ndparks.com
701-766-4015
💲🍴🚻🚶🚻

38 Sullys Hill National Game Preserve *(Page 202)*
www.fws.gov/sullyshill
701-766-4272
❓💲🚻🚶🌊🚻

39 Icelandic State Park
(Page 202)
www.ndparks.com
701-265-4561
❓💲🚻🚶🌊🚻

ADDITIONAL SITES

6 Oak Grove Park
www.fargoparks.com
701-241-1350
❓🚻🚶🚻

In spring and fall, look for migrants in the cottonwoods and other riparian vegetation along the floodplain. Explore trails along the river for migrant flycatchers, vireos, thrushes, and warblers. The area across from El Zagal golf course is often quite productive. (At times in spring, high water on the Red River may limit access.)

7 Big Gumbo
www.bowmannd.com
701-523-5880
Several special species nest in this area, a sagebrush prairie landscape. From Marmarth, take Camp Crook Road, which parallels the river. Bird along this route or on side roads, watching for Ferruginous Hawk, Golden Eagle, Sage Grouse, Long-billed Curlew, Loggerhead Shrike, Horned Lark, Brewer's Sparrow, Lark Bunting, and Chestnut-collared Longspur.

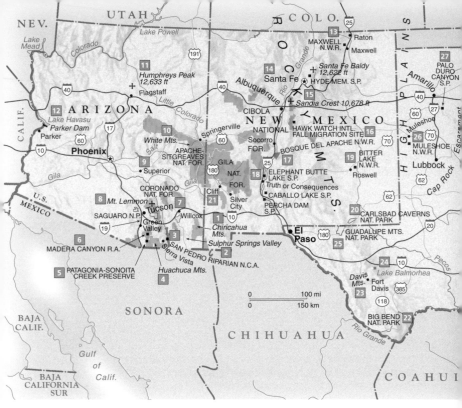

SOUTHWEST

- Arizona
- New Mexico
- Western Texas

THE TYPICAL TRAVELER IS LIKELY TO VISUALIZE THE southwestern deserts through a wide-angle lens: broad panoramas of arid terrain covered in spined cactus and mesquite, with rugged hills on the horizon, all seen in harsh midday light. The birder's image is more tightly cropped: a dry wash in the soft light of a cool morning, with the calls of wrens, thrashers, and sparrows against the crunch of sand underfoot.

Birders know that the Southwest has far more than deserts. Cottonwood-lined streams create oases where Gray Hawk and Green Kingfisher nest. Mountains near the Mexican border host regional specialties such as Elegant Trogon and Red-faced Warbler, in lush canyons shaded by oaks and junipers. High country is home to Blue Grouse, American Three-toed Woodpecker, Clark's Nutcracker, and Gray Jay, resident in forests of Douglas-fir, spruce, and aspen. Refuges and reservoirs shelter waders, waterfowl, and shorebirds.

The Southwest has two of America's finest birding locales. Southeastern Arizona ranks with the nation's best birding

destinations. Its "sky islands"—mountain ranges in a sea of desert—and riparian areas such as the San Pedro River shelter great diversity in a small area.

Another famed birding destination is Texas' Big Bend National Park. Its stark desert contrasts with green riparian areas and the striking Chisos Mountains. The tiny Colima Warbler lives here and only here in the U.S., rewarding hikers who climb to the oak woods where it sings its trilling song in spring and early summer.

Also visit New Mexico's southwestern corner for many of the same specialties found in Arizona, and travel to Bosque del Apache National Wildlife Refuge for remarkable concentrations of Sandhill Crane. The Texas Hill Country offers many western birds for Eastern visitors, including the endangered Golden-cheeked Warbler, which nests only in its oak-juniper woods. ■

Rose-throated Becard

SPECIAL BIRDS OF THE SOUTHWEST

Neotropic Cormorant	Violet-crowned Hummingbird	Brown-crested Flycatcher	Olive Warbler
Black-bellied Whistling-Duck	Blue-throated Hummingbird	Sulphur-bellied Flycatcher	Lucy's Warbler
Gray Hawk	Magnificent Hummingbird	Tropical Kingbird	Grace's Warbler
Common Black-Hawk	Lucifer Hummingbird	Thick-billed Kingbird	Red-faced Warbler
Harris's Hawk	Elegant Trogon	Rose-throated Becard	Painted Redstart
Zone-tailed Hawk	Green Kingfisher	Black-capped Vireo	Hepatic Tanager
Scaled Quail	Gila Woodpecker	Gray Vireo	Abert's Towhee
Montezuma Quail	Arizona Woodpecker	Mexican Jay	Rufous-winged Sparrow
Mountain Plover	Northern Beardless-Tyrannulet	Cave Swallow	Cassin's Sparrow
Whiskered Screech-Owl	Greater Pewee	Bridled Titmouse	Botteri's Sparrow
Elf Owl	Buff-breasted Flycatcher	Verdin	Yellow-eyed Junco
Spotted Owl	Vermilion Flycatcher	Black-tailed Gnatcatcher	McCown's Longspur
Broad-billed Hummingbird	Dusky-capped Flycatcher	Bendire's Thrasher	Pyrrhuloxia
		Crissal Thrasher	Varied Bunting
		Phainopepla	Bronzed Cowbird

ARIZONA

- Highland birds in the Chiricahua and Santa Rita Mountains
- Riparian species along the San Pedro River and Sonoita Creek
- Waterbirds in the Lake Havasu area

Blue sky over Cave Creek Canyon, Arizona

A glance at a map shows why southeastern Arizona ranks as a top birding destination: Notable birds, both regular breeders and strays, can be expected this close to the Mexican frontier. But you need a three-dimensional view truly to understand the region's allure. Then you see how mountains rise abruptly from the desert, creating a wide range of habitats in a relatively small area, home to equally diverse bird life.

1 The **Chiricahua Mountains** are on every list of the country's best birding sites. From US 80 just north of Rodeo, New Mexico, drive west on Portal Road. Just west of the hamlet of Portal, bear southwest toward **Cave Creek Canyon** on

Forest Road 42. At the **Coronado National Forest** station, check the hummingbird feeders. Along the road and inthe campgrounds ahead, look for breeding birds including the elusive Montezuma Quail; Acorn, Ladder-backed, and Arizona Woodpeckers; Dusky-capped and Brown-crested Flycatchers; Plumbeous Vireo; Mexican Jay; Virginia's Warbler; Black-headed and Blue Grosbeaks; and Bullock's and Scott's Orioles.

Turn left into the **South Fork Picnic Area,** a legendary birding locale. In late spring and summer find the Elegant Trogon, a regional specialty. Find Peregrine Falcon; Band-tailed Pigeon; Cordilleran and Sulphur-bellied Flycatchers; Hutton's Vireo; Bridled Titmouse; Black-throated Gray, Grace's, and Red-faced Warblers; Painted Redstart; and Hepatic Tanager.

Back on the main road; ascend the Chiricahuas on a twisting road to Onion Saddle; keep left (south) here and continue to **Rustler Park.** At these heights, nesting birds include Northern Goshawk (rare), Northern Pygmy-Owl, Greater Pewee, Steller's Jay, Violet-green Swallow, Mexican Chickadee (this is the best spot for this species), Pygmy Nuthatch, Olive and Grace's Warblers, Western Tanager, and Yellow-eyed Junco.

2 To the west of the Chiricahuas, the **Sulphur Springs Valley** is an excellent winter birding destination. Here are great numbers of wintering Sandhill Crane—often more than 10,000, some years twice that—and raptors. Waterfowl and shorebirds are seen seasonally on shallow lakes that form in the flat basin; in winter you'll find large mixed flocks of sparrows (Brewer's, Vesper, and White-crowned are the dominant species) and Lark Bunting. To reach one crane-viewing site, drive east from Willcox on Ariz. 186. Turn south on Kansas Settlement Road and drive to **Willcox Playa.** To reach another, begin in Elfrida, 25 miles north of Douglas. Take Central Highway 6 miles south to Davis Road, drive west a mile, then go south on Coffman Road to **Whitewater Draw Wildlife Area.** At either site, cranes gather each night and leave in the morning to feed in surrounding fields. Watch, too, for Northern Harrier; Bald and Golden Eagles; and Harris's, Red-tailed, and Ferruginous Hawks. Also look for resident Scaled Quail and Crissal and Bendire's Thrashers.

3 The **San Pedro Riparian National Conservation Area** stretches 40 miles along the San Pedro River, running north from the Mexican border, east of Sierra Vista. **San Pedro House,** 7 miles east of Sierra Vista on US 90, is the area's visitor center, and the site of a hummingbird-banding station in spring and fall. Trails from San Pedro House provide excellent birding in spring and summer: See Gambel's Quail, Gray Hawk, Yellow-billed Cuckoo, Vermilion Flycatcher, Verdin, Crissal Thrasher, Lucy's Warbler, Yellow-breasted Chat, Summer Tanager, Abert's Towhee, and Pyrrhuloxia. Find tiny Green Kingfisher (rare) at **Kingfisher Pond,** south of San Pedro House, and Tropical Kingbird, of localized distribution in Arizona. In winter check the San Pedro House feeders; the nearby scrub is full of sparrows and Green-tailed Towhees.

ELEGANT TROGON

Trogons compose a colorful family of mostly tropical species, including Resplendent Quetzal of Central America, one of the world's most spectacular birds. The Elegant Trogon is one of the most sought-after specialties of southeastern Arizona. Its hoarse co–ah call is heard in spring and early summer in Cave Creek and Madera Canyons, among other wooded riparian sites. The species is much rarer in southwestern New Mexico. Its larger relative the Eared Quetzal is found only rarely in southeastern Arizona mountains. ∎

4 Just west of Sierra Vista, the **Huachuca Mountains** are another celebrated birding site. Put the Nature Conservancy's **Ramsey Canyon Preserve** high on your list, but call for reservations first, as parking is limited. The hummingbird feeders are busy here, and a trail up the canyon through oaks and junipers offers sight of many birds listed for the Chiricahuas, including Elegant Trogon, Acorn and Arizona Woodpeckers, Sulphur-bellied Flycatcher, Mexican Jay, and Painted Redstart. Eared Quetzal, a larger relative of the Elegant Trogon, rarely seen north of Mexico, is an occasional late summer, fall, or winter visitor above Ramsey Canyon.

Nearby **Fort Huachuca** is a military base that allows birders to explore its birdy highlands. Inside the fort's main gate, take the road to Garden Canyon (check for Montezuma Quail). The best known birding areas lie beyond. **Scheelite Canyon,** less than a mile past the upper picnic area, has long been home to a pair of Spotted Owl, regularly seen along the trail leading up from the road; take care not to disturb them. Continue up the road to **Sawmill Canyon.** Here you may find Elegant Trogon; Greater Pewee; Buff-breasted Flycatcher; Olive, Grace's, and Red-faced Warblers; Painted Redstart; and Yellow-eyed Junco. In late summer, see flocks of migrant warblers.

5 Part of pretty Sonoita Creek, which flows past the town of Patagonia, is protected in the Nature Conservancy's **Patagonia-Sonoita Creek Preserve,** reached by driving north from

Ariz. 82 on Fourth Avenue. Turn southwest at Pennsylvania Avenue; after crossing the creek, continue to the preserve entrance. Along the trails here in spring and summer you may find nesting birds including Gray Hawk, Yellow-billed Cuckoo, Bell's Vireo, Northern Beardless-Tyrannulet, Vermilion and Brown-crested Flycatchers, Black Phoebe, Bridled Titmouse, Curve-billed Thrasher, Lucy's Warbler, and Summer Tanager—a few highlights. In winter the sanctuary may be quiet, but it hosts Hammond's and Dusky Flycatchers, Green-tailed Towhee, and possibly a Green Kingfisher.

About 4 miles southwest of Patagonia on Ariz. 82 lies a picnic area birders call the **Patagonia roadside rest area.** In spring and summer, this is usually the best spot in the United States to find Rose-throated Becard, a flycatcher relative that is very rare and local north of Mexico. The birds build large hanging nests in sycamores along Sonoita Creek, across the highway. (Obey the "No Trespassing" signs here.) Other birds in the area include Thick-billed Kingbird, Canyon and Rock Wrens, and Rufous-crowned Sparrow.

A few miles farther southwest on Ariz. 82, turn north at the entrance to **Patagonia Lake State Park.** Drive through the campground to the upper end of the lake, the start of the **Sonoita Creek Trail.** The park is best known for Neotropic and Double-crested Cormorants year-round. In winter, several species of grebes and ducks, including Common Merganser, may be present. The trail leads through mesquite scrub and riparian areas good in winter for Hammond's and Dusky (riparian), Gray (mesquite), and Ash-throated (mesquite) Flycatchers, and for typical lowland birds all year. Nutting's Flycatcher and Black-capped Gnatcatcher are two rarities that have been found here.

6 Southeast of Green Valley, **Madera Canyon Recreation Area** in the Santa Rita Mountains offers the chance to see many regional specialties. Madera Canyon Road bends south from White House Canyon Road. Within the first mile you'll cross two bridges over usually dry creek beds, or washes. Walking the second of these, Florida Wash, you can find typical desert breeding species including Gambel's Quail, Greater Roadrunner, Bell's Vireo, Verdin, Cactus Wren, Black-tailed Gnatcatcher, Curve-billed and Crissal Thrashers, Phainopepla, Rufous-winged and Black-throated Sparrows, Pyrrhuloxia, and Varied Bunting. In grassland farther along the road, the look-alike Cassin's and Botteri's Sparrows sing after midsummer rains renew the vegetation.

In the woods of the lower canyon, check trails for Acorn and Arizona Woodpeckers, Sulphur-bellied Flycatcher, Plumbeous and Hutton's Vireos, Mexican Jay, Bushtit, Hepatic Tanager, Black-headed Grosbeak, and Bronzed Cowbird. Feeders at the lodge offer fabulous hummingbird-watching. Madera Canyon is known for its owls: Find

Western Screech-Owl in the lower canyon, Whiskered Screech-Owl in the oaks of the middle canyon, and Flammulated Owl along trails higher up, past the end of the road. Tiny Elf Owl nests in telephone poles near the old lodge site. At the end of Madera Canyon Road, take trails up toward 7,600-foot Josephine Saddle and 9,453-foot Mount Wrightson. On the ascent see Elegant Trogon; Greater Pewee; Cordilleran Flycatcher; Steller's Jay; Pygmy Nuthatch; Black-throated Gray, Grace's, and Red-faced Warblers; Western Tanager; and Yellow-eyed Junco.

Giant saguaro cactus in Saguaro National Park, near Tucson

7 Find good desert and mountain birding just outside the Tucson city center. To the west, **Arizona-Sonora Desert Museum** provides an excellent introduction to both bird life and the overall environment of this region. Part zoo and part botanic garden, the museum hosts many wild birds on its extensive grounds, from Gambel's Quail scuttling through the scrub to Cactus Wren singing its chugging song to Gila Woodpecker on the feeders. To reach the museum, take Speedway Boulevard west from I-19 to Gates Pass Road and Kinney Road (the route is well marked). After visiting here, continue northwest on Kinney Road to the **Tucson Mountain District** of **Saguaro National Park** for more desert birding. Birding in the desert is best early in the morning or late in the evening. Gila Woodpecker and Gilded Flicker excavate holes in the giant saguaros, and Elf Owl roosts in old cavities.

8 In northeastern Tucson, following Tanque Verde Road east from Kolb Road brings you to the Catalina Highway, which leads uphill 30 miles to the top of 9,157-foot **Mount Lemmon,** part of **Coronado National Forest.** Driving this road takes you from desert, with Gila Woodpecker and Phainopepla, through middle elevations, with Acorn

Woodpecker and Black-throated Gray Warbler, to pine and Douglas-fir highlands, with Hairy Woodpecker and Mountain Chickadee. You won't find Elegant Trogon in these Santa Catalina Mountains, but looking in the proper habitat will turn up other regional specialties such as Zone-tailed Hawk; Magnificent Hummingbird; Arizona Woodpecker; Greater Pewee; Dusky-capped Flycatcher; Mexican Jay; Bridled Titmouse; Pygmy Nuthatch; Western Bluebird; Olive, Grace's, and Red-faced Warblers; Painted Redstart; and Yellow-eyed Junco. Check campgrounds and recreation areas as you drive up Mount Lemmon to see the widest range of species. At overlooks, you may see a Peregrine Falcon, White-throated Swift, or Common Raven sailing along.

9 On US 60 near Superior, about 50 miles east of Phoenix, the **Boyce Thompson Southwestern Arboretum** displays plants from deserts and arid areas around the world. It's a great place to get excellent looks at typical desert species, and the varied plantings attract interesting migrants (often including eastern vagrants) and winter residents. Look here for White-winged and Inca Doves, Gila and Ladder-backed Woodpeckers, Hutton's Vireo, Rock and Canyon Wrens, Curve-billed Thrasher, Canyon and Abert's Towhees, Northern Cardinal, and Pyrrhuloxia. Check **Ayer Lake** for occasional waterbirds such as Sora or Common Moorhen. Hummingbirds are attracted to all sorts of blooms; look for the beautiful little Costa's in spring and summer.

10 The **White Mountains** of east-central Arizona offer a chance to see montane species (some of which usually have the adjective "elusive" before their names) as well as lower elevation birds. From Eagar, just south of Springerville, drive 5 miles west on Ariz. 260, then south toward the South Fork Campground in the **Apache-Sitgreaves National Forest** (closed Dec.-April). Look for Western Scrub-Jay, Pinyon Jay, and Mountain Bluebird along the road, and for Gray Catbird in riparian areas along the Little Colorado River, which the road crosses in 2 miles. American Dipper nests by the river.

Return to Ariz. 260 and drive west about 12 miles to Ariz. 273; turn south and go 4 miles to the turn to Sunrise Peak ski area and campground. The forest here, on the **White Mountain Apache Reservation,** is home to Blue Grouse, Williamson's and Red-naped Sapsuckers, American Three-toed Woodpecker, Cordilleran Flycatcher, Gray Jay, Clark's Nutcracker,

Mountain Chickadee, Red-breasted and Pygmy Nuthatches, Brown Creeper, Golden-crowned Kinglet, Townsend's Solitaire, Virginia's and Grace's Warblers, Western Tanager, and Pine Grosbeak (rare). At night, listen for the hollow hoots of Flammulated Owl. To find another good spot, continue south on Ariz. 273 about 5 miles to a forest road on the west (close to the Sheep Crossing Campground), leading to the trail up 11,590-foot **Mount Baldy.** Only the intrepid will hike to the top, but the trail, along the West Fork Little Colorado River, offers fine birding.

HUMMINGBIRD HAVEN

In the United States, southeastern Arizona is the number one hummingbird hot spot. At least a dozen species can be found here at times. The best places to look are feeders in such hummer hangouts as Cave Creek, Ramsey, and Madera Canyons, and in Patagonia. While brilliantly colored males are readily identifiable, females can be a challenge. Fortunately, birds at feeders often return regularly, allowing close observation of characteristics such as bill length and shape, tail color, and call notes. The greatest variety of species is present in late summer. ■

11 Quite naturally, high-country birds are also the attraction at **Humphreys Peak,** at 12,633 feet Arizona's tallest mountain and the high point on the rim of an ancient volcano now forming the San Francisco Mountains. From Flagstaff, drive northwest about 7 miles to well-marked Snow Bowl Road, which leads to the ski area. A chair-lift operating in summer provides easy access to the slopes of 12,356-foot **Agassiz Peak,** and a hiking trail leads to the top of Humphreys. Along the road and around the ski area you may find Flammulated Owl, Williamson's and Red-naped Sapsuckers, Dusky Flycatcher, Clark's Nutcracker, Mountain Chickadee, Hermit Thrush, Dark-eyed Junco, and many of the other species listed above for the White Mountains.

12 Although most birders think first of Arizona's deserts and mountains, some of its best rarities have come from along the Colorado River, especially from around Parker Dam and **Lake Havasu.** Fall and winter are the best times to bird this area. From Parker, drive north 19 miles on Ariz. 95 to the dam, checking the river for ducks and other waterbirds. Barrow's Goldeneye is seen regularly in winter in the river below the dam, and gulls congregate at the dam itself. Follow Ariz. 95 north and scan the huge lake for geese, ducks, loons (Common is most frequent, but Red-throated, Pacific, and Yellow-billed have been seen), and grebes (Horned is sometimes found along with Eared, Western, and Clark's).

ARIZONA | MORE INFORMATION

RARE BIRD ALERT
Phoenix 602-832-8745
Tucson 520-798-1005

1 Coronado National Forest *(Page 207)*
www.fs.fed.us/r3/coronado
520-364-3468
⬛⬛⬛⬛

2 Sulphur Springs Valley *(Page 207)*
www.explorecochise.com
800-862-5273

3 San Pedro Riparian National Conservation Area *(Page 207)*
www.blm.gov/nlcs
520-458-3559
⬛⬛⬛⬛⬛⬛
See San Pedro House; Kingfisher Pond.

4 Ramsey Canyon Preserve *(Page 208)*
www.nature.org
520-378-2785
⬛⬛⬛⬛
Also offers a bed-and-breakfast and naturalist-led field trips.

4 Fort Huachuca *(Page 208)*
www.army.mil
520-533-7083
⬛⬛⬛

5 Patagonia-Sonoita Creek Preserve *(Page 208)*
www.nature.org
520-622-3861

Patagonia Lake State Park *(Page 209)*
www.pr.state.az.us
520-287-6965
⬛⬛⬛⬛
Birding boat tours on Sat. a.m., weather permitting; hike Sonoita Creek Trail.

Madera Canyon Recreation Area *(Page 209)*
www.fs.fed.us/r3/coronado
520-281-2296
⬛⬛⬛⬛⬛⬛

Arizona-Sonora Desert Museum *(Page 210)*
www.desertmuseum.org
520-883-2702
⬛⬛⬛⬛⬛⬛

Saguaro National Park *(Page 210)*
www.nps.gov/sagu
520-733-5158
⬛⬛⬛⬛⬛

Coronado National Forest *(Page 210)*
www.fs.fed.us/r3/coronado
520-749-8700
⬛⬛⬛⬛⬛⬛

9 Boyce Thompson Southwestern Arboretum *(Page 211)*
arboretum.ag.arizona.edu
520-689-2811
⬛⬛⬛⬛⬛⬛

10 Apache-Sitgreaves National Forest *(Page 212)*
www.fs.fed.us/r3/asnf
520-333-4301
⬛⬛

11 Humphreys Peak *(Page 212)*
www.fs.fed.us/r3/coconino
928-527-3600

12 Lake Havasu *(Page 212)*
www.golakehavasu.com
928-453-3444

NEW MEXICO

- Mountain species on Sandia Crest
- Waterfowl and Sandhill Crane at Bosque del Apache National Wildlife Refuge
- Southwestern specialties in the Gila National Forest

Sandia Crest, a popular birding location for mountain species northeast of Albuquerque

13 Travelers on I-25 in northeastern New Mexico can find good birding just minutes from the interstate at **Maxwell National Wildlife Refuge,** noted for migrant waterfowl, winter raptors, and some interesting breeding species. From Maxwell, drive north less than a mile on N. Mex. 445, turn west on N. Mex. 505, and drive 2.5 miles to the refuge entrance.

The three main lakes here can host more than 90,000 waterfowl at the peak of fall migration. Among the most common are Snow, Cackling, and Canada Geese; Gadwall; Mallard; Northern Pintail; Bufflehead; Common Goldeneye; and Common Merganser. Most years, Canada Goose, Gadwall, Mallard, and Blue-winged and Cinnamon Teals remain to nest, along with Pied-billed, Eared, and Western Grebes; American Avocet; and Wilson's Phalarope. In migration and in winter, look for raptors including Bald Eagle and Rough-legged Hawk, along with occasional Ferruginous Hawk, Golden Eagle, and Prairie Falcon. Northern Harrier and Swainson's and Red-tailed Hawks nest in the area.

In summer, practice your observation skills on look-alike Cassin's and Western Kingbirds; the Eastern Kingbirds here are much easier to identify. You might see the long-legged little Burrowing Owl nesting, along with Vesper, Savannah, and Grasshopper Sparrows; Blue Grosbeak; and Yellow-headed Blackbird. In winter, American Tree Sparrow is common.

14 Many high-country birds extend their ranges south into New Mexico along the Rocky Mountains, and roads to ski areas near Santa Fe and Albuquerque provide easy access to montane habitat. If you're in Santa Fe, stop at the **Randall Davey Audubon Center** at the end of Upper Canyon Road for advice. See Black-chinned and Broad-tailed Hummingbirds (not in winter), Steller's Jay (winter), Western Scrub-Jay, Black-billed Magpie, Juniper Titmouse, and Spotted and Canyon Towhees.

Proceed up **Santa Fe Scenic Byway** (N. Mex. 475) toward the Santa Fe Ski Area. Stop at **Hyde Memorial State Park** to look for Steller's Jay, Mountain Chickadee, Red-breasted and Pygmy Nuthatches, Brown Creeper, and Western Tanager. As the road climbs, watch for a parking area at **Aspen Vista,** where a hiking trail makes for easy walking. Clark's Nutcracker gives its harsh *kra-a-a* call, and a Blue Grouse may appear. The road ends at the ski area parking lot, and the **Windsor Trail** leads to 12,622-foot Santa Fe Baldy. Williamson's Sapsucker, American Three-toed Woodpecker, Gray Jay, Ruby-crowned Kinglet, Townsend's Solitaire, Pine Grosbeak, Red Crossbill, and Pine Siskin are among the birds you'll see on the way.

15 Look for many of these montane species on the way up to 10,678-foot **Sandia Crest**, northeast of Albuquerque. Drive east on I-40, north on N. Mex. 14, then northwest on N. Mex. 536, or Sandia Crest Byway, up into the Sandia Mountains. In **Cibola National Forest**, listen for Black-headed Grosbeak at Sulphur Canyon picnic area, as well as the fluting of Hermit Thrush. Other nesting species you'll find as you ascend include Band-tailed Pigeon, White-throated Swift, Red-naped Sapsucker, Dusky and Cordilleran Flycatchers and Virginia's and Grace's Warblers. In winter, all three species of rosy-finches may be found around the summit parking lot. Back down in Albuquerque, the Rio Grande creates a narrow green oasis along the city's west side. Set in a riparian forest of cottonwoods and willows, the **Rio Grande Nature Center State Park** offers fine birding just minutes from I-40. Take Rio Grande Boulevard north from I-40 and turn left on Candelaria Road.

GREATER ROADRUNNER

Its generic name, *Geococcyx*, means "ground cuckoo," and that's just what the Greater Roadrunner is: a large cuckoo that flies only rarely and for short distances, preferring to stay on terra firma. Common throughout much of the Southwest, the Greater Roadrunner often stops and seems to inspect humans who are watching it, expressively raising and lowering its bushy crest. A roadrunner's legs are thick and strong, and this bird, which is carnivorous, uses its fabled speed to catch snakes, lizards, insects, small birds, and rodents. ■

Breeding birds you'll see include Gambel's Quail, Western Screech-Owl, Black-chinned Hummingbird, Western Wood-Pewee, Black and Say's Phoebes, Ash-throated Flycatcher, Bewick's Wren, Black-capped Chickadee, Blue Grosbeak, Bullock's Oriole, and Lesser Goldfinch. A pond here is home to Wood Duck, Pied-billed Grebe, Great Blue Heron, Black-crowned Night-Heron, and other waterbirds. In spring and fall, the Rio Grande *bosque* (Spanish for "woodland") is a corridor for migratory birds; vagrant eastern species have been seen. Check the nature center feeders in fall and winter.

16 Visitors are welcome at the **Hawk Watch International Fall Migration Site** in the Manzano Mountains southeast of Albuquerque. Here southbound migrant raptors fly low over the watch site on Capilla Peak. Drive west from N. Mex. 56 in Manzano, toward Capilla Peak Campground. Near the fire tower by the campground, walk west on the **Gavilan Trail** a half mile to the site. Most years, some 5,000 hawks pass this point in September and October, and 1998 saw more than 9,000! Peak migration comes in late September and early October, with Sharp-shinned, Cooper's, and Red-tailed Hawks, and American Kestrel the most commonly sighted. Also seen are Northern Harrier, Northern Goshawk, Swainson's Hawk, Golden Eagle, Merlin, and Peregrine and Prairie Falcons.

17 New Mexico's most famous birding spot lies along the Rio Grande 90 miles south of Albuquerque. The 57,000 acres of **Bosque del Apache National Wildlife Refuge** stretch along the river. Its varied habitats—comprising wetlands, riparian cottonwood-and-willow woods, cropland, and arid uplands—have attracted over the years 320 species. One bird, though, has come to symbolize the refuge: Sandhill Crane winters here in flocks numbering in the thousands. Nearby Socorro holds a Festival of the Cranes each November, one of the most popular birding festivals in America. Waterbirds frequent the refuge year-round. Huge flocks of Snow Goose (40,000 or more) winter here, along with Ross's and Canada and occasional Greater White-fronted Geese. At least 15 species of ducks—perhaps 50,000 individuals—can be found. Pied-billed, Eared, Western, Clark's, and Horned Grebes can appear in migration. American White Pelican, Neotropic and Double-crested Cormorants, bitterns, herons, egrets, White-faced Ibis, Virginia Rail, Sora, Common Moorhen, and American Coot either nest or appear regularly. In spring, late summer, and fall, Black-necked Stilt and American Avocet breed. Migrant shorebirds may be numerous if water levels are low.

Twenty or more Bald Eagles winter in the refuge, and a few Golden Eagles are around during the year. Chihuahuan and Common Ravens nest here and can be told apart if a gust of wind reveals the white bases of the former's neck feathers. Bosque del Apache is a fine place for visitors to observe desert birds such as Gambel's Quail, Greater Roadrunner, Lesser and Common Nighthawks, Common Poorwill, Black-chinned Hummingbird, Ladder-backed Woodpecker, Ash-throated Flycatcher, Verdin, Bushtit, Curve-billed Thrasher, Black-throated Sparrow, and Pyrrhuloxia, the crested finch resembling the female Northern Cardinal. Auto tour routes and observation platforms allow views of the refuge habitats.

18 Farther south, dams on the Rio Grande create Elephant Butte and Caballo Reservoirs where loons, grebes, diving ducks, gulls, and terns are seen from fall through spring. To reach a favored viewpoint over **Elephant Butte,** New Mexico's largest lake, take the Elephant Butte exit from I-25 and drive east 8 miles to the lake. Turn north to North Monticello Point, part of **Elephant Butte State Park.** In winter, see assorted ducks, Common Loon, Horned Grebe, Western and Clark's Grebes, and Bald Eagle. Rarities have ranged from Brown Pelican to Sabine's Gull. Paralleling the Rio Grande, N. Mex. 51 leads to the main part of the park and its lookouts of the lower lake.

The Caballo exit from I-25 provides access to fine birding sites. Drive north and immediately east to reach **Caballo Dam** and **Caballo Lake State Park.** The dam offers good viewing of the lake and Rio Grande for winter waterbirds and Bald Eagle. This spot has been the state's best for gulls, and American White Pelican and Neotropic Cormorant (resident) are seen. Clark's Grebe breeds here. Below the dam see interesting land birds migrating and wintering. Western Screech-Owl, Verdin, Cactus and Rock Wrens, Phainopepla, and Rufous-crowned Sparrow are here year-round. N. Mex. 187 south from I-25 leads to **Percha Dam State Park,** a favorite of local birders. The riparian vegetation attracts an array of migrants and wintering songbirds. Eastern and western strays show up. Residents include Gambel's Quail, Ladder-backed Woodpecker, Verdin, and Curve-billed and Crissal Thrashers (spring–summer only).

19 In southeastern New Mexico, northeast of Roswell, **Bitter Lake National Wildlife Refuge** is a noted spot for shorebirds. A natural lake and several man-made ones vary in levels during the year, attracting geese and ducks in fall migration. Tens of thousands of Sandhill Crane may flock here in November. Grebes, American White Pelican, Neotropic and Double-crested Cormorants, herons, gulls, and terns frequent these wetlands seasonally. An 8.5-mile auto tour route passes several refuge lakes and an observation platform at Bitter Lake.

Spring, late summer, and fall are the peak times for shorebird variety. Migrants include Greater and Lesser Yellowlegs; and Western, Least, Semipalmated, White-rumped (late spring), Baird's, and Stilt Sandpipers. Snowy Plover, Black-necked Stilt, and American Avocet nest on the refuge. It is New Mexico's only regular breeding site for Least Tern. Grasslands shelter winter sparrows. Chestnut-collared Longspur is a common migrant and winter resident.

20 **Carlsbad Caverns National Park** offers nature lovers treats in addition to its underground wonders: At dusk, nearly 500,000 Mexican free-tailed bats leave the cave entrance to hunt insects, and the cave mouth is home to the largest colony of Cave Swallow in the U.S., from March to October.

From the main park entrance, drive 6 miles south on US 62/180 and turn east on County Road 418 to reach **Rattlesnake Springs.** This section of the park is famed as one of the state's best "vagrant traps," or sites that attract rare strays; more than 300 species have been seen here. The springs have a long history of use by Native Americans and early settlers and today create a desert oasis that rewards a birding visit. Notable nesting birds here include Yellow-billed Cuckoo,

Vermilion Flycatcher, Bell's Vireo, Yellow-breasted Chat, Summer Tanager, Northern Cardinal, Pyrrhuloxia, Indigo and Painted Buntings, and Orchard and Hooded Orioles. In winter, eastern species found with some regularity include Eastern Phoebe, Eastern Bluebird, and Brown Thrasher.

21 In southwestern New Mexico, Silver City is the gateway to excellent birding areas. Nesting species found in the **Gila National Forest** north of town include Flammulated and Spotted Owls; Acorn Woodpecker; Greater Pewee; Cordilleran Flycatcher; Plumbeous, Hutton's, and Warbling Vireos; Steller's, Mexican, and Pinyon Jays; Mountain Chickadee; Bridled and Juniper Titmice; Red-breasted and Pygmy Nuthatches; Ruby-crowned Kinglet; Western Bluebird; Hermit Thrush; Olive, Virginia's, Black-throated Gray, Grace's, and Red-faced Warblers; Painted Redstart; Hepatic and Western Tanagers; and Red Crossbill.

For a sampling of these species, take Little Walnut Road north from US 180 in Silver City 4 miles to the **Little Walnut Picnic Area,** at 6,600 feet. After birding here, return to Silver City and take N. Mex. 15 north 13 miles, climbing to the **Cherry Creek Campground** and then to the **McMillan Campground.** Two miles farther, a side road leads up 9,001-foot **Signal Peak.**

Return to Silver City and take US 180 northwest 25 miles; turn southwest toward Bill Evans Lake. In 3.5 miles, go right at a Y on a gravel road that ends at the national forest's **Gila Bird Habitat,** a riparian area on the Gila River with an array of nesting species. Look for Wild Turkey; Montezuma Quail; Common Black-Hawk; Yellow-billed Cuckoo; Elf Owl; Willow, Vermilion, and Brown-crested Flycatchers; Bridled and Juniper Titmice; Lucy's Warbler; Yellow-breasted Chat; Summer Tanager; Abert's Towhee; Northern Cardinal; and Pyrrhuloxia. You may see Common Merganser in the river, and check the skies for an occasional Zone-tailed Hawk "masquerading" as a Turkey Vulture. The first Gray Hawk was seen near here in 1998, and there are hopes that as the habitat develops this species may begin breeding in the area.

Return to US 180 and continue northwest 4 miles to Cliff. Take N. Mex. 211 east a short distance and turn north on N. Mex. 293 (Box Canyon Road). Continue on this paved, then gravel road about 7 miles to the Nature Conservancy's **Gila Riparian Preserve.** At the confluence of Mogollon Creek and the Gila River, you'll have another chance at finding many of the same species listed above for Gila Bird Habitat.

NEW MEXICO | MORE INFORMATION

RARE BIRD ALERT
Statewide 505-323-9323

13 Maxwell National Wildlife Refuge *(Page 214)*
www.fws.gov/southwest
505-375-2331
[?] [†††]

14 Randall Davey Audubon Center
(Page 215)
www.audubon.org
505-983-4609
[?] [$] [†††] [👤] [♿]

From here take the Santa Fe Scenic Byway toward Santa Fe Ski Area.

14 Hyde Memorial State Park *(Page 215)*
www.emnrd.state.nm.us
505-983-7175
[?] [$] [†††] [👤] [~] [♿]

Hike trail at Aspen Vista— with potential Clark's Nutcracker sightings—and take smaller Windsor Trail up to Santa Fe Baldy.

15 Cibola National Forest
(Page 215)
www.fs.fed.us/r3/cibola
505-281-3304
[$] [†] [†††] [👤] [♿]

15 Rio Grande Nature Center State Park
(Page 216)
www.emnrd.state.nm.us
505-344-7240
[?] [$] [†††] [👤] [♿]

16 Hawk Watch International Fall Migration Site
(Page 216)
www.hawkwatch.org
505-255-7622
[👤]
Also known as the Manzano Hawk Watch Site; take the Gavilan Trail to the site.

17 Bosque del Apache National Wildlife Refuge *(Page 216)*
www.fws.gov/southwest
505-835-1828
[?] [$] [†††] [👤] [~] [♿]

18 Elephant Butte State Park *(Page 217)*
www.emnrd.state.nm.us
505-744-5421
[?] [$] [†††] [👤] [~] [♿]

8-mile dirt road to North Monticello Point is extremely rough; four-wheel-drive vehicles are recommended.

18 Caballo Lake State Park *(Page 217)*
www.emnrd.state.nm.us
505-743-3942
[?] [$] [†††] [👤] [♿]

Take N. Mex. 187 south from I-25 to Percha Dam State Park, a local birding favorite.

19 Bitter Lake National Wildlife Refuge *(Page 218)*
www.fws.gov/southwest
505-622-6755
[†††] [👤] [~] [♿]

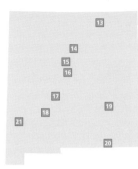

20 Carlsbad Caverns National Park *(Page 218)*
www.nps.gov/cave
505-785-2232
[?] [$] [†] [†††] [👤] [~] [♿]

Take US 62/180 south to County Rd. 418 to Rattle-snake Springs, a noted "vagrant trap." (It attracts rare strays.)

21 Gila National Forest
(Page 219)
www.fs.fed.us/r3/gila
505-388-8201
Take Walnut Road north from US 180 to visit Walnut Picnic Area (6,600 ft.) and Signal Peak (9,001 ft.).

21 Gila Riparian Preserve *(Page 219)*
www.nature.org
505-988-3867

WESTERN TEXAS

- Desert and mountain species at Big Bend National Park
- Western birds and specialties in the Hill Country

One of the most remote parks in the lower 48 states, **Big Bend National Park** is high on the list of the country's best birding destinations. This 800,000-acre park, located where the Rio Grande makes a "big bend" north on its way to the Gulf of Mexico, boasts dramatic mountain and desert scenery and a fine list of special birds. Most of the park is Chihuahuan desert, where Scaled Quail, Verdin, Cactus Wren, Black-tailed Gnatcatcher, Black-throated Sparrow, and Pyrrhuloxia are the typical birds in a habitat of creosote bush, lechuguilla, ocotillo, and cactus. But riparian areas thrive along the Rio Grande and in the park's Chisos Mountains, which are forested in oak, juniper, and Arizona cypress. Birders prefer visiting late April through early June, when breeders are present and singing.

Entering the park from the north along a long desert highway (make sure your car is serviced), you might see a Lesser Nighthawk flying low, or a colorful Scott's Oriole flashing by.

McKittrick Canyon, site of an excellent birding trail in Guadalupe Mountains National Park, east of El Paso

221

Stop at the visitor center at Panther Junction, then go east to **Rio Grande Village** to explore the campgrounds. You'll probably be greeted by a Greater Roadrunner. Watch the sky for Gray Hawk. Check the cottonwoods for White-winged and Inca Doves, Golden-fronted and Ladder-backed Woodpeckers, Black Phoebe, Vermilion and Ash-throated Flycatchers, Bell's Vireo, Summer Tanager, Painted Bunting, and Orchard and Hooded Orioles. Western Screech- and Elf Owls usually nest here; ask a park naturalist for reliable locations.

Your next stop should be the **Chisos Mountains Basin,** from which trails lead into the high country. On the way, watch for blooming century plants, tall green spikes with masses of yellow flowers. In and near the basin, it's possible to see four or five species of hummer at one plant, including Blue-throated and Magnificent (both may come down from higher areas), Lucifer, Black-chinned, and Broad-tailed; Rufous arrives after breeding in late summer. On the **Window Trail,** look for Black-capped Vireo (scarce, but nests here), Rock and Bewick's Wrens, Hepatic Tanager, Spotted and Canyon Towhees, Rufous-crowned and Black-chinned Sparrows, Black-headed Grosbeak, Varied Bunting, and Lesser Goldfinch.

The strenuous hike to **Boot Spring** is one of America's classic birding quests. The object is Big Bend's signature species, the Colima Warbler, a bird that nests nowhere else in the U.S. but these Chisos Mountains. Leave early in the morning; climb to Laguna Meadow, continuing on the **Colima Trail** to Boot Canyon and returning down the **Pinnacles Trail.** It's a round-trip of 9.5 fairly hard miles, but you'll see fabulous scenery and a great list of birds, including, from mid-April through June, almost certainly a Colima. Other species are Zone-tailed Hawk, Band-tailed Pigeon, White-throated Swift, Magnificent Hummingbird, Acorn Woodpecker, Cordilleran Flycatcher, Hutton's Vireo, Mexican Jay, and Bushtit. Those who can't make it all the way to Boot Canyon can usually find Colima Warbler lower on the Pinnacles Trail or in **Laguna Meadow** (check here for Black-chinned Sparrow), though a hike of 3 miles or so (one way) is necessary to reach the bird's habitat. Flammulated Owl nests in the high Chisos, but a permit to camp overnight, and luck, are necessary to find one.

Other fine birding sites include **Blue Creek Canyon,** which is good for Lucifer Hummingbird, Gray Vireo, Canyon Wren, Phainopepla, Rufous-crowned Sparrow, and Varied Bunting. Walk up the canyon from the old ranch house for a mile or more. Check the **Sam Nail Ranch** (a desert oasis where anything might show up) and the **Cottonwood Campground** (look for Hooded Oriole here, and, in nearby scrub, Lucy's Warbler).

23 A hundred miles north of Big Bend, the **Davis Mountains** offer beautiful scenery, and frustration, since very few areas are publicly accessible. As you approach **Davis Mountains State Park** from Fort Davis along Tex. 118, watch for Common Black-Hawk, which nests along Limpia Creek. The park is a good spot to find the elusive Montezuma Quail, which is not so elusive when it comes to feeders or water in the campground. Other species to look for include Zone-tailed Hawk, Golden Eagle, Prairie Falcon, Greater Roadrunner, White-throated Swift, Acorn Woodpecker, Say's Phoebe, Western Scrub-Jay, Rock and Canyon Wrens, and Western Bluebird. Stop at the **Madera Canyon Picnic Area** for a chance at species such as Band-tailed Pigeon, Williamson's Sapsucker (winter), Gray Flycatcher, Plumbeous Vireo, Mountain Chickadee, Grace's Warbler, and Hepatic Tanager. Check hummingbird feeders, as several species may be found, including rarities.

24 Water is found in the desert at **Lake Balmorhea,** a private 573-acre impoundment between Balmorhea and Toyahvale. From fall through spring, a check might reveal Common Loon, grebes (including both Western and Clark's), and a variety of ducks, gulls, and terns; herons and shorebirds frequent the shore at times. As the only lake for many miles, Balmorhea has attracted some rare waterbirds over the years, from Yellow-billed Loon to Elegant Tern.

25 Texas' highest point is found near the New Mexican border in **Guadalupe Mountains National Park,** where Guadalupe Peak rises to 8,749 feet. Like Big Bend, the park features desert and mountain peaks, and so hosts a broad range of species. Here are some birds that nest nowhere else in Texas. High-elevation birds include Band-tailed Pigeon; Flammulated, Spotted, and Northern Saw-whet Owls; Olive-sided and Cordilleran Flycatchers; Plumbeous and Warbling Vireos; Steller's Jay; Mountain Chickadee; Pygmy Nuthatch; Brown Creeper; House Wren; Hermit Thrush; Virginia's and Grace's Warblers; Western Tanager; Dark-eyed Junco; and Pine Siskin. The strenuous hike up to The Bowl will give you a chance at these birds, though the owls are, of course, not likely in daylight. For low- and mid-level species, take the relatively easy hike up **McKittrick Canyon,** one of the state's most beautiful spots. Watch for Black-chinned Hummingbird, Gray Vireo, Western Scrub-Jay, Juniper Titmouse, Green-tailed Towhee, Rufous-crowned Sparrow, and Black-headed Grosbeak. At higher areas of ponderosa pine, look for Blue-throated Hummingbird, Grace's Warbler, and Hepatic Tanager.

ZONE-TAILED HAWK

With its mostly black coloration, long wings held in a shallow V, and habit of soaring lazily, the Zone-tailed Hawk looks amazingly like a Turkey Vulture in flight. This similarity is believed to aid the Zone-tailed in hunting, since small rodents and birds may allow it to approach closely, mistaking it for the nonthreatening, carrion-eating vulture. When you're in the Zone-tailed's range of southern Arizona to the Rio Grande Valley of Texas, check Turkey Vultures carefully to make sure you don't miss its much less common mimic. ∎

26 **Muleshoe National Wildlife Refuge,** 20 miles south of the town of the same name, is an important wintering ground for Sandhill Crane, as well as home to migrant and wintering waterfowl and migrant shorebirds. Water levels in refuge lakes depend on rainfall, and so bird numbers can vary greatly from year to year. Thousands of waterfowl may be present, along with 10,000 or more Sandhill Crane. In drought years numbers can be far lower, though some cranes are always found October through February. Nesting birds at Muleshoe include Scaled Quail, Greater Roadrunner, Ladder-backed Woodpecker, Ash-throated and Scissor-tailed Flycatchers, Curve-billed Thrasher, and Cassin's Sparrow. Look for Burrowing Owl at the prairie-dog town near refuge headquarters and for nesting Snowy Plover and American Avocet by the lake. In winter, find Ferruginous or Rough-legged Hawks and Golden Eagle soaring overhead.

27 The tabletop-flat High Plains of the Texas Panhandle terminate dramatically along the Caprock Escarpment, where the terrain falls hundreds of feet in rugged canyons to the Rolling Plains region. Here, in **Palo Duro Canyon State Park,** southeast of Amarillo, you'll find gorgeous Painted Bunting singing from shrubs all over the park. Walk trails or explore campgrounds in spring and summer for Wild Turkey; Scaled Quail; Mississippi Kite; Greater Roadrunner; Golden-fronted and Ladder-backed Woodpeckers; Say's Phoebe; Ash-throated Flycatcher; Western Scrub-Jay; Black-crested Titmouse; Bushtit; Rock, Canyon, and Bewick's Wrens; Rufous-crowned and Lark Sparrows; Blue Grosbeak; and Bullock's Oriole. Stunning **Lighthouse Trail,** a 6-mile round-trip, has good birding.

28 The **Hill Country** west of Austin and San Antonio is a ruggedly picturesque landscape drained by clear, bluff-lined rivers. The Hill Country is known as the nesting-season home of the endangered Black-capped Vireo and Golden-cheeked Warbler. The strikingly patterned vireo breeds from northern Mexico and Texas' Big Bend east and north into Oklahoma, but the warbler nests only in central Texas, where estimates of its population range from 8,000 to 15,000 pairs.

The Hill Country is the approximate eastern limit of regular occurrence of several western birds, among them Scaled Quail; Common Poorwill; Golden-fronted and Ladder-backed Woodpeckers; Black and Say's Phoebes; Vermilion and Ash-throated Flycatchers; Western Scrub-Jay; Verdin; Bushtit; Cactus, Rock, and Canyon Wrens; Long-billed and Curve-billed Thrashers; Canyon Towhee; Black-throated Sparrow; Pyrrhuloxia; Scott's Oriole; and Lesser Goldfinch.

Golden-cheeked Warbler, which looks a bit like its close relative the Black-throated Green Warbler, requires a specific breeding habitat of mature oak-juniper woods. (It incorporates juniper bark in its nest.) Residential and ranching development has been a factor in its decline. The effort to protect the warbler and the Black-capped Vireo has, in part, resulted in the **Balcones Canyonlands National Wildlife Refuge,** northwest of Austin. Still being developed and with limited public access, the refuge has recently opened nature trails and viewing areas. A vireo site is found on RR (Ranch Road) 1869 about 8 miles west of Liberty Hill. Continue west to RR 1174 and drive south 2.3 miles to a nature trail where the warbler can be found. Call the refuge before visiting for up-to-date information. The refuge is also the easternmost breeding area in the United States for Vermilion Flycatcher, Bushtit, Canyon Towhee, and Black-throated Sparrow.

You'll have far better luck finding both Black-capped Vireo and Golden-cheeked Warbler if you learn their songs before searching. The warbler's song consists of four or five notes with the buzzy quality of its relatives the Black-throated Green and Townsend's Warblers. The vireo's song is a squeaky series of two- or three-note phrases, shorter than that of Bell's Vireo, which may be found in similar scrubby habitat. Male Golden-cheekeds begin to sing in mid-March, when they arrive from their wintering grounds; they leave the Hill Country by the end of July. The vireo arrives beginning in late March, lingering into September before heading south again, although it's difficult to find in late summer.

Golden-cheeked Warbler also nests in **Emma Long Metropolitan Park** just west of Austin (take Tex. 2222 NW from Tex. 360 and turn W on City Park Rd.). **Turkey Creek Trail** is the best site for the warbler. A favorite Austin location for shorebirds and waterfowl is **Hornsby Bend Biosolids Management Facility** (on FM 973, just N of Tex. 71). The ponds are good for waders and ducks, and when conditions are right, shorebirding can be excellent. Black-bellied Whistling-Duck nests here. Check the woods near the Colorado River for migrants in season.

White-winged Dove perched on ocotillo, Big Bend National Park

29 Thirty miles west of Austin, **Pedernales Falls State Park** is an excellent spot to find Golden-cheeked Warbler. Birds are often seen and heard along the **Hill Country Nature Trail**, which is also a good place to experience the area's common plants. Other breeding species here are Greater Roadrunner, Black-chinned Hummingbird, Golden-fronted and Ladder-backed Woodpeckers, Vermilion and Ash-throated Flycatchers, Western Scrub-Jay, Verdin, Bushtit, Rock and Canyon Wrens, and Rufous-crowned Sparrow. Green Kingfisher is sometimes seen along the Pedernales River.

30 Farther south, **Lost Maples State Natural Area** near Vanderpool was named for its bigtooth maples, growing in sheltered canyons here at the eastern edge of their range. The park is home to several rare, endemic, or unusual species, from plants to fish to amphibians, but birders visit to see Green Kingfisher (uncommon and irregular), Black-capped Vireo, and Golden-cheeked Warbler, all of which nest here. Check with rangers for spots where these birds have been seen. In looking for the kingfisher, keep in mind how tiny it is compared to the familiar Belted Kingfisher. It perches quietly on small branches low over the water. Often it's seen only as a virtual blur flying up or down the Sabinal River, maybe uttering a squeaky little *tick* call note. Lost Maples is also good for many of the western species listed for Pedernales Falls. Nesting here are Ash-throated and Great Crested Flycatchers, Eastern Wood-Pewee, Yellow-throated Vireo, Painted Bunting, Scott's Oriole, and Lesser Goldfinch.

WESTERN TEXAS | MORE INFORMATION

RARE BIRD ALERT
Statewide 713-369-9673
Abilene 915-691-8981
Austin 512-926-8751
San Antonio 210-308-6788

22 Big Bend National Park *(Page 221)*
www.nps.gov/bibe
915-477-2251

Call about boat tours; service your car before traveling here. Key birding sites are Rio Grande Village, Chisos Mountains Basin, Window Trail, Boot Spring, Laguna Meadow, Blue Creek Canyon, Sam Nail Ranch, and Cottonwood Campground.

23 Davis Mountains State Park *(Page 223)*
www.tpwd.state.tx.us/spdest
915-426-3337

Stop at Madera Canyon Picnic Area; visit Lake Balmorhea (near Balmorhea) to seek Western and Clark's Grebes.

25 Guadalupe Mountains National Park *(Page 223)*
www.nps.gov/gumo
915-828-3251

A highlight is McKittrick Canyon.

26 Muleshoe National Wildlife Refuge *(Page 224)*
www.fws.gov/southwest
806-946-3341

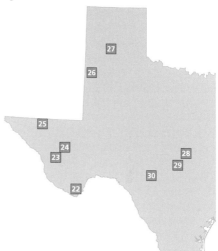

27 Palo Duro Canyon State Park *(Page 225)*
www.tpwd.state.tx.us/spdest
806-488-2227

A good bird walk is Lighthouse Trail.

28 Balcones Canyonlands National Wildlife Refuge *(Page 224)*
www.fws.gov/southwest
512-339-9432

28 Emma Long Metropolitan Park *(Page 226)*
www.ci.austin.tx.us/parks
512-346-1831

Find Golden-cheeked Warbler on Turkey Creek Trail.

28 Hornsby Bend Biosolids Management Facility *(Page 226)*
www.hornsbybend.org
512-929-1000

29 Pedernales Falls State Park *(Page 227)*
www.tpwd.state.tx.us/spdest
830-868-7304

On Hill Country Nature Trail, find native birds and plants.

30 Lost Maples State Natural Area *(Page 227)*
www.tpwd.state.tx.us/spdest
830-966-3413

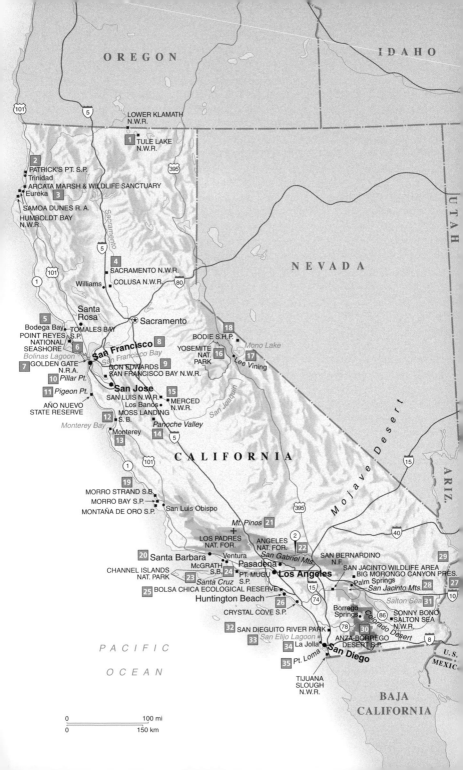

OREGON

IDAHO

101

5

LOWER KLAMATH
N.W.R.

1 TULE LAKE
N.W.R.

395

2
PATRICK'S PT. S.P.
Trinidad
ARCATA MARSH & WILDLIFE SANCTUARY
Eureka **3**

SAMOA DUNES R. A.
HUMBOLDT BAY
N.W.R.

5

Sacramento

1

101

Williams

4
SACRAMENTO N.W.R.
COLUSA N.W.R.

80

NEVADA

Santa
Rosa

5 Bodega Bay
TOMALES BAY
POINT REYES   S.P.
NATIONAL
SEASHORE   **6**
Bolinas Lagoon
7 GOLDEN GATE
N.R.A.
10 Pillar Pt.
11 Pigeon Pt.
AÑO NUEVO
STATE RESERVE

★ Sacramento

San Francisco **8**
San Francisco Bay

9
DON EDWARDS
SAN FRANCISCO BAY N.W.R.

San Jose

15
SAN LUIS N.W.R.
Los Banos
MOSS LANDING
S. B.
12 S.B.
Monterey Bay
13 Monterey
14
Panoche Valley
5

18 BODIE S.H.P.
Mono Lake
16 YOSEMITE
NAT.
PARK
17 Lee Vining

15
MERCED
N.W.R.

San Joaquin

CALIFORNIA

1

101

19
MORRO STRAND S.B.
MORRO BAY S.P.
MONTAÑA DE ORO S.P.
San Luis Obispo

395

Mt. Pinos **21**
+
LOS PADRES
NAT. FOR.
ANGELES
NAT. FOR.
2

San Bernardino
N.F.
22
SAN BERNARDINO

40

29

20 Santa Barbara
Ventura
McGRATH
S.B. **24**
PT. MUGU
S.P.
CHANNEL ISLANDS
NAT. PARK
23 Santa Cruz
25 BOLSA CHICA ECOLOGICAL RESERVE
Huntington Beach
CRYSTAL COVE S.P.
26

San Gabriel Mts.
Pasadena
Los Angeles

15

SAN JACINTO WILDLIFE AREA
BIG MORONGO CANYON PRES.
Palm Springs
San Jacinto Mts. **28**
27
10

Salton Sea
31

74
Borrego
Springs
Colorado Desert
86
SONNY BONO
SALTON SEA
N.W.R.

Mojave Desert

15

ARIZ.

UTAH

32 SAN DIEGUITO RIVER PARK
33 San Elijo Lagoon
La Jolla
34
Pt. Loma **35**
San Diego

78
30
ANZA-BORREGO
DESERT S.P.

8

U.S.
MEXICO

TIJUANA
SLOUGH
N.W.R.

BAJA
CALIFORNIA

PACIFIC
OCEAN

0   100 mi
0   150 km

CALIFORNIA

ALIFORNIA HAS A GREATER VARIETY OF TERRAIN THAN any other state. Within its 800-mile range are Mojave Desert scrub, redwood forests, Pacific Ocean cliffs, and Sierra Nevada peaks. Such diversity means a correspondingly long list of birds. More than 600 species have been found here— about 70 percent of the total seen in the lower 48 states.

- Northern California
- Southern California

Of its specialties (below) the California Quail and California Thrasher are common and easily seen. The threatened California Gnatcatcher and the endangered California Condor are harder to find. The Island Scrub-Jay and the Yellow-billed Magpie are special specialties: neither has been seen in another state or country.

Birding highlights include the Salton Sea, where odd water-birds flock; pelagic trips from Monterey Bay, where seabirds wander in from around the globe; Yosemite National Park, where high-country birds nest; and Point Reyes National Seashore, where land birds and waterbirds share the area. ■

Yellow-billed Magpie

SPECIAL BIRDS OF CALIFORNIA

Chukar	Pacific Golden-Plover	Black Swift	
Greater Sage-Grouse	Mountain Plover	Anna's Hummingbird	
Blue Grouse	Wandering Tattler	Costa's Hummingbird	California Gnatcatcher
Mountain Quail	Black Turnstone	Allen's Hummingbird	Varied Thrush
California Quail	Surfbird	Red-breasted Sapsucker	Wrentit
Ross's Goose	Rock Sandpiper	Nuttall's Woodpecker	California Thrasher
Eurasian Wigeon	Heermann's Gull	White-headed Woodpecker	Le Conte's Thrasher
Barrow's Goldeneye	Mew Gull	Black-backed Woodpecker	Phainopepla
Pacific Loon	Thayer's Gull		Hermit Warbler
Black-footed Albatross	Yellow-footed Gull	Pacific-slope Flycatcher	California Towhee
Buller's Shearwater	Elegant Tern	Cassin's Vireo	Black-chinned Sparrow
Black-vented Shearwater	Common Murre	Hutton's Vireo	Sage Sparrow
Ashy Storm-Petrel	Pigeon Guillemot	Island Scrub-Jay	Golden-crowned Sparrow
Black Storm-Petrel	Marbled Murrelet	Yellow-billed Magpie	Tricolored Blackbird
Brandt's Cormorant	Xantus's Murrelet	Chestnut-backed Chickadee	Hooded Oriole
Pelagic Cormorant	Cassin's Auklet	Oak Titmouse	Scott's Oriole
California Condor	Rhinoceros Auklet	Verdin	Gray-crowned Rosy-Finch
White-tailed Kite	Tufted Puffin		Lawrence's Goldfinch
Black Rail	Spotted Owl		
Clapper Rail	Great Gray Owl		

NORTHERN CALIFORNIA

- Excellent diversity at Point Reyes National Seashore
- Seabirds at Año Nuevo and other coastal sites
- Pelagic trips from Monterey Bay
- Mountain species at Yosemite National Park

The Rocky Coast at Patrick's Point State Park, home to several species of nesting seabirds

1 Wildlife refuges with lots of wintering waterfowl are certainly not rare in the United States; neither is it unusual to find numbers of Bald Eagle and other raptors congregating in such places to feed on sick and injured ducks and geese. Even so, the **Klamath Basin National Wildlife Refuges Complex** stands out for the spectacle it offers, with more than a million waterfowl present at times during fall migration. Common species include Tundra Swan; Greater White-fronted, Snow, Ross's, Cackling, and Canada Geese; and a host of dabbling and diving ducks. In addition, the Klamath Basin is home to the greatest concentration of wintering Bald Eagle in the lower 48 states, with most years seeing peak populations ranging from 500 to 1,000 birds.

The six refuges in this complex straddle the California-Oregon border north and south of Klamath Falls, Oregon. Two refuges in California, **Lower Klamath National Wildlife Refuge** and **Tule Lake National Wildlife Refuge,** make the best destinations, since most others are either closed to the public or difficult to access. To reach Lower Klamath from the town of Tulelake, drive northwest on Calif. 139 for 4 miles, turn west on Calif. 161, and drive 10 miles. For the latter, turn south off Calif. 161 onto Hill Road 2 miles west of the Calif. 139/161 junction. Auto tour routes at both refuges lead through wetlands where you'll enjoy looking over masses of birds from fall through spring (though midwinter freeze-up pushes many birds farther south). With luck you might find a rarity such as Emperor Goose (best chance in fall at Tule Lake), Trumpeter Swan, Long-tailed Duck, or Barrow's Goldeneye. Eurasian Wigeon is uncommon but regular in flocks of American Wigeon. In addition to Bald Eagle, look for other winter raptors including Red-tailed (nests) and Rough-legged Hawks, Golden Eagle (nests), Merlin, and Peregrine Falcon, and for that diminutive predator, the Northern Shrike.

Lower Klamath and Tule Lake refuges are more than winter birding sites. Great numbers of herons, waterfowl, and other waterbirds breed here, including many ducks; Pied-billed, Eared, Western, and Clark's Grebes; American White Pelican; Great and Snowy Egrets; White-faced Ibis; Virginia Rail; Sora; Snowy Plover; Black-necked Stilt; American Avocet; Long-billed Curlew; Wilson's Phalarope; and Caspian, Forster's, and Black Terns. Other nesters include California Quail, Sandhill Crane, Short-eared Owl, Ash-throated Flycatcher, Western Scrub-Jay, and Tricolored and Yellow-headed Blackbirds—and this is just a sampling.

2 There's excellent seabird-watching, and good land birding, too, at **Patrick's Point State Park,** west of US 101, 5 miles north of Trinidad. Follow the **Rim Trail,** and from the cliffs of this rocky headland look for Common Murre, Pigeon Guillemot, Cassin's and Rhinoceros Auklets, and with luck Tufted Puffin (April–July); and for wintering sea ducks including all three scoters; Red-throated, Pacific, and Common Loons; Brandt's, Double-crested, and Pelagic Cormorants; and Brown Pelican. Black Oystercatcher nests here, and three other "rocky shorebirds"—Wandering Tattler, Black Turnstone, Surfbird—are present except in early summer. In woods you'll find resident California Quail, Band-tailed Pigeon, Anna's Hummingbird, Pileated Woodpecker, Black Phoebe, Hutton's Vireo, Gray and Steller's Jays, Chestnut-backed Chickadee, Bushtit, Varied Thrush, Wrentit. Nesting-season birds include

Allen's Hummingbird, Olive-sided and Pacific-slope Flycatchers, Orange-crowned and Wilson's Warblers, Western Tanager, and Black-headed Grosbeak.

 Not far to the south, in Arcata, turn west on Calif. 255, then soon turn south on I Street to enter the **Arcata Marsh and Wildlife Sanctuary.** Here, extensive trails border wetlands where you'll find waders, ducks, and other marsh birds, as well as migrant shorebirds. The sanctuary sits alongside **Humboldt Bay,** one of California's most productive birding areas. From fall through spring, many loons, grebes, and waterfowl can be present. The eelgrass beds here attract migrant Brant, and mudflats along the shoreline draw migrant and wintering shorebirds.

San Francisco and the Golden Gate Bridge, as seen from the Marin Headlands, Golden Gate National Recreation Area

From Eureka, take Calif. 255 west from US 101 then go south on New Navy Base Road to the **Samoa Dunes Recreation Area,** where a viewing platform overlooks the bay and Pacific coast. For more birding, return to US 101. About 6.5 miles south take Hookton Road west to a section of **Humboldt Bay National Wildlife Refuge,** or keep west to **Table Bluff County Park,** both of which provide more bay views.

 Moving inland from the coast, you'll find huge flocks of wintering waterfowl at the **Sacramento National Wildlife Refuge Complex,** about 100 miles north of Sacramento. Ross's and Snow Geese are abundant here in winter. Greater White-fronted and Cackling Geese are common, and waterfowl reach into the hundreds of thousands from October through February. **Sacramento National Wildlife Refuge** (take Norman Rd. exit from I-5, drive east and immediately north on the frontage road) and **Colusa National Wildlife Refuge** (from Williams, E on Calif. 20) have auto tour routes for viewing geese, ducks, and other marsh and waterbirds. These wetlands also attract migrant shorebirds and nesting ducks, herons, and rails. Look in spring and summer for breeding American Bittern; Great and Snowy Egrets; Black-crowned Night-Heron; White-faced Ibis; Common Moorhen; Black-necked Stilt; and American Avocet. Yellow-billed Magpie is found here year-round.

5 Back on the coast, the area around **Bodega Bay,** about 20 miles southwest of Santa Rosa, ranks with the region's best seabirding sites. Just north of Bodega Bay, turn west off Calif. 1 on Eastshore Road and then west again onto Westside Road, to Bodega Head. Scan the bay for loons, grebes, and ducks from fall through spring, and for Brant in spring. Black-crowned Night-Heron nests at the **Hole-in-the-Head Picnic Area,** and **Westside County Park** offers good bay views. At **Bodega Head,** check the rocks for resident Black Oystercatcher and migrant Wandering Tattler, Ruddy and Black Turnstones, Surfbird, and other shorebirds. Migrant and wintering ducks may include Harlequin Duck, scoters, or Long-tailed Duck. Pelagic Cormorant, Western Gull, and Pigeon Guillemot nest on rocky cliffs. Return to Calif. 1, drive south, and in about a mile veer west onto Smith Brothers Road to check the bay for ducks, migrant shorebirds, and gulls. Just to the south, turn west off Calif. 1 onto Doran Beach Road to reach **Doran County Park,** another fine shorebirding site.

6 **Point Reyes National Seashore** earns its superb birding reputation on several levels. You'll find many characteristic land birds of the area in forests (walk the **Bear Valley Trail**), scrub, and fields, including California Quail, Anna's and Allen's (late winter–summer) Hummingbirds, Nuttall's Woodpecker, Pacific-slope Flycatcher (spring–summer), Hutton's Vireo, Chestnut-backed Chickadee, Oak Titmouse, Pygmy Nuthatch, Wrentit, and California Towhee. Spots such as Limantour Beach can have concentrations of migrant shorebirds; walk along the spit, and take the **Estero** and **Muddy Hollow Trails** north past ponds good for waterbirds. Walk to **Abbott's Lagoon,** on Pierce Point Road, to look for winter and migrant waterfowl, and visit **Drake's Estero** for waders and shorebirds.

The lighthouse area is a great lookout for Red-throated and Pacific Loons, Sooty Shearwater (summer), Brown Pelican (summer–fall), scoters (fall–spring), and Brandt's and Pelagic Cormorants. Find Black Oystercatcher, Common Murre, Pigeon Guillemot, and Rhinoceros Auklet. Where Sir Francis Drake Blvd. turns toward the lighthouse, drive east toward Chimney Rock. At **Drake's Bay** see sea ducks, loons, and grebes.

Point Reyes offers special birding challenges, too. The rare Spotted Owl may be seen at adjacent **Tomales Bay State Park,** where trails provide good land birding, and the bay hosts Osprey and migrant and winter waterfowl. Pacific Golden-Plover is often found in pastures from fall through spring.

Check along Sir Francis Drake Blvd. near the road to Drake's Beach. Look also for wintering raptors and rare longspurs here. Isolated patches of trees, including those around dairy farms, are famed migrant and vagrant traps (fall and late spring), when all sorts of eastern migrants show up. Overcast or foggy conditions are best for migrants. (Dairy ranches are private; use discretion.) Point Reyes is a large and heavily birded area, so ask park naturalists about recent sightings and best locations for the time of your visit. Just to the south, **Bolinas Lagoon** is excellent for waders, waterfowl, and resident Osprey. From Olema, drive south on Calif. 1 about 9 miles, then south on Olema-Bolinas Road, scanning the water. Check the lagoon from pull-offs along Calif. 1 south of this road. Just north of Calif. 1 here, **Audubon Canyon Ranch** (open mid-March–mid-July) is home to a Great Blue Heron colony and to Great and Snowy Egrets nesting in redwood trees. An observation platform provides a great view of the families.

ACORN WOODPECKER

The strikingly attractive Acorn Woodpecker is notorious for its habit of storing acorns in small holes it drills in the bark of trees, or in other wood from utility poles to buildings. One tree may be used year after year and have thousands of holes. Woodpeckers wedge the nuts in tightly to protect them from other birds and squirrels. Common throughout western and central California, this "clown-faced" bird also feeds on insects, sap, and fruit. ■

7 In fall, visit the Marin Headlands area of the **Golden Gate National Recreation Area** (take the Alexander Ave. exit from US 101 N of Golden Gate Bridge and drive W), where Battery 129 on Conzelman Road is known to birders as "Hawk Hill." In September and October, thousands of raptors, including Osprey; Northern Harrier; accipiters; Red-shouldered, Broad-winged (uncommon), and Red-tailed Hawks; Golden Eagle; Merlin; and Peregrine Falcon pass over the region's most famous hawk-watching site. Visitors to San Francisco without time to travel far from the city will also find **Marin Headlands** a pleasant place to see typical area birds such as California Quail, Chestnut-backed Chickadee, and Wrentit, and exploring its coastline and **Rodeo Lagoon** will always turn up waterbirds.

8 Many an out-of-state visitor has seen his or her first Glaucous-winged Gull, Anna's Hummingbird, Western Scrub-Jay, Chestnut-backed Chickadee, Bushtit, Pygmy Nuthatch, Wrentit, or California Towhee at **Golden Gate Park.**

To this list can be added nesting Allen's Hummingbird and wintering Mew Gull, Red-breasted Sapsucker, Varied Thrush, and Golden-crowned Sparrow. Wooded areas in the western part of this park offer the best land birding, but local bird-watchers keep an eye on all the park lakes for waterfowl and gulls. Eurasian Wigeon appears here regularly in winter.

Next drive just to the northwest, where the **Cliff House** area of the Golden Gate National Recreation Area provides an excellent viewpoint for finding seabirds and shorebirds year-round. Black Oystercatcher is a nesting resident on the rocks below, and other "rocky shorebirds" are present except in mid-summer. Look for Brandt's and Pelagic Cormorants, Brown Pelican, gulls (Western nests here, and Heermann's is present much of the year), Elegant Tern (in summer), Common Murre, Pigeon Guillemot (absent in winter), and any number of other waterbirds, including possible wintering Harlequin Duck, scoters, and Long-tailed Duck. Try walking down to the old Sutro Baths, where waterfowl rest on ponds.

9 Waders, waterfowl, shorebirds, and other wetlands species can be found at the south end of San Francisco Bay. To reach the **Don Edwards San Francisco Bay National Wildlife Refuge,** take the Paseo Padre Pkwy./Thornton Ave. exit from Calif. 84, just east of the Dumbarton Bridge; drive south to the entrance. The **Tidelands Trail,** a 1-mile loop, traverses marshland where dabbling ducks, Pied-billed and Eared Grebes, American Bittern, Great and Snowy Egrets, Common Moorhen, Black-necked Stilt, and American Avocet are present all year. Follow Marshlands Road (closed Apr.–Aug. to protect nesting Snowy Plover) to the **Shoreline Trail** along the bay, where you might see a Clapper Rail—or a Black Rail at high tides in winter. The trail leads north 4 miles to **Coyote Hills Regional Park,** where more trails provide access to freshwater marsh. White-tailed Kite might be seen here or at the refuge.

To reach another unit of the national wildlife refuge, at Milpitas take Calif. 237 west from I-880, then turn north on Zanker Road, and continue to the Environmental Education Center. The **Mallard Slough** and **Alviso Slough Trails** are excellent birding walks for wetlands species. For more of the same kind of marsh habitat, take Embarcadero Road east from US 101 in Palo Alto, on the west side of the bay, to **Palo Alto Baylands Preserve,** where birders also look for Clapper Rail and, at high tide in winter, for the elusive Black Rail and Nelson's Sharp-tailed Sparrow.

10 Following Calif. 1 south from the Bay Area along the Pacific coast will take you past a number of excellent sites for observing seabirds and shorebirds. Just north of Half Moon Bay, drive west through the community of Princeton toward **Pillar Point,** a fine spot from which to scan the sea for loons, grebes, sea ducks, and alcids, and the rocky coast for shorebirds. The harbor here should be checked for waterfowl as well as seabirds; Brant can be common in spring. Check gull flocks for Thayer's, occurring regularly but in small numbers.

YELLOW-BILLED MAGPIE

Endemic to central and northern California, the Yellow-billed Magpie is a common resident of the rangelands and foothills of central California, of the Northern Central Valley, and of coastal valleys south to Santa Barbara County. Scan oaks in orchards and parks or on the borders of grasslands for this magpie's signature yellow bill and yellow patch of bare skin around the eye. Listen for its whining *mag,* or *chuck* notes. It roosts and feeds in flocks, and nests in loose colonies. ■

11 About 20 miles south, turn west off Calif. 1 toward the lighthouse at **Pigeon Point,** one of the coast's very best seabird lookouts. Stop along the road north of the lighthouse for the best viewing, and keep in mind that this sort of birding can be exciting or dull, depending on circumstances of weather and luck. On good days, the sea and sky can be alive with ducks, loons, cormorants, gulls, and alcids from the common Common Murre to something as unusual as an Ancient Murrelet (winter) or Tufted Puffin (summer). In migration, a west wind pushes birds closer to shore. Pigeon Point is an excellent spot for Marbled Murrelet and for pelagics such as Sooty Shearwater (summer–fall); each spring a few Black-footed Albatrosses are seen from shore here.

Just 6 miles south is **Año Nuevo State Reserve,** famed for its colony of elephant seals, and for good birding. Brandt's and Pelagic Cormorants, Black Oystercatcher, Pigeon Guillemot, and Cassin's and Rhinoceros Auklets nest on cliffs and/or offshore islands, and the bluffs are a good viewpoint for seabird-watching. Marbled Murrelet might be found out beyond the surf line. Land birding at Año Nuevo is interesting as well. Nesting birds include California Quail, White-tailed Kite, Band-tailed Pigeon, Acorn Woodpecker, Black Phoebe, Hutton's Vireo, Steller's Jay, Swainson's Thrush, California Thrasher, Wrentit, Wilson's Warbler, Spotted and California Towhees, White-crowned Sparrow, and Lesser Goldfinch.

Anywhere along this stretch of coast in fields and marshes look for Tricolored Blackbird. The rare Black Swift breeds in sea caves at Año Nuevo, though only at dawn or dusk might you see them leaving or returning to the nests; during the day they travel long distances to feed on insects high in the sky.

12 As you skirt Monterey Bay and approach the town of Moss Landing from the north along Calif. 1, turn west on Jetty Road toward **Moss Landing State Beach,** where migrant shorebirds can be abundant in marshes and on mudflats. Set up your spotting scope here and scan the bay for loons, grebes, cormorants, sea ducks, and whatever other waterbirds might be present from fall through spring. Because the seafloor drops off quickly to deep water in Monterey Bay, pelagic species such as shearwaters, storm-petrels, and jaegers may approach close to land. To reach **Elkhorn Slough National Estuarine Research Reserve,** which can have an excellent diversity of waterfowl and shore-birds, continue south on Calif. 1 toward Moss Landing. Drive east on Dolan Road 3.5 miles, turning north on Elkhorn Road—the entrance is 2 miles ahead. In addition to water-birds, land birding can be rewarding along the reserve trails.

13 Some of America's most famous pelagic trips leave from **Fisherman's Wharf** in Monterey, heading out to deep water for looks at oceanic species seldom or never seen from shore. Trips are offered by several tour companies, the most active of which is **Shearwater Journeys**. The list of possible species depends on the destination and time of year, ranging from year-round near certainties such as Black-Footed Albatross, Sooty Shearwater, Common Murre, and Rhinoceros Auklet to rarities such as Laysan Albatross and Streaked, Wedge-tailed, and Manx Shearwaters. Fall is best for diversity of species including Buller's and Black-vented Shearwaters and four species of storm-petrels. The January issue of the American Birding Association's newsletter, *Winging It,* includes a listing of nationwide pelagic trips with target species. Consult it for trip sponsors' expected sightings, or check with the trip organizers as far in advance as possible.

In Monterey, the city's municipal wharf (N off Del Monte Ave.) provides a view of the harbor and bay. As you continue southwest toward Point Pinos along Ocean View Boulevard, stop to look for Black Oystercatcher and other rocky shore-birds, and to scan the bay. From **Point Pinos** you can often see a good number of seabirds such as shearwaters and alcids.

14 Moving inland, a driving tour through the **Panoche Valley** can bring good birding from late fall through early spring (summers are very hot and dry, and bird activity is low). To reach it, take the Little Panoche Road/Shields Avenue exit from I-5 about 20 miles south of Los Banos and drive west.

Little Panoche Road curves to the south to join Panoche Road in about 20 miles; from here (when the road is dry) you can drive east back to I-5. While this isn't exactly the middle of nowhere, it is an isolated drive, so make sure that you're prepared and that your car is in good condition. Four miles from I-5, stop at **Little Panoche Reservoir** to see what might be around (Tricolored Blackbird is possible), and then continue west, looking for Chukar (rare); California Quail; White-tailed Kite; Ferruginous and Rough-legged Hawks; Prairie Falcon; Greater Roadrunner; Burrowing Owl; Lewis's and Nuttall's Woodpeckers; Loggerhead Shrike; Yellow-billed Magpie; Horned Lark (check flocks for rare winter longspurs); Bushtit;

Yosemite National Park's Bridalveil Falls, where the very local Black Swift nests

Mountain Bluebird; California Thrasher; Phainopepla, Rufous-crowned, Vesper, and Lark Sparrows; and Lesser and Lawrence's Goldfinches. Mountain Plover, one of the special birds of the area, is getting harder to find, but diligent searching in short-grass areas might turn up a small wintering flock between early November and early March.

15 Not far north, in the San Joaquin Valley, several wildlife areas attract masses of wintering waterfowl and host nesting waterbirds in the warmer months. To reach **Merced National Wildlife Refuge** from Los Banos, take Calif. 152 east 18 miles, turn north on Calif. 59, drive 6.5 miles, and turn west on Sandy Mush Road. For **Los Banos Wildlife Area**, take Calif. 165 north from Los Banos; in 3 miles go east on Henry Miller Avenue. For **San Luis National Wildlife Refuge** get back on Calif. 165 north, then drive northeast 2 miles on Wolfsen Road.

At these sites and in the surrounding agricultural fields you'll find wintering Tundra Swan; Greater White-fronted,

Snow, Ross's, Cackling, and Canada Geese; ducks; and Sandhill Crane (mostly at Merced). Look also for Bald Eagle and Ferruginous and Rough-legged Hawks, among other raptors. Migrant shorebirds make a spring, late summer, or fall visit to these areas worthwhile. Long-billed Curlew is present year-round. A small sampling of nesting species includes Wood Duck (at San Luis), Western and Clark's Grebes, American Bittern, Great and Snowy Egrets, White-faced Ibis, White-tailed Kite, Northern Harrier, Swainson's Hawk, Burrowing Owl, Yellow-billed Magpie, and Tricolored and Yellow-headed (uncommon) Blackbirds.

16 One of America's most beautiful natural areas, **Yosemite National Park** is also one of California's most popular destinations—a fact that causes personnel some concern as they try to maintain the park's wild character despite throngs of visitors. Birders who go to Yosemite (the best time is between early June and August—earlier in lower-elevation areas) tend to get up early, and those who do will have an advantage here not only in bird-finding but in crowd-avoiding. The effort will be worthwhile, because Yosemite offers a fine list of montane species. Some, such as Vaux's and White-throated Swifts, Hammond's and Dusky Flycatchers, Clark's Nutcracker, Mountain Chickadee, Brown Creeper, Western Tanager, and Fox and Lincoln's Sparrows, are easy to find in proper habitat. But it takes a bit of luck to walk up on a Blue Grouse along a forest trail, or to spot a Black-backed Woodpecker chipping away at the bark of a lodgepole pine, or to look up just in time to see Northern Goshawk soaring overhead.

Drive **Glacier Point Road,** south of Yosemite Valley, to look for forest birds such as Band-tailed Pigeon; Williamson's Sapsucker; White-headed and Pileated Woodpeckers; Olive-sided Flycatcher; Cassin's Vireo; Golden-crowned Kinglet; Townsend's Solitaire; Hermit Thrush; Nashville, Black-throated Gray, and Hermit Warblers; Pine Grosbeak; and Red Crossbill. A morning walk along the entrance road to Bridalveil Campground will bring looks at a good number of these species. Yosemite has many expansive meadows, in or around which you may find Mountain Quail, Calliope Hummingbird (Rufous doesn't nest but is common as a summer migrant), Red-breasted Sapsucker (look in aspens and willows around meadow edges), Mountain Bluebird, and MacGillivray's and Wilson's Warblers.

Great Gray Owl is one of the park's special species, and

fortunate birders sometimes spot one perched in a tree at the edge of a meadow such as McGurk or Peregoy on Glacier Point Road or Crane Flat in the western part of the park. (If you're lucky enough to see this impressive bird, enjoy it from a distance—don't approach for a "better look.") Flammulated Owl can be heard giving its hollow hoots in late May and June, but it is rarely ever seen. The threatened Spotted Owl calls earlier in the year in old-growth forest, and it is even less frequently seen.

Another much sought-after bird, the scarce Black Swift, nests near waterfalls. **Bridalveil Falls** is a favorite spot to look for this large swift, but be there at dawn or just before dusk to see

Tufa formations at Mono Lake, near Lee Vining

the birds leaving or returning to their nests. Sometimes Black Swift can be seen from Glacier Point, flying with the much more common White-throated. Hiking into the tundra around **Tioga Pass,** or behind the dam at Ellery Lake, just east of there, may bring a sighting of Gray-crowned Rosy-Finch; early summer offers the best chance.

17 Eastward near the Nevada border, **Mono Lake** is famed not only for the number of migrants that appear here in summer and fall, but for the spectacular landscape of weirdly shaped towers of calcium-carbonate deposits called tufa, formed when the water level of this highly salty and alkaline lake was higher. Your first stop should be at the **Mono Basin National Forest Scenic Area Visitor Center** on US 395 just north of Lee Vining, where you can get maps and information. Four miles north of Lee Vining, turn east on Cemetery Road to reach **Mono Lake County Park,** the best spot on the lake for a variety of birds. Here you can check the cottonwoods and willows along DeChambeau Creek for nesting American Kestrel, Great Horned Owl, Northern Flicker, Western Wood-Pewee, Warbling Vireo, Yellow Warbler, Black-headed Grosbeak, and Bullock's Oriole, and for migrants in spring and fall. Then take the boardwalk to the lake, passing through a wetland where Green Heron, Virginia Rail, Sora, and Common Snipe nest.

California Gull nests at Mono Lake in a colony of around 50,000 birds, making this species easy to find from spring through fall. The lake also sees enormous concentrations of migrant phalaropes. In summer, Wilson's Phalarope arrives by the tens of thousands, joined in late July by Red-necked Phalaropes. As these shorebirds feed on flies and their larvae, building up fat reserves before continuing their southward migration, their numbers can reach 150,000. As the phalaropes depart, Eared Grebe arrives in the hundreds of thousands, at times covering the water in immense flocks totaling more than a million birds. Shorebirding can be excellent at Mono, as well, though rising water levels are changing the lake's configuration and inundating areas that once were mudflats.

Returning to Lee Vining, drive south on US 395 about 5 miles, then east on Calif. 120; in 4 miles turn north toward the **South Tufa** area. In the sagebrush scrub, look for Common Nighthawk, Say's Phoebe, Loggerhead Shrike, Western Scrub-Jay, Bushtit, Mountain Bluebird, Sage Thrasher, Green-tailed Towhee, and Brewer's and Sage Sparrows. Viewpoints here, as anywhere around the lake, can provide looks at a range of migrant and wintering waterfowl.

Two areas near Mono Lake offer the chance to see Greater Sage-Grouse. To visit a lek, where males "dance" to court females in spring, drive south on US 395; 5 miles past Calif. 203, turn northeast on Benton Crossing Road. Go 1.1 miles, veer east, and in 0.7 mile east again. In a mile you'll come to a road leading south 0.3 mile to the lek. Be here before dawn from late March to early May to see the courtship display.

18 Greater Sage-Grouse are also seen in summer at **Bodie State Historic Park**, 20 miles northeast of Lee Vining. Six miles north of town, turn east on Calif. 167. As you travel this road, watch for Pinyon Jay. In 6.5 miles, turn north on Cottonwood Canyon Road. It leads to the park in about 10 winding miles. Grouse are often seen walking around this ghost town in spring and (especially) summer. Other times you might run across one by walking through sagebrush in the area (also good for Common Nighthawk, Mountain Bluebird, Sage Thrasher, and Brewer's Sparrow), but call ahead for road conditions in bad weather. You can also reach Bodie via US 395 north from Lee Vining 17 miles, turning east on Calif. 270.

SOUTHERN CALIFORNIA

- Coastal birds at Morro Bay
- Highland species at Mount Pinos and the San Gabriel Mountains
- Migrants and desert birds at Anza-Borrego Desert State Park
- Waterbirds and rarities at the Salton Sea

Montane habitat on California's Mount Pinos

19 One of the landmarks of the central California coast, **Morro Rock** lifts its rugged cliff face 578 feet above the surf of Morro Bay. To reach it, drive north on Embarcadero, which runs beside the water in the town of Morro Bay, and turn west on Coleman Drive. Park in the south lot, from which you can scan the rock in spring and summer for Peregrine Falcon nesting on the cliffs. Brandt's and Pelagic Cormorants, Pigeon Guillemot, White-throated Swift, Violet-green Swallow, and Canyon Wren also breed here. Watch for the sea otters, which often can be seen near shore.

In Morro Bay, take Main Street south; skirt the bay southward to **Morro Bay State Park.** Great Blue Heron, Snowy Egret, and Black-crowned Night-Heron nest in a heronry north of the Morro Bay Natural History Museum. Past the museum, turn south to a marina from which you can scan the bay for waterbirds. Look for Brant (attracted to eelgrass beds) and American White Pelican in winter, Brown Pelican year-round, and at any time of the year for sea ducks, loons, grebes, gulls, and terns. Elegant Tern, a visitor from breeding grounds farther south, can be seen in late summer and fall.

Continuing through the park, you'll reach South Bay Blvd. To look for Snowy Plover, turn north to Calif. 1, drive 2.3 miles, and go west on Atascadero Road to its end. Walk the sandy beach of **Morro Strand State Beach** northward to find this little shorebird. Otherwise, drive 1.6 miles south, turn west on Santa Ysabel Avenue for 0.9 mile, turn north on Third Street to the bay. Here you can visit the **Morro Coast Audubon Overlook** and have another chance to check the bay for Willet, Whimbrel, Long-billed Curlew, Marbled Godwit, and other shorebirds, as well as the waterbirds mentioned above.

Return to South Bay Blvd, drive south to Los Osos Valley Road, turn west, and follow signs to **Montaña de Oro State Park,** an excellent year-round birding spot. Walk the **West Hazard Canyon Trail** or the **Campground Loop,** checking the pines and streamside vegetation for resident Anna's Hummingbird, Nuttall's Woodpecker, Hutton's Vireo, Chestnut-backed Chickadee, Bewick's Wren, Wrentit (more often heard than seen), California Thrasher, and Spotted and California Towhees. In nesting season look for Allen's Hummingbird and Pacific-slope Flycatcher; in winter for Ruby-crowned Kinglet, Blue-gray Gnatcatcher, and Golden-crowned Sparrow. On the the **Bluff Trail,** a 3-mile walk along the coast, scan the Pacific for loons, grebes, and sea ducks. Check the rocks for cormorants and "rocky shorebirds" such as Black Oystercatcher, Wandering Tattler, Black Turnstone, and Surfbird; the Black Oystercatcher is present all year, while the last three birds are fall-through-spring visitors

20 In Santa Barbara, take Mission Canyon Road north to reach the **Santa Barbara Museum of Natural History, Rocky Nook County Park,** and the **Santa Barbara Botanic Garden.** Oak woods at these sites host typical birds of the region, from California Quail to California Thrasher to California Towhee. Residents include Anna's Hummingbird, Acorn and Nuttall's Woodpeckers, Black Phoebe, Hutton's Vireo, Western Scrub-Jay, Oak Titmouse, Wrentit, Orange-crowned Warbler, Spotted Towhee, and Lesser Goldfinch. Among the nesting-season species are Black-chinned and Allen's Hummingbirds, Pacific-slope and Ash-throated Flycatchers, Black-headed Grosbeak, and Hooded Oriole. The 5.5 miles of trails at the botanic garden also give an excellent lesson in California native plants. Drive west on Foothill Road (Calif. 192) to Calif. 154; then head north to the crest of San Marcos Pass, turning east on **East Camino Cielo Road,** to **Los Padres National Forest.** A local birders' favorite, this picturesque route can produce Mountain Quail, Band-tailed Pigeon, California Thrasher, Greater Roadrunner, Wrentit, and Rufous-crowned Sparrow year-round; in spring and summer look for Costa's Hummingbird, Common Poorwill (in predawn and at dusk), Black-chinned Sparrow, and Lazuli Bunting. Drive east at least 7 miles to La Cumbre Peak, where you also might find Townsend's Solitaire in the winter.

CALIFORNIA CONDOR

One of the most famous endangered birds in the U.S., the California Condor was in such low numbers in the 1980s that the less than ten wild birds remaining were taken from their southern California range and added to a captive-breeding program. Condors have now been reintroduced into southern California. Controversy follows their recovery, and many wonder if the bird will find a place in a world so greatly changed from wilderness condition. ■

21 Higher-elevation species are the reward for a spring or summer visit to **Mount Pinos** in **Los Padres National Forest.** Leave I-5 at the Frazier Park exit just north of Gorman, and drive west; in 6.5 miles bear right on Cuddy Valley Road, and in about 5 miles turn south on Mount Pinos Road. Explore side roads as you drive up the mountain. Two favorite birding stops are **McGill Campground,** about 5 miles up, and **Iris Meadow,** near the Chula Vista Campground at the end of the paved road. You should walk the old road 1.5 miles to the 8,831-foot summit as well. Among the many birds nesting in the area are Mountain Quail, Band-tailed Pigeon, Northern Pygmy-Owl, White-throated Swift, Calliope Hummingbird, Red-breasted Sapsucker, White-headed Woodpecker, Olive-sided and Dusky Flycatchers, Steller's Jay, Clark's Nutcracker, Mountain Chickadee, Oak Titmouse, Pygmy Nuthatch, Western Bluebird, Yellow-rumped Warbler, Western Tanager, Green-tailed Towhee, the large-billed subspecies of Fox Sparrow, Purple and Cassin's Finches, and Lawrence's Goldfinch.

22 A detour eastward: Most of these same highland birds can be found on a trip into the **San Gabriel Mountains** north of Los Angeles in the **Angeles National Forest.** From I-210 northwest of Pasadena, take Calif. 2 (Angeles Crest Highway) to the north. Explore some of the picnic areas and camp-grounds as you ascend along 34 miles of winding road to

Buckhorn Campground at 6,500 feet. Here look for Nuttall's Woodpecker, Oak Titmouse, Wrentit, and California Thrasher at mid-elevations. As you climb, check spots such as **Charlton Flat** and the **Chilao Visitor Center** for Mountain Quail, White-headed Woodpecker, Dusky Flycatcher, Cassin's and Hutton's Vireos, Steller's Jay, Western Tanager, and Lawrence's Goldfinch. Even higher, you might find Clark's Nutcracker, Townsend's Solitaire, Hermit Warbler, or Red Crossbill.

23 The oceanside town of Ventura is the embarkation site for boat trips to **Santa Cruz Island** in **Channel Islands National Park,** known to birders as the only place in the world where the Island Scrub-Jay can be found. Once a race of the Scrub Jay shown in most field guides, this species can sometimes be found in a grove of eucalyptus trees and other exotic plantings near the landing site at Scorpion Anchorage. If not, try finding them by walking a mile up the seasonal stream to the west to stands of oaks and ironwood trees in the narrowing canyon above. Better yet, schedule your trip to be one that lands at **Prisoners Harbor,** where the jays are easily found near the dock.

Cruises to Santa Cruz aren't just for the jay. Among the pelagic species you might see are Sooty Shearwater (spring–fall), Black-vented Shearwater (early fall, early spring), Ashy and Black Storm-Petrels (May–October), Least Storm-Petrel (late summer), Xantus's Murrelet (spring), and Common Murre and Cassin's and Rhinoceros Auklets (late fall–early spring). Other migrant seabirds include Red-necked and Red Phalaropes and Pomarine and Parasitic Jaegers. Black Oystercatcher and Pigeon Guillemot nest on Santa Cruz; the oystercatcher is a permanent resident. Santa Cruz and other Channel Islands are also home to the nonmigratory race of Allen's Hummingbird. For information, contact the Channel Islands National Park or the boat concessioner, **Island Packers**, at Ventura Harbor.

24 A short distance south on Harbor Boulevard, **McGrath State Beach** can have excellent shorebirding. Take the nature trail to the mouth of the Santa Clara River and look over mudflats for Black-necked Stilt, American Avocet, Willet, Marbled Godwit, and Elegant Tern (summer–fall), among other species. Snowy Plover nests in the sand dunes, and some rarities may appear.

Drive south on the Pacific Coast Highway (PCH) past the Point Mugu Naval Air Station, and watch for parking at Point

Mugu, within **Point Mugu State Park.** Mugu Rock is a favorite lookout from fall through spring for seabirds. The salt marsh and tidal flats bordering the PCH just north of the rock are often teeming with waterfowl, herons, and shorebirds.

25 In Orange County, **Bolsa Chica Ecological Reserve** is a top wetland birding site. On the east side of the PCH, 4 miles south of Seal Beach, the reserve hosts nesting Snowy Plover; Black-necked Stilt; American Avocet; Caspian, Royal, Elegant, Forster's, and Least Terns; and Black Skimmer. The Belding's subspecies of Savannah Sparrow lives in cordgrass areas. Find herons and these shorebirds: Black-bellied and Semipalmated Plovers, Willet, Long-billed Curlew, Marbled Godwit, Red Knot, and Western and Least Sandpipers, common from midsummer through spring. Waterfowl throng the reserve in winter, and from fall through spring you might find Pied-billed, Horned, Eared, Western, and Clark's Grebes.

26 A few miles farther south on the PCH, **Huntington Beach Pier** is a lookout for seabirds in early morning. Snowy Plover and Least Tern nest at nearby **Huntington State Beach.** Just south of Newport Bay, turn left (north) on Jamboree Road and, in 0.2 mile, west on Back Bay Drive. This road passes alongside **Upper Newport Bay Ecological Reserve,** where mudflats, marsh, and open water attract waders, waterfowl, shorebirds, gulls, and terns. Clapper Rail is here. In about a mile, stop at the Big Canyon area; find endangered California Gnatcatcher in the coastal sage scrub near the pond across the road (listen for a rising and falling kittenlike mew). The endangered coastal race of Cactus Wren sings its chugging song on the bluffs. Visit the new interpretive center, opened in 2000, for local birding advice. Back on the PCH, go south. Three miles from Jamboree Road, turn west into the Pelican Point area of **Crystal Cove State Park.** Trails through coastal sage scrub may reveal California Gnatcatcher. South along the east side of the PCH, miles of trails lead through coastal sage scrub, grassland, and woods; residents include California Quail, White-tailed Kite, Greater Roadrunner, Anna's Hummingbird, Black Phoebe, Western Scrub-Jay, Bushtit, Wrentit, California Thrasher, and Spotted and California Towhees.

27 Moving from the coast to the desert: The lush oasis of **Big Morongo Canyon Preserve** north of Palm Springs attracts a noteworthy array of breeding species. To reach it, drive north from I-10 on Calif. 62 for 10.5 miles to Morongo Valley; turn southeast on East Drive. See the preserve entrance on the east. In its woodlands and marsh areas in spring and summer, you'll find Virginia Rail, Black-chinned and Costa's Hummingbirds, Ladder-backed and Nuttall's Woodpeckers, Black and Say's Phoebes, Vermilion and Brown-crested (scarce) Flycatchers, Cassin's and Western Kingbirds, Bell's Vireo (rare), Verdin, Cactus and Marsh Wrens, Blue-gray and Black-tailed Gnatcatchers, Phainopepla, Lucy's Warbler (rare), Yellow-breasted Chat, Summer Tanager, Black-throated Sparrow, Blue Grosbeak, Lazuli Bunting, Hooded and Scott's Orioles, and Lesser and Lawrence's (irregular) Goldfinches.

28 Though surrounded by desert, Palm Springs is not far from coniferous forest in the **San Jacinto Mountains.** One picturesque route has been designated the **Palms to Pines Scenic Byway** for its linkage of desert and highland habitats. Traveling between two such worlds will bring a correspondingly wide range of birds. From Palm Springs, take Calif. 111 to Palm Desert and turn south on Calif. 74. Stop at the Bureau of Land Management's visitor center outside town for information.

From the desert, where Costa's Hummingbird, Ladder-backed Woodpecker, Verdin, Cactus Wren, Phainopepla, and Black-throated Sparrow reside, ascend into pinyon-juniper scrub; within **San Bernardino National Forest** stop along the roads near **Lake Hemet** for a chance at Pinyon Jay. Check **Hurkey Creek Campground** for White-headed Woodpecker. At Mountain Center turn north on Calif. 243, and at Idyllwild hike the trail up Mount San Jacinto at **Mount San Jacinto State Park.** Here, look for Mountain Quail, Band-tailed Pigeon, White-headed Woodpecker, Red-breasted Sapsucker (scarce), Steller's Jay, Mountain Chickadee, Oak Titmouse, Pygmy Nuthatch, Townsend's Solitaire, Purple and Cassin's Finches, and Pine Siskin. In summer, see Olive-sided and Dusky Flycatchers, Western Tanager, and Black-headed Grosbeak. Calif. 243 winds back down to I-10 at Banning.

29 Drive 6 miles west on I-10, take Calif. 60 west, and in 8 miles turn south on Theodore Street, continuing south on Davis Road (this dirt road can be difficult or impassable in wet weather). In 4.6 miles, turn east to **San Jacinto Wildlife Area,** a restored remnant of the once much larger wetlands of the San Jacinto Valley. Breeders here include Pied-billed Grebe, varied ducks, California Quail, Virginia Rail, Common

Moorhen, Black-necked Stilt, American Avocet, Greater Roadrunner, Burrowing Owl, Rufous-crowned and Sage Sparrows, Blue Grosbeak, and Tricolored and Yellow-headed Blackbirds. Fall and winter bring waterfowl; raptors such as Ferruginous Hawk, Golden Eagle, and Prairie Falcon; and Mountain Bluebird. In winter look for scarce Mountain Plover and longspurs in the agricultural fields.

Island Scrub-Jay, found only on Santa Cruz Island

30 The vast, rugged expanse of **Anza-Borrego Desert State Park,** California's largest state park at 600,000 acres, harbors desert species and migrants. First stop at the visitor center in Borrego Spring, and then drive north to the **Borrego Palm Canyon Campground.** Here a walk on the 3-mile round-trip nature trail could turn up Gambel's Quail, Greater Roadrunner, Ladder-backed Woodpecker, Verdin, Cactus and Canyon Wrens, Black-throated Sparrow, and Hooded and Scott's Orioles. This is a popular trail, so arrive early. To look for Lucy's Warbler (spring–early summer), drive east on Palm Canyon Drive and turn south on Borrego Springs Road (Calif. S3); about 2 miles after this road turns east, go north on Yaqui Pass Road to its end and search the desert scrub. You'll also find Black-tailed Gnatcatcher and Phainopepla here, and in winter Brewer's Sparrow.

Return to Borrego Springs Road and drive south to **Tamarisk Grove Campground,** to find Long-eared Owl (irregular; ask the park ranger for recent owl news). Then take the road west across Borrego Springs Road to the **Yaqui Well Nature Trail** for spring and fall migrants, and for California Quail, White-winged Dove, Anna's and Costa's Hummingbirds, Ladder-backed Woodpecker, Black-tailed Gnatcatcher, California Thrasher, and Phainopepla. Seek the scarce and elusive Le Conte's Thrasher by taking Calif. 78 east from Tamarisk Grove and turning northwest on Borrego Springs Road. In under a mile cross the wash along **San Felipe Creek,** which is a good place to search.

For another Le Conte's Thrasher site, take the dirt road north off Calif. S22, just east of the intersection of Henderson Canyon Road and Calif. S22 in northeastern Borrego Springs. Drive 3 miles and investigate the sparse scrub on the southwest side of **Clark Dry Lake.** The thrasher is most likely to be singing in early morning in late winter and early spring.

31 The **Salton Sea** has a history as unusual as its reputation among birders is high. Formed in 1905 when an accidental break in a canal diverted water into the dry alkaline basin of the Imperial Valley, this saline lake (saltier than the Pacific) covers 380 square miles. At 200 feet below sea level, the area can be one of the hottest in the U.S. in summer. Such a body of water in the desert attracts waterbirds of all sorts.

If you're approaching the Salton Sea from the west on Calif. 78, turn north on Calif. 86 to Salton City, Salton Sea Beach, and Desert Shores, towns where you can make your way to the sea's west shore to check for waterbirds including Yellow-footed Gull, a specialty here. The gull is present from late June to early winter.

Go south on Calif. 86, and 12 miles south of the intersection with Calif. 78, exit east on Bannister Road, then turn north on Vendel Road to reach **Unit 1** of the **Sonny Bono Salton Sea National Wildlife Refuge.** In winter find Snow and Ross's Geese and Long-billed Curlew. Herons, egrets, and White-faced Ibis are present year-round. Check the roadside for Burrowing Owl. Return to Calif. 86, turn east, drive 5 miles to Westmoreland, then turn north on Forrester Road, which becomes Gentry Road and leads to the refuge headquarters.

Take the **Rock Hill Nature Trail** to check freshwater marshes and the sea for waterfowl (fall–spring), Western and Clark's Grebes, American White and Brown Pelicans, Wood Stork (summer), Clapper Rail (nesting), Virginia Rail and Sora (fall–spring), shorebirds, gulls, and terns. Land birds include Gambel's Quail, Common Ground-Dove, Lesser Nighthawk (at dusk), Verdin, Cactus Wren, Phainopepla, and Abert's Towhee.

For another good waterbird spot, take Gentry Road south of refuge headquarters to McKendry Road and go west to **Obsidian Butte.** It's also good in winter for Savannah Sparrow of the large-billed subspecies; birders search out this sparrow hoping it may someday be reclassified as a separate species.

Next, take Sinclair Road a mile east from the headquarters and turn north on Garst Road to the **Red Hill** area at the Alamo River mouth, another excellent place for sighting waterbirds. (The road west to the marina offers a good viewpoint.) This is one of the best areas around the sea for Yellow-footed Gull.

Drive east on Sinclair Road to Calif. 111 and turn south to the town of Calipatria. Drive 2.7 miles past the intersection with Calif. 115, then turn east to **Ramer Lake,** part of **Imperial Wildlife Area** (avoid in fall hunting season). Drive around the lake and go east on Quay Road, south on Kershaw Road, east on Titsworth Road, and south on Smith Road to **Finney Lake,** another unit of the wildlife area. At both lakes you'll find a good assortment of waterbirds. Finney Lake also has some of the region's best desert scrub, which attracts Lesser Nighthawk, Verdin, Cactus Wren, Black-tailed Gnatcatcher, Crissal Thrasher (rare), and Abert's Towhee.

BIRDS, PLANTS, AND FIRES

The California coastal habitat called chaparral has dense shrubby vegetation adapted to regular fires. Several birds make this habitat their home, including California Quail, Wrentit, California Thrasher, and California Towhee. Fires and demand for real estate have led to the destruction of both chaparral and the lower-elevation habitat coastal sage scrub, The most famous bird of the latter habitat is the threatened California Gnatcatcher. ∎

Drive north on Calif. 111 through Calipatria about 8 miles to Niland. Turn west on Noffsinger Road and drive 3.3 miles to Davis Road. Drive both north and south on Davis to explore wetlands and roads running west to the Salton Sea. (Avoid in hunting season and wet weather.) For another good viewpoint, go north on Davis Road to Calif. 111; drive north for 6.5 miles and turn south to Niland Marina. The shoreline vegetation here may have wintering large-billed subspecies of Savannah Sparrow.

32 Moving back toward the coast on I-15, drive 7 miles south of Escondido to West Bernardo Drive, which goes west, then south for 0.3 mile. Park in the lot and walk the **Piedras Pintadas Interpretive Trail** near Casa de las Campanas retirement center into the **San Dieguito River Park's Bernardo Bay Natural Area at Lake Hodges.** The lake has waterbirds (fall–spring); but specialties are the threatened California Gnatcatcher and Sage Sparrow, found in coastal sage scrub along the trail. See California Quail, White-tailed Kite, Golden Eagle, White-throated Swift, Anna's Hummingbird, Cassin's Kingbird, Cactus Wren, Wrentit, California Thrasher, and California Towhee.

33 Back on the shores of the Pacific, north of San Diego, exit I-5 on Lomas Santa Fe Drive going toward Solana Beach, and in 0.7 mile turn north on North Rios Avenue to its end at **San Elijo Lagoon.** The coastal sage scrub fringing the lagoon along the path to the east is home to California Gnatcatcher, as well as Cassin's Kingbird, Wrentit, California Thrasher, California Towhee, and Lesser Goldfinch. Large numbers of waders, waterfowl, shorebirds, and terns frequent the lagoon, as well.

34 To the south, the rugged coastline at **La Jolla** attracts the "rocky shorebird" group—Wandering Tattler, Black Turnstone, and Surfbird—from fall through spring. Take Ardath Road west from I-5 to where it merges with Torrey Pines Road. In a little less than a mile, turn right onto Prospect Place, then right onto Coast Blvd. toward Scripps Park and the lifeguard station, favorite lookouts for seabird-watching. Red-throated, Pacific, and Common Loon; Black-vented Shearwater; Brandt's and Pelagic Cormorants; gulls; and terns might be seen in winter. Sooty Shearwater is often spotted off-shore from spring through fall.

35 In San Diego, take Calif. 209 southwest from I-5 toward **Cabrillo National Monument** and **Point Loma.** This peninsula boasts migrants and vagrants in spring and fall. Check trees and shrubs in **Fort Rosecrans National Cemetery,** a mile north of the national monument, and around the monument's visitor center and along its 2-mile **Bayside Trail.** Along the trail you'll find California Quail, Anna's Hummingbird, Ash-throated Flycatcher, Bushtit, California Thrasher, Wrentit, and Rufous-crowned Sparrow. Go south toward the Point Loma Light Station and follow the road west and back north to parking lots on the cliffs, lookouts for seabirds and rocky shorebirds.

Back on I-5, drive south and take Calif. 75 (Palm Avenue) west toward Imperial Beach. In 1.3 miles turn north on Tenth Street to reach spots for viewing the south end of **San Diego Bay.** Gull-billed, Caspian, Elegant, and Least Terns and Black Skimmer nest here, and herons, shorebirds, and gulls are present year-round. Go west and north on Calif. 75 (Silver Strand Blvd.); find a parking spot on the east for scanning the bay.

Return south on I-5 to the Coronado Avenue exit. Go west on Coronado (which turns into Imperial Beach Blvd.) to Third Street, which leads to the marsh and the visitor center for **Tijuana Slough National Wildlife Refuge.** After obtaining information here, drive west to Seacoast Drive and go south to its end. Check the marsh and tidal channels, and walk along the beach south to more marshes and mudflats at the mouth of the Tijuana River, just a couple miles from the Mexican border. Winter waterfowl, herons, shorebirds, gulls, and terns can be found here in large numbers, and the endangered local race of Clapper Rail lives in the marsh. The beach at the river's mouth is good for Snowy Plover and Least Tern. Access another part of the area by driving south on Fifth Street from Imperial Beach Blvd. and following a trail southward toward the river.

CALIFORNIA | MORE INFORMATION

RARE BIRD ALERT
Northern 415-681-7422
Southeast 909-793-5599
Southern 818-952-5502

1 Klamath Basin (P. 230)
klamathbasinrefuges.fws.gov
530-667-2231

2 Patrick's Point (P. 231)
www.parks.ca.gov
707-677-3570

3 Arcata Marsh (P. 232)
www.arcatacityhall.org
707-826-2359

3 Samoa Dunes (P. 232)
www.redwoodvisitor.org
707-825-2300

3 Humboldt Bay (P. 232)
www.fws.gov/pacific
707-733-5406

4 Sacramento NWR
(P. 232)
www.fws.gov/pacific
530-934-2801

6 Point Reyes (P. 233)
www.nps.gov/pore
415-663-1092

6 Tomales Bay (P. 233)
www.parks.ca.gov
415-669-1140

**6 Audubon Canyon
Ranch** (P. 234)
www.egret.org
415-868-9244

7 Golden Gate NRA
(P. 234)
www.nps.gov/goga
415-556-0560

8 Golden Gate Park
(P. 234)
www.parks.sfgov.org
415-831-2745

9 Don Edwards (P. 235)
www.fws.gov/desfbay
510-792-0222

9 Coyote Hills (P. 235)
www.ebpakrs.org
510-795-9385

**9 Palo Alto Baylands
Preserve** (P. 235)
www.abag.ca.gov
650-329-2506

11 Año Nuevo (P. 236)
www.anonuevo.org
650-879-0227

12 Moss Landing (P. 237)
www.parks.ca.gov
831-384-7695

12 Elkhorn Slough (P. 237)
www.elkhornslough.org
831-728-2822

13 Shearwater Journeys
(P. 237)
www.shearwaterjourneys
.com; 831-637-8527

**15 Merced and San Luis
NWRs** (P. 238)
www.fws.gov/pacific
209-826-3508

16 Yosemite NP (P. 239)
www.nps.gov/yose
209-372-0200

17 Mono Basin *(P. 240)*
www.monolake.org
760-647-3044
🚻 ⓢ 🏕 🚶 ⛵ ♿
Call for winter hours.

18 Bodie SHP *(P. 241)*
www.parks.ca.gov
760-647-6445
🚻 ⓢ 🏕 ♿

19 Morro Bay *(P. 242)*
www.parks.ca.gov
805-772-2694
🚻 ⓢ 🍴 🏕 🚶 ⛵ ♿

19 Montaña de Oro SP
(P. 243)
www.parks.ca.gov
805-528-0513
🚻 🏕 🚶

**20 Santa Barbara
Museum** *(P. 243)*
www.sbnature.org
805-682-4711
🚻 ⓢ 🏕 🚶 ♿

**20 Santa Barbara
Botanic Garden** *(P. 243)*
www.sbbg.org
805-682-4726
🚻 ⓢ 🏕 🚶

21 Los Padres NF *(P. 244)*
www.fs.fed.us/r5/lospadres
805-245-3731
ⓢ 🚶 ♿

22 Angeles NF *(P. 244)*
www.fs.fed.us/r5/angeles
626-574-5200
🚻 ⓢ 🍴 🏕 🚶 ⛵ ♿

23 Channel Islands *(P. 245)*
www.nps.gov/chis
805-658-5730
🚻 🏕 🚶 ♿
Contact Island Packers, 805-642-1393, for cruise info.

24 McGrath Beach *(P. 245)*
www.parks.ca.gov
850-899-1400
🚻 ⓢ 🏕 🚶 ♿

24 Point Mugu *(P. 246)*
www.parks.ca.gov
818-880-0350
ⓢ 🏕 ♿

25 Bolsa Chica *(P. 246)*
www.dfg.ca.gov
714-846-1114
🚻 🏕 🚶 ♿

26 Huntington Beach
(P. 246)
www.parks.ca.gov
714-536-1454
🚻 ⓢ 🍴 🏕 ♿

**26 Upper Newport Bay
Reserve** *(P. 246)*
www.dfg.ca.gov
949-640-6746
🏕 🚶 ⛵ ♿

26 Crystal Cove *(P. 246)*
www.parks.ca.gov
949-494-3539
🚻 ⓢ 🍴 🏕 🚶 ♿

27 Big Morongo Canyon
(P. 246)
www.bigmorongo.org
760-363-7190
🏕 🚶 ♿

28 San Bernardino *(P. 247)*
www.fs.fed.us/r5
909-383-5588
🚻 🍴 🏕 🚶 ⛵ ♿

28 Mount San Jacinto SP
(P. 247)
www.sanjac.statepark.org
909-659-2607
🚻 🏕 🚶 ♿

**29 San Jacinto Wildlife
Area** *(P. 247)*
www.dfg.ca.gov
909-654-0580
ⓢ 🏕 🚶 ⛵ ♿

30 Anza-Borrego *(P. 248)*
*www.anzaborrego
.statepark.org;*
760-767-5311
🚻 ⓢ 🏕 🚶 ♿

**31 Sonny Bono Salton
Sea Refuge** *(P. 249)*
www.pacific.fws.gov
760-348-5278
🚻 🏕 🚶 ♿

**35 Cabrillo National
Monument** *(P. 251)*
www.nps.gov/cabr
619-557-5450
🚻 ⓢ 🍴 🏕 🚶 ♿

35 Tijuana Slough *(P. 251)*
www.fws.gov/pacific
619-575-3613
🚻 🏕 🚶 ♿

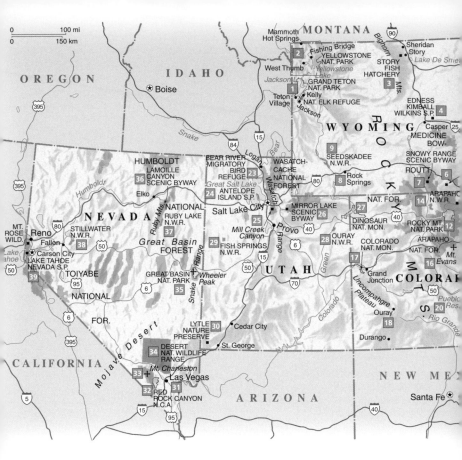

CENTRAL ROCKIES

- Wyoming
- Colorado
- Utah
- Nevada

SOME OF THE BIRDING HIGHLIGHTS of this expansive and diverse region are very high, indeed. In Colorado's Rocky Mountain National Park, for example, Trail Ridge Road ascends past tree line to alpine tundra at more than 12,000 feet, an elevation that can leave you breathless in more ways than one. Lucky birders sometimes find White-tailed Ptarmigan or Brown-capped Rosy-Finch near the highway—and even the not-so-lucky will find spectacular scenery. The view of Long's Peak and the Continental Divide from Trail Ridge rates at the top in a state of magnificent panoramas. Colorado's Mount

Evans Scenic Byway, southern Wyoming's Snowy Range Scenic Byway, Utah's Mirror Lake Scenic Byway, and Nevada's Great Basin National Park are just a few of the other highland areas where Clark's Nutcrackers and Mountain Bluebirds brighten already stunning landscapes. Find noisy Steller's Jay, and elusive Blue Grouse, too.

In Colorado, birders at Pawnee National Grassland may see McCown's Longspurs perform their song flights, or see the declining species Ferruginous Hawk and Mountain Plover. Dinosaur National Monument, on the Colorado-Utah line, hosts Gray Flycatcher, Pinyon Jay, and Juniper Titmouse. A portion of Nevada's Desert National Wildlife Refuge ranks with the best desert-oasis "migrant traps" in the country.

Fine wetlands in this region include the renowned Bear River Migratory Bird Refuge, on Utah's Great Salt Lake west of Brigham City; Wyoming's Seedskadee National Wildlife Refuge; and Nevada's Lahontan Valley. In the Arkansas River Valley of eastern Colorado, waders and shorebirds frequent a series of shallow lakes that dot the High Plains. ■

Sage Thrasher

SPECIAL BIRDS OF THE CENTRAL ROCKIES

Clark's Grebe	Snowy Plover	Gray Flycatcher	
Trumpeter Swan	Mountain Plover	Gray Vireo	Black-chinned Sparrow
Barrow's Goldeneye	Wilson's Phalarope	Pinyon Jay	Sage Sparrow
Ferruginous Hawk	Flammulated Owl	Chihuahuan Raven	McCown's Longspur
Chukar	Great Gray Owl	Juniper Titmouse	Chestnut-collared Longspur
Himalayan Snowcock	Boreal Owl	Sage Thrasher	Gray-crowned Rosy-Finch
Greater Sage-Grouse	Black Swift	Curve-billed Thrasher	
White-tailed Ptarmigan	Lewis's Woodpecker	Le Conte's Thrasher	Black Rosy-Finch
Blue Grouse	Williamson's Sapsucker	Phainopepla	Brown-capped Rosy-Finch
Lesser Prairie-Chicken	American Three-toed Woodpecker	Virginia's Warbler	
		Cassin's Sparrow	Pine Grosbeak

WYOMING

- Mountain and wetland birds at Grand Teton National Park
- Waterbirds and grassland species in the Torrington area
- High-elevation species along the Snowy Range Scenic Byway

The Snowy Range Scenic Byway, an excellent high-elevation birding route west of Laramie

1 The jagged peaks, glacier-carved valleys, and tree-lined lakes of Grand Teton National Park and the surrounding area make it a beautiful birding spot, and diverse habitats make it a rewarding one. From marshes and riparian vegetation along the Snake River to sagebrush flats, and from spruce-fir forest to alpine tundra, there's a lot to keep a birder busy.

From Jackson, it's a short drive north off Broadway to the **National Elk Refuge,** where wetlands are home to migrant and breeding waterfowl including Trumpeter Swan and Sandhill Crane. Keep watch for Prairie Falcon, Long-billed Curlew, and Mountain Bluebird. On US 89/191 just north of town, the Jackson Hole and Greater Yellowstone Information Center sits beside a marsh with various waterbirds. Farther north, highway pull-offs allow scanning of refuge wetlands.

Drive northward into **Grand Teton National Park.** After crossing the Gros Ventre River, turn east on the Gros Ventre Road toward Kelly. You might find Greater Sage-Grouse in the sagebrush flats here, and Mountain Bluebird, Sage Thrasher, Green-tailed Towhee, and Brewer's and Savannah Sparrows. The park campground 4 miles up the road can have Western Wood-Pewee, Cordilleran Flycatcher, Warbling Vireo, Tree and Violet-green Swallows, Black-capped Chickadee, Yellow Warbler, and Bullock's Oriole. At the nearby Jackson Hole Airport, the sagebrush north of the entrance road is a good place to find Greater Sage-Grouse. In spring, males "dance" at courtship grounds here. Ask park personnel for information.

In summer, find Black Rosy-Finch, a park specialty, by taking the aerial tramway from Teton Village to the top of **Rendezvous Mountain,** 10,446 feet high. These little finches prefer rocky areas and cliff faces, especially near snowbanks. Check cirques and snowfields. To return, try hiking **Granite Canyon Trail** back down. It's a 12.4-mile walk with an elevation change of more than 4,000 feet—but it's all downhill.

From the park's Moose Visitor Center, drive north on the main park road (closed in winter). On trails at **Jenny** and **String Lakes** and up to **Hidden Falls,** find nesting species of western montane forests, such as Northern Goshawk, Blue Grouse, Williamson's and Red-naped Sapsuckers, Dusky Flycatcher, Gray and Steller's Jays, Clark's Nutcracker, Mountain Chickadee, Red-breasted Nuthatch, American Dipper, Ruby-crowned Kinglet, Townsend's Solitaire, Swainson's and Hermit Thrushes, Yellow-rumped Warbler, Western Tanager, Pine Grosbeak, Cassin's Finch, and Pine Siskin. Farther north, **Signal Mountain Road** has the same species.

Ahead lies some of the park's best birding. At the **Jackson Lake Dam** scan for loons, grebes, and waterfowl. Check the **Oxbow Bend Turnout, Willow Flats Overlook,** and **Christian Pond** for wetland and meadow species such as Trumpeter Swan, Barrow's Goldeneye, Common Merganser, Western Grebe, American White Pelican, American Bittern, Osprey, Northern Harrier, Bald Eagle, Sora, California Gull, Calliope Hummingbird, Willow Flycatcher, Marsh Wren, MacGillivray's and Wilson's Warblers, and Lincoln's Sparrow.

2 In the northwest corner of the state, **Yellowstone National Park** encompasses 2.2 million acres of forest, grassland, and wetlands. There are plenty of birds to see here, especially for Easterners making their first trip West. Checking varied habitats at differing elevations will turn up typical species such as Cinnamon Teal; Broad-tailed Hummingbird; Red-naped

Sapsucker; Olive-sided, Hammond's, and Dusky Flycatchers; Gray and Steller's Jays; Clark's Nutcracker; Black-billed Magpie; Violet-green Swallow; Mountain Chickadee; Swainson's Thrush; MacGillivray's Warbler; and Western Tanager. With luck, you will see Blue Grouse, Northern Goshawk, Williamson's Sapsucker, Pine Grosbeak, and Red Crossbill. For these, time on the trails pays off. After you've seen Old Faithful, some of the park's best birding can be found by driving 73 miles from West Thumb, on Yellowstone Lake, east and north to Tower and west to Mammoth Hot Springs. As you skirt **Yellowstone Lake** to Fishing Bridge a bit beyond, scan for Trumpeter Swan, Barrow's Goldeneye, Common Loon, American White Pelican, Double-crested Cormorant, California Gull, as well as Osprey and Bald Eagle.

BURROWING OWL

With its fierce yellow eyes and long legs adapted to terrestrial life, the Burrowing Owl is one of the most appealing birds of the plains. It often bobs up and down rather comically while standing on the ground. Though still widely distributed through much of the West, this species has suffered serious declines nearly everywhere it occurs. The owl nests in holes dug by prairie dogs and other burrowing animals, and the destruction of prairie dog colonies is dwindling Burrowing Owl populations. ■

Heading north along the **Yellowstone River,** find White-throated Swift flying through canyons and American Dipper flitting from rock to rock along rapids. Where roads cross meadows stop and check surrounding trees for Great Gray Owl. You could spot a Sandhill Crane nesting or a beautiful sky-blue Mountain Bluebird. In sagebrush areas, look for Sage Thrasher and Brewer's Sparrow.

American Three-toed and Black-backed Woodpeckers frequent burned woodland, and the Yellowstone fires of 1988 provided vast areas of such habitat. Ask park naturalists about the chances of seeing these often elusive species.

3   In north-central Wyoming, the small town of **Story** and nearby **Lake De Smet** constitute a popular birding destination. In Story, Wyo. 194 (Fish Hatchery Road) leads west to **Story Fish Hatchery,** set in ponderosa pine forest; find nesting Broad-tailed Hummingbird; Dusky Flycatcher; Plumbeous Vireo; Mountain Chickadee; Red-breasted, White-breasted, and Pygmy Nuthatches; Ruby-crowned Kinglet (and Golden-crowned in winter); and Yellow-rumped Warbler. Drive back east into town and turn south on County Road 145 (Wagon

Box Monument Road). Find Calliope Hummingbird (spring–early summer) along **South Piney Creek.** As you continue south down the road alongside **Little Piney Creek,** nesting birds include Veery, Yellow and MacGillivray's Warblers, American Redstart, Ovenbird, Common Yellowthroat, and Lazuli Bunting. In grasslands to the south, see Sharp-tailed Grouse and Bobolink.

4 If you're in Casper in spring or fall, walk along the **Platte River Parkway** to view migrants. A paved, 2.5-mile trail along the Platte River, it can be accessed from Crossroads Park, off Poplar Street, or from the Bryan Stock Trail Bridge over the Platte to the east. East of Casper, off US 20/26/87, **Edness Kimball Wilkins State Park** is also excellent in migration and hosts riparian breeding species such as Red-headed Woodpecker, Western and Eastern Kingbirds, Blue Jay, Yellow Warbler, Black-headed Grosbeak, Lazuli Bunting, and Bullock's Oriole.

5 The region around Torrington, near the Nebraska border, is noted for waterbirds and grassland species. The ponds and marshes at **Table Mountain Wildlife Habitat Management Area** host waterfowl, migrant shorebirds, and at times thousands of Snow Geese. American Bittern and Snowy Egret are here (summer), and Great and Cattle Egrets may be seen. Black-crowned Night-Heron, Virginia Rail, Sora, American Avocet, and Wilson's Phalarope breed. Wyoming's first Great-tailed Grackle nest was found here in 1998. Cars aren't allowed before Memorial Day, so walk in. Avoid hunting season.

Grasslands here shelter McCown's and Chestnut-collared Longspurs. On back roads through the plains, see Swainson's and Ferruginous Hawks, Burrowing Owl, Western and Eastern Kingbirds, Horned Lark, and Lark Bunting.

6 One of the best places for waterbirds in southern Wyoming is the **Hutton Lake National Wildlife Refuge,** southwest of Laramie. Take Wyo. 230 southwest from I-80 about 10 miles; turn east on County Road 37 and drive 7 miles to County Road 34. Turn northeast and drive to the entrance. It has no facilities and roads are primitive. Don't visit in wet weather or winter. Driving through grassland to the refuge, watch for McCown's Longspur. Inside, check the five small lakes for waterfowl, migrant grebes, American White Pelican, gulls, and terns. In April, 20,000 ducks may throng the wetlands. Nesting species include Canvasback; Redhead; Ruddy Duck; Pied-billed, Eared, and Western Grebes; Northern

Harrier; Virginia Rail; Sora; American Avocet; Forster's and Black Terns; Marsh Wren; Vesper, Lark, and Savannah Sparrows; Yellow-headed Blackbird; and Snowy Egret (summer). In summer and early fall, see large numbers of shorebirds.

7 West of Centennial, the **Snowy Range Scenic Byway** (Wyo. 130) through **Medicine Bow-Routt National Forest** ascends to 10,847-foot Snowy Range Pass before heading down the western side of the Medicine Bow Mountains. From late May into October, see nesting species such as Blue Grouse; Olive-sided, Dusky, and Cordilleran Flycatchers; Gray and Steller's Jays; Clark's Nutcracker; Mountain Chickadee; Red-breasted Nuthatch; American Dipper; Townsend's Solitaire; Swainson's and Hermit Thrushes; Orange-crowned and Yellow-rumped Warblers; White-crowned Sparrow; and Pine Grosbeak.

Stop at the visitor center a mile west of Centennial, then continue about 7 miles to the turn north to **Brooklyn Lake.** About 3.5 miles west on Wyo. 130, turn north to **Lewis Lake** for more birding. From here you can hike up 12,013-foot **Medicine Bow Peak,** where you'll find nesting American Pipit and Brown-capped Rosy-Finch.

8 You'll find a far different landscape south of **Rock Springs,** From the Flaming Gorge Road exit (exit 99) on I-80 west of town, drive south on US 191 for 4.2 miles, turn west on Little Firehole Road, and go south to meet Firehole Canyon Road, where you can turn east back to US 191. Stop often on this route to find Gray and Ash-throated Flycatchers; Plumbeous Vireo; Western Scrub-Jay; Pinyon Jay; Juniper Titmouse; Bushtit (rare); Rock, Canyon (rare), and Bewick's Wrens; Blue-gray Gnatcatcher; Sage Thrasher; Virginia's and Black-throated Gray Warblers; and Scott's Oriole (rare).

9 From I-80, take Wyo. 372 north about 28 miles, a mile past Wyo. 28, to **Seedskadee National Wildlife Refuge.** Here at any time of year see waterbirds attracted to Green River marshes and land birds of riparian and arid terrain. In summer see several species of ducks, Western Grebe, American White Pelican, Great Blue Heron (a heronry is on the refuge), White-faced Ibis, Osprey, Bald Eagle (more common in winter), Northern Harrier, Swainson's Hawk, Golden Eagle, Prairie Falcon, Sora, Sandhill Crane, Short-eared Owl, Warbling Vireo, Mountain Bluebird, Sage Thrasher, Vesper and Sage Sparrows, and Yellow-headed Blackbird.

WYOMING | MORE INFORMATION

RARE BIRD ALERT
Statewide 307-265-2473

1 National Elk Refuge
(Page 256)
nationalelkrefuge.fws.gov
307-739-9322

**1 Grand Teton National
Park** *(Page 256)*
www.nps.gov/grte
307-739-3300

*Birding highlights are at
Granite Canyon Trail, Jenny
and String Lakes, Hidden
Falls, Signal Mountain Road,
Jackson Lake Dam, Oxbox
Bend Turnout, Willow Flats
Overlook, and Christian Pond.*

**2 Yellowstone National
Park** *(Page 257)*
www.nps.gov/yell
307-344-7381

*Interior of park closed to
vehicles early Nov.–late April.
Birding highlights include
Yellowstone Lake and
Yellowstone River.*

3 Story Fish Hatchery
(Page 258)
gf.state.wy.us
307-683-2234

*Birding highlights include
the town of Story, Lake
DeSmet, South Piney and
Little Piney Creeks.*

**4 Edness Kimball
Wilkins State Park**
(Page 259)
www.wyoparks.state.wy.us
307-577-5150

*Take the Platte River Park-
way in spring and fall to view
migrants.*

**5 Table Mountain and
Rawhide Wildlife Habitat
Management Areas**
(Page 259)
gf.state.wy.us
307-777-4600

**6 Hutton Lake National
Wildlife Refuge** *(Page 259)*
www.fws.gov/refuges
970-723-8202

**7 Medicine Bow-Routt
National Forest**
(Page 260)
www.fs.fed.us/r2/mbr
307-745-2300

*This park is a birding high-
light on the Snowy Range
Scenic Byway, which leads to
birding spots at Brooklyn
Lake, Lewis Lake, and
Medicine Bow Peak.*

8 Rock Springs
(Page 260)
*www.rockspringswyoming
.net*
307-362-3771

**9 Seedskadee National
Wildlife Refuge** *(Page 260)*
seekskadee.fws.gov
307-875-2187

Open June–Oct.

COLORADO

- Prairie birds in the Pawnee and Comanche National Grasslands
- Highland species at Rocky Mountain National Park
- Arid-country birds at Colorado National Monument

Pawnee Buttes on the Pawnee National Grassland, home of nesting Golden Eagles and Prairie Falcons

Colorado means mountains to many people, and it's certainly true that the Rockies offer fabulous scenery, great recreational opportunities, and wonderful birding. In addition to mountain sites, several sites in the High Plains reward traveling birders with sought-after regional specialties, migrants—and more wide-open sky than some people see in an average year.

10 Just 25 minutes north of I-70 via US 385, **Bonny Lake State Park,** on the shores of Bonny Reservoir, attracts waterbirds and some eastern species unusual in this area; it's also a fine spot to look for vagrant warblers and other songbirds in spring. Check cottonwoods and willows at the **Foster**

Grove Campground on the north shore, and the **Wagon Wheel Campground** on the south shore, for Wild Turkey, Yellow-billed Cuckoo, Red-headed and Red-bellied Woodpeckers, Eastern Kingbird, Warbling Vireo, Blue Jay, Gray Catbird, Brown Thrasher, Lazuli and Indigo Buntings, Orchard and Bullock's Orioles, and migrants. Scan the reservoir from the dam for waterfowl and grebes. When low water in late summer exposes mudflats, watch for migrant shorebirds. Around the lake, you may find Loggerhead Shrike, Eastern Bluebird, several species of sparrows, and Dickcissel. Bonny is a popular hunting, fishing, and recreation area; plan your visit accordingly.

11 East of Fort Collins, the **Pawnee National Grassland** attracts birders who drive back roads through the rolling shortgrass steppe country from late April through early July looking for Swainson's and Ferruginous Hawks; Mountain Plover; Long-billed Curlew; Burrowing Owl; Lark Bunting; Cassin's, Brewer's, and other sparrows; and McCown's and Chestnut-collared Longspurs. The area northwest of Briggsdale is a productive one, and with a map of the Pawnee you can explore on your own for hours (noting that much private property is mixed with federal land). Your best bet, though, is to get a copy of the grassland's birding-route map, available at the office in Greeley or at **Crow Valley Recreation Area** just north of Briggsdale off County Road 77. While you're at the latter spot, check the riparian vegetation along Crow Creek for migrants and breeders such as Yellow-billed Cuckoo, Western and Eastern Kingbirds, Northern Mockingbird, Brown Thrasher, and Orchard and Bullock's Orioles.

Lark Bunting and McCown's Longspur are quite easy to find in many places on the grassland, especially when males are performing their song flights (see sidebar, p. 264), and seeing Ferruginous Hawk is a matter of keeping your eyes on the sky and having a bit of luck. Burrowing Owl is found in prairie dog towns, and because these little rodents have suffered losses recently from plague and persecution, it might pay to ask Pawnee personnel about likely locations. Mountain Plover can be tricky to find—look in habitat where vegetation height is less than 4 inches, as well as in prairie dog towns. Chestnut-collared Longspur prefers grass a bit longer than McCown's and is usually not as easy to see. For one likely spot, take US 85 north of Ault for 16 miles, turning east into the **Central Plains Experiment Range.** Stop along the entrance road and walk the field just to the south.

Northeast of Keota, Golden Eagle and Prairie Falcon nest on cliffs at picturesque **Pawnee Buttes;** close approach is prohibited from March through June. Observe from a distance; you might see either of these species anywhere in the area.

SINGING IN THE AIR

Male birds in forested areas perch in trees when they sing, to help their song carry farther, or to make themselves more conspicuous. Prairie birds have no such perches, so many have evolved song flights: They sing while hovering or flying slowly. In Pawnee National Grassland in late spring and early summer, see and hear Horned Lark, Lark Bunting, and McCown's and Chestnut-collared Longspurs displaying song flights over the plain. ■

12 There could hardly be a more beautiful spot to search for high-country birds than the varied **Rocky Mountain National Park,** encompassing more than 400 square miles of meadows, coniferous woodland, and tundra, all lying astraddle the Continental Divide. The park's famed **Trail Ridge Road** (open from Memorial. Day to mid-October) ascends through spruce-fir forest to run for several miles above tree line, offering an alpine experience for those unable to climb. Other roads provide access to varied habitats. For those who enjoy hiking, the potential for exploration—and for birding—can be limitless.

Entering the park from Estes Park at the Beaver Meadows entrance, turn south toward Bear Lake. At Moraine Park, turn west to the **Cub Lake Trail** and walk through the marshy riparian area of the Big Thompson River and up the valley toward the lake. Look for Northern Pygmy-Owl (rarely seen, but listen for the "scolding" notes of songbirds mobbing an owl they've spotted in daylight), Broad-tailed Hummingbird, Williamson's and Red-naped Sapsuckers, Northern Flicker, Western Wood-Pewee, Plumbeous Vireo, Steller's Jay, Black-billed Magpie, Violet-green Swallow, Black-capped and Mountain Chickadees, Pygmy Nuthatch, Townsend's Solitaire, MacGillivray's and Wilson's Warblers, Western Tanager, Lincoln's Sparrow, and Black-headed Grosbeak, among others. (Farther north, the road to the **Endovalley Picnic Area** offers excellent spots for most of these species.)

Backtrack to Bear Lake Road, where, past Hollowell Park, you'll be driving along **Glacier Creek.** Stop anywhere here, sit on a streamside rock, and the odds are pretty good that an American Dipper will fly by before long. Farther on, the flat, easy loop around **Sprague Lake** is a good place to look for many of the same birds mentioned for the Cub Lake Trail. The road climbs to end at 9,475 feet at **Bear Lake,** where Hammond's Flycatcher, Gray Jay, Clark's Nutcracker, Yellow-rumped Warbler, Pine Grosbeak, and Cassin's Finch might be found. Looking south from the parking lot at dusk, some people have been lucky enough to see Black Swifts flying toward nesting sites behind nearby waterfalls.

From Bear Lake, and from **Glacier Gorge Junction** back down the road a short distance, some of the park's nicest trails proceed through deep forests to such stunning destinations as **Mills Lake, The Loch,** and **Odessa Lake.** Many of the park's special birds, such as Northern Goshawk, Blue Grouse, Northern Pygmy-Owl, Williamson's Sapsucker, American Three-toed Woodpecker, Pine Grosbeak, and Red Crossbill, are present but irregular in occurrence. To see them, just walk the trails and stay alert—the more you walk, the better your chances.

The same can be said for White-tailed Ptarmigan, that elusive tundra resident. If you trudge along trails above tree line long enough, you'll find this chickenlike bird in its brownish summer plumage. From Bear Lake, the trail up to **Flattop Mountain** and **Hallett Peak** is as good as any. If you're not ready for a strenuous hike, ptarmigan are regularly found along Trail Ridge Road, as are Horned Lark and American Pipit.

Take this awesomely scenic route west from Deer Ridge Junction, stopping at **Rainbow Curve,** just past the "Two Miles Above Sea Level" sign, to enjoy the view and the Gray Jays and Clark's Nutcrackers that are always present. Soon you'll enter the tundra world; about 2 miles from Rainbow Curve, watch for a parking area for the **Old Ute Trail** on the south. You might find ptarmigan by hiking a bit of this trail, or farther on at the **Tundra Nature Trail** at the popular Rock Cut area. (Be aware that simply walking at this elevation requires great exertion and can be dangerous for those with health problems.) Brown-capped Rosy-Finch is also found along Trail Ridge Road at times, but can be quite elusive. Look in rocky areas and along the edges of snow fields. The Lava Cliffs area, a short distance west, is often productive. Continue to the Alpine Visitor Center for rest rooms and refreshment. Just beyond, at **Medicine Bow Curve,** a trail from the parking area leads northeast across the tundra. Ptarmigan are sometimes seen a quarter mile or so along this path, downhill near the wind-stunted shrubs.

13 Colo. 14 running from Fort Collins to Walden, the **Cache la Poudre-North Park Scenic Byway,** follows the Cache La Poudre River through the **Roosevelt National Forest,** where picnic areas and trails offer the chance to see montane species and watch American Dippers dip on river rocks. The road crests at 10,276-foot **Cameron Pass,** a spot where the very elusive Boreal Owl can sometimes be heard on quiet nights in spring and fall. Walk the dirt road leading south from the pass (if snow levels make this possible), and also check the area around **Joe Wright Reservoir,** about 3 miles east, where the owl has been heard.

Eared Grebes nesting at Arapaho National Wildlife Refuge in north-central Colorado

14 In the intermontane basin called North Park, south of Walden, **Arapaho National Wildlife Refuge** is home to birds of dry sagebrush, ponds, and marsh, and migrating shorebirds can throng shallow wetlands. Nesting ducks of many species are abundant, and when you drive the 6-mile tour route in summer, you'll see Eared Grebe; Northern Harrier; American Avocet; Willet; Wilson's Phalarope; Forster's and Black Terns; Sage Thrasher; Brewer's, Vesper, and Savannah Sparrows; and Yellow-headed and Brewer's Blackbirds. Drive the road from refuge headquarters north back to Colo. 14, along the Illinois River, and watch for Willow Flycatcher, Mountain Bluebird, Tree Swallow, and Yellow Warbler—and for moose, which you may find feeding in riparian areas. The sage flats along this road are particularly good for Sage Thrasher and sparrows. Walk a little, and you could find Greater Sage-Grouse as well.

You might be lucky enough to see sage-grouse in the refuge, but for the best chance, call the North Park Chamber of Commerce (970-723-4600) and ask about tours to leks (courtship grounds) in April and May. On the western edge of Walden, be sure to scan **Walden Reservoir** for waterbirds and migrant shorebirds. Franklin's and California Gulls nests here.

15 In the Denver area, **Barr Lake State Park** has recorded nearly 350 species over the years, testament to its habitat attractive to waterbirds and migrants. Bald Eagles have begun nesting at the lake, and other breeders include Blue-winged, Cinnamon, and Green-winged Teals; Pied-billed and Western Grebes; Double-crested Cormorant; Great Blue Heron; Snowy and Cattle Egrets; Black-crowned Night-Heron; American Avocet; Say's Phoebe; Western and Eastern Kingbirds; Horned Lark; Common Yellowthroat; and American Goldfinch. Barr is an irrigation lake where the shoreline advances and recedes with water use; in late summer and fall, shorebirding can be excellent on mudflats. In both spring and fall check trees and shrubs along the lake's south and east sides for migrant songbirds. A 9-mile trail circles the lake.

16 Within **Arapaho National Forest,** the **Mount Evans Scenic Byway** south of Idaho Springs climbs nearly to the top of 14,264-foot Mount Evans. Open from around Memorial Day to Labor Day, the drive offers a better chance than does Rocky Mountain National Park's Trail Ridge Road to witness Brown-capped Rosy-Finch. A few miles before the top, stop at **Summit Lake** (at 12,830 feet, it is the only handicapped-accessible alpine lake in Colorado) to look for the rosy-finches, which frequent rocky places, cliffs, and the edges of snowbanks. American Pipit nests on this alpine tundra, and if luck is truly with you, a White-tailed Ptarmigan just might put in an appearance.

Fewer than 4 miles west as the Common Raven flies, **Guanella Pass** is a good place to see White-tailed Ptarmigans in their pure-white winter plumage (see sidebar, p. 268). Tightly twisting, partly paved, partly gravel County Road 381 runs south from Georgetown on I-70 to Grant on US 285, topping out at 11,669 feet at the pass. This is not a trip to undertake when bad weather threatens. From the parking area at the pass, scan the hillside to the southeast. Sometimes birders see ptarmigans from their cars, but other times they may have to walk toward the hill and explore a bit to find them. Before or after this winter trip, you should drive around Georgetown and check feeders for Gray-crowned, Black (uncommon), and Brown-capped (also uncommon) Rosy-Finches, Pine and Evening Grosbeaks, and Cassin's Finch. Chances are best when there's lots of snow cover.

17 Westward nearly to Utah, just south of I-70 and west of Grand Junction, **Colorado National Monument** delights the eye with sculptured cliffs of red sandstone and deep canyons cutting into the Uncompahgre Plateau. Pinyon pine and juniper create habitat far different from the fir and pine forests of the Rockies. Here the list of nes ing birds includes Gambel's Quail, Black-chinned Hummingbird, Gray and Ash-throated Fly-catchers, Gray Vireo (uncommon), Western Scrub-Jay, Pinyon Jay, Juniper Titmouse, Bushtit, Blue-gray Gnatcatcher, Black-throated Gray Warbler (uncommon), Black-throated Sparrow, and Lazuli Bunting. The **Devils Kitchen** picnic area and 0.75-mile trail, near the east entrance to the park, provide a good introduction to the area. Other trails range from 0.25 to 8.5 miles. Along scenic **Rim Rock Drive**, watch for Golden Eagles, Peregrine and Prairie Falcons, White-throated Swift, and Mountain Bluebird, and listen for the songs of Rock, Canyon, and Bewick's Wrens. The pinyon-juniper habitat around **Saddlehorn Campground** is another fine birding location.

WHITE-TAILED PTARMIGAN

All birds molt at least once a year to replace worn feathers. The grouselike White-tailed Ptarmigan, of high elevations, molts three times annually, changing its plumage to match its environment. In winter, its white feathers blend with snow–covered terrain; in summer, mottled brown and white give camouflage on tundra where patches of snow and ice linger; more white appears in the fall plumage. The birds are elusive, but approachable once located. ■

18 The mountain town of **Ouray,** which calls itself the Switzerland of America, has a reputation among birders as one of the best places to see the scarce and elusive Black Swift. The species nests at **Box Canyon Falls Park**, located just a half mile south of town off US 550, and can be seen on the rock face at the base of the falls, which drop 285 feet off sheer cliffs. Be here in early morning or just before dusk, because the birds spend the day feeding away from nest sites.

Continue on County Road 361, along Canyon Creek up toward Yankee Boy Basin, to look for nesting Blue Grouse; Williamson's and Red-naped Sapsuckers; Hammond's, Dusky, and Cordilleran Flycatchers; Gray Jay; Clark's Nutcracker; Mountain Chickadee; Orange-crowned and MacGillivray's Warblers; and Pine and Evening Grosbeaks.

19 In Fountain, south of Colorado Springs, **Fountain Creek Regional Park and Nature Center** (north of town, west of US 85) rates highly with local birders for its spring and fall songbird migration. A 2.5-mile-long park stretching along the cottonwood-lined creek, it also hosts a good variety of breeding birds such as Wood Duck, Great Blue and Green Herons, Virginia Rail, Sora, Red-headed Woodpecker, Western and Eastern Kingbirds, Violet-green Swallow, Yellow Warbler, Common Yellowthroat, Lazuli Bunting, Bullock's Oriole, and Lesser and American Goldfinches. Stop at the nature center for advice and to check the nearby marsh. Then drive to the north part of the park, where you can investigate the area's ponds, marshes, and riparian woods for more good birding.

20 The region around **Pueblo Reservoir** combines lake, shallow ponds, riparian areas, and pinyon-juniper habitat, a variety that makes it an excellent birding destination, productive for fall and winter waterbirds, migrants, and local breeders. From the intersection of Colo. 96 and Colo. 45 in Pueblo, take Colo. 96 west 2.5 miles and turn north to **Valco Ponds State Wildlife Area,** along the Arkansas River below the reservoir dam.

Explore the riverbank (a trail follows the river eastward) and wetlands for migrant songbirds and summering Wood Duck, Osprey, Mississippi Kite, Yellow-billed Cuckoo, Red-headed Woodpecker, Blue Jay, Bewick's and House Wrens, Blue-gray Gnatcatcher, Northern Mockingbird, Brown Thrasher, Blue Grosbeak, and Lazuli and Indigo Buntings. Don't be shocked if you see the gorgeous Mandarin Duck here: Introduced from Asia, this exotic species breeds along the river. In fall and winter, check the ponds for ducks and gulls.

Return to Colo. 96 and drive west 3 miles to **Lake Pueblo State Park,** on Pueblo Reservoir. From fall into spring, use lookout points at reservoir marinas and at the dam to scan for ducks, loons, grebes (six species have been present simultaneously), and gulls. Several Bald Eagles usually winter here. In breeding season, pinyon-juniper areas both south and north of the lake host Scaled Quail, Greater Roadrunner, Western Scrub-Jay, Pinyon Jay, Juniper Titmouse, and Bushtit.

21 Following US 50 and the Arkansas River eastward from Pueblo onto the plains leads to some fine birding sites. Lakes and reservoirs along the way are also good spots. From Ordway, drive east 1.9 miles on Colo. 96 and turn north to **Lake Henry,** where grebes, herons, and shorebirds are present

from spring through fall, and waterfowl and gulls congregate in fall and winter. The woodland on the west side of the lake attracts migrant songbirds in spring and fall.

Not far southeast, **Lake Cheraw** (north of La Junta) is bisected by Colo. 109. A good birding site year-round, it can be excellent for migrant shorebirds. Northwest of Lamar, US 287 passes several shallow lakes, of which the most popular for birding may be **Nee Noshe Reservoir,** just east of the highway, and **Neeso Pah Reservoir,** to the west. At any or all of these lakes you may find nesting Western and Clark's Grebes, Snowy Plover, Black-necked Stilt, and American Avocet.

22 The **Comanche National Grassland** south of Springfield is best known for its Lesser Prairie-Chicken leks, where males gather in spring to "dance" for females at dawn. This scarce species is found in Colorado only in Baca and Prowers Counties, where its leks are on high spots in sage-grassland. If you plan to explore this area, contact the Comanche office in advance for a map and travel advice. To reach one traditional lek site, take County Road J east from Campo 8 miles to County Road 36. Go south 2 miles to County Road G and turn east for 4 miles. Just before a road culvert, turn south through a gate and drive 1.2 miles. The lek is on the west side of the road. The prairie-chickens perform from mid-March into May. You should arrive well before dawn and take care not to disturb them. This habitat is also home to Scaled Quail, Northern Bobwhite, Ferruginous Hawk, and Lark Bunting.

To reach the national grassland's **Carrizo Canyon Picnic Area,** which has many local specialties, drive west from Campo on County Road J for 15 miles to County Road 13. Go north 3 miles to County Road M and drive west about 8.5 miles to the turnoff south to the picnic area. Look for Long-billed Curlew, Burrowing Owl (in prairie dog towns), Cassin's Kingbird, Chihuahuan Raven, and Cassin's and Grasshopper Sparrows. In the canyon, you may see Scaled Quail; Mississippi Kite; Greater Roadrunner; Black-chinned Hummingbird; Ladder-backed Woodpecker; Ash-throated Flycatcher; Juniper Titmouse; Bushtit; Rock, Canyon, and Bewick's Wrens; Curve-billed Thrasher; Spotted and Canyon Towhees; and Rufous-crowned Sparrow. Return to County Road M and go west 4 miles to County Road J. Take it south through **Cottonwood Canyon,** a great place to find Lewis's Woodpecker. Continue through the canyon 7 miles, then reach County Road 5, and follow it northeast back to County Road M.

COLORADO | MORE INFORMATION

RARE BIRD ALERT
Statewide 303-424-2144

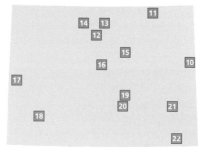

10 Bonny Lake State Park
(Page 262)
parks.state.co.us
970-354-7306
🔵 🚻 🚶 ♿

**11 Pawnee National
Grassland** *(Page 263)*
www.fs.fed.us/r2/arnf
970-353-5004
❓ 🚻 🚶 〰️ ♿

**11 Central Plains
Experiment Range**
(Page 263)
www.ars.usda.gov
970-897-2226

**12 Rocky Mountain
National Park**
(Page 264)
www.nps.gov/romo
970-586-1206
❓ 🔵 🏕️ 🚻 🚶 〰️ ♿
Toll road open Mem. Day–
Columbus Day. Trails closed
mid-April–late May.

**13 Roosevelt National
Forest** *(Page 266)*
www.fs.fed.us/r2/arnf
970-498-1100
❓ 🚻 🚶 〰️ ♿

**14 Arapaho National
Wildlife Refuge** *(Page 266)*
arapaho.fws.gov
970-723-8202
🚻 🚶 〰️ ♿
*Auto tour route and most
other roads closed in winter.*

15 Barr Lake State Park
(Page 267)
parks.state.co.us
303-659-6005
❓ 🔵 🚻 🚶 ♿

**16 Arapaho National
Forest** *(Page 267)*
www.fs.fed.us/r2/arnf
303-567-2901
❓ 🔵 🚻 🚶 〰️ ♿

**17 Colorado National
Monument** *(Page 268)*
www.nps.gov/colm
970-858-3617
❓ 🔵 🚻 🚶 〰️ ♿

**18 Box Canyon Falls
Park** *(Page 268)*
www.ouraycolorado.com
970-325-4464
❓ 🔵 🚻 🚶

**19 Fountain Creek
Regional Park and Nature
Center** *(Page 269)*
adm.elpasoco.com/parks
719-520-6745
❓ 🚻 🚶 ♿

**20 Valco Ponds State
Wildlife Area** *(Page 269)*
gppbt.org
719-561-4909

**20 Lake Pueblo State
Park** *(Page 269)*
parks.state.co.us
719-561-9320
❓ 🔵 🚻 🚶 〰️ ♿

21 Lake Henry
(Page 269)
parks.state.co.us
303-297-1192

**22 Comanche National
Grassland** *(Page 270)*
www.fs.fed.us/r2/psicc
719-523-6591
🚻

UTAH

- Waterfowl and shorebirds on the Great Salt Lake
- Highland sites along the Mirror Lake Scenic Byway
- Migrants and varied breeders at Ouray National Wildlife Refuge

American White Pelicans at Bear River Migratory Bird Refuge, west of Brigham City

Utah's **Great Salt Lake** ranks with the West's wonders. The largest natural lake in the U.S. west of the Mississippi, it stretches northwest of Salt Lake City 2,000 square miles. Expanses around the lake are covered in marshland attractive to nesting and migratory waterbirds. The lake has no outlet; losing water only through evaporation it has accumulated such a high concentration of salts that no fish can survive here.

23 The most famous birding area on the lake—indeed, one of the most famous in the West—is **Bear River Migratory Bird Refuge,** west of Brigham City. As you drive to the refuge, you'll cross marshes adjoining the Bear River where waterfowl

and wading birds can be abundant. In fact, the birding can be better along the road than in the refuge itself. Look especially for Snowy Plover and Long-billed Curlew.

Bear River refuge suffered great damage in the mid-1980s when the Great Salt Lake rose 7 to 11 feet above normal level, destroying habitat. The refuge reopened in the early 1990s, and it is again a birding hot spot. From the old headquarters site, a 12-mile loop auto tour route passes ponds and marshes diked to control water level and salinity.

In spring and summer, find Western and Clark's Grebes and nesting Black-necked Stilt, American Avocet, and Willet. Observe several species of ducks, Ring-necked Pheasant, Eared Grebe, American White Pelican, Double-crested Cormorant, Great Blue Heron, Snowy and Cattle Egrets, Black-crowned Night-Heron, White-faced Ibis, Northern Harrier, Virginia Rail, Sora, California Gull, Forster's and Black Terns, Horned Lark, Marsh Wren, and Savannah and Song Sparrows.

Migration brings thousands of ducks stopping to feed, and up to 50,000 Tundra Swans in November. In summer and fall, shorebirds include Greater and Lesser Yellowlegs, Marbled Godwit, Western and Least Sandpipers, Long-billed Dowitcher, and Wilson's and Red-necked Phalaropes. Peak shorebird variety occurs during August.

24 **Antelope Island State Park** occupies the largest island in the Great Salt Lake. The island and its causeway harbor migrant waterbirds and shorebirds. In summer and fall, brine flies swarm the shoreline, and tiny brine shrimp provide a food source. The result is vast congregations of Eared Grebes, shorebirds including Snowy Plover and Wilson's and Red-necked Phalaropes, and gulls. From the island and causeway, birders scan the open lake for migrant and wintering waterfowl. At the state park, look for Chukar, Burrowing Owl, Common Poorwill, Say's Phoebe, Rock and Canyon Wrens, Sage Thrasher, and Brewer's and Sage Sparrows. Bridger Bay Beach is good for swimming, and 16 miles of backcountry trails allow hiking and wildlife viewing.

To the south, **Farmington Bay Waterfowl Management Area** has many of the same waders, waterfowl, and shorebirds as Bear River refuge. The marshes here have nesting Western and Clark's Grebes, Great Blue Heron, and Snowy Plover, and 200,000 ducks may be present in fall. Driving and/or walking are allowed on some dikes at certain times of year, but parts of the area are closed seasonally to lessen disturbance of the birds.

25 Part of Utah's great diversity of habitats is the high country of the Rocky Mountains. From Salt Lake City, it is easy to access nesting birds of the mountains in the **Wasatch-Cache National Forest.** From Utah 190, take 3800 South Street east up into **Mill Creek Canyon.** Along the road find White-throated Swift; Black-chinned and Broad-tailed Hummingbirds; Red-naped Sapsucker; Olive-sided, Dusky, and Cordilleran Flycatchers; Plumbeous and Warbling Vireos; Steller's Jay; Clark's Nutcracker; Mountain Chickadee; American Dipper; Townsend's Solitaire; Swainson's and Hermit Thrushes; Orange-crowned, Virginia's, and MacGillivray's Warblers; Western Tanager; Green-tailed Towhee; Song and Lincoln's Sparrows; Black-headed Grosbeak; and Cassin's Finch. Most of these birds can be seen in **Big Cottonwood Canyon,** 5 miles south. From Wasatch Boulevard, drive on Utah 190 east into the canyon. **Spruces Recreation Area,** at 7,400 feet, is a good birding stop. About 14 miles up the canyon, bear right to Brighton. Behind the general store is a trail around **Silver Lake.** Continue 1.5 miles to **Lake Solitude,** for more birding.

26 East of Salt Lake City, take Utah 150, or the **Mirror Lake Scenic Byway,** from Kamas east and north toward Wyoming. It crosses the Uinta Mountains, the highest east-west range in the lower 48. Stop at **Trial Lake,** at 9,500 feet, to find Blue Grouse, Williamson's Sapsucker, American Three-toed Woodpecker, Olive-sided and Hammond's Flycatchers, Gray and Steller's Jays, Clark's Nutcracker, Mountain Chickadee, Brown Creeper, Townsend's Solitaire, Pine Grosbeak, Cassin's Finch, Red Crossbill, and Pine Siskin. In 3 miles, at Bald Mountain Pass, turn toward **Bald Mountain Trail,** where you'll find Black Rosy-Finch. Check rocky slopes for this little bird, which nests only above timberline. Find American Pipit at around 10,700 feet. The 2-mile trail (best July–October) to Bald Mountain's 11,943-foot summit, offers fabulous views of Uinta peaks. In 3 more miles, the **Mirror Lake** campground and picnic area is another popular birding spot. Walk a short spur trail that leads to the **Highline Trail** and glimpse Blue Grouse, Calliope Hummingbird, Mountain Bluebird, American Three-toed Woodpecker, and possibly Northern Goshawk and Golden Eagle soaring overhead.

27 Over on the Colorado state line east of Vernal, **Dinosaur National Monument** is a fine place to see birds, as well as the bones of the creatures that may have been their ancestors.

Outside the Dinosaur Quarry building is an arid, rocky landscape of sagebrush, pinyon pine, and juniper; breeding birds include White-throated Swift; Black-chinned and Broad-tailed Hummingbirds; Say's Phoebe; Plumbeous Vireo; Western Scrub-Jay: Pinyon Jay; Juniper Titmouse; Rock, Canyon, and House Wrens; Mountain Bluebird; Virginia's and Black-throated Gray Warblers; Spotted Towhee; Chipping, Lark, and Sage Sparrows; Lazuli Bunting; and Bullock's Oriole.

At **Josie Morris Cabin**, 10 miles past Dinosaur Quarry, rugged box canyons shelter riparian and pinyon-juniper birds. On the nature trail at Split Mountain Campground, or along the Green River, find Golden Eagle, Prairie Falcon, and Peregrine Falcon, which is still making its comeback from endangered status. Take the **Harpers Corner Scenic Drive** to look for Greater Sage-Grouse. In spring, ask naturalists about viewing the birds' leks (courtship grounds) outside the park.

28 Downstream on the Green River, **Ouray National Wildlife Refuge** ranks with Utah's best birding sites. The marshes and impoundments of this 11,987-acre refuge serve as an oasis in a desert region where rainfall averages only about 7 inches a year. Drier habitat around the wetlands adds to the diversity of possible species. As you drive south from US 40 toward the refuge on Utah 88, stop and check the sage flats to the east for Brewer's and Sage Sparrows. At **Pelican Lake,** check for waders and for shorebirds in migration. Continue south another 6 miles to the Ouray refuge entrance on the east.

On the 9-mile auto tour route, look for nesting waterbirds including Canada Goose; ducks, including all three teal, Redhead, Common Merganser, and Ruddy Duck; Pied-billed, Eared, Western, and Clark's Grebes; Double-crested Cormorant; American Bittern; Great Blue Heron; Snowy Egret; Black-crowned Night-Heron; White-faced Ibis; Virginia Rail; Sora; Black-necked Stilt; American Avocet; Wilson's Phalarope; and Forster's and Black Terns. The observation tower at Sheppard Bottom gives an area overview.

Burrowing Owl may be seen at the prairie dog town on the tour route. Other species include Ring-necked Pheasant, Northern Harrier, Say's Phoebe, Western and Eastern Kingbirds, Horned Lark, Loggerhead Shrike, Sparrows, and Lazuli Bunting, Marsh Wren, Yellow Warbler, and Yellow-headed Blackbirds. Find Lewis's Woodpecker (spring–fall) by driving south on Utah 88 to **Ouray** and crossing the bridge over the Green River to check the cottonwoods.

29 Out—far out—in west-central Utah, **Fish Springs National Wildlife Refuge** is another desert oasis, where springs and seeps provide water for a 10,000-acre marsh complex, attracting ducks; nesting grebes; waders, including American Bittern, Great Blue Heron, and Snowy Egret; Willet; and Long-billed Curlew. Sage Thrasher is a possibility in desert scrub, as is Black-throated Sparrow. In fall and winter, Tundra Swan is common, and some Trumpeter Swans winter here.

The birds of Fish Springs are tempting, but travelers should be advised that reaching it requires a long drive on gravel roads through uninhabited desert—a journey requiring preparation. From Salt Lake City, take I-80 west to Utah 36 (Tooele exit). Travel south about 27 miles to the old Pony Express route and follow this approximately 63 miles to the refuge.

30 The most famous birding spot in southwestern Utah is not one of the well-known national parks or monuments, but the small **Lytle Nature Preserve,** off the beaten track just a few miles from both Nevada and Arizona. Here several birds of the Mojave Desert extend their ranges into Utah, and a small creek creates a riparian oasis in an arid landscape of shrub-dotted cliffs. From St. George, drive west on US 91 through Santa Clara; at Shivwits, continue on US 91 southwestward toward Arizona. About 7 miles from Shivwits, reach Utah Hill, the crest of the Beaver Dam Mountains. Gray Vireo and Black-chinned Sparrow have been seen here in spring and early summer. Watch for Western Scrub-Jay and Scott's Oriole. In 4 more miles, at Cattle Cliff, turn west onto a dirt road, following signs to the preserve. Reservations aren't needed for day visits, but call in advance for camping information and fees.

Birds you might find include Gambel's Quail; White-winged Dove; Greater Roadrunner; Costa's Hummingbird; Ladder-backed Woodpecker; Vermilion, Ash-throated, and Brown-crested Flycatchers; Black Phoebe; Loggerhead Shrike; Bell's Vireo; Verdin; Cactus and Bewick's Wrens; Black-tailed Gnatcatcher; Crissal Thrasher; Lucy's Warbler; Summer Tanager; Abert's Towhee; Black-chinned Sparrow; Hooded and Scott's Orioles; and Lesser Goldfinch. Several trails lead up the wash and into the low hills, passing through cottonwoods, desert scrub, and old fields and an orchard from the days when this was a working ranch. Look down occasionally, instead of always up for birds, and you might be lucky enough to spot a Gila monster, that beautiful, orange-and-black poisonous lizard of the southwestern desert.

UTAH | MORE INFORMATION

RARE BIRD ALERT
Statewide 801–538-4730

23 Bear River Migratory Bird Refuge *(Page 272)*
www.fws.gov/bearriver
435-723-5887

24 Antelope Island State Park *(Page 273)*
www.utah.com/stateparks
801-773-2941

24 Farmington Bay Waterfowl Management Area *(Page 273)*
www.wildlife.utah.gov
801-451-7386

25 Wasatch-Cache National Forest
(Page 274)
www.fs.fed.us/r4/wcnf
801-524-3900

Administers Mill Creek Canyon, Big Cottonwood Canyon, and Mirror Lake Scenic Byway areas. In Spruces Recreation Area visit Silver Lake and Lake Solitude.

26 Mirror Lake Scenic Byway *(Page 274)*
www.utah.com/byways
Take this byway to Trial Lake, Bald Mountain Pass, and Mirror Lake.

27 Dinosaur National Monument *(Page 274)*
www.nps.gov/dino
970-374-3000

Past Dinosaur Quarry, visit Josie Morris Cabin, then take Harpers Corner Scenic Drive.

28 Ouray National Wildlife Refuge
(Page 275)
ouray.fws.gov
435-789-0351

Check for shorebirds at Pelican Lake.

29 Fish Springs National Wildlife Refuge
(Page 276)
fishsprings.fws.gov
435-831-5353

30 Lytle Nature Preserve
(Page 276)
mlbean.byu.edu/lytle
801-378-5052

NEVADA

- High-elevation birds on Mount Charleston
- Famed desert oasis at the Corn Creek Field Station
- Wetland species in the Lahontan Valley

The picturesque landscape of Red Rock Canyon National Conservation Area, near Las Vegas

31 If you're visiting Las Vegas and you're more interested in birding than betting, several spots give you an escape. To see a selection of typical desert birds, visit **Sunset Regional Park,** just 3 miles east of the southern end of The Strip. The park is developed mainly for recreation, but check remaining areas of natural scrub to the south for Gambel's Quail and possibly a Greater Roadrunner. Look for Ladder-backed Woodpecker, Verdin, Bewick's Wren, Black-tailed Gnatcatcher, Crissal Thrasher, Phainopepla, and Abert's Towhee all year, joined in nesting season by Ash-throated Flycatcher, Bell's Vireo, Lucy's Warbler, and Hooded and Bullock's Orioles. Check the park pond for migrant waterfowl and swallows.

Drive east on Sunset Road for 6 miles, and a half mile after crossing Boulder Boulevard (Nev. 582), turn north on Moser Drive to the 90-acre **Henderson Bird Viewing Preserve.** The preserve is managed to benefit migrant and nesting waterbirds, resulting in one of Nevada's best birding hot spots. Highlights include migrant waterfowl, shorebirds, gulls, and terns

Wetland species include Cinnamon Teal, Ruddy Duck, Great and Snowy Egrets, Virginia Rail, Ring-billed and California Gulls, and Belted Kingfisher. Also find Black and Say's Phoebes, Horned Lark, Verdin, Bushtit, and Rock Wren. In nesting season see Black-chinned Hummingbird, Common Yellowthroat, Blue Grosbeak, and Yellow-headed Blackbird.

32 A half hour west of Las Vegas, **Red Rock Canyon National Conservation Area** (take Charleston Boulevard west and proceed on Nev. 159) offers good birding for Mojave Desert species. From the Bureau of Land Management visitor center, take the 13-mile drive through the rocky hills. At **Pine Creek Canyon** see Chukar; Gambel's Quail; Black-chinned, Anna's, and Costa's Hummingbirds; Ladder-backed Woodpecker; Ash-throated Flycatcher; Gray Vireo; Western Scrub-Jay; Juniper Titmouse; Bushtit; Cactus and Canyon Wrens; Blue-gray and Black-tailed Gnatcatchers; Spotted Towhee; and Black-chinned and Black-throated Sparrows. Farther south on Nev. 159, riparian areas at **Spring Mountain Ranch State Park** and **Wheeler Camp Spring** have Crissal Thrasher, Summer Tanager, and Hooded Oriole. At Nev. 160, drive west to Mount Potosi Road; turn south and check the habitat for Gray Vireo, Black-chinned Sparrow, and Scott's Oriole (May–June).

33 Take US 95 northwest from Las Vegas and turn west on Nev. 157, which ascends Kyle Canyon toward **Mount Charleston** in the **Humboldt-Toiyabe National Forest.** Near the top drive north on Nev. 158 to Nev. 156, then descend Lee Canyon back to US 95. This 41-mile drive leads from desert through pinyon-juniper woods up through ponderosa pine forest to spruce-fir habitat; see birds ranging from the desert Cactus Wren to the highland Mountain Chickadee. You can see Pinyon Jay on the middle level. Explore picnic areas and trails for Broad-tailed Hummingbird, Red-naped Sapsucker, Olive-sided Flycatcher, Plumbeous Vireo, Steller's Jay, Clark's Nutcracker, Pygmy Nuthatch, Brown Creeper, Townsend's Solitaire, Hermit

Thrush, Virginia's and Grace's Warblers, Western Tanager, Dark-eyed Junco, Cassin's Finch, and Red Crossbill. In spring and early summer, find Flammulated Owl, Whip-poor-will, and Common Poorwill.

WILSON'S PHALAROPE

Wilson's Phalarope is one of many shore-birds that nest far from ocean shores. In breeding season it is found on shallow lakes throughout the Great Plains and Great Basin. In fall migration huge flocks gather at spots such as Utah's Great Salt Lake and Mono Lake in California. As is true for all phalaropes, in Wilson's the sex roles are reversed: The female is more colorful than the male, and it's the latter that incubates the eggs and raises the young. ∎

34 East off US 95 between Nev. 156 and Nev. 157, enter **Desert National Wildlife Range;** at 1.6 million acres, it's the largest refuge in the lower 48 and dedicated to preserving bighorn sheep. Birders visit **Corn Creek Field Station,** 4 miles from US 95. Here, spring-fed ponds and lush vegetation create an oasis. On the way in, check the desert scrub for Le Conte's Thrasher and Brewer's and Sage Sparrows. In spring and fall, find flycatchers, vireos, thrushes, warblers, and sparrows. Ash-throated Flycatcher and Phainopepla are found, too. The primitive, lonely Mormon Wells Road leads up to coniferous woods with good birding. (Check with refuge staff first.)

35 **Great Basin National Park** was established in 1986 to protect part of the southern Snake Mountain Range and surrounding desert. A drive up to its highest point at 13,063-foot Wheeler Peak lets visitors experience the range of life zones within Great Basin and nearby lands, from sagebrush into forests of spruce and aspen, upward to terrain where bristlecone pines give way to rocky peaks. These pines are more than 3,000 years old; one is almost 5,000.

Take **Wheeler Peak Scenic Drive** from the visitor center to the Wheeler Peak Campground at 10,000 feet. From seeing Western Scrub-Jay, Pinyon Jay, Mountain Chickadee, Juniper Titmouse, Bushtit, Sage Thrasher, and Green-tailed Towhee at the bottom, soon hear the *kra-a-a* of Clark's Nutcracker, and spot Steller's Jay, Red-breasted Nuthatch, Brown Creeper, American Dipper, Golden-crowned and Ruby-crowned Kinglets, Mountain Bluebird, Townsend's Solitaire, Yellow-rumped and MacGillivray's Warblers, and Dark-eyed Junco. Also find Blue Grouse, Northern Goshawk, Northern Pygmy-Owl, Calliope Hummingbird, Williamson's and Red-naped

Sapsuckers, Hammond's and Dusky Flycatchers, Cassin's Finch, and Pine Siskin. Spot Golden Eagle soaring, and see Canyon Wren along cliffs. Try the 2.7-mile **Alpine Lakes Loop,** or the 4.3-mile climb to the top of Wheeler Peak.

36 Mountain birds are the attraction of the **Lamoille Canyon Scenic Byway** in Humboldt-Toiyabe National Forest. The drive begins near Lamoille, southeast of Elko, and winds up the canyon into the Ruby Mountains. As you go, look for Blue Grouse, Clark's Nutcracker, Mountain Bluebird, Townsend's Solitaire, Virginia's Warbler, Western Tanager, and White-crowned Sparrow. At road's end, trails head up above the timberline, where American Pipit and Black Rosy-Finch nest.

But the famed bird of the Ruby Mountains is the exotic Himalayan Snowcock, an Asian species introduced as a game bird in the 1960s and surviving in what must be close to its native Himalayan heights. To try to find it you must hike at least 2 miles, gaining 800 feet in elevation, to the **Island Lake** area. The **Liberty Pass** and **Wines Peak** areas also shelter the birds. Visit mid-July through August, when snow has left the trails, but there's no guarantee you'll find the scarce species.

37 In a high valley on the east side of the Ruby Mountains, **Ruby Lake National Wildlife Refuge** has nesting and migrant waterbirds. From Elko, take Nev. 227 to Nev. 228. Drive south 28 miles, and cross the mountains on the Harrison Pass Road (look for Lewis's Woodpecker), then drive south to refuge headquarters. Some 160 springs flow into the area from the Ruby Mountains, creating a marsh where a variety of waterfowl breed—including Trumpeter Swan, introduced from Montana. Find Pied-billed and Eared Grebes, American Bittern, Great and Snowy Egrets, Black-crowned Night-Heron, White-faced Ibis, Northern Harrier, Virginia Rail, Sora, Sandhill Crane, Black-necked Stilt, American Avocet, Long-billed Curlew, Forster's and Black Terns, Short-eared Owl, Tree and Violet-green Swallows, Marsh Wren, and Orange-crowned and MacGillivray's Warblers. In sagebrush and shrubby areas, look for Gray Flycatcher, Western Scrub-Jay, Juniper Titmouse, and Brewer's and Vesper Sparrows.

38 Wetlands near **Fallon,** in western Nevada, are home to nesting and migrant waterfowl, heron, and shorebirds. Located in the **Lahontan Valley,** a basin filled by a glacial lake at the end of the last ice age, these lakes and marshes vary yearly in size and depth. Collectively, the Lahontan Valley wetlands compose one of the West's most important waterbird habitats.

To reach **Stillwater National Wildlife Refuge,** take US 50 east from Fallon 5 miles and continue east on Nev. 116 for 11 miles. In spring and fall migration, tens of thousands of shorebirds may feed here. Find Western and Least Sandpipers, Long-billed Dowitcher, and Red-necked Phalarope. Also see Black-necked Stilt, American Avocet, and Wilson's Phalarope. Nesting birds include ducks such as Gadwall, Cinnamon Teal, and Redhead; Eared, Western, and Clark's Grebes; Great, Snowy, and Cattle Egrets; Black-crowned Night-Heron; White-faced Ibis; and Forster's Tern. American White Pelicans are common from spring through fall. Fall migration can bring vast numbers of geese and ducks, including perhaps half the Pacific flyway's Canvasbacks, and 6,000 Tundra Swans in late fall. Many Tundras remain in winter, as do Bald Eagles; look also for wintering Rough-legged Hawk, Golden Eagle, Prairie Falcon, and Northern Shrike. From Fallon, drive south on US 95 for 8.8 miles, turn east on Pasture Road, and drive 2 miles to **Carson Lake,** another part of the region's wetland complex with terrific birding most of the year. This is a managed hunting area, so you must check in at the entrance before birding. Access is restricted during the fall waterfowl season. Migrant waterfowl and shorebirds highlight Carson Lake. Three viewing towers allow easy scanning of the area.

39 The coniferous forests around lovely Lake Tahoe, southwest of Reno, host montane species from the raucous Steller's Jay to the unassuming little Dark-eyed Junco. **Lake Tahoe Nevada State Park,** on the lake between Incline Village and Carson City, is a good place to start exploring. At **Spooner Lake,** trails lead up into the mountains; the **Tahoe Rim Trail** follows the crest of the Carson Range. There are less strenuous trails, too. White-headed Woodpecker is possible in these forests, as are Williamson's, Red-naped, and Red-breasted Sapsuckers. Watch also for Blue Grouse; Band-tailed Pigeon; Calliope and Broad-tailed Hummingbirds; Hammond's, Dusky, and Cordilleran Flycatchers; Mountain Chickadee; Pygmy Nuthatch; Yellow-rumped and Hermit Warblers; Western Tanager; Cassin's Finch; and Red Crossbill. For more birding, take Nev. 431 north from Incline Village, stopping at recreation areas in the Humboldt-Toiyabe National Forest along the way. Trails lead westward into the **Mount Rose Wilderness** area, for those seeking a solitary backcountry experience.

NEVADA | MORE INFORMATION

RARE BIRD ALERT
Northwest 702-324-2473
South 702-390-8463

31 Sunset Regional Park
(Page 278)
www.co.clark.nv.us
702-455-8293

**31 Henderson Bird
Viewing Preserve**
(Page 279)
www.cityofhenderson.com
702-565-4264

*Also known as the Henderson
sewage ponds.*

**32 Red Rock Canyon
National Conservation
Area** *(Page 279)*
www.discovernlcs.org
702-363-1921

**32 Spring Mountain
Ranch State Park**
(Page 279)
parks.nv.gov/smr
702-875-4141

**33 Humboldt-Toiyabe
National Forest**
(Page 279)
www.fs.fed.us/r4/htnf
702-873-8800

*Visit Mount Charleston and
Lee Canyon for good birding.*

**34 Desert National
Wildlife Range** *(Page 280)*
www.nvwf.org
702-646-3401

*At Corn Creek Field Station,
find an oasis and good birding
in the desert scrub.*

**35 Great Basin National
Park** *(Page 280)*
www.nps.gov/grba
775-234-7331

*Enjoy Wheeler Peak Scenic
Drive and take the Alpine
Lakes Loop.*

**36 Lamoille Canyon
Scenic Byway** *(Page 281)*
*Leads to Island Lake area;
also visit Liberty Pass and
Wines Peak.*

**37 Ruby Lake National
Wildlife Refuge** *(Page 281)*
pacific.fws.gov/refuges
775-779-2237

**38 Stillwater National
Wildlife Refuge** *(Page 282)*
www.fws.gov/stillwater
775-423-5128

*Find waterfowl and shorebirds
in this Lahontan Valley wetlands area.*

38 Carson Lake
(Page 282)
www.ndow.org
775-423-3171

**39 Lake Tahoe Nevada
State Park** *(Page 282)*
parks.nv.gov/lt
702-831-0494

*Take trails from Spooner
Lake, including Tahoe Rim
Trail. To the north explore
Mount Rose Wilderness area.*

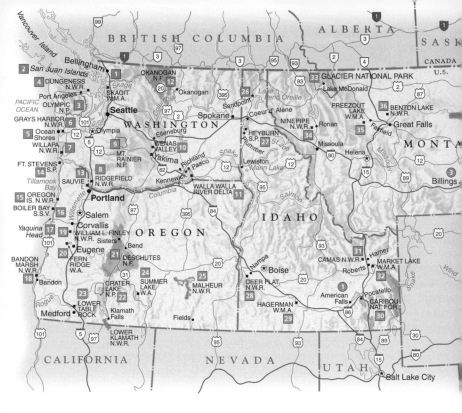

NORTHWEST

- Washington
- Oregon
- Idaho
- Montana

JUST AS IT DOES IN MANY AREAS, WATER DEFINES SOME OF the best and most characteristic birding opportunities in the Northwest. The Pacific Ocean meets land in beautiful scenes of rock and sand along the Washington and Oregon coasts, and water in the form of abundant rainfall fuels the lush greenery of Washington's Olympic National Park. Varied Thrush sings here, and American Dipper haunts rocky mountain streams. Spotted Owl still calls in areas where dense old-growth forest remains.

Farther east, rainfall dwindles so much that semidesert conditions prevail in some areas. Arid-country species add appealing variety to regional birding, and where water does occur in the midst of desert terrain, it can attract substantial numbers of breeders and migrants.

Lakes and marshes host great flocks of waterfowl at Montana's Freezout Lake Wildlife Management Area, Idaho's Camas National Wildlife Refuge, Washington's Ridgefield

National Wildlife Refuge, and many other sites throughout the region. Where waterfowl gather, birders assemble to look for eagles and large falcons. The Skagit and Samish Flats area in northwestern Washington is famed for sightings of the powerful Gyrfalcon, and the Klamath Basin, on the Oregon-California border, serves as winter home to hundreds of Bald Eagles.

This region stretches more than a thousand miles from corner to corner. Habitats include coniferous forest, riparian woodland, sagebrush shrub-steppe, oak chaparral, coastal salt marsh, and others providing good birding throughout the year. Whether your idea of fun is scanning for rare seabirds on a pelagic trip, hiking up rugged mountains to tundra in search of White-tailed Ptarmigan, or driving through a wildlife refuge to marvel at masses of geese, you'll find the Northwest full of possibilities. ■

Varied Thrush

SPECIAL BIRDS OF THE NORTHWEST

Trumpeter Swan
Eurasian Wigeon
Harlequin Duck
Barrow's Goldeneye
Spruce Grouse
Blue Grouse
White-tailed Ptarmigan
Pacific Loon
Black-footed Albatross
Pink-footed Shearwater
Buller's Shearwater
Fork-tailed Storm-Petrel
Brandt's Cormorant
Pelagic Cormorant
Gyrfalcon

Pacific Golden-Plover
Black Oystercatcher
Black Turnstone
Surfbird
Sharp-tailed Sandpiper
Rock Sandpiper
Mew Gull
Thayer's Gull
Common Murre
Pigeon Guillemot
Marbled Murrelet
Ancient Murrelet
Cassin's Auklet
Rhinoceros Auklet
Tufted Puffin
Spotted Owl

Boreal Owl
Black Swift
Vaux's Swift
Rufous Hummingbird
Calliope Hummingbird
Red-breasted Sapsucker
White-headed Woodpecker
American Three-toed Woodpecker
Black-backed Woodpecker
Pacific-slope Flycatcher
Cassin's Vireo
Northwestern Crow
Chestnut-backed Chickadee

Boreal Chickadee
Varied Thrush
Wrentit
Sage Thrasher
Sprague's Pipit
Townsend's Warbler
Hermit Warbler
Sage Sparrow
Baird's Sparrow

WASHINGTON

- Waterfowl and raptors at Skagit Flats
- Shorebirds and seabirds at Ocean Shores
- Diverse nesting birds in the Wenas Valley area

Near the Hoh River in Olympic National Park

Skagit and Samish Flats in northwestern Washington—an area of agricultural fields, wetlands, and bay shore near the mouths of the Skagit and Samish Rivers—is famous for its large wintering flocks of waterfowl, including both Trumpeter and Tundra Swans and great numbers of Snow Geese, as well as for excellent viewing of raptors. Among the latter group, the star is Gyrfalcon, a prized sighting anywhere south of the Arctic, but seen regularly here in winter. Bald Eagle, Red-tailed and Rough-legged Hawks, Peregrine Falcon, and Short-eared Owl also frequent this area in winter. Northern Harrier can be found in area fields, and Sharp-shinned or Cooper's Hawk may flash by. Snowy Owl is seen occasionally.

At **Padilla Bay National Estuarine Research Reserve** and **Bayview State Park,** you can scan the bay for wintering Brant, scoters, and other waterfowl. Huge flocks of Dunlin, sometimes numbering well over 10,000, winter in the vicinity.

Large flocks of Snow Geese winter near the headquarters of **Skagit Wildlife Management Area,** along with lesser numbers of Trumpeter and Tundra Swans, Greater White-fronted Goose, and assorted dabbling ducks. Bald Eagle and other raptors can turn up anywhere in the area.

2 The **San Juan Ferry,** which makes stops in the San Juan Islands as it travels from Anacortes, Washington, to Sidney, British Columbia, is an easily accessible seabird trip. You might observe sea ducks; four species of wintering loons (Yellow-billed rare); grebes; Double-crested and Pelagic Cormorants; Bonaparte's, Heermann's, Mew, Thayer's, Glaucous-winged, and other gulls; and the alcids Common Murre, Pigeon Guillemot, Marbled and Ancient Murrelets, and Rhinoceros Auklet. Bald Eagle nests on the islands and can be seen any time of year.

3 The northern entrance to **Olympic National Park** provides easy access to high-country birds. If possible, make the trip to the Hurricane Ridge Visitor Center early in the morning for more bird activity and less traffic. Along the way, watch for Blue Grouse, Northern Pygmy-Owl (seldom seen, but listen for small birds "scolding" if they've found an owl perched in daylight), Vaux's Swift, Red-breasted Sapsucker, Olive-sided and Pacific-slope Flycatchers, Cassin's (uncommon) and Hutton's Vireos, Gray and Steller's Jays, Winter Wren, Common Raven, Chestnut-backed Chickadee, Townsend's Solitaire, Hermit and Varied Thrushes, Yellow-rumped and Townsend's Warblers, Western Tanager, Dark-eyed Junco, Pine Grosbeak, and Red Crossbill. Walk the **Hurricane Hill Nature Trail,** and check open areas for nesting Horned Lark and American Pipit. If it's open, drive the dirt road to **Obstruction Peak** for more birding and fabulous vistas.

4 **Dungeness National Wildlife Refuge** is a long sandspit reaching out into the Strait of Juan de Fuca, creating a bay where waterfowl gather from fall through spring. Some birders walk the 5 miles to the lighthouse to find waterbirds and shorebirds, but much can be seen closer in. **Marina Drive** also offers some good places to see Brant, ducks, loons, gulls, and terns (one of the best viewpoints is from the Three Crabs restaurant).

5 Washington birders consider the **Ocean Shores** area among the state's top birding sites. This seaside town occupies a peninsula at the north entrance to Grays Harbor, where beaches, marshes, and jetties attract a variety of seabirds and shorebirds. Side roads lead to a long Pacific Ocean beach where shorebirds and gulls can always be seen. At the southwestern corner of the peninsula, check the jetty for "rocky shorebirds": Black Oystercatcher and, from late summer through spring, Surfbird, Black Turnstone, and Rock Sandpiper. Inshore waters will have ducks (all three species of scoter), loons, grebes, cormorants (including Brandt's), and alcids such as Common Murre and Rhinoceros Auklet. Brown Pelicans appear in summer and fall, when Sooty Shearwater passes offshore in great numbers.

GYRFALCON

A breeding bird of the Arctic, the Gyrfalcon sometimes travels south to the northern U.S. in winter, where a sighting is always exhilarating. Large and powerful enough to capture ptarmigans and even geese, the Gyr is irregular in its wanderings in search of prey. One of the best spots to look for this rare bird is near the mouths of the Skagit and Samish Rivers in northwestern Washington, where one or more Gyrfalcons usually spend part of the winter feeding on waterfowl in farmlands and wetlands. ■

Walk from the parking area on Damon Point Road for good shorebird habitat. From Whimbrel to Least Sandpiper, the diversity of species can be extensive. In early fall, watch for both American and Pacific Golden-Plovers, look-alike birds formerly considered races of the same species. Wherever there are concentrations of shorebirds, be alert for Peregrine Falcon hunting for a meal. Check the marina for ducks, loons, and grebes, and stop at the nearby **Ocean Shores Environmental Interpretive Center.**

6 From late April through early May, the opportunity to see hundreds of thousands of massed shorebirds attracts birders to **Grays Harbor National Wildlife Refuge**, just west of Hoquiam. Park across from the airport café and walk west on the paved road leading to the refuge's **Sandpiper Trail.** The majority of spring migrants are Western Sandpipers; other common species include Black-bellied and Semipalmated Plovers, Ruddy Turnstone, Red Knot, Least Sandpiper, Dunlin (large flocks winter here), and Short-billed and Long-billed Dowitchers. Fall migration doesn't see the same concentration of birds as spring, but the refuge is still worth a visit. Best viewing occurs within two hours of high tide.

On the south side of Grays Harbor, **Westport** is the embarkation point for popular commercial pelagic trips that cruise

40 miles or more offshore. Trips last from 9 to 13 hours. Expected species on all trips include Black-footed Albatross, Northern Fulmar, Fork-tailed Storm-Petrel, Common Murre, Cassin's and Rhinoceros Auklets, and Tufted Puffin, while seasonal sightings include Laysan Albatross; Pink-footed, Buller's, and Short-tailed Shearwaters; South Polar Skua; all three species of jaeger; Sabine's Gull; Black-legged Kittiwake; and Arctic Tern.

7 Between Tokeland and Raymond, you'll have many chances to pull off the road and scan **Willapa Bay** for waterbirds and shorebirds. Stop at Bruceport Park for more bay views. Shorebird viewing can be good near the headquarters of **Willapa National Wildlife Refuge.** Ask about visiting the nearby **Lewis Unit** of the refuge, where winter waterfowl can be abundant.

Intrepid birders searching for rarities, and ready for a hike, visit the **Leadbetter Point Unit** of Willapa refuge. In **Leadbetter Point State Park,** trails lead to the tip of the peninsula. Snowy Plover breeds on the ocean side, but nesting areas are closed seasonally to protect the birds. Large numbers of shorebirds frequent this area in migration (mostly on the bay side) in late summer and fall, sometimes including rarities such as Pacific Golden-Plover, Sharp-tailed Sandpiper, and Ruff. There's always something to see, from Brown Pelican in summer, to Sooty Shearwater in summer and fall, to flocks of Brant in spring migration.

8 "Geese, geese, geese," is how one Washington birder describes winter at **Ridgefield National Wildlife Refuge.** Swans and ducks might be added to that, along with Bald Eagle and other raptors, and Sandhill Crane. Tens of thousands of waterfowl winter here, including Tundra Swan (with occasional Trumpeter), Snow and Canada Geese, American Wigeon (look for a few Eurasian Wigeon as well), Mallard, Northern Shoveler, Northern Pintail, Green-winged Teal, Common Merganser, and others. You can scan wetlands and fields from several parking areas. North of town, another refuge entrance offers access to a 1.9-mile loop nature trail; this area can be excellent for winter sparrows. Nesting birds here include several species of duck, Great Blue Heron, Bald Eagle, Virginia Rail, Sora, Willow and Pacific-slope Flycatchers, Western Scrub-Jay, Marsh Wren, Warbling Vireo, and Yellow Warbler.

9 At **Mount Rainier National Park,** look for birds of middle and high elevations on the slopes of this snow- and ice-capped volcano. All areas of the park are open from July through Labor

Day, and most are accessible from Memorial Day into October; in spring and fall, call to check the status of roads and trails.

In the southeastern part of the park, trails along the Ohanapecosh River pass through old-growth forest of Douglas fir and western red cedar. Along the short **Trail of the Patriarchs** or the longer **Eastside Trail**, watch for Olive-sided Flycatcher, Gray and Steller's Jays, Chestnut-backed Chickadee, Townsend's Solitaire, Varied Thrush, Yellow-rumped and Townsend's Warblers, Western Tanager, and Pine Siskin. With luck you might see Blue Grouse, Hammond's Flycatcher, Cassin's Vireo, Purple Finch, Hermit Warbler, or Evening Grosbeak. Look for American Dipper along the river. To the north, the popular Sunrise Visitor Center provides access to trails leading above timberline, where White-tailed Ptarmigan and Gray-crowned Rosy-Finch breed. The **Wonderland Trail** near the White River entrance station is the park's best spot for Hermit Thrush.

In the southwest, Harlequin Duck frequents the Nisqually River at the Sunshine Point Campground. The **Trail of Shadows** at Longmire may have Band-tailed Pigeon and Red-breasted Sapsucker, as well as interesting migrants. As you're driving, look also for Vaux's Swift, Clark's Nutcracker, and Mountain Bluebird; Rufous Hummingbird is common in summer in wildflower-dotted meadows.

10 In nesting season, the **Wenas Valley,** northwest of Yakima, hosts a fine diversity of species. Washington birders converge here on Memorial Day weekend for a camp-out and field trips. Check **Wenas Lake** for waterfowl; a walk upstream from the lake might provide Gray Catbird and Yellow-breasted Chat. Continue up the valley to Audubon Road, which leads to a campground called the **Hazel Wolf Wenas Bird Sanctuary,** in honor of a longtime Washington environmental leader.

This route includes riparian areas with aspen groves, brushy hillsides, and open ponderosa pine forest. By searching these habitats, you may find such species as Blue Grouse; Vaux's Swift; Calliope Hummingbird; Red-naped Sapsucker; Least (rare in aspens), Gray, Dusky, and Pacific-slope (riparian) Flycatchers; Western and Mountain Bluebirds; Veery; Nashville Warbler; Black-headed Grosbeak; Lazuli Bunting; and Bullock's Oriole. Check in pines around the campground for White-headed Woodpecker (a specialty of this area), Mountain Chickadee, Pygmy Nuthatch, Western Tanager, and Cassin's Finch. By returning to North Wenas Road and following it north and east (it becomes Umtanum Road) to Ellensburg, you'll pass through arid sagebrush country where you may find Rock Wren, Sage Thrasher, and Brewer's Sparrow.

11 You'll find one of the region's best inland shorebird sites just southeast of the Tri-Cities area of Richland, Kennewick, and Pasco. The **Walla Walla River Delta**, at the confluence of the Walla Walla and Columbia Rivers, hosts an excellent assortment of fall migrants, with peak numbers between mid-August and mid-September. To reach the best viewing location, turn west on a gravel road opposite the entrance to the U.S. Army Corps of Engineers' Madame Dorian Park; cross the railroad tracks and go down to the water. A telescope is essential here, and some birders wade out on the mudflats to get better looks. Washington's only breeding American White Pelican nests on an island nearby, along with Caspian Terns. Gulls can be common here (Glaucous winters in small numbers), and both Trumpeter (uncommon) and Tundra Swans appear in migration. In winter, the area hosts diving ducks, 15 to 20 Bald Eagles, and an occasional Merlin or Peregrine Falcon.

12 In the **Okanogan National Forest,** the **Hart's Pass** area is known as an important raptor migration route and a productive spot for many high-elevation species. Look for nesting Harlequin Duck on Lost River Road, along the east side of the Methow River. Golden Eagles soar most summer days on the updrafts along Goat Wall; in spring and summer, Least Flycatcher, Red-eyed Vireo, and American Redstart can be found in riverside cottonwoods. The road climbs to Hart's Pass, Washington's highest drivable point. Along the way look for Blue Grouse (both coastal and northern Rockies race), Black (scarce) and Vaux's Swifts, and four species of chickadee (Black-capped, Mountain, Chestnut-backed, and Boreal). Later in summer, both Red and White-winged Crossbills are possible. Meadows at high elevations have Savannah, Fox, and White-crowned Sparrows, with Lincoln's in wet areas.

Late September is the best time for southbound raptors at the pass, including possible Northern Harrier, Cooper's Hawk, Northern Goshawk, Golden Eagle, Merlin, and Peregrine Falcon. A walk on the **Pacific Crest National Scenic Trail** here could turn up Gray Jay, Clark's Nutcracker, Mountain Bluebird, Hermit Thrush, American Pipit, Pine Grosbeak, and Pine Siskin. Several woodpecker species are possible in this area, including American Three-toed, Black-backed, and Pileated, as well as Williamson's and Red-naped Sapsuckers.

WASHINGTON | MORE INFORMATION

RARE BIRD ALERT
Statewide 425-454-2662
Southeast 208-882-6195
Lower Columbia Basin
 509-943-6957

1 Bayview State Park
(Page 287)
www.parks.wa.gov
360-757-0227

**2 Washington State
Ferries** *(Page 287)*
www.wsdot.wa.gov/ferries
206-464-6400

**3 Olympic National
Park** *(Page 287)*
www.nps.gov/olym
360-565-3130

4 Dungeness NWR
(Page 287)
pacific.fws.gov/refuges
360-457-8451

**5 Ocean Shores
Environmental
Interpretive Center**
(Page 288)
*www.oceanshores
interpretivecenter.com*
360-289-4617

6 Grays Harbor NWR
(Page 288)
www.fws.gov/pacific
360-268-5222

*Shorebird festival with work-
shops, lectures, and guided
field trips during peak migration. Westport is the embarkation point for popular
commercial pelagic trips,
which last 9–13 hours. Call
360-733-8255 for a schedule.*

7 Willapa NWR
(Page 289)
www.fws.gov/pacific
360-484-3482

**7 Leadbetter Point
State Park** *(Page 289)*
www.parks.wa.gov
360-642-3078

8 Ridgefield NWR
(Page 289)
www.fws.gov/pacific
360-887-4106

*Portions of refuge closed
seasonally Oct.–May.*

**9 Mount Rainier
National Park** *(Page 289)*
www.nps.gov/mora
360-569-2211

**10 Hazel Wolf Wenas
Bird Sanctuary** *(Page 290)*
*www.nwlink.com/~cyrus
/wenas.html*

11 Walla Walla *(Page 290)*
www.wallawalla.org
509-525-0850

**12 Okanogan National
Forest** *(Page 291)*
www.fs.fed.us/r6/oka
509-826-3275

*The road to Hart's Pass is
narrow and steep and is
closed to trailers. Be advised
that the high-country season
is short (mid-July–early
Oct.); be prepared for stormy
weather any time.*

OREGON

- Waterfowl, raptors, and gulls at Sauvie Island
- Excellent seabird-watching along the coast
- Diverse nesting birds and migrants at Malheur National Wildlife Refuge

Wizard Island rising from the water at Crater Lake National Park, where roads and trails provide easy access to highland birds

13 Minutes from Portland, **Sauvie Island** earns its birding reputation as a home for wintering waterfowl, raptors, Sandhill Crane, gulls, and sparrows, as well as for migrant shorebirds. Get a map, and a checklist at the **Sauvie Island Wildlife Area** headquarters. The south half of the island is private, while most of the north is in the wildlife area. Access to the wildlife area is restricted from October through mid-April, but much can still be seen from roads and observation areas.

In fall and winter, tens of thousands of waterfowl congregate here, including Greater White-fronted, Cackling, Canada (abundant) and Snow Geese; Tundra Swan; and 15 or more species of ducks, the most common of which are Wood Duck, American Wigeon (look for Eurasian Wigeon as well), Mallard, Northern Shoveler, Northern Pintail, Green-winged Teal, Bufflehead, Common Merganser, and Ruddy Duck. Sandhill Crane is common in spring and fall migration, and has been increasing as a wintering bird. Bald Eagle may be the most publicized wintering raptor (as many as 20 or more may be present), but look also for Northern Harrier; Sharp-shinned, Cooper's, Red-tailed, and Rough-legged Hawks; and an occasional Peregrine Falcon, among other possibilities. In late summer, drive roads in the wildlife area looking for mud-flats where shorebirds rest and feed. The Coon Island observation area is one good spot, and the Eastside Viewing Platform on Reeder Road is another.

14 One of Oregon's finest birding sites, **Fort Stevens State Park,** sits on the south bank where the Columbia River meets the Pacific Ocean. Though seabirds and shorebirds are its claim to fame, it's also attracted many rare songbirds over the years, especially vagrants from the east. The favorite spot in the park is the **south jetty** of the Columbia River. To reach it, go to parking lot C, where a viewing platform is nearby. Around high tide in spring, and especially fall, shorebirds congregate below. The rare Sharp-tailed Sandpiper has been seen from September to October, though its habitat has deteriorated in recent years. Walking out on the jetty from fall through spring brings views of sea ducks; loons (Red-throated, Pacific, and Common); grebes; Brown Pelican (summer–fall); Sooty Shearwater (summer–fall); Brandt's, Double-crested, and Pelagic Cormorants; gulls; terns; and alcids (members of the auk family such as Pigeon Guillemot and Common Murre). Pomarine and Parasitic Jaegers and Black-legged Kittiwake are sometimes spotted close to shore. After visiting the jetty, check **Trestle Bay,** where there's an observation bunker.

The state park's beaches are Oregon's best locations for both American and Pacific Golden-Plovers in fall migration. The beaches are also among the best places to look for winter rarities such as Gyrfalcon, Snowy Owl, and Snow Bunting; Lapland Longspur can be found annually in winter. Nesting birds include Wood Duck, Osprey, Bald Eagle, Pacific-slope Flycatcher, Winter and Marsh Wrens, Wrentit, and Orange-crowned Warbler.

15 Excellent birding sites dot the length of the beautiful Oregon coastline, and as you travel US 101 you'll pass many state parks, recreation sites, and scenic viewpoints. All but one of the more than 1,400 rocks, reefs, and islands that you see out in the Pacific Ocean make up **Oregon Islands National Wildlife Refuge,** which protects breeding or resting areas for more than a million seabirds (among them Brandt's, Double-crested, and Pelagic Cormorants; Black Oystercatcher; Western and Glaucous-winged Gulls; Common Murre; Pigeon Guillemot; Rhinoceros Auklet; Leach's Storm-Petrel; and Tufted Puffin).

One of the best coastal sites is **Tillamook Bay.** Visit the public marina in Garibaldi to scan for waterbirds of all sorts, and check the cove where the Miami River enters the bay just east of town for migrant shorebirds at low tide. In Tillamook, turn north on Bayocean Road toward Cape Meares; to the east will be good views of the bay. Where this road turns west in about 5 miles, continue north to **Bayocean Peninsula,** a spit of land separating Tillamook Bay from the Pacific. From the parking lot, walk east to the bay; shorebirding can be exciting here, especially around high tide in late summer and fall. The shrubs and coniferous woodland are productive for migrant songbirds, and Bald Eagle and Peregrine Falcon are often spotted.

Return to Bayocean Road and drive west to **Cape Meares National Wildlife Refuge** and **Cape Meares State Park.** From the lighthouse, scan for all manner of seabirds, from loons and ducks to an occasional Fork-tailed Storm-Petrel and, in August, great flocks of Sooty Shearwaters passing offshore. Cormorants, Common Murre, Pigeon Guillemot, and Tufted Puffin are among the nesting species on the cliffs and sea rocks below. Just south, the community of Oceanside and Oceanside Beach State Wayside provide views of **Three Arch Rocks National Wildlife Refuge,** a half mile offshore (you'll need a scope), home of the state's largest colony of Tufted Puffins and the largest Common Murre colony south of Alaska, with more than 200,000 birds some years.

16 Many Oregonians consider **Boiler Bay State Scenic Viewpoint** the best seabird-watching site in the state. Here you might find loons, shearwaters, all three scoters, gulls (look for Black-legged Kittiwake in spring and fall), and alcids. Many rarities have been seen at this spot, particularly during and after storms. On rocks below, you may find Black Oystercatcher and, from fall through spring, Black Turnstone, Surfbird, and Rock Sandpiper.

17 Cliffs and offshore rocks in **Yaquina Head Outstanding Natural Area** are home to nesting Brandt's and Pelagic Cormorants, Black Oystercatcher, gulls, Pigeon Guillemot, Common Murre, and Tufted Puffin. The area's rocky headland

offers a 93-foot lighthouse—a good place to scan for migrant and winter seabirds. Oregon State University's **Hatfield Marine Science Center** offers exhibits of sea life, and its nature trail leads to viewpoints of Yaquina Bay, where from fall through spring you'll find loons, grebes, Brant, ducks, shorebirds, and gulls. A nearby road following the south shore of the estuary outlet leads west to a jetty that in winter often provides close looks at Harlequin and Long-tailed Ducks among many other waterbirds.

MARBLED MURRELET

In the controversy over logging in the remaining old-growth forests of the Pacific Northwest, the bird most often mentioned is the Spotted Owl. Though less celebrated, a small seabird, the Marbled Murrelet, also depends on this threatened resource. It nests high in mature redwoods, Douglas firs, and other conifers along the Pacific coast as far south as central California. Mottled brown in breeding season, it molts to black and white plumage in winter. It lives in small numbers just offshore year-round. ∎

18 **Bandon Marsh National Wildlife Refuge** is outstanding for migrant shorebirds. Just before and after high tide are the best birding times. In Bandon, the south jetty at the Coquille River mouth is another fine site for seabird- and shorebird-watching. Take Beach Loop on the west side of town to **Coquille Point** (part of Oregon Islands National Wildlife Refuge), where you'll find Tufted Puffins and other nesting seabirds on the beautiful offshore rocks.

19 In the Willamette Valley, **William L. Finley National Wildlife Refuge** is one of several areas set aside to provide wintering habitat for the large dusky race of Canada Goose. The refuge's fields, oak savanna, and woodland of bigleaf maples and Douglas fir make it one of the state's finest birding destinations. Finley offers excellent viewing of waterfowl and raptors (including an occasional Peregrine Falcon) from fall through spring. Greater White-fronted, Cackling, and Snow Geese, Tundra Swan, and many species of ducks join the abundant Canada Goose in cropland and wetlands. Diversity of habitat makes Finley excellent for all-around birding, including spring songbird migration and, depending on water levels, shorebird migration.

20 Noted for a variety of waterbirds, **Fern Ridge Wildlife Area** (8 miles west of Eugene on Ore. 126) hosts many nesting species, including Wood Duck, Pied-billed Grebe, American Bittern, Osprey, Acorn Woodpecker, Purple Martin,

Yellow-headed Blackbird, Yellow-breasted Chat, and Lesser Goldfinch. In recent years, this has been the only nesting site in western Oregon for Western Grebe and Black Tern, and Red-shouldered Hawk is an occasional visitor fall through spring.

21 Ponderosa pine dominates upland forests on the eastern slope of the Cascade Range (which is drier than the western slope). Nesting birds of the pine forest can be found at **Indian Ford Campground** in the **Deschutes National Forest.** Indian Ford Creek runs through this local favorite birding area, offering riparian species as well. Explore the creek vicinity and surrounding forest for Northern Pygmy-Owl; Calliope Hummingbird; Williamson's and Red-naped Sapsuckers; White-headed Woodpecker (a specialty); Hammond's and Dusky Flycatchers; Cassin's and Warbling Vireos; Mountain Chickadee; Pygmy Nuthatch; Townsend's Solitaire; Orange-crowned, Townsend's, and MacGillivray's Warblers; Green-tailed Towhee; Fox Sparrow; Cassin's Finch; and Red Crossbill.

22 **Crater Lake National Park** is one of the most beautiful, and most popular, recreational areas in Oregon. Its blue lake in the caldera of a dormant volcano is a spectacle in itself. Birders know it as a place with easy access to mid- and high-elevation species of coniferous forest and alpine habitats. Some of these species—Olive-sided and Hammond's Flycatchers, Gray and Steller's Jays, Clark's Nutcracker, Mountain Chickadee, Townsend's Solitaire, and Hermit Thrush among them—are fairly easy to find. Others require searching or a bit of luck, including Blue Grouse, Great Gray and Northern Saw-whet Owls, American Three-toed and Black-backed Woodpeckers, and Gray-crowned Rosy-Finch. Driving Rim Road and hiking the easier trails such as **Godfrey Glen** can turn up a good number of these species. The strenuous hike up **Garfield Peak** offers a better chance at finding the rosy-finch.

23 A far different landscape awaits you at **Lower Table Rock,** a Nature Conservancy preserve just north of Medford. The upper portions of Lower Table and nearby **Upper Table Rocks** are remnants of lava flows that occurred nearly 7 million years ago, and the relatively dry habitats here include grassland; woodlands of oak, madrone, and ponderosa pine; and shrub chaparral on the slopes. As you climb the trail to the top, look in spring and summer for Mountain Quail, Acorn Woodpecker, Loggerhead Shrike (rare), Hutton's Vireo, Western

Scrub-Jay, Oak Titmouse, Blue-gray Gnatcatcher, Wrentit, Western Bluebird, California Towhee, and Lesser Goldfinch.

24 **Summer Lake Wildlife Area** offers wetlands in an arid landscape and seasonally attracts waterfowl, herons, and shorebirds. Pick up a map of the area at the headquarters, and then drive the wildlife loop. During nesting season you can find Western and Clark's Grebes, American White Pelican, Double-crested Cormorant, Great and Snowy Egrets, Black-crowned Night-Heron, White-faced Ibis, Sandhill Crane, Snowy Plover (look for this small shorebird on alkali flats), Black-necked Stilt, American Avocet, Willet, Wilson's Phalarope, and Caspian and Forster's Terns. In migration, Snow Goose arrives in numbers, along with Tundra Swan and 15 or more species of ducks. Watch here for Trumpeter Swan, some from the nearby Malheur National Wildlife Refuge.

25 Similar to Summer Lake but on a grander scale, **Malheur National Wildlife Refuge** ranks with Oregon's finest and most popular birding sites. This 187,000-acre refuge hosts large numbers of migrant birds (up to 300,000 Snow and Ross's Geese, hundreds of thousands of ducks, and thousands of Sandhill Cranes in spring and fall migration).

In spring and fall, Malheur is great for migrants and serves as an excellent "vagrant trap." For this sort of birding, check especially the headquarters area, Benson Pond, P-Ranch, and the Page Springs Campground. (**Fields,** nearer the Nevada border, is another classic migrant and vagrant trap.) The list of nesting species at this site is long, including Trumpeter Swan; Chukar; five species of grebes; American White Pelican; American Bittern; Snowy Egret; White-faced Ibis; Swainson's and Ferruginous Hawks; Golden Eagle; Prairie Falcon; Sandhill Crane; Snowy Plover; Franklin's Gull; Long-billed Curlew; Caspian, Forster's, and Black Terns; Burrowing and Short-eared Owls; Common Poorwill; Sage Thrasher; Black-throated (scarce) and Sage Sparrows; and Bobolink.

At dawn from March to May, male Greater Sage-Grouse perform their thrilling courtship "dance" at leks, or traditional courtship areas, near the refuge.

Birding is usually slow in winter (though Bald Eagle and Rough-legged Hawk are seen commonly); spring and fall are the best times to visit. Waterfowl numbers peak in late March and April, and migrant shorebirds can be plentiful in spring, late summer, and early fall.

OREGON | MORE INFORMATION

RARE BIRD ALERT
Statewide 503-292-0661
Northeastern 208-882-6195

13 Sauvie Island Wildlife Area *(Page 293)*
www.dfw.state.or.us
503-621-3488
🅢 🍴 👥 ♿

Closed Oct.–mid-Apr. A livestock feed plant on the island attracts wintering gulls. This is one of the best places in the country to find Thayer's Gull.

14 Fort Stevens SP
(Page 294)
www.oregonstateparks.org
503-861-1671
❓ 🅢 👥 🚶 ♿

15 Oregon Coastal Refuges *(Page 294)*
www.fws.gov/oregoncoast
541-867-4550
❓ 👥 🚶 ♿

Administers Oregon Islands, Cape Meares, Three Arch Rocks, and Bandon Marsh NWRs and Cape Meares SP.

16 Boiler Bay State Scenic Viewpoint
(Page 295)
www.oregonstateparks.org
541-265-4560
👥 ♿

17 Yaquina Head Outstanding Natural Area *(Page 295)*
www.blm.gov/nlcs/ona
541-574-3100
❓ 🅢 👥 🚶 ♿

17 Hatfield Marine Science Center *(Page 296)*
hmsc.oregonstate.edu
541-867-0100
❓ 👥 🚶 ♿

18 Bandon Marsh NWR
(Page 296)
www.fws.gov/oregoncoast
541-347-1470

19 William L. Finley NWR
(Page 296)
www.fws.gov/refuges
541-757-7236
❓ 👥 🚶 ♿

20 Fern Ridge Wildlife Area *(Page 296)*
www.dfw.state.or.us
541-935-2591
👥 🚶 🔭 ♿

Seasonal access restrictions in place. Stop at Perkins Peninsula Park to scan the lake, then continue less than a mile to a pull-off on the north with views of a marshy area. Clear Lake Rd. takes you to the dam area. In winter, mudflats attract migrant shorebirds.

21 Deschutes NF
(Page 297)
www.fs.fed.us/r6
541-383-5300
🅢 👥 🚶

22 Crater Lake NP
(Page 297)
www.nps.gov/crla
541-594-3100
❓ 🅢 🍴 👥 🚶 🔭 ♿

23 Lower and Upper Table Rocks *(Page 297)*
www.nature.org
503-230-1221
👥 🚶

24 Summer Lake Wildlife Area *(Page 298)*
www.dfw.state.or.us
541-943-3152
❓ 👥 🔭 ♿

8.3-mile wildlife loop; some areas closed Oct.–Jan.

25 Malheur NWR
(Page 298)
www.fws.gov/pacific
541-493-2612
❓ 👥 🚶 🔭 ♿

IDAHO

- Lookouts for viewing rare migrants on Pend Oreille Scenic Byway
- Waterfowl and shorebirds at Deer Flat National Wildlife Refuge
- Varied breeders and migrants at Camas National Wildlife Refuge

A staff member displaying a Peregrine Falcon at the World Center for Birds of Prey, near the Deer Flat National Wildlife Refuge outside Boise

26 Glacier-carved Lake Pend Oreille, Idaho's largest lake, winds among mountains covered in evergreen forest in the northern panhandle. At 43 miles long and more than 1,100 feet deep, it offers plenty of room for a wide variety of waterbirds. Visit the **Sandpoint City Beach** to check the upper part of the lake. During the most productive period of fall through spring, you may find numbers of loons, grebes, and waterfowl here, and the beach area itself can host migrant shorebirds, gulls, and terns. Fewer birds are present in winter than at migration peaks, but interesting rarities can appear in that season, and Bald Eagle is usually here.

The **Pend Oreille Scenic Byway** goes from Sandpoint to Clark

Fork, near the Montana border. All along the way you'll find lookouts to scan the lake for waterbirds, including such rare migrants as Greater Scaup, Long-tailed Duck (both possible in late fall), and Barrow's Goldeneye. Western Grebe, Double-crested Cormorant, Osprey, and Bald Eagle nest on the lake.

27 **Heyburn State Park** encompasses 7,800 acres of woods, marshes, and lakes to the south of famed Coeur d'Alene Lake. At Plummer Creek, stop at a wildlife viewing area overlooking a marsh, where you may see nesting Wood Duck, Mallard, Pied-billed and Red-necked Grebes, and Marsh Wren. From here, the easy **Lake Shore Trail** runs east to Hawley's Landing Campground, with good marsh and lake views on the way. Continue to the Chatcolet Use Area, where the popular **Indian Cliff Trail** climbs from cedar-hemlock forest into woods of ponderosa pine and Douglas fir. Here you'll find Northern Pygmy-Owl (scarce), Cassin's Vireo, Chestnut-backed Chickadee, Pygmy Nuthatch, Townsend's Solitaire, and Yellow-rumped and Townsend's Warblers. The trail has excellent views of the lakes, including Osprey nests along the St. Joe River.

Return to Idaho 5 and drive east along **Chatcolet Lake.** Pull-offs along the road provide viewing opportunities for migrant waterfowl and wintering Bald Eagle. At shallow **Benewah Lake,** wild rice attracts waterfowl and other wildlife. Great Blue Heron nests in the vicinity, remaining throughout winter as long as there's open water.

28 Easily accessible from Boise, **Deer Flat National Wildlife Refuge** is known for large concentrations of waterfowl in migration and winter, interesting nesting birds, and shorebirds in fall migration. Of the two refuge units, birders most often visit the one surrounding **Lake Lowell.**

From the park at the east end of the dam and from the headquarters, you can scan Lake Lowell for a wide variety of waterbirds. Geese and ducks can number in the tens of thousands in spring and fall. The most common species usually include Canada Goose (check the smaller numbers of Snow Geese for rare Ross's), American Wigeon, Mallard, Northern Pintail, and Green-winged Teal; Tundra Swan is an uncommon migrant. Bald Eagle gathers around the lake in winter; Golden is less common but is seen often. Late summer can bring postbreeding Great and Snowy Egrets and White-faced Ibis. Nesting birds here include Redhead; Eared, Western, and Clark's Grebes; Black-crowned Night-Heron; Virginia

Rail; Sora; American Avocet; Ring-billed and California Gulls; and Caspian and Black Terns.

When mudflats are exposed, migrant shorebirds can be abundant. Examine flocks of the commoner species for rare American Golden-Plover (fall), Snowy Plover (spring), and Stilt Sandpiper (late summer).

CALLIOPE HUMMINGBIRD

The smallest North American bird is of course a member of the hummingbird clan: the Calliope, a summer resident of meadows and clearings in northwestern highlands. Both sexes have a very short bill and tail, and the male sports a distinctive gorget that often looks striped, iridescent purple over white. In his courtship display, the male flies in a shallow U-pattern, showing off as well as he can with a body only a bit more than 3 inches long. ∎

29 **Hagerman Wildlife Management Area** is home to great concentrations of waterfowl in winter and a variety of other species in wetland vegetation and surrounding grassland, trees, and shrubs. From a highway rest area on the east side of US 30 about 2 miles south of Hagerman, scan for geese, ducks, and Tundra Swan (Trumpeter is found as a migrant) attracted to spring-fed waters that remain largely open throughout winter. Mallard and Canada Goose are the primary species, present in thousands. Other common wintering ducks include Wood Duck, Gadwall, American Wigeon, Northern Shoveler, Northern Pintail, Redhead, Ring-necked Duck, Lesser Scaup (watch for occasional Greater), Bufflehead, and Common Goldeneye. Wintering Bald and Golden Eagles and Red-tailed and Rough-legged Hawks are seen frequently. Once in the wildlife management area, walk along the levees for more viewing opportunities. In nesting season, the area hosts Gray Partridge, California Quail, Pied-billed Grebe, Ruddy Duck, Black-crowned Night-Heron, Virginia Rail, Spotted Sandpiper, Plumbeous and Warbling Vireos, Horned Lark, Common Yellowthroat, Marsh Wren, Yellow-breasted Chat, Spotted Towhee, Yellow-headed Blackbird, and Bullock's Oriole, among many other species.

30 Areas in the **Caribou National Forest** make for a productive birding trip in nesting season. From Pocatello, take South Main Street southeast; then turn south on Bannock Highway (Forest Road 231). Just past a cattle guard, walk the old road east up **Kinney Creek.** Look for Common Poorwill; Calliope and Broad-tailed Hummingbirds; Gray and Dusky Flycatchers; Plumbeous Vireo; Western Scrub-Jay; Juniper

Titmouse; Blue-gray Gnatcatcher; Orange-crowned, Virginia's, Yellow, Black-throated Gray, and MacGillivray's Warblers; Green-tailed and Spotted Towhees; and Lesser Goldfinch.

At the **Cherry Springs Nature Area**, trails are good for many of the same species, along with forest- and riparian-habitat birds such as Ruffed Grouse, Willow Flycatcher, Black-capped Chickadee, Gray Catbird, Cedar Waxwing, Yellow-breasted Chat, Fox Sparrow, and Black-headed Grosbeak. Higher-elevation breeding birds at the **Scout Mountain Campground** include Blue Grouse, Flammulated and Northern Saw-whet Owls, Northern Pygmy-Owl, Red-naped Sapsucker, Hairy Woodpecker, Hammond's and Cordilleran Flycatchers, Clark's Nutcracker, Mountain Chickadee, Red-breasted Nuthatch, Golden-crowned and Ruby-crowned Kinglets, Brown Creeper, Swainson's and Hermit Thrushes, Western Tanager, Lincoln's Sparrow, and Red Crossbill.

31 **Camas National Wildlife Refuge** is known for concentrations of migratory waterfowl, as well as for some notable breeding species. In addition, trees near the refuge headquarters serve as a "migrant trap" not only for western species but for strays from the East. Along with Canada Goose and many varieties of ducks nesting here, look also for Trumpeter Swan in the lakes and marshes south of the headquarters. Peregrine Falcon was reintroduced in 1983 and can be seen on the refuge throughout the year. Ferruginous Hawk, a declining species throughout the West, is an uncommon breeder, and both Bald and Golden Eagles are seen here regularly.

Nesting waders and waterbirds include Eared and Western Grebes; American White Pelican; Double-crested Cormorant; American Bittern; Great Blue Heron; Great, Snowy, and Cattle Egrets; Black-crowned Night-Heron; Sandhill Crane; White-faced Ibis; Black-necked Stilt; American Avocet; Willet; Long-billed Curlew; and Wilson's Phalarope. In the grasslands and scrub, look for Gray Partridge; Ring-necked Pheasant; Common Nighthawk; Horned Lark; Sage Thrasher; and Vesper, Savannah, and Grasshopper Sparrows.

32 Only a short drive south, **Market Lake Wildlife Management Area** offers lots of waterfowl in migration and nesting wetlands species from grebes and waders to Marsh Wren and Yellow-headed Blackbird. Several large marshy impoundments, accessible by road or by walking dikes, allow viewing of waterfowl, shorebirds, gulls, and terns.

IDAHO | MORE INFORMATION

RARE BIRD ALERT
North 208-882-6195
South 208-236-3337
Southwest 208-368-6096

26 **Sandpoint** *(Page 300)*
www.cityofsandpoint.com
/Parks_Rec
208-263-3613

27 **Heyburn State Park**
(Page 301)
www.idahoparks.org/parks
208-686-1308

28 **Deer Flat National
Wildlife Refuge** *(Page 301)*
www.fws.gov/refuges
208-467-9278

*Though it's not a birding
site, the World Center for
Birds of Prey (208-362-8687;
www.peregrinefund.org),
south of Boise, repays a tour
with close looks at some of
the rarest and most beautiful
raptors on earth. The center
is operated by the Peregrine
Fund.*

29 **Hagerman Wildlife
Management Area**
(Page 302)
fishandgame.idaho.gov
/cms/wildlife/wma
208-324-4350

30 **Caribou National
Forest** *(Page 302)*
www.fs.fed.us/r4
208-524-7500

*Administers Kinney Creek
and Cherry Springs Nature
Areas.*

31 **Camas National
Wildlife Refuge**
(Page 303)
pacific.fws.gov/refuges
208-662-5423

32 **Market Lake Wildlife
Management Area**
(Page 303)
fishandgame.idaho.gov
/cms/wildlife/wma
208-228-3131

ADDITIONAL SITES

1 **American Falls**
www.americanfallschamber
.org
208-226-7214
*Waterbirds, shorebirds, and
Bald Eagles make a visit to
American Falls a productive
one. From the marina, you
can scan the reservoir for
loons, grebes, and waterfowl
in spring and fall. From midsummer through fall, visit
mudflats along the reservoir,
which attract large numbers
of shorebirds and occasional
herons, egrets, and White-
faced Ibis. Drive through
town to view the Snake River
below the dam and find river
viewpoints past the town*

*landfill. The river attracts
ducks and gulls from fall
through spring, along with
several Bald Eagles, which
roost in riverside trees, and
migrant Osprey. Look for
Common and Barrow's
Goldeneyes; Hooded, Com-
mon, and Red-breasted
Mergansers; and an occasional surprise such as scoters or
Oldsquaw.*

MONTANA

- Rocky Mountain species at Glacier National Park
- Migrant waterfowl and shorebirds at Freezout Lake
- Prairie species at Bowdoin National Wildlife Refuge

33 **Glacier National Park,** Montana's most popular natural area, has excellent birding. Simply driving the **Going-to-the-Sun Road** over Logan Pass and stopping at picnic areas and overlooks can bring sightings of Red-naped Sapsucker; Northern Flicker; Hammond's Flycatcher; Gray and Steller's Jays; Clark's Nutcracker; Winter Wren; Golden-crowned and Ruby-crowned Kinglets; Townsend's Solitaire; Hermit, Swainson's, and Varied Thrushes; Cedar Waxwing; Townsend's, Yellow-rumped, and MacGillivray's Warblers; Western Tanager; Black-headed Grosbeak; Red Crossbill; and Pine Siskin. Walking trails might turn up less common birds such as Blue Grouse, American Three-toed Woodpecker, or Pine Grosbeak. Osprey and Bald Eagle nest in the park; watch for them around any of the lakes.

Look for American Dipper at the road bridge that crosses McDonald Creek just north of **Lake McDonald.** Watch for Barrow's Goldeneye (uncommon) on the lake and for Harlequin

Sparkling water and mountain vista of Montana's Glacier National Park

Duck anywhere along the creek above this point. At the **Avalanche Creek** picnic area, look for the rare Black Swift, which nests on nearby cliffs. Vaux's Swift also nests in this area. At **Logan Pass,** walk the trail across the tundra for a chance to see White-tailed Ptarmigan, American Pipit, and Gray-crowned Rosy-Finch. This popular spot has a small parking lot, so arrive early.

Wet meadows along **Inside North Fork Road** may have nesting Le Conte's Sparrow; try about a half mile up the **Camas Creek Trail.** Continuing up toward **Rogers Lake** may bring a sighting of a Boreal Chickadee. Mountain, Chestnut-backed, and Black-capped Chick-adees also nest in the park. Check meadows along the road for Great Gray Owl. Past Polebridge is an area that burned in 1988, where you might find Black-backed Woodpecker. Also, Clay-colored Sparrow has nested here, as has Northern Hawk Owl (rare).

AMERICAN THREE-TOED WOODPECKER

A s its name states, the American Three-toed Woodpecker has only three toes; all other U.S. woodpeckers, except for the closely related Black-backed, have four. Both American Three-toed and Black-backed are found in coniferous forests in western mountains and prefer to feed on dead trees with bark still loosely attached. In this part of the country (check recently burned areas), the American Three-toed is generally more common than the Black-backed. ∎

34 A viewing area and a short nature trail off US 93 make it easy to observe some of the nesting and migrant birds at **Ninepipe National Wildlife Refuge.** Breeders on and around the reservoir here include Canada Goose; several species of ducks; Red-necked, Eared, and Western Grebes; Double-crested Cormorant; American Bittern; Great Blue Heron; Osprey (which often try nesting on platforms); Sora; American Avocet (uncommon); Marsh Wren; and Yellow-headed Blackbird.

In fall and winter, raptor viewing can be excellent in this vicinity, though numbers fluctuate with populations of rodents and other prey. Look for Bald Eagle, Northern Harrier (nests), Red-tailed (nests) and Rough-legged Hawks, Golden Eagle, Peregrine and Prairie Falcons, and Short-eared Owl (nests)— and hope for a rarity such as Gyrfalcon or Snowy Owl. Swainson's Hawk, an uncommon breeder, is absent in winter.

35 As you approach **Freezout Lake Wildlife Management Area** from Fairfield, a high point on US 89 offers a view of one of Montana's finest birding sites, where spectacular numbers of waterfowl stop to rest in spring and fall migration, and many species of waterbirds breed. In early spring, Canada Goose and

Tundra Swan arrive in the area by the thousands, along with 15 to 20 species of ducks. Look for Eurasian Wigeon, uncommon but regular here in spring. Tens of thousands of Snow Geese arrive in March; scan the flocks for the smaller Ross's Goose.

In late April and May, Freezout hosts a variety of migrant shorebirds. Remaining to nest will be Killdeer, Black-necked Stilt, American Avocet, Willet, Upland Sandpiper, Long-billed Curlew, Marbled Godwit, and Wilson's Phalarope. Other breeding waterbirds include Green-winged Teal; Ring-necked Duck; all six Montana species of grebes; American Bittern; Black-crowned Night-Heron; Sora; Franklin's, Ring-billed, and California Gulls; and Common, Forster's, and Black Terns. American White Pelican summers but doesn't breed. Look in grasslands for nesting Gray Partridge; Ring-necked Pheasant; Northern Harrier; Short-eared Owl; Clay-colored, Vesper, and Savannah Sparrows; Lark Bunting; and Chestnut-collared Longspur. Waterfowl are abundant around the wetlands in fall.

36 **Benton Lake National Wildlife Refuge** is known for most of the same waterfowl and marsh birds as Freezout. The refuge auto tour route passes wetlands alive in breeding season with grebes, ducks, American Coot, gulls (including thousands of nesting Franklin's), and terns. Migrant shorebirds can be abundant. Look for Burrowing Owl on the prairie, along with Sharp-tailed Grouse (males "dance" on their leks in spring), Northern Harrier, Upland Sandpiper, Short-eared Owl, Sprague's Pipit (occasional), Savannah and Grasshopper Sparrows, as well as Chestnut-collared Longspur. Swainson's Hawk is common here except in winter; Ferruginous Hawk and Gyrfalcon occasionally appear. Rough-legged Hawk is a frequent winter visitor.

37 Offering wetlands habitat in an environment that receives only a foot of rain a year, **Bowdoin National Wildlife Refuge** attracts migrant and breeding waterfowl and shorebirds. Sought-after grassland species also reward a trip to this refuge. Where the fluting song of Western Meadowlark sounds over short-grass and mid-grass prairie, look for Sprague's Pipit and Baird's Sparrow. McCown's and Chestnut-collared Longspur perform their song flights in spring and early summer. Sharp-tailed Grouse, Burrowing Owl, Horned Lark, and a variety of sparrows in addition to Baird's also nest on the prairie.

The refuge auto tour route circles Lake Bowdoin, allowing looks at breeding birds including Western and Clark's Grebes; American White Pelican (abundant here); Great Blue Heron;

Black-crowned Night-Heron; White-faced Ibis; Franklin's, Ring-billed, and California Gulls; and Common and Black Terns. Close study of shallow-water areas or mudflats in late summer and early fall can turn up a great variety of shorebirds.

38 In eastern Montana the Missouri River has been impounded as the huge **Fort Peck Lake.** The tailwaters of the **Fort Peck Dam** attract large numbers of gulls in late fall and winter. Fourteen species have been identified here, including Mew and Great Black-backed. November and December are the best months to check gatherings of the gulls, which include Ring-billed, California, and Herring, to try to identify Thayer's, Glaucous (both regular), and other uncommon to rare species.

A few eastern birds can be found around Fort Peck at the edge of their normal nesting range. Check around the campground along the Missouri River downstream from the dam for Orchard and Baltimore Orioles (as well as the western Bullock's), and watch the skies overhead around town for Chimney Swift. Drive north to the river and turn west through a gate into a wooded area. Red-headed Woodpecker, Blue Jay, Eastern Bluebird, and Field Sparrow nest here; Black-and-white Warbler has been seen in summer and may breed here.

Piping Plover breeds around Fort Peck Lake, and can often be seen with a spotting scope from the west end of the dam in spring and summer. For a chance to find nesting Least Tern, drive to the **Bear Creek Recreation Area** on the lake.

39 In April, male Sharp-tailed Grouse perform their earnest courtship displays at **Medicine Lake National Wildlife Refuge.** Reserve a space in a blind, and watch from just a few feet away as male grouse strut in their tail-up, spread-wing posture.

Here in the transition zone between tallgrass and short-grass prairies, nesting birds include grassland species such as Gray Partridge; Ring-necked Pheasant; Upland Sandpiper; Burrowing and Short-eared Owls; Sprague's Pipit; Clay-colored, Vesper, Lark, Savannah, Grasshopper, Baird's (a specialty), Le Conte's (a local breeder in Montana), and Song Sparrows; Lark Bunting; and Chestnut-collared Longspur. Look for these as you drive the auto tour route, and scan the coves and islands of Medicine Lake for breeding ducks, grebes, American White Pelican (the colony on Big Island is one of the most important in the U.S.), American Avocet, Wilson's Phalarope, gulls, and terns. The threatened Piping Plover nests at the water's edge. In migration, flocks of Sandhill Cranes and thousands of waterfowl rest here.

MONTANA | MORE INFORMATION

RARE BIRD ALERT
Statewide 406-721-9799
Big Fork 406-756-5595

33 Glacier National Park
(Page 305)
www.nps.gov/glac
406-888-7800

Some roads closed in winter

34 Ninepipe National Wildlife Refuge *(Page 306)*
www.fws.gov/bisonrange /Ninepipe
406-644-2211

Parts of the refuge are closed during nesting season (mid-Mar.–mid-July) and hunting season (Sept.–Jan.).

35 Freezout Lake Wildlife Management Area
(Page 306)
fwp.state.mt.us/habitat /wma/freezout.asp
406-467-2646

36 Benton Lake National Wildlife Refuge *(Page 307)*
bentonlake.fws.gov
406-727-7400

37 Bowdoin National Wildlife Refuge *(Page 307)*
bowdoin.fws.gov
406-654-2863

38 Fort Peck Dam and Lake *(Page 308)*
www.nwo.usace.army.mil /html/Lake_Proj
406-526-3411

39 Medicine Lake National Wildlife Refuge
(Page 308)
medicinelake.fws.gov
406-789-2305

The auto tour route is open May–Sept. Call the refuge office a week or more in advance to reserve space in a blind.

ADDITIONAL SITES

❷ Westby
geocities.com/westbymt
406-385-2445
Birders eager to see songbirds visit this small town, where the very small Onstad Memorial Municipal Park seems to act as a magnet for migrants. Westby lies in the prairie pothole region, surrounded by hundreds of glacier-formed ponds and marshes. Such rarities as Yellow Rail and Le Conte's and Nelson's Sharp-tailed Sparrows nest in these wetlands, and Piping Plover breeds on alkali ponds.

❸ Billings
ci.billings.mt.us
406-252-4016
If you happen to be in Billings during spring or fall migration, a visit to Two Moon County Park can be worthwhile. This riparian area on the Yellowstone River is popular with local birders, who search its trees, shrubby vegetation, and wetlands for migrant flycatchers, vireos, wrens, thrushes, warblers, sparrows, and a variety of other species.

INDEX

ABOUT THE AUTHORS

Mel White's earliest birding memory is of a Western Tanager he saw on a family vacation to Arizona when he was six years old. Four decades later, he still recalls this meeting of boy and bird when he considers the pleasures of travel—the delight in the new, whether expected or un-, and the transforming moment when a vision that existed only in the imagination is replaced by the real thing in binoculars. An Arkansas native and a former newspaper reporter and magazine editor, Mel White is now a free-lance writer specializing in travel and nature. A contributing editor for *National Geographic Traveler,* he writes frequently for other National Geographic Society publications and is author of *A Birder's Guide to Arkansas* and *Exploring The Great Texas Coastal Birding Trail.* His assignments have taken him from New Zealand to Amazonia to the Swiss Alps—and he geneerally manages to find time for bird-watching no matter where he goes.

Paul Lehman, perhaps more than any other birder, has traveled virtually to every nook and cranny of North America, using his background in geography and bird distribution to compile bird lists in every state and province. A past editor of ABA's *Birding* magazine, he has written extensively on avian distribution and identification. He has been a principal consultant on several popular field guides, most recently chief consultant for the range maps in the *National Geographic Field Guide to the Birds of North America* and *National Geographic Complete Birds of North America.* He was chief editor of the ABA /Lane volume *A Birder's Guide to Metropolitan Areas of North America* and currently serves as associate editor for *North American Birds.* A former lecturer in physical geography and environmental studies at the University of California in Santa Barbara, he continues to give talks on weather, bird distribution, migration, and vagrancy.

ABOUT THE CONSULTANT

Jonathan Alderfer a respected field ornithologist and one of America's top birding artists, is the chief consultant for the National Geographic Society's Birding Program. He is editor of the recent *National Geographic Complete Birds of North America* and is chief consultant for the upcoming *National Geographic Field Guide to the Birds of North America* (5th edition). He is former associate editor of the American Birding Association's magazine *Birding* and his art appears in publications and galleries across the nation.

ILLUSTRATIONS CREDITS

All the bird paintings are from the *National Geographic Society Field Guide to the Birds of North America, Third Edition* © *1999,* reprinted with permission of the National Geographic Society.

Cover, Annie Griffiths Belt.
2-3, Richard Cummins; 4-5, Jerry & Marcy Monkman/EcoPhotography.com; 12, Tom Payne; 17, Jerry & Marcy Monkman/EcoPhotography.com; 18, Bill Silliker, Jr.; 20, Susan Cole Kelly; 23, Barrett & MacKay Photography; 28, Susan Cole Kelly; 31, Tim Fitzharris/Minden Pictures; 36, Al Messerschmidt/Folio, Inc.; 42, Johann Schumacher Design; 47, Steven Holt/Stockpix.com; 52, Irene Hinke-Sacilotto; 56, Heather R. Davidson; 62, Tom Till; 67, Kelly Culpepper/Transparencies, Inc.; 72, James P. Blair/NGS Image Collection; 77, Byron Jorjorian; 80, Jeff Foott/Bruce Coleman, Inc.; 84, Randy Wells/Getty Images; 86, Rick Poley; 88, Larry Ulrich; 91, Bates Littlehales/NGS Image Collection; 96, Bruce Clarke/Transparencies, Inc.; 100, Willard Clay; 104, Robert P. Falls, Sr.; 108, John Elk III/Bruce Coleman, Inc.; 112, John Cancalosi/nature-pl.com; 118, James P. Blair/NGS Image Collection; 123, Joel Sartore/NGS Image Collection; 125, Gary Kramer; 134, Ruth Hoyt/Close to Nature; 138, Rob Curtis/The Early Birder; 142, Clint Farlinger; 146, Steve Solum/Bruce Coleman, Inc.; 150, Wayne Nelson/Earth Images; 156, Ed Simpson/Getty Images; 160, David Muench/Getty Images; 164, Kent & Donna Dannen; 169, Carr Clifton/Minden Pictures; 170, John Heidecker; 172, Gene Boaz; 178, John Elk III; 184, Herbert Stormont/Unicorn Stock Photos; 189, Scott T. Smith; 194, Michael Frye; 199, James P. Blair/NGS Image Collection; 206, Larry Sansone; 210, Paula Borchardt; 214, Laurence Parent; 221, Laurence Parent; 226, David J. Sams; 230, George Wuerthner; 232, Michael Sewell/Visual Pursuit; 238, Larry Sansone; 240, Chuck Place/Place Stock Photography; 242, Larry Sansone; 248, George H.H. Huey; 256, John Elk III; 262, Stephen & Michele Vaughan; 266, Cathy & Gordon ILLG; 272, Wendy Shattil/Bob Rozinski; 278, Maxine Cass; 286, Charles Gurche; 293, Bruce Jackson; 300, William H. Mullins; 305, Brian F. Small.

ADDITIONAL READING

New England

A Birder's Guide to Maine, Elizabeth Pierson, Jan Erik Pierson, and Peter D. Vickery (Down East Books, 1996)

A Birder's Guide to New Hampshire, Alan Delorey (American Birding Association, 1996)

A Birder's Guide to Eastern Massachusetts (Bird Observer, American Birding Association, 1994).

Birding Cape Cod (Cape Cod Bird Club and Massachusetts Audubon Society, 1990).

Bird Walks in Rhode Island, Adam J. Fry (Backcountry Publications, 1992).

Connecticut Birding Guide, Buzz Devine and Dwight G. Smith (Thomson-Shore, 1996).

Bird Finding in New England, Richard K. Walton (David R. Godine, 1988).

Mid-Atlantic

Where to Find Birds in New York State: The Top 500 Sites, Susan Roney Drennan (Syracuse University Press, 1981).

City Cemeteries to Boreal Bogs: Where to Go Birding in Central New York, Dorothy W. Crumb and James Throckmorton (eds.) (Onondaga Audubon Society, 1996).

A Guide to Bird Finding in New Jersey, William J. Boyle, Jr. (Rutgers University Press, 1986).

Birder's Guide to Pennsylvania, Paula Ford (Gulf Publishing, 1995)

Finding Birds in the National Capital Area, Claudia Wilds (Smithsonian Institution Press, 1992).

South Atlantic

A Birder's Guide to Virginia, David W. Johnston (compiler) (American Birding Association, 1997).

Birds of the Blue Ridge Mountains, Marcus B.

Simpson, Jr. (University of North Carolina Press, 1992).

Finding Birds in the National Capital Area, Claudia Wilds (Smithsonian Institution Press, 1992).

A Birder's Guide to Coastal North Carolina, John O. Fussell III (University of North Carolina Press, 1994)

Finding Birds in South Carolina, Robin M. Carter (University of South Carolina Press, 1993)

A Birder's Guide to Georgia, Joel R. Hitt and Kenneth Turner Blackshaw (eds.) (Georgia Ornithological Society, 1996).

Florida

A Birder's Guide to Florida, Bill Pranty (American Birding Association, 1996).

South-Central States

A Birder's Guide to Alabama, John Porter (ed.) (University of Alabama Press, 1999).

Birder's Guide to Alabama and Mississippi, Ray Vaughn (Gulf Publishing, 1994).

A Birder's Guide to Arkansas, Mel White (American Birding Association, 1995).

Eastern Texas

A Birder's Guide to the Texas Coast, Harold R. Holt (American Birding Association, 1993).

A Birder's Guide to the Rio Grande Valley, Harold R. Holt (American Birding Association, 1992).

A Birder's Guide to Texas, Edward A. Kutac (Gulf Publishing, 1989)

Birding Texas, Roland H.Waver and Mark A. Elwonger (Falcon Press, 1998)

Heartland

A Birder's Guide to Minnesota, Kim R. Eckert (Williams Publications, Inc., 1994).

Traveler's Guide to Wildlife in Minnesota, Carrol L. Henderson et al. (Minnesota Department of Natural Resources, 1997).

Wisconsin's Favorite Bird Haunts, Daryl D. Tessen (ed.) (Wisconsin Society for Ornithology, 1989).*A Guide to the Birding Areas of Missouri*, Kay Palmer (ed.) (Audubon Society of Missouri, 1993).

A Guide to Bird Finding in Kansas and Western Missouri, John L. Zimmerman and Sebastian T. Patti (University Press of Kansas, 1988).

Birds of the St. Louis Area (Webster Groves Nature Study Society, 1998).

North-Central States

Bird Finding Guide to Michigan, C.T. Black and C. Roy Smith (compilers) (Michigan Audubon Society, 1994).

Birding in Ohio, Tom Thompson (Indiana University Press, 1994).

Birds of the Indiana Dunes, Kenneth J. Brock (Indiana University Press, 1997).*reat Birding Trips of the West*, Joan Easton Lentz (Capra Press, 1989).

The Plains

A Guide to Bird Finding in Kansas and Western Missouri, John L. Zimmerman and Sebastian T. Patti (University Press of Kansas, 1988).

Southwest

A Birder's Guide to Southeastern Arizona, Richard Cachor Taylor (American Birding Association, 1995).

Birds in Southeastern Arizona, William A. Davis and S.M. Russell (Tucson Audubon Society, 1995).

New Mexico Bird Finding Guide, Dale A. Zimmerman *et al.* (eds.) (New Mexico Ornithological Society, 1997).

Birding Texas, Roland H. Wauer and Mark A. Elwonger (Falcon Press, 1998).

A Birder's Guide to Texas, Edward A. Kutac (Gulf Publishing, 1989).

A Birder's Guide to the Rio Grande Valley, Mark Lockwood *et al.* (American Birding Association, 1999).

California

A Birding Northern California, Jean Richmond (Mt. Diablo Audubon Society, 1985). *Birder's Guide to Northern California*, LoLo and Jim Westrich (Gulf Publishing, 1991).

San Francisco Peninsula Birdwatching, Cliff Richer (ed.) (Sequoia Audubon Society, 1996).

A Birder's Guide to Southern California, Brad Schram (American Birding Association, 1998).

Central Rockies

A Birder's Guide to Wyoming, Oliver K. Scott (American Birding Association, 1993).

Birds of Yellowstone, Terry McEneaney (Rinehart, 1988).

Finding the Birds of Jackson Hole, Bert Raynes and Darwin Wile (Darwin Wile, 1994).

A Birder's Guide to Colorado, Harold R. Holt (American Birding Association, 1997).

Birding Utah, D. E. McIvor (Falcon Press, 1998). Covers 112 sites in Utah.

Northwest

A Guide to Bird Finding in Washington, Terence R. Wahl and Dennis R. Paulson (T.R. Wahl, 1991)

The Birder's Guide to Oregon, Joseph E. Evanich, Jr. (Portland Audubon Society, 1990).

A Birder's Guide to Idaho, Dan Svingen and Kas Dumroese (eds.) (American Birding Association, 1997).

The Birder's Guide to Montana, Terry McEneaney (Falcon Press, 1993).

Hawaii and Alaska

Enjoying Birds in Hawaii, H. Douglas Pratt (Mutual Publishing, 1993).

A Bird Finding Guide to Alaska, Nick Lethaby (Nick Lethaby, 1994).

NATIONAL GEOGRAPHIC
GUIDE TO BIRDING HOT SPOTS
OF THE UNITED STATES
Mel White with Paul Lehman

PUBLISHED BY
THE NATIONAL GEOGRAPHIC SOCIETY

John M. Fahey, Jr., *President & Chief Executive Officer*

Gilbert M. Grosvenor, *Chairman of the Board*

Nina D. Hoffman, *Executive Vice President; President, Books & School Publishing*

PREPARED BY THE BOOK DIVISION

Kevin Mulroy, *Senior Vice President and Publisher*

Kris Hanneman, *Illustrations Director*

Marianne R. Koszorus, *Design Director*

Carl Mehler, *Director of Maps*

Barbara Brownell Grogan, *Executive Editor*

STAFF FOR THIS BOOK

Barbara Brownell Grogan, *Editor*

Jennifer Seidel, *Text Editor*

John C. Anderson, *Illustrations Editor*

Cinda Rose, *Art Director*

Lauren Pruneski, *Assistant Editor*

Cameron Zotter, *Production & Design Assistant*

Jehan Aziz, Matt Chwastyk, Sven M. Dolling, Steven D. Gardner, Thomas L. Gray, Sean M. Groom, Keith R. Moore, Michelle H. Picard, Nicholas P. Rosenbach, Gregory Ugiansky, Martin S. Walz, *Map Research & Production*

Rebecca Hinds, *Managing Editor*

Gary Colbert, *Production Director*

Lewis Bassford, *Production Project Manager*

Meredith Wilcox, *Illustrations Specialist*

MANUFACTURING AND QUALITY CONTROL

Christopher A. Liedel, *Chief Financial Officer*

Phillip L. Schlosser, *Managing Director*

John T. Dunn, *Technical Director*

Vincent P. Ryan, *Director*

Chris Brown, *Manager*

Maryclare Tracy, *Manager*

Founded in 1888, the National Geographic Society is one of the largest nonprofit scientific and educational organizations in the world. It reaches more than 285 million people worldwide each month through its official journal, NATIONAL GEOGRAPHIC, and its four other magazines; the National Geographic Channel; television documentaries; radio programs; films; books; videos and DVDs; maps; and interactive media. National Geographic has funded more than 8,000 scientific research projects and supports an education program combating geographic illiteracy.

For more information, please call 1-800-NGS LINE (647-5463) or write to the following address:

National Geographic Society
1145 17th Street N.W.
Washington, D.C. 20036-4688
U.S.A.

Log on to nationalgeographic.com; AOL Keyword: NatGeo.

For information about special discounts for bulk purchases, please contact National Geographic Books Special Sales: ngspecsales@ngs.org

Library of Congress Cataloging-in-Publication Information available upon request. ISBN 0-7922-5483-X

National Geographic Guide to Birding Hotspots of the United States was originally published in two volumes: *National Geographic Guide to Birdwatching Sites: Eastern U.S. (1999)* and *National Geographic Guide to Birdwatching Sites: Western U.S (1999)*